ACTS

ACTS

The Autobiography of
WOLFGANG
WAGNER

Translated from the German by
JOHN BROWNJOHN

WEIDENFELD & NICOLSON
London

First published in Great Britain in 1994 by
Weidenfeld & Nicolson

The Orion Publishing Group Ltd
Orion House
5 Upper Saint Martin's Lane
London WC2H 9EA

ISBN 0 297 81349 8

A catalogue record for this book is available
from the British Library

Filmset by Selwood Systems, Midsomer Norton

Printed in Great Britain by
Butler & Tanner Ltd, Frome and London

CONTENTS

ILLUSTRATIONS

The curtain call after Wolfgang Wagner's first Bayreuth production, *Lohengrin*, 1953 (presse-foto-gebauer, Bayreuth)

Birgit Nilsson rehearsing Isolde with producer Wolfgang Wagner, 1957 (Bayreuther Festspiele, photo Falk)

Hans Knappertsbusch and Wolfgang Wagner, 1951 (Bayreuther Festspiele, photo Renner)

Wolfgang Wagner with Karl Böhm, 1963 (presse-foto-gebauer, Bayreuth)

Herbert von Karajan with Wolfgang Wagner at Wahnfried, 1952 (Foto Leo Schneiderhahl, Nuremberg)

Between pp. 180–181

Wolfgang Wagner rehearsing *Die Walküre* with Gwyneth Jones, 1973 (Bayreuther Festspiele, photo Rauh)

Donald McIntyre being congratulated by Wolfgang Wagner after his hundredth Bayreuth performance (Foto Klaus Tritschel, Bayreuth)

Rehearsing *Parsifal* in 1993, with Placido Domingo, Deborah Polaski and James Levine (Bayreuther Festspiele, photo Rauh)

Pierre Boulez, Wolfgang Wagner and Patrice Chéreau, 1976 (Bayreuther Festspiele, photo Rauh)

The team that staged *The Ring* in 1983: Peter Hall, Georg Solti and William Dudley (Bayreuther Festspiele, photo Rauh)

Harry Kupfer and Daniel Barenboim rehearsing *The Ring*, 1988 (Bayreuther Festspiele, photo Rauh)

The soloists' 'singing school' for *Die Meistersinger*, 1981 (Bayreuther Festspiele, photo Rauh)

Die Meistersinger (Act III), 1981 (Bayreuther Festspiele, photo Lauterwasser)

Parsifal (Act I, Scene 2), 1975 (Bayreuther Festspiele, photo Rauh)

Lohengrin (Act I), 1967 (Bayreuther Festspiele, photo Rauh)

Parsifal (Act I, Scene 2), 1989 (Bayreuther Festspiele, photo Schulze)

The Ring (*Götterdämmerung*, Act I, Scene 2), 1960 (Bayreuther Festspiele, photo Rauh)

The Ring (*Das Rheingold*, Scene 4), 1970 (Bayreuther Festspiele, photo Rauh)

The Ring (*Die Walküre*, Act II), 1970 (Bayreuther Festspiele, photo Rauh)

The Ring (*Siegfried*, Act II), 1970 (Bayreuther Festspiele, photo Rauh)

The Ring (*Siegfried*, Act III, Scene 2), 1970 (Bayreuther Festspiele, photo Rauh)

The Ring (*Götterdämmerung*, Act II), 1970 (Bayreuther Festspiele, photo Rauh)

The Ring (*Götterdämmerung*, finale), 1970 (Bayreuther Festspiele, photo Eysell)

The last photograph of Winifred Wagner with her surviving children, 1979 (Julius G. Schmidt, Saarbrücken)

Gudrun and Wolfgang Wagner with their daughter Katharina, 1984 (Foto Klaus Tritschel, Bayreuth)

Gudrun and Wolfgang Wagner at the opening of the Franz Liszt Museum
  in Haus Wahnfried, 1993 (presse-foto-gebauer, Bayreuth)

On pp. 138–9
Two drawings illustrating the relationship between the auditorium, orchestra
  and stage for Wolfgang Wagner's second production of *The Ring*, 1970

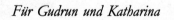

Für Gudrun und Katharina

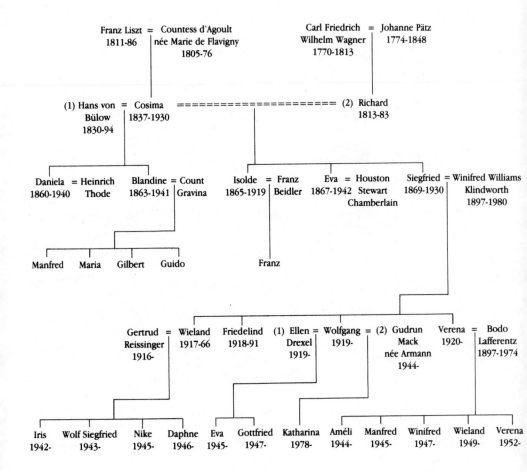

Franz Liszt = Countess d'Agoult
1811-86 | née Marie de Flavigny
1805-76

Carl Friedrich = Johanne Pätz
Wilhelm Wagner | 1774-1848
1770-1813

(1) Hans von = Cosima ===================== (2) Richard
Bülow 1837-1930   1813-83
1830-94

Daniela = Heinrich   Blandine = Count   Isolde = Franz   Eva = Houston   Siegfried = Winifred Williams
1860-1940 Thode   1863-1941 Gravina   1865-1919 Beidler 1867-1942 Stewart 1869-1930   Klindworth
                                                                        Chamberlain   1897-1980

Manfred   Maria   Gilbert   Guido   Franz

Gertrud = Wieland   Friedelind   (1) Ellen = Wolfgang = (2) Gudrun   Verena = Bodo
Reissinger 1917-66   1918-91   Drexel   1919-   Mack   1920-   Lafferentz
1916-   1919-   née Armann   1897-1974
                                                        1944-

Iris   Wolf Siegfried   Nike   Daphne   Eva   Gottfried   Katharina   Améli   Manfred   Winifred   Wieland   Verena
1942-   1943-   1945-   1946-   1945- 1947-   1978-   1944-   1945-   1947-   1949-   1952-

FOREWORD

People have for years been asking me to commit my experiences to paper for the benefit of my contemporaries and even, perhaps, of posterity. I long declined to do so, partly on the grounds that my present and future commitments left me far too little spare time, and partly because I had no intention of adding to the vast amount of literature on Wagner and Bayreuth already in existence. But one cannot always abide by one's resolutions, even the best of them, so I eventually bowed to the cogent arguments and pleas of my publisher, Lord Weidenfeld.

I did not fully realize what I had let myself in for until I started work, because my leisure hours are very few, and I was determined not to put together a kaleidoscope of anecdotes and intimate disclosures of the kind purveyed by so many volumes of memoirs. If this book were to have any point at all, I knew that it would have to be factually watertight without becoming excessively dry. This entailed very thorough research. The extent of the available material seemed prodigious, and I was naturally compelled to be selective because it would have been humanly impossible to plug every gap.

The considerations that governed my choice were subjective, and many people may regret – or even welcome – my omission of this episode or that. My ultimate determinants could only be the general, autobiographical framework of my story and the authenticity of what I recounted in detail. As anyone who dips into this book will realize, my experiences and activities were closely connected with the existence and history of the Bayreuth Festival from a very early stage. The older I become the less I can divorce the two spheres, each of which does, to a certain extent, emanate from the other. As for authenticity, it was not my ambition to perpetuate and prolong the endless series of stereotyped ideas, prejudices, half-truths or total lies about myself and Bayreuth, nor to refute them point by point. I have simply adhered to the facts themselves.

If, in addition to conveying my personal characteristics, it conveys something of Bayreuth's immense vitality, and of my unremitting efforts to preserve the festival, I shall consider that this book has fulfilled its purpose. That it came into being in its present form is due not least to my numerous assistants and comrades-in-arms. My sincere thanks to them all.

W.W.

1

A PERSONAL STATEMENT

Being one of Richard Wagner's grandsons and the third-born of four reversionary heirs invested with equal testamentary rights, I was, and still am, associated with an unusual heritage. The purpose of this book is to explore its value and significance, past and present.

I was born in 1919, and thus into an age characterized by hope and disappointment, material losses and extremes of social inequality – but also by endeavours to evolve a stable, durable democracy of which much was expected by many. They included people of all political persuasions: pacifists and revanchists, scorners of traditional values and exaggerators of their own worth, chauvinists and supporters of the League of Nations.

Experience of the Second World War, which ended in Germany's unconditional surrender and almost reduced the country to a bombed-out ruin, provided me with a sufficient reason for closely examining my own position and debating whether it was still worthwhile, necessary and justifiable to make an active commitment to the Bayreuth Festival – perhaps, even, to make it my life's work.

What clinched my own and my brother's decision to revive the Festival was a wish to rid our grandfather's œuvre of the distortions occasioned by its misappropriation by 'nationalists', and by a misunderstanding of the history of its reception, and to hazard an attempt to present his works as if they had been created only yesterday. This meant submitting them to objective, unprejudiced critical analysis and examining their musical, thematic and dramatic structure with a view to discovering whether and how the artistic synthesis Richard Wagner had in mind should be presented in all its spiritual universality; that is to say, in a manner capable of acquainting people of today with the complexity of the timeless problems inherent in his works and in the conflicts portrayed by them. Any attempt to do this meant a return *ad fontes* – to the original source, to the œuvre itself – and to the exposure of its human core. Wagner's *'Hier gilt's der Kunst!'* [What matters here is art], taken from *Die Meistersinger*, could not have been more apt in 1951, the year the festival re-opened after the war. His works dealt with great human themes such as love, power, treachery, compassion, fidelity, tolerance, and faith. To create this timeless validity he made use of myth: he turned his back on history, the favourite operatic material of his day, because it merely presented a series of fortuitous events, whereas myth revealed the essence of nature and humankind. The purpose of his decision was to evade the misunderstandings that stem from topical or political associations. His bold vision was one of conscious human responsibility and deliberate action presented on stage as a 'colourful reflection' of life.

In this respect he made artistic demands on the theatre that not only ran counter to the operatic conventions of the time but totally contradicted them. This was the real reason why he evolved his festival idea, and why he needed a special setting in which to fulfil it. He rejected the 'luxurious ostentation' of the theatrical buildings customary in his day, whose tiers and boxes segregated the audience according to class and status. His Festspielhaus at Bayreuth was to be a people's theatre modelled on the 'democratic round' of the Greek amphitheatre, an architectural symbol consistent with the democratic utopia that formed the basic content of his works. Work and theatre became an integrated whole, making 'Bayreuth' a counter-design, an alternative to the theatre of the time.

Wagner believed that, in 'Bayreuth', he had given the Germans a national art form of their own. However, the translation of his *Gesamtkunstwerk* concept into the theatrical reality of the Festspielhaus – with *Der Ring des Nibelungen* in 1876 and *Parsifal* in 1882 – left him far from satisfied that he had realized his ideal. His intentions far exceeded the scope of the contemporary theatre. After his death, his widow Cosima's achievement in perpetuating the festival and expanding its repertoire still merits recognition and admiration, even today; but her decision to make historicism the only style of presentation and her nationalistic ideologizing of Bayreuth had a disastrous effect. Although she buttressed her claim to authenticity by invoking 'the Master's wishes', it was based on a total misconception. Her reversion to history signified a renunciation of myth and was thus completely at odds with Wagner's central endeavour. She distorted the artistic idea underlying the festival into a political ideology. Her strictly ideological approach rigidified, and this inherent misconception, disseminated by the publicists of the so-called 'Bayreuth circle', became a sanctified, taboo tradition. As O.G. Bauer wrote, 'The terms "Bayreuth" and "Wahnfried" no longer stood for the festival and its artistic intentions, but for a limited Germanic ideology: nationalistic, conservative, and anti-democratic.'

My father's time as director of the festival also laboured under this tradition, but it was additionally overshadowed by political events, in particular the First World War and the decade-long closure of the Fest-spielhaus. He was unable to stage any new productions there until the end of his life, and it was my mother who put his scenic reform into effect from 1933 onwards. The baneful tradition of the Bayreuth ideology culminated, under the Third Reich, in its misappropriation for the Party's propaganda purposes, although my mother's artistic freedom, in her capacity as festival director, remained inviolate.

When Haus Wahnfried, the Wagner family home, which had been bomb-damaged in the Second World War, was reopened in 1976, my speech included a remark that has often been quoted since: 'I think that bomb *had* to fall.' I was not, of course, referring to the house that had been my parental home, but to the ideology and tradition that had become associated with its name. My decision to share in the adventure of a fresh start stemmed from the realization that Richard Wagner's œuvre is greater than those who have misconstrued and abused it.

1966: A DIFFERENT SITUATION

From 1951, when it restarted after the Second World War, my brother Wieland and I jointly directed the Bayreuth Festival as equal partners. Just how we came to do so, after a succession of eventful years, I shall describe at a later stage, detailing all the objections and opposition we encountered in the process – and many of the circumstances surrounding that process were curious in the extreme. We bore sole overall responsibility for planning and decision-making, productions and sets. Legal documents were not deemed valid unless signed by us both. Although we never resembled Castor and Pollux (we were not twins in any case), ours was a comprehensive and productive working partnership whose strength and durability transcended all our undeniable differences in character and temperament – and this despite the attacks and intrigues of those around us, whose envy often took the form of specious concern. We none the less succeeded in saving the Bayreuth Festival from financial and spiritual ruin and, over the years, in firmly reintegrating it, not only into the cultural life of post-war Germany, but into the worldwide cultural landscape. More will be said below of the multifarious problems and forms of resistance we had to contend with, and of the specific phenomenon that has come to be known, since the mid-1950s, as 'New Bayreuth'.

In June 1966, after fifteen years of joint endeavour, a grave development occurred: my brother became seriously ill and was unable to attend the rehearsals then in progress. It also seemed likely that his illness would prevent him from taking an active part in the festival itself. In spite of my forebodings, I naturally hoped that he would regain his health and refused to entertain the possibility that things might go from bad to worse. His illness created a difficult situation, because it meant that we would for the first time have to dispense with his services not only as one of the two festival directors but, more especially, as a producer – and the festival programme consisted exclusively of his own productions: *Tristan und Isolde, Parsifal, Tannhäuser,* and *Der Ring des Nibelungen.* The latter *Ring,* his second attempt to interpret the tetralogy, had been premièred in 1965 and was now to be repeated for the first time.

At the Festspielhaus, in contrast to many other theatres, it is not only possible but customary to take the lessons learned during a production's first year and incorporate them in subsequent years. Apart from successive improvements in matters of detail, this can also entail considerable changes in casts and sets. Far from being crystallized once and for all, interpretations of a work are subjected to constant criticism and change, so every production remains 'work in progress' in the best and most comprehensive sense. This does not, of course, mean that we begin by putting something on the stage and then allow ourselves a couple of leisurely years in which to eliminate perceived mistakes or remedy shortcomings. In the case of a work as complex and intricate as *The Ring,* which is performed on four successive nights, continuous reassessment and retouching are absolutely essential.

Without the constant presence of my brother, however, this could only be done with difficulty and to a limited extent. A further problem related to his *Parsifal* production, which had undergone many changes since 1951 and was this year to be conducted for the first time by Pierre Boulez – and Wieland, who had pinned great hopes on working with Boulez, had definitely intended to collaborate with him on an evolutionary trans-formation of the work.

So what was to be done? It was clear that my brother did not believe his two assistants of the previous year, Nikolaus Lehnhoff and Wolfram Dehmel, possessed sufficient authority to be entrusted with the difficult and manifold problems that would have to be overcome if they were to produce *The Ring* successfully and in accordance with his intentions. After careful consideration, therefore, Wieland gave the job to Peter Lehmann, who was also his assistant on *Parsifal.* Having worked at Bayreuth since 1960, Lehmann could claim several years' experience in the relevant field. He was also noted for his professional competence, and his tact and understanding enabled him to deal sensibly with a wide variety of people. The term devised for his function was 'scenic coach', which later appeared in print on the evening leaflets. He fully justified the trust placed in him, even though he had not originally assisted Wieland on *The Ring.* The decision to appoint Peter Lehmann was, however, bound to provoke friction and controversy between him, as the assistant in charge, and the two other assistants mentioned above, who repeatedly crossed swords with him. Lehmann's appointment also signified that my brother's wife, Gertrud Wagner, whom Wieland had not enlisted in the new, 1965 production, had been excluded for a second time. There is no indication that he ever at this time considered appointing her to carry on his work. It should be mentioned in this connection that his son Wolf-Siegfried, then in his early twenties, was supposed in 1966 to embark on a systematic study of the workings of the theatre and, more specifically, of the Bayreuth Festival itself. The plan was to employ him as a student lighting technician. His complete lack of professional training naturally precluded his employment as an assistant producer, nor had his father ever contemplated such a step.

Choreographic work on *The Ring*, and the Rhine Maidens' scenes in particular, was the responsibility of Renate Ebermann, whose main claim to fame was her morning keep-fit programme on Bavarian Radio, but who, at Bayreuth, contrived with notable skill to make herself unpopular with almost everyone. Peter Lehmann had a far from easy time of it, being forever exposed to the rancour of those whose pride had been hurt because they felt demoted and affronted.

On 17 June my brother left the Green Hill – as the site of the Festspielhaus is universally known – and the festival to undergo a course of medical treatment, but no one guessed at this stage that he would never return. Three days later he went into the hospital at Kulmbach, and from there he was transferred on 2 July to Munich. At my suggestion his long-time personal assistant Gabriele Taut accompanied him, both to Kulmbach and to Munich, so that she could keep him in constant touch with Bayreuth and current developments there, in which he continued to take a great interest. After my brother had been in hospital for some days, I instituted a regular evening conference after each rehearsal. This gave all concerned an opportunity to record any questions and concerns they thought it absolutely necessary to raise, and the tape was brought to Wieland immediately afterwards. My brother being ill and in need of rest, I was compelled to take this somewhat unusual step to spare him all needless annoyance and agitation. Previously, people had been telephoning whenever they chose and confronting him with matters of moment or pestering him with trivia, and some of them had patently taken full advantage of this favourable opportunity, as they saw it, to hatch plots of various kinds. None of this helped to improve his condition, of course – indeed, it probably made him even more painfully aware of his absence. He was far from indifferent to the fate of his productions, and the breathless tittle-tattle purveyed by many of his 'solicitous' callers could not fail to alarm him and inspire a sense of impotent irritation. He also asked for and was given recordings of musical rehearsals to enable him to follow and check them. These were delivered by Gabriele Taut, who also undertook the task of acquainting him with particular problems and items of information in a suitable form and at the appropriate juncture.

Gabriele Taut had worked in the office during the festival season since 1956, and in 1972 she took over its management during the season. Her predecessor, Gerhard Hellwig, musical director of the 'Schöneberger Sängerknaben' in Berlin, had rehearsed the Noble Pages in *Tannhäuser* in 1954 and 1955 and had been personal consultant and manager of the artistic planning office between 1957 and 1971. He could not, however, make the commitment to work at Bayreuth all year round. From 1 January 1974, Gabriele Taut assumed full-time management of the office and ran it with great efficiency.

The severity of the physical and mental strain to which Wieland was subjected is starkly conveyed by his reply to a telegram from the mayor of Bayreuth, in which the latter had complained to him about the public's exclusion from the dress rehearsal of *Parsifal* at Pierre Boulez's request: 'First, pursuant to information received from the doctors treating me, I respectfully request you to desist from sending me extremely disagreeable telegrams after the beginning of the nightly time of repose customary in all hospitals, thus depriving me of the night's sleep due to any patient. I am appalled that the members of Bayreuth's town council and the mayor of Bayreuth should display such an absolute lack of understanding of the exceptionally difficult circumstances under which the Bayreuth Festival has perforce to be held this year, and take the liberty of pointing out that, quite apart from this year's change of musical directors necessitated by Knappertsbusch's death, and not in respect of *Parsifal* alone, the well-known vacation problems of the entire company and stringent financial economy measures have together reduced rehearsals to a minimum unacceptable by any theatrical director in the world.'

Despite his sojourn in hospital and the limitations it imposed, Wieland naturally took a keen interest in everything to do with the festival, as I have already intimated, and was as active as his circumstances permitted. I was therefore able to discuss and obtain his endorsement of all our plans for the immediate future, and we managed to prepare or even conclude nearly all the contracts for 1967. Thus, the casting of the soloists for the next festival was jointly laid down and settled between us.

After the 1966 festival ended, Wieland was temporarily permitted to leave the hospital in Munich and return to Bayreuth. He at once became his old restless self again and proceeded to forge plans for the future. Having discussed the plan to make a television recording of his *Tannhäuser* production during his last working day on the Hill, he promptly resumed work on that project. He devoted much thought to the prospective Bayreuth Festival visit to Japan and immersed himself in its detailed planning. He also engaged in preparations for various guest performance offers whose acceptance he favoured. They included a production of *Lohengrin* which was scheduled to make its début at the New York Met. But, on 14 October, after several busy, crowded weeks, he had to return to Munich to continue his treatment as an in-patient, having previously done so as an out-patient.

On 15 and 16 October, a weekend, I visited him in Munich, where I stayed with my daughter. Also present at the lengthy bedside discussions I conducted with him on both days was Gerhard Hellwig, who had since 1957 been his personal adviser and head of the artistic planning office. Any matters we had been unable to settle at Bayreuth were discussed and clarified. All these related to current negotiations and were directly connected with festival business. This is attested by the fact that, late on the evening of 16 October, Wieland signed the 1967 contract with Birgit Cullberg, who had choreographed *Tannhäuser* since 1965 and whose employment on *Parsifal* was thereby extended. Filled with concern for my brother, I returned to Bayreuth the same night.

At 4.05 a.m. on 17 October Wieland Wagner died in Munich's 2nd Surgical University Clinic. He was only forty-nine.

As soon as I received the news I drove to the hospital with Dr Helmut Danzer, his schoolfriend and personal physician. There I met Wieland's wife Gertrud and some of his children. He himself was still lying in his private room, so I was able to take leave of him alone and in total silence.

I hesitate to describe my shock and distress, which gave way to a feeling of profound sorrow, because it is seldom possible adequately to express such a sense of loss without giving an impression of false sentimentality or adopting the tone of a formal obituary.

After bidding my brother a last, inexpressibly sad farewell I drove straight back to Bayreuth to arrange for his body to be brought there and to organize the funeral service, which was to take place in the Festspielhaus itself. Not surprisingly, there were so many matters to be dealt with in the next few days that I had little time or opportunity, for the moment at least, to devote my mind to the future. My brother's family also came at once to Bayreuth and assembled at Haus Wahnfried, their family home. After consulting together the same day, we jointly agreed on the form of the funeral service scheduled for 21 October, on the guests to be invited, and on all the matters connected with such a melancholy occasion. We drew up a plan whose detailed provisions covered the timing of the body's transfer from Munich on 18 October; its public lying-in-state on the stage of the Festspielhaus two days later to enable friends, acquaintances and the inhabitants of Bayreuth to pay their last respects; the exact course of the solemn commemorative gathering to be addressed by several speakers on 21 October; and the ensuing burial in the town cemetery, which only members of the family and close friends would attend. Meantime, telegrams and letters of condolence poured in from private individuals and public figures of all kinds, obituaries were published, and representatives of radio and television networks turned up to report on the proceedings. The sympathy evinced by all was as sincere as their dismay at this tragic stroke of fate was great. In Wieland's death, the theatre had sustained a loss that was universally mourned.

On the morning of 21 October, after the townsfolk and numerous visitors from elsewhere had paid their last respects, a party of specially invited mourners assembled on the stage of the Festspielhaus, which had been duly prepared for the occasion. Flying at half-mast above the theatre was the festival flag usually to be seen only in summer, a red W *à la* Dürer on a white ground. The safety curtain had been lowered, and before it stood the simple coffin surrounded by a sea of flowers and innumerable wreaths, some of which were affixed to lowered tie bars. Members of the festival orchestra and chorus, for whom a special platform had been erected, took their places on the right, guests on the left. The proceedings opened with the prelude to *Parsifal* conducted by Pierre Boulez. Ironically enough, this was the first and only time he shared the Festspielhaus stage with Wieland, who had undoubtedly meant to collaborate with him on refurbishing, not only *Parsifal*, but other productions of his. There followed speeches, all of them brief, by Mayor Hans Walter Wild of Bayreuth, Consul Dr Franz Hilger, president of the 'Association of Friends of Bayreuth', and Professor Dr Walter Erich Schäfer, general director of the Stuttgart Opera. After them came Ernst Bloch, Carl Orff, and Wolfgang Windgassen. The minister representing the Federal Republic was Hermann Höcherl, and the last of the addresses was given by Alfons Goppel, the Bavarian premier. The commemorative ceremony ended with the final chorus from Johann Sebastian Bach's *St Matthew Passion*, 'Wir setzten uns mit Tränen nieder', conducted by Wilhelm Pitz, the festival's chorus master. Wieland, it should be added, was the first member of the Wagner family for whom such a ceremony had been held at the Festspielhaus.

The tenor of the speeches was one of dismay – indeed, Ernst Bloch declared that everyone was 'more than shocked and horrified' by my brother's sudden death. No one from the family spoke, not even his sisters and I, who were then too overcome with grief to do so. I did, however, deliver a brief address in 1991, when a commemorative exhibition was opened on the 25th anniversary of Wieland's death. After that lapse of time, of course, I did not pay a formal tribute to him but presented some quite subjective views and thoughts on our work together. It was only then, after so many years had gone by, that I ventured to give public expression to the spiritual and emotional bond between us. For all our differences and all the normal dissensions of the time, and despite all the factitious stories told by third parties about supposedly irreconcilable antagonisms – and there have always been plenty such – the bond between us was one of brotherly love.

Very soon, only a few days after Wieland's funeral, mundane concerns reclaimed my attention with a vengeance. The problems confronting me were not only considerable but in some cases extremely awkward. It was inevitable that rumours should arise here and there about a potential or conceivable successor to my brother on the festival directorate. Wieland had thought it opportune to distance himself from his mother, particularly after her handover of the festival to the two of us, though she herself realized that her past disqualified her from further direct association with Bayreuth. Since, unlike him, I had never been as relentlessly cool towards our mother Winifred, but had in general striven to conciliate, or at least to maintain a mother-son relationship, it was even suspected that I proposed to involve her more closely in the affairs of the festival. I did not, however, contemplate this step at any stage, and my mother was equally aware of its absolute impossibility. It was only natural that she should have been deeply distressed by the untimely loss of her elder son, and that she was concerned about the festival's future, but she was quite objective and wholly alive to the consequences of Wieland's death. 'Put your trust in my son Wolfgang, whose sole and burdensome responsibility it now is to ensure the continued success of the festival, and help him to solve his problems!' She wrote this in a letter dated 24 October to the staff on the Hill. Having lost her husband, my father Siegfried, when she was just thirty-three years old, she was personally acquainted with the difficulties confronting anyone who assumed sole responsibility for an undertaking such as the Bayreuth Festival.

Winifred had entrusted my brother and me with the running of the festival in 1949, after long years of difficulties of which more will be said at a later stage. In view of these, and of the problems that had arisen when the management changed hands in earlier years, it became desirable that Wieland and I should ourselves conclude an agreement that would guarantee continuity and insure the festival against any needless disruption in the event that one of us dropped out. I and Dr Gottfried Breit, our legal and business adviser, managed to draft a partnership agreement that defined our relationship and mutual obligations. Lengthy negotiations finally produced a form of words to which my brother, too, signified his assent, and which he was willing to endorse. Wieland and I signed the document, which thus became legally valid, on 30 April 1962. Our mother, in her capacity as owner of the Festspielhaus, was also in agreement with the contract and approved it without more ado. It reaffirmed what had already appeared in her 1949 declaration of assignment, namely, that both partners enjoyed equal rights. Clause 5 stated: 'Both partners are jointly entitled and obligated to manage and represent the company.' Another very important clause, which became fully effective under the existing situation, stated that, in the event of one partner's death, his share should pass to the survivor. Clause 8: 'No dispute with the heirs will occur in this case [in the event of a takeover].' The agreement laid it down that the survivors should receive an appropriate annuity.

Prompted by certain misgivings and by the most diverse demands from various quarters including members of my family, whose singular powers of imagination all too often compensated for their regrettable failure to come to terms with incontrovertible facts, I kept in more or less continuous touch with Dr Breit. After another consultation at his Munich office on 10 November 1966, I went on to Stuttgart to see Dr Walter Schäfer, for many years a close and fatherly friend of mine and my brother's, to seek his advice on certain points of law as they related to the theatre. Our conversation very soon yielded a singularly intimate exchange of views on my late brother, about whom Dr Schäfer was later to write a sympathetic and perceptive book.

Dr Schäfer told me he considered it a great tragedy that financial necessity should have compelled Wieland, particularly in his later years, to stage so many second-hand copies of his Bayreuth productions at other theatres. This had deprived him of the time and energy to enrich his artistic endeavours in respect of our grandfather's work with new and expressive interpretations.

Conversation then turned to Wolf-Siegfried, Wieland's son, who, despite all the loving care lavished on him, had been a considerable source of worry to his father. Now twenty-three, he showed no signs of embarking on a serious course of training and was not studying on a regular basis, so Dr Schäfer offered to take him on at the Stuttgart Opera. This would have enabled him to familiarize himself with the full scope and ramifications of the theatre 'from the bottom up', but also with its far from always glamorous everyday reality, and thus to become gradually acquainted with the business. However, Wolf-Siegfried thought he could qualify himself for Bayreuth without studying hard or pursuing a comparable form of training, simply by acting as assistant to a few celebrated producers. He consequently declined this friendly and well-meant offer. Dr Schäfer, being extremely concerned about this Wagner of the next generation, was bitterly disappointed. Like Wieland, he considered it absolutely essential that Wolf-Siegfried should develop and perfect his practical knowledge by acquiring the theoretical tools of the trade. In a letter to Wolf-Siegfried dated 29 September 1966, a copy of which went to the financial department of the Bayreuth Festival and came to my notice in that way, Wieland had expressly urged his son to embark on a systematic course of training, since Wolf-Siegfried had at last, after a number of vague forays in other directions, definitely opted for a career in the theatre. Wieland clearly had no intention of training his son himself, because he requested his regular attendance at the Reinhardt seminar in Vienna, up to and including the final examinations. For his part, he offered to initiate all the requisite steps and handle all the formalities. Wieland's letter also contained very definite indications that he would in future be compelled to impose considerably tighter financial constraints on his children. He gave a very precise account of his resources because he wished to ensure, doubtless in view of his prolonged illness, that the chaos hitherto prevailing in his family's finances would not lead to total collapse. His financial problems were accumulating at an alarming rate, not least because the original budget for the house he had purchased at Keitum on the island of Sylt had been exceeded by roughly 200 per cent, part of the reason being Gertrud Wagner's unbridled and rather extravagant insistence on renovating it.

My brother urgently needed the guest performances, which brought him an additional income, in order to avert the disaster that so constantly threatened him like a Damoclean sword. He pinned great hopes, artistic as well as financial, on the Japanese project.

At the end of October 1966 I was contacted by the well-known artists' agent Martin Taubmann, whom I had known since 1950, with a view to discussing the outside productions approved or envisaged by Wieland and the form in which they were to be carried out. The Japanese project, in particular, needed clarifying as soon as possible, because *Die Walküre* and *Tristan und Isolde* were scheduled to be performed with the Bayreuth cast at the Osaka Festival in spring 1967. Martin Taubmann, who had arranged this tour, was understandably eager to get it settled from the contractual and administrative aspect. Wieland had met and entered into personal negotiations with the director of the festival, Mrs Murayama, in Munich at the beginning of the month. I myself had taken no part in these talks and had held aloof from the initial preparations because I thought my brother's demands were excessive and unwarranted. Given that Bayreuth's own financial circumstances, though not disastrous, were straitened enough to restrict us to basic necessities, I considered his overweening attitude towards another festival unjustified and disapproved of it accordingly.

My original dissociation from the Japanese tour prompted an intervention on the part of my brother's widow, who rather impulsively and precipitately sought to assert her right and duty to exploit it for her family's personal and financial benefit. Confusion having arisen from her ignorance and her superficial misinterpretations of a simple and straightforward state of affairs, Mrs Murayama invited me and Martin Taubmann to Zurich to clear the air and reach a final, effective and appropriate settlement of all outstanding differences. This was not the first nor the last time I encountered such complications, some of which proved far harder to deal with. It seems clear that many members of the Wagner family and its offshoots have an innate tendency to provoke these. This, as we shall see, is eloquently attested by past history and present experience.

Our meeting with Mrs Murayama had been scheduled for 11/12 November 1966, the other participants being Gerhard Hellwig and Gabriele Taut. My sister-in-law Gertrud also travelled to Zurich for the occasion. I bumped into her as she was descending the stairs of our hotel accompanied by Walter Legge, an extremely talented man but one who inspired me with very mixed feelings born of our encounters in earlier years, as I shall describe. Gertrud, who did not attend the discussions, was represented at them by her then attorney, Herr von Castelberg.

Mrs Murayama had proceeded on the assumption that the tour, which had already been publicly announced, would be an official, Bayreuth Festival fixture. She intimated that the project would be doomed to failure unless the Bayreuth management took responsibility for it. There could be no question of dropping out at this stage, because preparations were already far advanced. The three parties concerned, that is to say, the Bayreuth Festival, the Osaka Festival, and Martin Taubmann, had to reach a feasible agreement and define the legal means of carrying it out in a clear and conclusive manner.

As scenic director I eventually appointed Peter Lehmann, who had acquitted himself extremely well in that capacity during the previous festival season. Gertrud Wagner could not be considered a candidate for the post because she had assisted on neither *Tristan* nor *Die Walküre*. Very obligingly and generously, Mrs Murayama agreed to pay her, as Wieland's widow, an 'honorarium' amounting to 75 per cent of the sum due to my brother. This left all concerned free to steer the detailed technical and practical arrangements for the Osaka tour in the right direction.

A Vienna production of *Der Fliegende Holländer* scheduled for March 1967 was assigned to Gertrud Wagner, who was engaged in her late husband's place on the understanding that she would direct the work in accordance with his ideas and precise instructions, not turn it into something of her own. Her success in Vienna was not, however, sufficient to warrant any claim to Bayreuth.

April 1967 saw the final settlement of all the other projects connected with Wieland's artistic estate in so far as they related to outstanding productions. This agreement, concluded on 19 April between my brother's heirs on the one hand and, on the other, the municipality of Bayreuth, the 'Association of Friends', and myself, was important from every point of view. It effected a generous settlement of my brother's financial liabilities, which had accrued from loans and extra withdrawals from our partnership under civil law, a substantial proportion of which I forbore to recover from his heirs, just as the 'Association of Friends', whose crucial role in our post-war re-establishment I will describe in due course, did everything possible to ease their financial situation in the most obliging manner. In addition to the foregoing provisions, however, all the signatories including Wieland's wife and her children acknowledged that, where the interpretation of his grandfather's works was concerned, Wieland Wagner's artistic estate was to be administered and utilized by the Bayreuth Festival alone. The heirs further undertook to refrain from making any statements that might tend to cast doubt on the facts as now contractually defined. Wieland's family also agreed not to produce any works by Richard Wagner until 30 August 1969.

The agreement was of equal relevance to the artists who had been engaged for the current year, most of whom had received contracts signed by my brother and me. They were now most insistent that all legal ambiguity be banished by creating a situation in which everyone knew where authority and responsibility rested. Indeed, some of them gave me to understand that they would not remain at Bayreuth or work there if one of Wieland's heirs had a say in things, because that would probably add fuel to the flames.

The six months between my brother's death and this agreement were taken up with intensive consultations and discussions between me and representatives of the public, public authorities, and, above all, board members and trustees of the 'Association of Friends of Bayreuth'. Although there was never the slightest doubt that sole charge of the festival had passed to me under the partnership agreement of 1962, we were concerned lest Bayreuth be imperilled by a kind of 'schism' arising from the firmly held but erroneous ideas of Wieland's heirs and the squabbles so closely associated with them.

One development that alarmed us and intensified our misgivings was a Norddeutscher Rundfunk television interview between Gertrud Wagner and Berndt W. Wessling on 8 December 1966. Wessling was a journalist with whom Wieland, who was not alone in protesting against his forms of presentation, had clashed in the past. Five days after this spectacular television appearance, which had aired the family's tensions and dissensions in public, I held a meeting whose purpose was to preclude any recurrence of such dubious publicity and instil a sense of realism. Gertrud agreed that she would, with immediate effect, refrain from making any more remarks in the same vein because, quite apart from being defamatory, they could only harm the festival. It was not until 16 December that my sister-in-law informed me in writing of her reasons for giving such an 'essential' interview, in which she had spent most of the time belittling my brother's achievements, the better to present a puzzled and incredulous world with a highly-coloured account of her imperishable contributions to New Bayreuth.

Although I had counted at first on their intelligence and goodwill, and later on their grasp of straightforward legal facts, it became steadily more apparent to me in the course of numerous conversations after Wieland's death that neither his widow nor his other 'heirs' had any serious intention of accepting situations and decisions disagreeable to them, and that they clung to arbitrary interpretations and applications of the agreements in force. Above all, they seemed to think it certain, indeed, an absolutely foregone conclusion, that they would be reintegrated into the running of the festival – and, what was more, in positions of authority.

I was left with no choice but to make statements to my sister-in-law, among others, which she construed as a personal humiliation to add to those which she felt she had already suffered in abundance at her late husband's hands and no longer wished to acknowledge – for instance, that he had ceased to enlist her services for the Bayreuth Festival. In the aforesaid letter of 16 December 1966 she wrote: 'Dear Wolf, I cannot forbear briefly to explain ... the crucial reason: your and Mama's hostile statements about me after Wieland's death – the disparagement of our last conversations and the spreading of lies about a divorce in an endeavour, after all that I had undergone, to deal me a final blow in some way or other.'

These developments clearly demonstrated that there was no possibility of common sense prevailing – a common sense that was badly needed if the Bayreuth Festival were to be realistically associated with one side of the family.

Had it not been essential to clear the air in this way, my 'spare-time' work – current preparations for the 1967 festival, which I now had to handle on my own – would have proceeded along 'normal' lines. I additionally had to carry out the spadework for my new production of *Lohengrin* and crystallize my plans for the sets in a manner satisfactory to myself, and I was naturally under pressure to supply the workshops with my sketches and designs in good time. There were also gaps in the cast list to be filled. At the Festspielhaus on 8 November, in the thick of the above turmoil, I had to audition Donald McIntyre. In consultation with my *Lohengrin* conductor, Rudolf Kempe, who knew him from England, I engaged McIntyre to sing Telramund. It was a part that launched him on his subsequent, meteoric international career.

Such, in short, were the events and preoccupations with which I had to contend in the aftermath of Wieland's death. Under the circumstances I believe that to have concluded the family agreement of 19 April and to have completed the bulk of the festival's work in progress – all in the space of six months – was no small achievement. But now, of course, I bore the responsibilities of the festival's sole director, and time alone would tell how those responsibilities would be discharged.

I badly needed a spell of calm contemplation in which to reflect on what had to be done and what changes were necessary in the wake of my brother's death. Taking advantage of the only time available, five days at the end of October 1966, I retired with my wife to the Chiemsee in Upper Bavaria, where I remained incommunicado and devoted the brief respite to self-examination. It was an attempt, by putting some physical distance between myself and Bayreuth, to gain the detachment I needed in order to conduct a leisurely review of the problems that were crowding in on me.

3

ON TIME AND SPACE

After the first Bayreuth Festival in 1876 Wagner took stock of the situation. Although he had only fulfilled his ideas and aims to a very limited extent and was far from satisfied with the artistic quality of the performances, he cherished the hope that he would be able to present them in a new and quite different form the following year. Against this, there was the huge loss that had been incurred, which loomed over the festival like a thunder-cloud and threatened its continued existence. Great efforts had to be made to reduce and defray this deficit, notably by Wagner himself, who conducted a series of concerts in London.

Experience of the new theatre, *The Ring*, and, last but not least, of audience reaction, had taught him numerous lessons during the first festival. These spilled over into his composition and into the première of *Parsifal*, his 'farewell to the world', which took place in 1882. He felt that the sixteen performances given that year had brought him considerably closer to his festival ideal.

On 18 November 1882 he wrote to his patron King Ludwig II of Bavaria concerning the future of Bayreuth. The years 1883 and 1884 were to be devoted exclusively to as many performances as possible of *Parsifal*. Wagner assumed that the income from admission fees – he would have to sell tickets contrary to his original intention, which had been to admit the public free of charge – would provide 'a basis for the accumulation of as large a fund as possible'. And this in turn would provide the wherewithal, as time went by, to present all his works from *Der Fliegende Holländer* onwards 'at our stage festival theatre in such a manner that those performances can be handed down to the next generation as models of correctness'.

Where his successor was concerned, he hoped – as he wrote in the same letter to the king – to be able to enjoy some ten more years of active life, by which time his son would be of age, for it was to him alone that he would entrust the 'spiritual and ethical preservation' of his work:

'... whereas I know of no one else to whom I could entrust my office.'
His dream never came true. Barely three months later, on 13 February
1883, he died in Venice, the city where he had dreamed it.

His unexpected departure from 'life's stage' had repercussions on the
festival that were tragic from every point of view. From now on, *Parsifal*
was celebrated as a requiem and every detail of its performance declared
sacrosanct.

In 1886, *Parsifal* alone having been performed in 1883 and 1884, as
Wagner had foreseen, his widow Cosima officially took charge of the
festival and staged her own first production, *Tristan und Isolde*. Step by step
over the next two decades or so, she built up the whole of the Bayreuth
repertoire, ranging from first performances of *Die Meistersinger* (1888),
Tannhäuser (1891), and *Lohengrin* (1894), and a second complete staging of
Der Ring des Nibelungen (1896), to a production of *Der Fliegende Holländer* in
1901.

This dogged and persevering process of development, during which the
festival became consolidated and institutionalized, was undeniably her
greatest service to Bayreuth. She was, however, wholly un-Wagnerian in
her insistence on preserving productions unchanged and thereby building
up an inviolable tradition which nothing and no one could challenge. She
did not consider it her function to create anything new or trend-setting.

Her guiding principle, in a nutshell, was as follows: she endeavoured to
reconstruct on the Bayreuth stage those performances that had taken place
during Wagner's lifetime and, in certain cases, with his direct participation,
some of which, like the Munich premières of *Tristan und Isolde* (1865) and
Die Meistersinger (1868), he had then considered exemplary. She was, however,
selective in her rejection of anything she considered currently inappropriate,
which she remedied as she thought fit. She also enriched her productions
with personal knowledge. In so doing she enlisted the services of sundry
specialists, among them her two sons-in-law: my aunt Daniela's husband,
the art historian Henry Thode, and aunt Eva's husband Houston Stewart
Chamberlain, whose aura and influence were far more ideological than
artistic.

Under Cosima's aegis the *Bayreuther Blätter*, edited from 1878 onwards by
Hans von Wolzogen, steadily developed into a bastion of out-and-out
'*Deutschtum*' [German chauvinism]. Wagner, whose initial enthusiasm for
the German Empire of 1871 quickly waned, had regarded it with growing
scepticism and disillusionment. This is apparent from a letter he wrote to
Ludwig II on 10 February 1878, in which he remarked that few people
had been quick to realize 'that the aridity of Prussian political thought was
to be imposed on us as a German imperial principle!' Now, after his death,
Bayreuth unreservedly espoused the political ideology of the Wilhelminian

imperium. Cosima Wagner, often disparaged as a 'foreigner', embraced 'Germanism' in a bloated, extravagant manner and infused the festival with nationalistic elements never envisaged or intended in that way by her late husband, as his articles and letters – and, above all, his scores – testify with sufficient eloquence. Bayreuth forgot or ignored the demand he had made of art: 'Just as Greek art embodied the ethos of a fine nation, so must the art of the future transcend all national barriers and embody the spirit of free humanity; its national features must be no more than an ornament, the charm of individual diversity, not an inhibiting restriction.' Those words became the keynote of New Bayreuth.

Unlike Wagner, Cosima no longer construed 'Bayreuth' as an alternative to the theatre of his day. To her, it represented the unsurpassable and only legitimate exemplar *per se*. She did not consider it necessary to realize Wagner's visions by studying the extremely fruitful developments that were taking place in other theatres, still less by submitting them to unprejudiced analysis, so she ignored them. There was no question at Bayreuth of accepting Adolphe Appia's theoretical approach to Wagner productions, which he evolved in critical opposition to the Bayreuth style, and which Gustav Mahler and Alfred Roller translated into exemplary productions at the Vienna State Opera early this century. Cosima's limited artistic horizon is particularly well illustrated by the arrogant 'Norn's decree' she wrote to Chamberlain on 13 May 1896: 'Appia seems unaware that *The Ring* was performed here in '76, and that, consequently, there is nothing more to be devised in the way of scenery and direction.' Her authority, legitimized by her life's companionship with Wagner and his personal communications to her, was generally accepted without demur. Invoked and consulted whenever someone sought information about Wagner, she regarded herself as the high priestess of the Wagner cult. For her, Wagner's spirit hovered over the Festspielhaus like the dove of the Holy Grail. The theatre was her temple.

In the autumn of 1955, when I visited Albert Schweitzer at Günsbach, he told me that Wagner's work had gained such full acceptance and legitimacy by the time Cosima took over the festival that it did not need defending, still less justifying. Schweitzer also said that he had never understood the 'enemy image' which Cosima had artificially created for herself, and which found expression in a form of anti-Semitism that was, in her view, justified by the pamphlet *Judaism in Music*.

My grandfather's attitude to anti-Semitism was ambivalent and inconsistent. In addition to a number of extremely reprehensible and distressing verbal aberrations that owe their notoriety to constant repetition, past and present, one could cite many contrasting and more enlightened statements and, above all, many examples of actual behaviour, that bespeak the very opposite of a fanatical anti-Semite. But Cosima, in her prejudice, deliberately suppressed this other side. The same applies to her husband's stated ideas in the diaries she kept with such scrupulous care, which were intended for her only son, Siegfried, who never saw them. 'R. said yesterday: "If I ever wrote again about the Jews, I should say I have nothing against them; it's simply that they joined us Germans too soon; we weren't yet stable enough to assimilate that element"' (22 November 1878); 'Summarizing his verdict on the Jews, he said: "Here, at least, they were emancipated a generation too soon"' (25 November 1878); 'Personally, he said, he has had some very good Jewish friends, but it was pernicious to emancipate and grant them equal status before we Germans amounted to something' (27 December 1878); '...R. then reverts to the subject of Jews as actors – to think that he could still write in '53 that there weren't any, and now! And the way they treated our language!' (17 September 1881).

In 1908, when my father Siegfried Wagner took over the management of the festival from his mother, he could not, unfortunately, be familiarized with the task and prepared for it by his father, as the latter had intended, but was largely dependent on his mother's schooling. He was not, however, a blind or blinkered Bayreuth 'initiate', because his first love had been architecture, which he studied for a short time. During a tour of the Far East in 1892, which took him all the way to China, he voluntarily decided to undertake the systematic development of his musical talents and propensities. His teacher was Engelbert Humperdinck, and he received friendly advice from the Bayreuth conductors Hans Richter, Hermann Levi, and Felix Mottl. In 1894, when Mottl was unexpectedly taken ill during a Bayreuth performance of *Lohengrin* and none of the other festival conductors was available, Siegfried conducted the third act. He did not, however, make his real début until the 1896 festival, when he successfully conducted Cosima's 'new edition' of *The Ring* alongside veteran conductors like Richter and Mottl.

It was no easy matter to grow up under the aegis of Cosima, the imperious queen of Bayreuth, and her devoted, submissive courtiers, who fished in troubled waters on their own account, nor to be an only, idolized son in the 'care' of four half-sisters. In my opinion, he managed to fulfil and for many years sustain his preordained role as heir to Bayreuth only because he was an amiable, intelligent, self-contained man who showed great understanding and sympathy for others.

His first five independent festival years prior to the outbreak of the First World War were largely a continuation of Cosima's work where staging was concerned, though there was a perceptible change in choral direction. He had, however, developed lighting technique into his own special field during his years as an assistant, if only because his mother had been compelled to neglect this aspect of stage production by her impaired and deteriorating eyesight. It was not until his latter years at Bayreuth, after the festival reopened in 1924, that my father finally cut his personal and artistic 'umbilical cord' and emerged from a phase governed by ossified pseudo-traditions.

Mention must be made, in connection with my father, of Bayreuth's special system of financial administration. The payment of royalties, which had hitherto been treated in various ways, was standardized by the Berne Convention of 1886 for the protection of works of art. Since Wagner was one of the most-performed stage composers at the turn of the century, both at home and abroad, the family were relieved of all the money worries that had so plagued my grandfather.

In return for the salary remitted to Wagner from his privy purse, King Ludwig II had been granted the rights in all Wagner's works subsequent to 1864. In accordance with this provision, Munich's Court Theatre paid no royalties. On 20 February 1874, when work on the Festspielhaus was halted by lack of money, the king saved the project from certain ruin by granting 'the governing body of the Stage Festival' a loan of 100,000 thalers. Drawing on the festival budget, Wagner and his heirs gradually redeemed this loan with repayments amounting to 216,152 marks 42 pfennigs.

The first festival incurred a disastrous loss of approximately 148,000 marks. All efforts to the contrary, nearly 100,000 marks were still outstanding at the beginning of 1878, so there was no immediate prospect of repeating the festival; in other words, the Bayreuth première of *Parsifal*, then in process of composition, was receding into the indefinite future. At this stage, after long and fruitless negotiations, Cosima addressed a fervent appeal to the king. It had the desired effect. Adolf von Gross, Haus Wahnfried's financial administrator, concluded the agreement on Wagner's behalf on 31 March 1878. It was a contract that embodied an interest-bearing loan and guaranteed that the Munich Court Orchestra and other personnel would be available for the first performance of *Parsifal* at Bayreuth. In return, Wagner would release *Parsifal* to Munich. Although he was now entitled to receive royalties on all performances of his works from Munich as well as elsewhere, these were to be set against his indebtedness until it was discharged. On 24 October 1879 the king waived his right to a Munich première of *Parsifal* and formally agreed that it 'shall only be given at Bayreuth'.

By 1901 the Wagners had paid off their debts. Unfortunately, they were neglectful and short-sighted enough in the ensuing years to omit to improve and reconstruct the Festspielhaus, which had been built as a temporary expedient, in such a way that it would stand up to continuous use. They also failed to introduce the innovations essential to performances of works that were, from the technical aspect alone, immensely difficult to stage. Their financial investments were so 'skilfully' managed that the family fortune, which had considerably appreciated, was almost wiped out by the First World War and inflation. This imposed a heavy burden on my father, because he could no longer afford to renew sets whose replacement was long overdue. At the reopening in 1924, but even in 1925, he had to make do with some of the old canvas scenery, which was falling to pieces.

He was compelled to husband his resources with extreme care and make economies. He had, with a heavy heart, to forgo a new production in 1924/5 in order to finance the major extension behind the main stage area needed for the 'rock wagons', the three-dimensional scenery of the successive *Ring* revival, and the construction of new technical workshops. By the 1928 festival he had managed to acquire a new lighting system equal to all the demands made on it. With the aid of this and new scenery he was able to realize all the 'light-painting' ideas that had been impracticable during the pre-war years. His long-cherished wish to stage a new production of *Tannhäuser*, which had not been performed since 1904, could not be fulfilled until my mother and his friends set up the so-called 'Tannhäuser Fund' to mark his sixtieth birthday.

Winifred, twenty-eight years his junior and a thoroughgoing realist, drew my father's attention to the curious fact that, even as an adult, he was still under the financial tutelage of Adolf von Gross. Cosima had made over to my father her fifty per cent share in Haus Wahnfried, its appurtenances, contents and furnishings (including the whole of the Wahnfried archives) in 1913, together with her interest in the Festspielhaus, its contents and outbuildings, and the festival working capital. Neither my mother nor I myself could ever understand why Adolf von Gross's power of attorney persisted into the 1920s, regardless of the fact that the property had changed hands. It was revoked at my mother's resolute instigation, though not, of course, without some resistance.

When, in 1930, my mother succeeded my father at the age of thirty-three, she also inherited a great many worries. Demand for tickets in 1933 was poor, owing to the absence of visitors from abroad. At the end of the 1920s she and my father had jointly developed something that would now be termed a marketing concept. A mailing list was built up, and certain professional groups, notably doctors and lawyers, were sent circular letters encouraging them to attend the festival. In 1929 a balcony was installed between the rearmost lower tier of boxes and the gallery above. This was reserved for the press, whose representatives were regularly circularized after the manner of a news agency. I remember being 'conscripted' as a schoolboy to operate the addressograph at home. It blackened my fingers with printer's ink, indelible traces of which can still be detected to this day on a piece of furniture in my home.

The professional competence of the young woman now in charge of the festival was strongly questioned at first, by Wilhelm Furtwängler among others, but my father had pronounced her capable of running it in their joint testament. Her first year in sole, independent charge of the festival was 1931, which 'merely' repeated the previous year's programme – not, as one still sees it frequently stated, 1933.

After attending a Berlin performance of *Lohengrin* in 1929, my father had intimated to my mother that, should he have to drop out for any reason, he thought Tietjen and Preetorius would be the men to assist her. She followed that advice after his death: having no directorial ambitions herself, she engaged Heinz Tietjen, who also acted as her artistic adviser, and employed Emil Preetorius to design new sets. Her own share in this division of labour, one that accorded with her real abilities, was that of organizer. As the person who bore overall responsibility, she ensured that the business ran smoothly and built up an ensemble of great artistic distinction.

Her stage design reform differed from the usual, countrywide 'state naturalism' (Dietrich Mack) in its artistic pretensions. She would never have considered employing a designer like Benno von Arendt, later the 'Reich stage designer' who botched the festival meadow in *Die Meistersinger* into an avenue of flags reminiscent of Nazi Party rallies. Heedless of vehement protests, she saw to it that the ancient *Parsifal* scenery of 1882, which had become a museum piece, vanished into the limbo where it had long belonged. But Siegfried had already introduced substantial changes earlier on, for instance to the flower garden in 1911. In 1924, while still a trainee, the stage designer Kurt Söhnlein mentioned in his diary that, when the festival was over, Siegfried had thanked him for his assistance and 'asked me to think of a design for the "Klingsor tower" [in Act II of *Parsifal*] for 1925, because the old, existing one was "the most boring piece of scenery in Bayreuth".'

Public outrage at the 'sacrilege' perpetrated by Winifred on the remaining two-thirds of *Parsifal* intensified. It was spearheaded by her sisters-in-law, Daniela and Eva, whose supporters included Richard Strauss and Toscanini. Orthodox Wagnerians from democratic Switzerland appealed for help to the government as personified by Adolf Hitler, of all people. It was categorically demanded that the scenery 'on which the Master's eye had rested' should be preserved – to all eternity, one presumes. My mother entrusted the zealous Daniela with the direction of the last performances of the old production in 1933. I believe today that this move was undoubtedly meant to demonstrate the sheer impossibility of conserving a production for decades on end, unchanged and without the smallest divergence from the original. A 'reverent' assistant producer amused himself by painstakingly proving beyond doubt that Daniela herself had made sixty-four 'errors', but my mother's clever ploy failed to silence the protests once they had been unleashed. I find it ironical that history should have repeated itself after the 1973 festival, when I had perforce to abandon my brother's *Parsifal* sets after twenty-two years and undertook the task of designing new ones. In that instance, however, the protesters had no authoritarian state to enlist as an arbiter.

The *Parsifal* furore of 1933/4 was very characteristic of the family atmosphere that had been smouldering in and around Wahnfried since Winifred entered it on her marriage to my father. Her sisters-in-law, Eva and Daniela, took umbrage at my youthful mother's failure to participate in the cult and rituals surrounding Cosima, the old doyenne. She was too unconventional for them. They accused her of bringing up her children in what today would be termed an 'anti-authoritarian' manner. They also reproached her because I and my brother and sisters had behaved 'unbecomingly' in the family box during a performance of *Parsifal* and had failed to show sufficient awestruck respect for such a sacred Bayreuth relic.

The only thing my mother had in common with her sisters-in-law was membership of the Nazi Party, which all three had joined at an early stage. Winifred Wagner's relationship with Adolf Hitler was a singular one. Her adoptive parents, the Klindworths, had reared her in the spirit of German nationalism and the ideology of the 'Bayreuth circle'. She was eighteen years old when she married my father during the First World War and moved into Wahnfried. After Germany's defeat in 1918, the Kaiser's abdication, and the proclamation of a republic, many people of nationalistic and conservative views found it hard to come to terms with the new, Weimar-style democracy. My mother, who shared this standpoint, defined it thus: 'The lamentable outcome of the war in 1918 had smashed Germany externally and, internally, set off a series of revolutionary surges that incited German against German and claimed countless lives. It had further subjected us all to the misery of unemployment and, in its train, hunger, cold, disease, and, ultimately, the rigours of inflation. In consequence, the heart of every right-minded German bled at the shame and disgrace that had descended on us, and longed for one thing only: that all Germans should join hands across the dozens of political parties and, with heartfelt faith in the future, collaborate in bringing about the genesis of a new German Reich.'

In the early 1920s Adolf Hitler, then just over thirty and a self-styled writer, had become 'acceptable' in the politico-literary salons of the cultivated Munich bourgeoisie, which included the art publishers Bruckmann and Hanftstaengl and the piano manufacturer Bechstein and their wives. My mother had, as she herself put it, an idealistic conception of faith in the 'national revival' propagated by Hitler, but she involved herself little in Party activities because she was uninterested them.

My mother first met Adolf Hitler when he visited Wahnfried on 1 October 1923. She never made any secret of the fact that she was instantly fascinated by his personality, and that this occasion marked the beginning of a lifelong friendship. It was also Hitler's first encounter with Wahnfried's resident ideologist, Houston Stewart Chamberlain, who had been married to my Aunt Eva since 1908. Hitler later said of Chamberlain that he had forged the spiritual sword with which they (the National Socialists) were now fighting. As for Chamberlain, who was deeply impressed, he wrote to Hitler a few days after his visit: 'It testifies to Germany's vitality that she should, in her hour of greatest need, have given birth to a Hitler.' I still find it inexplicable that my mother, who in general had such an unerring sense of reality, could have believed in such nonsense. A 'citation' addressed to my father by Hitler on 5 May 1924 thanked him and Winifred for their 'electoral assistance'.

In her written statements, my mother always took it as read that she and her husband shared the same political outlook. I must simply accept her testimony in this respect because I was, of course, too young to form an opinion, and she never mentioned the subject in later years.

My father did not join the Nazi Party, a decision he based on consideration for his position as festival director. He died on 4 August 1930, so he did not live to see the National Socialists come to power or the way they misused that power. Chamberlain, apostrophized as 'the Prophet of the Third Reich', also died before the accession of his Aryan Messiah.

On the first day of the 'Thousand-Year Reich' (it actually survived for 4,482 days) I was in bed recovering from one of my numerous childhood ailments. My mother brought me a portable wireless set, which was roughly the size of a machine that could now destroy the whole world by remote control, so that I could listen to the latest news: the appointment as Reich Chancellor of Adolf Hitler, known to those at Wahnfried, and to us children in particular, by his pseudonym 'Wolf'. I well remember her saying that he would probably suffer the same fate as his predecessors as head of government, none of whom had remained in office for long, because his majority was insufficient to enable him to govern effectively. It seems strange and paradoxical that my British-born mother, with her democratic cast of mind and profound aversion to authoritarianism, should have been taken in by a dictator. That, in my opinion, was the central contradiction in her personality. For her, Hitler was first and foremost the private individual with whom she got on well, to whom she felt bound by ties of friendship, and for whom she preserved a 'Nibelung loyalty' to the bitter end.

My mother took advantage of their close friendship to augment the independence of the festival and of herself as its director. She never joined the Reich Theatre Chamber, nor was the Bayreuth Festival ever declared 'important to the Reich', still less a 'Reich festival'. She enjoyed the special status of someone with direct access to the seat of power.

Having learned and inherited her conception of her role from my father, she would not make any artistic concessions, for instance to contemporary taste. Bayreuth's modernization and the recognition it earned her were attributable to her own efforts, not to her membership of the Party. She did, however, suffer Nazi propaganda to flaunt the festival's reputation and, so to speak, employ it as a stage on which to mount its own performances.

This cast doubt on the artistic freedom that was so fiercely defended inside the theatre. The propaganda associated with Bayreuth worked only because it extracted whatever suited its own purposes from the universality of Wagner's œuvre – a selective mode of procedure similar to Cosima's.

Adolf Hitler's passion for Wagner served to legitimize his own political mission, because he used Wagner's conception of a national art form for the benefit of his personal ideology. German art was whatever the National Socialists proclaimed it to be. Apart from Wagner, the artists who were accorded this 'honour' included Beethoven and Franz Liszt, the Austro-Hungarian composer with the French lifestyle – in fact a theme from the latter's symphonic poem *Les Préludes* was misused as the victory fanfare that preceded special radio announcements during the Second World War. One has only to compare the achievements of Wagner or Beethoven with those of the Third Reich's officially approved exponents of painting, sculpture, music, drama, or architecture – all of them second-hand products alternating between banality and megalomania – to perceive the full extent of that misappropriation and misuse.

I cannot put it better than Ernst Bloch, with whom my brother and I were on friendly terms: 'The Nazis' music isn't the prelude to *Die Meistersinger*, it's the Horst-Wessel-Lied; they have no other claim to fame, nor can or should they be credited with any other.'

As a son I always had great respect and regard for my mother, just as I always defended and supported her after the war, when the festival's transfer was under negotiation. She reared her four children in the spirit of liberalism and without subjecting them to the compulsion of overweening authority, which she taught them to mistrust. She also granted each of us the freedom to develop and exploit our particular talents. She never exerted any pressure on us to adopt her political beliefs. I myself neither shared them, nor did I ever join the Nazi Party. My mother's political orientation remains a fateful spiritual burden which I must bear to the end of my days, the more so since, with typical Welsh obstinacy, she never deviated from it. That her political creed was not and is not my own has, I feel, been sufficiently demonstrated by my decades of work for the Bayreuth Festival. I have overcome the past, not by making public statements to the media, but as festival director.

There are no skeletons in Wahnfried's cupboard. All documents relating to the festival's political and ideological history have either been published or are, at the very least, accessible to anyone interested in the subject. I draw a line between my mother's political beliefs and the credit she deserves for having handed over the Bayreuth Festival to me and my brother in a renovated, consolidated state and, thus, for having enabled us to perpetuate and renovate it in our turn. We were always aware that, over and above our own activities on the festival's behalf, one of our aims must be to join with her in clearly and unequivocally regulating and ensuring its continued existence.

4

GROWING UP

Now that I have essayed an outline of the primary considerations that have played a major and decisive part in my life, it is time to pay tribute to and, in a more relaxed and somewhat unorthodox manner, conduct a review of those who were responsible for my physical existence and have ultimately played an appreciable part in determining the course of my life.

The ideological criteria of the Third Reich compelled every German 'privileged' to live in it to make an extensive and exhaustive study of his or her family tree. In the case of my family, too, these investigations brought to light some interesting and curious particulars.

I can best describe my illustrious and less than illustrious pedigree as a genetic patchwork quilt, for my paternal and maternal ancestors not only hailed from all parts of old Europe but followed a wide diversity of occupations.

My father Siegfried was born at 'Tribschen' in Switzerland on Sunday, 6 June 1869. On 17 June his mother Cosima received a sympathetic letter from her legitimate spouse, Hans von Bülow, which held out the hope that, after their divorce (which took place on 18 July 1870), and after the official, church wedding of my father's natural parents (they eventually married at Lucerne on 25 August 1870), he could – as Wagner chose to express it in a letter – 'inherit his father's name and preserve his works for posterity'. After his baptism on 4 September 1870, therefore, my father's names – Helferich Siegfried Richard Wagner – became his by legal right because, in accordance with local custom, he was registered at Lucerne as having been born three months after he actually saw the light.

Cosima's mother, Marie de Flavigny, a banker's daughter from the (Aryan!) house of Bethmann in Frankfurt, was married off by her parents to the much older Comte d'Agoult, with whom she lived in Paris. To complete her marital bliss, she took several years off between 1835 and 1844 and, in 1835, 1837, and 1839, gave birth to three children by Franz

Liszt, 'the tiger of the keys'. Like her son-in-law-to-be, Richard Wagner, she felt an urge to mount the barricades in a literal sense: he did so at Dresden in 1849, she at Paris in 1870. They also wrote under pseudonyms, his being 'K. Freigedank' and hers 'Daniel Stern'.

Privy Councillor Johann Wolfgang von Goethe, whose second name was given me in the hope that he would protect and vouch for me like some super-godfather, once had dealings with my great-grandmother Johanne Rosine, Richard Wagner's mother, in his capacity as minister of state to Grand Duke Carl August of Weimar. The daughter of a master baker named Pätz from Weissenfels, she had caught the eye of a Saxonian general, Prince Constantin, who was none other than the pleasure-loving younger brother of the Grand Duke of Weimar, while delivering some breakfast rolls to his quarters during manœuvres. Prince Constantin not only looked upon her kindly but thought her a suitable candidate for apprenticeship to a milliner in the Brühl at Leipzig – a princely mark of favour calculated to extract some favours from her in return. When these bore no 'fruit', Privy Councillor von Goethe took a decision that spared the Grand Duke's exchequer, because she received no payments after her discharge.

Carl Friedrich Wagner, a police officer based in the Brühl, must obviously have found the 'Pätz girl' just as desirable, because he married and fathered eight children on her, of whom Richard was the youngest. Carl Friedrich died six months after Richard's birth. Nine months later Rosalie married Ludwig Heinrich Christian Geyer, a portrait painter, actor, and poet. The Wagner children, being minors, took the name of their stepfather for practical reasons. Richard retained it until his confirmation, thereby fostering the myth that he was really Geyer's son.

One of Friedrich Nietzsche's many favours to my grandfather was to hazard that a *Geyer* [vulture] was almost an *Adler* [eagle]. Among certain racially obsessed Nazis favourable to Nietzsche's philosophical ideas, this reinforced the hope that they could establish such a close link between Richard Wagner and the undesirable 'Jew' Geyer (who was demonstrably nothing of the kind) that the former would no longer accord with their programmatic and apodictic 'conception of art'. Wagner may, as a musical dramatist, have fitted uneasily into the National Socialist *Weltanschauung*, but to dismiss him as having 'Jewish connections' is as futile as the far-fetched attempt by Houston Stewart Chamberlain and my step-aunt Daniela to establish his descent from St Elisabeth, which some members of the family would gladly have used to upgrade themselves.

Never having learned much about the activities of my many paternal ancestors from central Germany, who included tax collectors, sacristans, organists, schoolmasters, and musicians of varying ability, I can now turn with an easy mind to my mother's forebears. What is striking about them –

and they were scattered across Denmark, Sweden, Germany, England, and Wales – is the variety of occupations they pursued. They included engravers, joiners, tailors, insurance agents, clergymen, poets, and at least one active socialist.

My maternal grandmother, Emily Florence, *née* Karop, was an actress. She married John Williams, an author and journalist twenty-two years her senior. My mother, christened Winifred Marjorie, lost them both within eighteen months of her birth. Karl Klindworth and his wife, to whom she was related, took care of the orphaned girl from 1907 onwards and later adopted her.

Klindworth, a pupil of Liszt's, wrote piano arrangements of Wagner's works and was, among other things, conductor of the Berlin Philharmonic. Through him my mother not only came into contact with the 'Bayreuth circle' but gained her first impressions of the cultural activity associated with it. She married my father on 18 March 1915, when she was eighteen and he forty-six.

She astonished the Bayreuthers and gave them plenty of food for gossip by producing four children in quick succession: Wieland in 1917, Friedelind in 1918, me in 1919, and Verena in 1920. Later on, as if these peculiar circumstances were not enough, she became friends with Adolf Hitler.

My memories of my first six years of life are coloured by what others have told me, and also by rereading an American questionnaire of the post-1945 period. While I cannot recall coming into the world as a breech birth, I became aware of the possible consequences later on. It may explain a great deal, for childhood ailments were very much part of my early life. Not yet home from hospital, I developed pneumonia because of carelessness on the part of the nursing staff, an illness that very soon earned me my first recuperative holiday near Kiel in the north of Germany. As a four-year-old I did not take in enough to be an imaginative reporter, so I cannot present an authentic account of what passed between Adolf Hitler and my parents during his first visit to Wahnfried on 1 October 1923. The accounts that exist of his visit to Chamberlain, on the other hand, the uncle by marriage who lived across the way from Wahnfried in a house given to him and my Aunt Eva by Siegfried and Cosima, may be interpreted and exploited in many ways.

At Easter 1926, when I was six-and-a-half, I was sent as custom prescribed to the local primary school, which was attached to a teacher training college. In accordance with the prevailing curriculum, I was to be infused with the discipline expected of all German males, if not considered their supreme virtue.

Four years later I passed my secondary school entrance examination. My father congratulated me on this feat with the jocular words 'I didn't think you had it in you!' – not that this prevented him from thinking me instantly capable of gracing a university chair.

There is little to tell of my time at secondary school, which I left at Easter 1937. My outside interests were so diverse that I inevitably found school an affliction, a tiresome and pointless subsidiary activity. I often suffered from ailments of varying seriousness at this period and was anything but overambitious, so I was relegated and left the school after seven years with a six-year diploma.

During our mother's absences we children were looked after by our nurse, Emma, and by Liselotte Schmidt, Winifred's secretary from 1931 until her death in 1938, who helped us with our homework and supervised our piano practices.

The classical education of those days concentrated on the Roman Empire and its victorious campaigns, so history lessons confined themselves to enumerating a series of military exploits. If only for that reason, I was appalled by the prospect of having to remain at school until I matriculated. Classical secondary schools had always been a prime source of candidates for a career, distinguished or undistinguished, as an officer in the armed forces. Having no inclination or ambition to become an officer, I thought that the three additional school years with which I was threatened could be put to better use by discharging my obligations to the state and getting my spell in the Arbeitsdienst [Labour Service] and my two years as a conscript behind me.

Later on, when I joined the Third Reich's field-grey ranks, I summarized my attitude to military life in conversation with a general whom I was driving across the parade ground at Bayreuth. When the colonel escorting him disclosed who I was, he asked if I proposed to become a reserve officer. My prompt response to his well-meant question was: 'No, Herr General, there have to be civilians who pay the taxes the armed forces live on.'

Whenever our parents were not abroad or away on business of various kinds, they devoted their spare time to us. Our communal breakfasts, lunches and four o'clock teas, of which the latter took the form of a minor ritual, afforded us plenty of opportunities for question-and-answer sessions. We four children fell naturally into two pairs, younger and older, so Wieland and Friedelind were allowed to take part in many more activities than Verena and I, at least while my father was still alive. In our daily dealings with each other, the result was that my elder sister ruled the roost and held the floor, which amused my father but often compelled my mother to tell her off. As I see it, Friedelind's contrary, rebellious attitude was a way of life in itself, and one she thought herself entitled on principle to maintain till the day she died. She always behaved in an ostentatious way and attracted everyone's attention, if only by the volume of sound she emitted. Someone once suggested that she ought to be called '*Krachlaute*' [roughly: 'Crash-Bang-Wallop'], not Friedelind, though her universal nickname was 'Mouse'.

Wieland was rather too reserved and reclusive – like my father – to find it easy to emulate Friedelind's defiant behaviour. Verena, the youngest and the pet of the family, had no difficulty in fitting in, while I myself appear to have injected a lighter note into the atmosphere by being unselfconsciously straightforward and uncomplicated.

The other three and I owed our knowledge of Bayreuth and the surrounding area to our father, who communicated his vast knowledge of art and history in an unobtrusive and readily digestible form. We also went on outings and longer trips together. It was with him and through him that I first saw Eisenach and the Wartburg, the fairy caves at Saalfeld, Würzburg, and, on our last major excursion together at Whitsun 1930, Neuburg on the Danube, Lindau, Meersburg, and Lake Constance. I particularly recall several visits to the theatre at Chemnitz, where we saw some of his operas staged. He died just before I turned eleven, unfortunately, so I was still devoid of the basic knowledge that would have enabled me to elicit anything really substantial and fundamental about Bayreuth and his own work. I did, of course, ask him in a childishly inquisitive way what this or that feature on stage signified, or why the singer playing Siegfried should kill such a huge beast like Fafner in such an idiotically clumsy manner.

We were too young and too fully occupied with school work to be present at many rehearsals and performances in the Festspielhaus, so my attendances were only sporadic. One of my most vivid and unforgettable memories is of a dress rehearsal of the finale of *Götterdämmerung* in 1925. The musical and technical aspects of the production had still to be precisely co-ordinated, it seemed, because one of the columns of the Gibichungs' hall, newly constructed in the round, suffered a premature collapse and toppled on to the cyclorama, which bore appliquéd wisps of cloud – not, at that time, projected images. This unintended special effect had an equally unintended result: it sent everyone at the rehearsal into paroxysms of laughter.

But however interesting and exciting events on stage might be, we children attached more importance to the many games of exploration and hide-and-seek we used to play in the Festspielhaus, particularly in the storerooms. It was our special delight to creep between the almost life-size figures of the gods awaiting their downfall, though my mother usually found it a difficult and time-consuming business to round us up and take us home to bed.

Resident on the top floor of Wahnfried until 1 April 1930, when she died at the ripe old age of ninety-two, was my grandmother Cosima. Her living quarters faced south and east. She spent most of her time on a *chaise-longue*, but the balcony of the south-facing room enabled her to be taken out into the sunlight and fresh air in a wheelchair. Her self-contained suite also comprised a small bedroom and her nurse's quarters, which were equipped with a bathroom and cooking facilities. We children and our parents slept in the rooms on the west side of the house.

My two aunts, Daniela and Eva, took it in turns to tend and entertain their mother. One of their chief concerns was to keep us children away from her. On the occasions when we were admitted to her presence for very brief visits, they were careful to see that we did not racket around too much on her outsize couch, that my sisters did not brush and comb her hair too roughly, and that we did not test the old lady's reflexes by tickling her feet too hard. Above all, though, my aunts were at pains to moderate our conversation and restrict it to whatever subjects they deemed appropriate.

When my father was in Bayreuth and visited his mother after tea, as he regularly did, he always liked to take one of us children with him. Cosima could hardly see a thing in her latter years, and conversation with her was interspersed with long silences. I sometimes spent these interludes playing chess with my father, who was usually good-natured enough to let me win.

Thanks to my mother's discretion and brilliant organization, though not to them alone, my father's sixtieth birthday proved to be a red-letter day for me as well as him, because my allotted role in the outdoor proceedings was that of barbecue supervisor. I not only served the guests with Franconian sausages grilled to perfection on glowing pine cones; I was my own best and happiest customer. That day my mother had no need – as sometimes happened when such sausages sizzled in the kitchen frying pan but were decorously served at table – to watch and warn me not to slip one of the delicacies into my pocket for subsequent consumption.

At festival time the public were granted access not only to the grounds in front of Haus Wahnfried but also, by way of a gate on the right, to our back garden and Wagner's grave. We were naturally free to romp around there without let or hindrance, so visitors often accosted us and asked, usually in unctuous, reverent tones, if we were Richard Wagner's grandchildren. Our favourite playground being one of the big neighbouring meadows, we startled and doubtless annoyed them by replying, 'No, we're cows.'

Because of certain supposedly health-giving nutritional theories espoused by my mother, we had for a while to survive on a vegetarian diet. In order to assuage our carnivorous appetites with sausages, which we usually bought on the way to school, we were obliged to earn some money. In one of our money-making ventures we took advantage of the 'Dürer Year', 1928, to hold a Dürer exhibition of our own. This was a collection of postcards and prints of the Nuremberg old master's works displayed on the wall of the gallery just inside Wahnfried's front door, which could be reached via the main steps. Interested visitors were charged a minimum admission fee of ten pfennigs. Wahnfried's historic downstairs rooms were open to the public at certain times, so we could count on a brisk demand for our exhibition, because anyone who viewed it could also gain a glimpse of a part of the house that was not normally accessible.

Another of our sources of income was the gardener's big wooden cart, which we fitted out with three small garden benches. Pilgrims to Wahnfried were thus afforded the opportunity to be hauled – as fare-paying passengers, of course – from the front gate to Wagner's grave and back by the Master's very own grandchildren.

We often greeted visitors, who regularly made courtesy calls by appointment at 11 a.m. on Sundays, with a 'ghost'. This welcome was mainly reserved for our pet hates. We tied a stick crosswise to a feather duster, dressed the result in a nightshirt, and attached our 'ghost' to the gallery banisters by a long string. When the maidservant answered the front door, visitors would be startled and dismayed to see it swoop down on them.

We did not, of course, come into contact with our aunts only when visiting our grandmother. Since they acquired an importance transcending their actual degree of kinship, particularly after my father's death, because of their dispute with my mother in her capacity as the new festival director, they merit somewhat closer examination here.

When they visited us at Wahnfried we often gave them a specially prearranged and 'ceremonious' reception: much to their annoyance, the gramophone would mark their arrival by blaring out the overture to *Orpheus in the Underworld* or the *Badenweiler March*.

I never knew the eldest of my aunts, Isolde, the first child of Richard Wagner and Cosima von Bülow, because she died in 1918, but I had a great deal to do with her son, my cousin Franz. Isolde had acquired a certain notoriety by reason of the so-called Beidler case of 1914, in which she claimed recognition as a legitimate Wagner offspring after her annual allowance had had to be reduced because the royalties from Wagner's works were drying up now that copyright in them, then limited to a term of thirty years, had expired. She lost.

Aunt Blandine, a genuine von Bülow child like Daniela, was my godmother. My grandfather had still been alive and present at her marriage to Count Biagio Gravina, a Sicilian, at Wahnfried on 25 August 1882. Their eldest son, Manfred, was my second godfather, and it was from him that I took my first forename. My second, Wolfgang, is the one by which I am usually known, and my third, be it noted for completeness' sake only, is

Martin after Martin Luther. What I most remember about Aunt Blandine, apart from her kind and friendly nature, is her considerable loss of memory in old age, because a child of my temperament sometimes balked at listening to the same things endlessly repeated.

Daniela possessed certain curious features that distinguished her from the others, if only outwardly. She had an exceptionally dark complexion, which earned her the nickname 'Moor', and eyes of two different colours, grey-blue and brown. After her divorce from Henry Thode she moved back into Wahnfried and remained there until shortly after the arrival of my mother, whom she lectured incessantly on how to comport herself in such 'hallowed halls'. She also tyrannized my mother by bullying her into playing piano duets and involving her in her obsessive ambition to rival the pianistic technique of her grandfather, Franz Liszt. My father soon realized how impossible a situation this was for his young wife, but before the budding conflict could attain a pitch of unendurable intensity Daniela reluctantly beat a retreat to Lisztstrasse, in the immediate vicinity of Wahnfried, where she lived in rented accommodation. She naturally continued to try to tell us children how to behave. In view of the very free-and-easy way in which our parents had brought us up, however, it was quite understandable that we did not take such a humourless know-it-all of an aunt too seriously.

My Aunt Eva's siblings had christened her '*Nadelkissen*' [Pincushion], a revealing nickname whose suitability was borne in on us, her nephews and nieces, whenever we came into contact with her. After the death of her husband, Chamberlain, one of us was invited to lunch with her one day a week, which meant that my turn came round once a month. Daniela took all her midday meals with Eva, so the conversation, if no one else was present, was a triangular one devoted more to the saving of our childish souls than to any subject that might have accorded with our rather different interests.

These lunches took place at No. 1 Wahnfriedstrasse, a building with a peculiar history. Not only was it Chamberlain's base of operations from 1908 until he died there in 1927, the crematorium for Cosima's correspondence with Richard and, from 1911 onwards, the 'vault' that held her diaries, but in August 1930 it became the headquarters of those who led the campaigns against my mother's festival directorship and, in 1976 in particular, against my own tenure of the same office. The chief and most active ringleader in the latter year was the archivist Gertrud Strobel, who was then in my employ and remained so thereafter.

The 'vault' was opened only once, and then only briefly, to give Du Moulin-Eckart access to the diaries and the authentic documentation that would enable him, in 1929, to publish his biography of the '*Hohe Frau*' [exalted or noble lady], which was influenced by my aunts and tailored to the Cosima 'myth'. In 1935 Eva Chamberlain presented the diaries to the municipality of Bayreuth 'as a gift to the Richard Wagner Memorial'; her will of 1939 stipulated that the diaries should, for thirty years after her death, remain unopened in a safe-deposit box at the Bayerische Staatsbank in Munich. She died in 1942.

As a result of Wahnfried's reconstruction from 1975 onwards, the collected items additional to the archives and not forming part of the Richard Wagner Foundation were transferred to No. 1 Wahnfriedstrasse, which had since Eva's death belonged to the municipality.

In April 1978, when I returned from presenting *Tristan* in Milan, I found to my great surprise, not to say indignation, that this collection had been broken up without my knowledge, and that much of it had been borne off to various places, many of which are still unknown to me.

After this brief foray into the future, back to my childhood.

Although we had inherited a miniature theatre equipped to present Wagner's works, it was played with less often than our Punch and Judy theatre. The *Ring* costumes in the well-known photographs of me and my brother and sisters dated from the childhood of my father and my aunts, but they did more to satisfy our childish love of dressing up than to kindle any personal or artistic ambitions. At all events, we found it far more fun when my father, in a jocular mood, blessed us *urbi et orbi* with a tea cosy on his head in lieu of the papal tiara, a blanket standing in for a cloak, and a walking stick for a crook. At hilarious moments like these, our half-century's difference in age melted away and his paternal gravitas went by the board. His untimely death changed a lot of things for us. Besides, we were growing up, developing interests and seeking mentors of our own, so we tended more and more to go our separate ways.

The numerous dogs that romped around with us were joined in their frolics by anything up to two full and fiercely competitive football teams recruited by Wieland, who was keen on the game, with the result that the field to the right of the avenue got completely churned up. My mother thereupon transferred the football field to the furthermost, south-west part of the grounds, where visitors to Wahnfried could not see it. Because she so disliked the incessant commotion these visitors caused in the part of our garden facing the Hofgarten, she gave them access to Wagner's grave from the Hofgarten itself. Another major change came about when she acquired some sandstone from the Geismarkt Barracks, which had been demolished, and had a wall constructed with it. Thanks to this wall, the house became known among the townsfolk as 'Burg Wahnfried' [Wahnfried Castle].

Winifred's building activities at Wahnfried are also well illustrated by their effect on me in my capacity as a chicken farmer. After my Uncle Chamberlain's death in 1927 I inherited his hen-coop, complete with enclosure, because Aunt Eva had no wish to keep it. The eggs laid by my twenty-odd hens were sold to my mother at the prevailing market price. I fed and tended the birds myself, though Friedelind temporarily assumed the far less arduous role of book-keeper. The proceeds had to cover the whole cost of the grain feed I needed in addition to the kitchen waste I carted over from Wahnfried. When she saw how conscientiously I looked after my birds, Winifred transferred my 'chicken farm' to the garden plot behind Wahnfried acquired by my father in 1928. This piece of land, which my brother used as his sports field, was later converted into a tennis court.

After my father's death his big study was turned into a self-contained archive for the storing of Wagner documents.

Winifred placed the private apartment on the first floor and a few guest rooms on the ground floor at the disposal of Toscanini and his family during his second and last year at Bayreuth. We children developed a very relaxed relationship with him because he had shown us great kindness and affection after our father's death in 1930, and we could drop in on him whenever we pleased.

Toscanini's affability to us fatherless children contrasted with his mode of working and his treatment of the orchestra. His explosive temperament expressed itself in broken batons and frequent eruptions of Italian abuse – indeed, his temper was such that the festival orchestra went on strike for the first and, happily, the last time in its history. My mother managed to calm everyone down, so the friction of the rehearsals was eventually banished from their minds by the musical results they obtained.

Like so many dramas, this one was accompanied by a kind of satyr play associated with Georg Köhler, the orchestra attendant who worked for the Bayreuth Festival from 1906 to 1959 and endeared himself to all the conductors he served. Georg came of Upper Franconian peasant stock and lived in neighbouring Bindlach. A short man with a slightly upturned moustache and hair that retained its flaxen colouring into old age, he collected broken batons and sold them as souvenirs. But that was not all: since most of the conductors employed him to buy them the batons of their choice, he was in a position to snap a few himself and increase his turnover considerably.

There may have been some justification for saying that Toscanini was a fascist on the podium. Many went so far as to claim that he had become an antifascist only because Mussolini surpassed him in the exercise of power.

In 1930, in addition to the new production of *Tannhäuser*, Toscanini conducted my father's production of *Tristan*, first seen in 1927 and then in its third year. In 1931 my mother engaged him for *Parsifal* in place of its conductor since 1901, Karl Muck, whose engagement she terminated after my father's death, and she also managed to get Wilhelm Furtwängler for *Tristan*.

In the autumn of 1930 Furtwängler came to Bayreuth to complete negotiations for the following year, accompanied by his legendary secretary Bertha Geissmar. Quite apart from their very different modes of verbal expression, Frau Geissmar's squat stature and nutcracker visage contrasted so comically with Furtwängler's tall, slim figure, long neck and characteristic head that we children could hardly contain our mirth.

The age of the 'working lunch' had not yet dawned, so my mother used to invite guests and business associates to eat with us at home. As youngsters we found this rather exciting, of course, because it enabled us to meet a lot of interesting people under informal circumstances and, at the same time, taught us something about the festival.

It was a tribute to my mother's talent for diplomacy that she managed to persuade two such musical antagonists as Toscanini and Furtwängler to work at the Festspielhaus simultaneously. As for the existence of a few photographs showing the two great conductors posing together, this must be accounted positively miraculous!

On one occasion, when my mother met Toscanini in Berlin, she went with him to the *Scala* music-hall, which was second in size only to the *Wintergarten* and one of the maestro's favourite haunts. Toscanini could not forbear to remark that Stenzel, the music-hall's conductor, displayed more rhythm and expression than Furtwängler. I was never told of an equally spiteful remark on Furtwängler's part, unfortunately, but that one alone serves to demonstrate the 'harmony' that reigned between the two confrères.

My mother's wide-ranging sphere of activities may also be inferred from the fact that, apart from going to the music-hall with Toscanini, she went to the cinema with Adolf Hitler and to the opera with Eugenio Pacelli, the papal nuncio who later became Pope Pius XII.

In 1894, to escape from the family squabbles at Wahnfried, my father had built a retreat on the site of some former staff quarters. In 1932/3, when my mother set about converting this into a guest-house after the old Wagner greenhouse had been pulled down, my hen-coop had to be removed to make room for a new one. My own special business enterprise was then installed on another plot of family-owned land on the festival hill. I never dreamed, when I went up there to feed my hens and collect their eggs, as I did almost daily, that in 1955 I would acquire the house adjacent to my new 'farm', complete with orchard, from the son of our former administrative director, Herr Schuler. Then, just as Frederick the Great owned his 'Sans-Souci', I owned my 'Sans-Famille'.

The building generally known today as the Siegfried Wagner House has been enlarged and modified several times since its original reconstruction in 1931/2. What mattered most to me about it in my childhood and adolescence was that my mother had a complete workshop installed for me in the cellar. I could saw and hammer away there to my heart's content, but I also had a metal workshop with a lathe and even a small forge. Having early displayed a considerable flair for handicrafts, I had already had a workshop in an attic at Wahnfried, though it was much more modestly equipped than my new one. My sisters had a dolls' kitchen up there, too, in which snacks and light meals could be prepared. Friedelind showed very little interest in it and Verena never was a great eater, so I ended up becoming the kitchen's principal user and chief beneficiary. I not only retained my fondness for cooking and kitchen utensils but have, over the years, become quite a good cook.

I and my friends Hermann and Emil were forever tinkering and pottering in the workshop. My mother would occasionally send over technicians from the Festspielhaus to lend a hand, with the result that I, in my turn, spent more and more time eagerly watching them at work in the Festspielhaus. Many of its installations were renovated and improved from 1932 onwards under the new technical director, Paul Eberhardt, and this was what kindled my great and enduring interest in the technical execution of artistic ideas.

My brother and I also had a communal dark-room situated in an erstwhile laundry room off the stairwell at Wahnfried.

After Toscanini had, at the end of May 1933, cabled my mother and revoked his firm undertaking of early April to conduct both that year and the next – a retraction too well known to merit comment here – Richard Strauss and his wife Pauline moved into the new guest-house, where they were joined for a while by his son Franz and his daughter-in-law Alice. Strauss, motivated by long-standing ties of friendship, had promptly agreed to conduct *Parsifal* in Toscanini's place. It should be added that he and his wife had jointly participated in the *Tannhäuser* production of 1894, he as conductor, she in the role of Elisabeth.

The name Strauss is associated in my mind with a series of incidents and utterances, some humorous, some thought-provoking, which are worth recalling here.

Richard Strauss enjoyed chatting with us children, so we were always at liberty to drop in unannounced. Frau Pauline, who obviously thought no other form of footwear sufficiently kind to floors and carpets, ensured that we would behave in an appropriately civilized manner by ordering us all some soft-soled slippers of the kind that were doubtless *de rigueur* at her home in Zöppritzstrasse, Garmisch.

When son Franz, known as Bubi, first visited his father at Bayreuth, he was too preoccupied to notice the ornamental pond, complete with dolphin fountain, that lay between him and his father. Bubi walked straight on and measured his length in two feet of water.

Richard Strauss remained extremely pleasant and affable, even while rehearsing at the Festspielhaus, a trait that utterly differentiated his manner from the deadly seriousness of his producer. The latter, as I have already said, was my Aunt Daniela, whom my mother, sick to death of her incessant niggling and harping on 'tradition', had maliciously entrusted with that year's *Parsifal*. On one occasion Strauss corrected the singer playing Gurnemanz at the point where he reproves the young Esquires: 'Hey! Ho! No forest wardens, you, but sleep wardens. At least wake up in the morning!' He did so as follows: 'Herr von Manowarda, do me a favour and don't sing that so dramatically. Gurnemanz is just a kind of head forester who's giving two young scamps a ticking-off.' Daniela was obviously in two minds whether to take offence at this or – something entirely alien to her – to smile and let it pass. She was also profoundly dismayed, needless to say, by Strauss's considerably faster tempi.

The last time my brother and I saw Richard Strauss was at Garmisch on his eighty-fifth birthday, 11 June 1949. On that occasion he restated his attitude to the aforesaid tempi in the presence of Alois Hundhammer, the Bavarian minister of culture. 'Yes, Herr Minister,' he said, 'that's the trouble with tradition. When I conducted *Parsifal* at Bayreuth in 1933, everyone said it was much too fast. When I asked if they'd attended the first performance at Bayreuth, they all had to say no, of course. But *I* had, because my father took me along, King Ludwig having lent Wagner the Munich Court Orchestra and he being a member of it. Wagner kept peering at Levi through that well-known peephole in the hood and telling him: "Don't drag so!" You know, Herr Minister, the longer they've played *Parsifal* there, the longer it's become.'

Richard Strauss was very fond of making little excursions in his six-litre Mercedes convertible, so he used to collect me when we both had time to spare and ask 'Wolferl' to show him 'something nice'. I had such a thorough knowledge of the surrounding countryside, thanks to my father, that I always found it easy to grant his request.

He was a great trencherman, as everyone knows, and my mother used to invite him to lunch when Pauline was away. Our meals were clearly insufficient for him, however, so – just to be on the safe side – he tended to stoke up beforehand at the Restaurant Bürgerreuth.

When none of the maestro's musicians or other potential card players volunteered to join him in a game of *skat* after work, because he usually won, my mother came to a special arrangement. Apart from providing the customary mountain of sandwiches and wash-tubful of ice-cold beer, she made good his victims' financial losses the next morning.

During my time in Berlin Strauss often attended performances of his own works. Heinz Tietjen took advantage of one of these occasions to ask him to take over the baton himself. While rehearsing one of his works he leafed through the score with a puzzled air: what he himself had written bore no relation to what he was conducting. The leader of the orchestra politely pointed out that a discrepancy had arisen between him and the orchestra. His laconic reply: 'Yes, it's easy enough to write it down, but to conduct it!'

After one performance at the Staatsoper Pauline was shuffling around in an armchair in the general administrator's office. Strauss was standing behind his wife and I facing her with Tietjen beside me. Pauline's relaxed sitting position presented us with a surprising spectacle: under her figure-hugging, sequin-covered gown she was wearing a woollen leotard, probably a relic of her long-forgotten days in the theatre. Strauss, who saw me grinning, said, 'Surprised, eh, Wolferl?'

But back to my experiences in and around the 'guest-house'.

My mother must have decided to encourage my bent for handicrafts, my activities as a small-scale chicken farmer, and my pronounced love of nature and everything to do with it, because she gave me, as a birthday present, a small hut in a field near Neunkirchen, seven kilometres from Bayreuth. Some of its components came from a small conservatory she had built for Toscanini in 1931, on the balcony of the Siegfried Wagner House, because the maestro was sensitive to temperature and my mother aimed to provide him with as much of his beloved Mediterranean warmth as possible. My hut was built on piles, so the rollers from the old travelling backcloths for Wagner's original production of *Parsifal*, which were not needed after 1933, came in very handy.

Poor Aunt Daniela! Thus ended some of the physical relics of your stepfather's theatrical estate – thus were pieces of materialized sanctity profaned by being driven into the ground like common-or-garden posts. *O tempora, o mores!* What had become of your meditative, prayerful pose beside Titurel's bier after the curtain fell? You drew the shroud over the horrid, waxen face of his stage-corpse and then, after a pause for reverent thought, when you had recovered your power of speech, told the company in a voice fraught with emotion, 'Thank you, ladies and gentlemen.' When, standing in the lee of a wobbly canvas column forming part of the temple of the Grail, I watched this scene after one of the five performances directed by her in 1933, I heard a member of the chorus remark, in the thickest of Berlin accents, 'I reckon the old nanny-goat's been eating soap.'

My mother and my brother tried to persuade Adolf Hitler to get my parents' joint will of 1929 changed under the new legal reassessment provisions, their aim being to amend its entailment and reversionary clauses so that my brother, by analogy with the estate inheritance law, would become sole heir of the Festspielhaus. Hitler rejected this request, however, because he obviously had no wish to interfere so drastically with an institution as world-renowned as the Bayreuth Festival, nor to be accused of disregarding the law of contract. Had this change come about, I would have been able to lead a good and acceptable existence, either as a respected Third Reich farmer who might have bequeathed his property to an heir, or as a stage technician with the Bayreuth Festival, in which case, as my brother's employee, I would have laboured on behalf of my grandfather's work in my own way.

One of our most important guides and mentors was my father's friend, Franz Stassen. He was Friedelind's godfather and the person who, in an unassuming and unselfish manner, encouraged Wieland's early essays in painting. Stassen never, as far as I can recall, missed a Bayreuth Festival. There were times when he seemed like a second father to us, because after our own father's death we could ask him all we wanted to know, not only about Wagner's works, but also about the German and foreign classics. A resident of Berlin, he proved himself an excellent cicerone when it came to showing us children around the Museumsinsel, the city of Berlin itself, Potsdam, and Brandenburg. Wieland and I toured northern Germany with him and, thanks to his companionship, came to know it well. He often accompanied us to the opera and theatre when we visited him. He also regularly attended performances of my father's works, with which he had a special affinity, and endeavoured to bring out their essential meaning in his drawings and illustrations. Stassen was a constant source of advice and support to me later on, when I was studying in Berlin, especially as he lived not far from me.

Alfred Roller visited Bayreuth for technical discussions prior to producing his designs for the 1934 *Parsifal*. One of my numerous childhood ailments had confined me to bed again, so Roller came to see me. In quite simple and readily understandable terms, he explained the purpose of a stage set and how it was executed. What I found particularly illuminating was his statement that the stage designer's primary consideration must be how to create a three-dimensional impression, which is not identical with the effect produced by a two-dimensional picture. Having originally been a painter, Roller was well aware that stage design is subject to entirely different laws. My father had mooted the possibility of his working at Bayreuth, but he had modestly declined. The fact that his employment by my mother accorded with Hitler's wishes was a fortunate coincidence. When Hitler eventually got a chance to speak with Roller, it emerged that an acquaintance had once given him a letter of introduction to Roller requesting the latter's help in getting him accepted by the Vienna Academy of Art, but that he, Hitler, had been too diffident to make use of it. It is pointless to speculate on what might have happened had Hitler's hopes of studying at the academy been realized thanks to Roller's good offices.

Unfortunately, Roller never fulfilled his artistic expectations at Bayreuth because his laryngeal cancer was too far advanced to enable him to do for the festival what he had formerly done for the stage. Had he been well enough to collaborate at Bayreuth on a long-term basis, the personal and artistic altercations between Wieland and Emil Preetorius would never have occurred.

Haus Wahnfried was emptying little by little. In 1932 my sister Friedelind had been sent for academic reasons, and not because it was patronized largely by the nobility, to Heiligengrabe, a boarding school at Pritzwalk, near Potsdam, where she remained until the spring of 1935. Thereafter, having obtained her intermediate school certificate, she continued her studies outside Bayreuth. Verena went off to board at the Luisenstift at Kötzschenbroda, near Dresden, and Wieland, who matriculated in 1936, completed his labour corps and military service before moving to Munich to study painting privately under Professor Staeger.

As children we followed an everyday routine little different from that of other families except when the festival was in progress. Until I joined up in 1938, holidays such as Easter, Whitsun and Christmas were usually spent *en famille*, and we also went on communal winter skiing vacations in Austria and Switzerland.

It was Friedelind who drove a definite wedge into our family solidarity. My mother financed her studies, which she pursued first in Sussex and later in Paris. She took advantage of her sojourn abroad to turn her back on Germany, and did not return to Bayreuth even when war broke out. Where her memoirs are concerned – she entitled them *Nacht über Bayreuth* [Night over Bayreuth, published in English as *Heritage of Fire*] – I will say only that the evidence available to me demonstrates that she erred on major points, both as regards the 'facts' described in her book and, later on, in her offensive public references to me. All that really mattered to me and my mother was her unqualified assent to the establishment of the Richard Wagner Foundation, which she instructed her attorney, Dr Bernhard Servatius, to attest on 2 May 1973. As I said in my speech on the occasion of her death in 1991, this was yet another illustration of the 'mass of contradictions' that her life had turned out to be. She approved the setting up of the foundation in company with her mother, the woman who had allegedly wanted her 'exterminated', and with me, whom she reviled as – among other things – 'power-hungry and weak'.

The festival had a so-called rest year in 1935, so the guest-house was unoccupied during the summer. In 1934, when taking leave of my mother after attending the cycle of performances, Adolf Hitler regretted that he would be unable to come to the festival in 1936 for want of accommodation. Bayreuth's Party members, and their local boss in particular, had intimated that he should not return to his previous lodgings in a house in Parkstrasse (opposite Wahnfried on the south side of the Hofgarten) because the owner was a freemason. My mother thereupon told him that, if he cared to do so and had nowhere else to go, he would be welcome to use our guest-house. This was how Hitler came to stay there in 1936, 1937, 1938, and 1939. To quote *Lohengrin*, Act II: 'Thus does misfortune enter this house!'

Hitler's presence in the grounds of Wahnfried during the festival season meant that he was, in the literal sense, our next-door neighbour. This being so, and the summer vacations being relatively quiet on the political front (as they still are), he extended his bohemianesque sociability to me and my brother and sisters by inviting us over. He was always impeccably polite to my mother, bowing and kissing her hand with all the formal courtesy of an old-fashioned Austrian gentleman. In conversation he would listen to us attentively, receptively, and without interruption. There were no uncontrolled outbursts in our presence, nor did he devalue any of our carpets by chewing them. One gained the inescapable impression that, in our company, he sought and possibly found some substitute for the family atmosphere that was denied him elsewhere. Because we children could speak out and ask him questions quite openly and uninhibitedly, our relations were uncomplicated and unaffected by that quasi-religious, awe-inspiring gulf that customarily separated him, a man regarded as the divinely appointed guardian of German honour and greatness, from the everyday world.

His staff at that time consisted of a few aides, his personal physician Dr Brand and his wife, some menservants, and his major-domo, Kannenberg, who was responsible not only for running the house but for his vegetarian master's physical well-being. Kannenberg also fulfilled the court jester's role on occasion by playing the squeeze-box. As far as I can remember, Joseph Goebbels and his wife Magda were often invited to stay as well. The bedrooms, which were anything but luxury suites, would be called rather modest by today's standards and quite unworthy of a visiting head of state.

Hitler's retinue, whose members stayed elsewhere, often included Otto Dietrich, his chief press officer. Dietrich would bring him press reports at any hour of the day or night, and I was particularly struck by their outsize lettering, which was produced with the aid of a special typewriter because

Hitler never liked wearing his glasses when others were present.

Albert Speer, who was also a frequent visitor to Bayreuth, would sometimes show Hitler drawings and models of building projects in the garden room of the guest-house – projects whose function was often still undetermined. We were sometimes permitted to examine these models, which usually consisted of façades alone. This surprised me, and on one such occasion I hazarded the following comment, borrowed from my grandfather: 'But this is the nature of the German ethos, that it builds from within.'

Julius Streicher, probably the most disreputable of all Hitler's subordinates, attended the festival in 1933 – for the first and last time. My mother told Hitler, very firmly, that she never wished to see such a 'proletarian' there again. This effectively precluded the appearance at Bayreuth of types like Martin Bormann.

I shall now touch briefly on a few of the topics discussed at our sporadic meetings with Hitler, which generally took place in the morning.

My brother was greatly concerned about the problem of 'degenerate art' as exemplified by the notorious Munich exhibition of 1937, especially as Goebbels himself had devoted a large-scale exhibition to the painter Edvard Munch a few years earlier. Hitler was evasive on the subject. He said that, after a phase of self-discovery, art of that kind would be able to be shown in Germany once more. It had not been destroyed, after all, merely sold off abroad and the proceeds used to purchase Old Masters for the benefit of German museums.

Once, when we asked him why he kept and tolerated so many toadies in his entourage, he said that it was really time to found a 'counter-party'. In the same connection, he admitted that he had very few outspoken and imaginative debaters on his staff and deplored having to deal all the time with deferential yes-men. He also lamented the fact that he knew only two genuinely independent-minded women, our mother and Leni Riefenstahl. In terms of personality, his *Reichsfrauenführerin* [Reich Women's Leader], Gertrud Scholtz-Klink, couldn't hold a candle to either of them. When we expressed incomprehension of Hermann Göring's foibles, he replied that ordinary folk wanted and needed a man of his type.

He often spoke with pleasure of our grandfather's works and their possible interpretations, and would sometimes expound his own ideas about them. As for the stubborn repudiation of Wagner by many Party members, notably Alfred Rosenberg, the Nazi mythologizer, he said that people had to be educated to Wagner's works in order to gain a sympathetic understanding of them, and that it might be possible to achieve this by a gradual process of transition from 'lighter works'.

He wanted to acquaint his *Volksgenossen* [the Nazi counterpart of the communist 'comrade'] with other countries and cultures (presumably, before they were sent forth to conquer them). This was to be done by means of 'Strength through Joy', the foreign travel organization run by the German Labour Front, and Hitler particularly mentioned its flagship, the *Wilhelm Gustloff*, in that connection. Dr Robert Ley, head of the German Labour Front, and my future brother-in-law Bodo Lafferentz, who was to marry my sister Verena, came to Bayreuth to see him on 'Strength through Joy' business.

As he had already done in *Mein Kampf*, Hitler used to state in company that great political objectives – the kind that brought power and renown – could only be attained by force, one example being the slaughter of thousands of Saxons by Charlemagne. These days, nobody gave a thought to all the genocidal atrocities perpetrated in the name of Christianity. The papacy and the Roman Catholic Church exemplified his ideal of consolidated power.

He once told us, among other things, that in 1932 the then representative of the Jewish religious community had assured him: 'Herr Hitler, open up the Party to us Jews and you'll have no problems of any kind.' When we vented our indignation at the anti-Semitic outrages committed on 9 November 1938, the so-called 'Night of Broken Glass', he told us that it was an independent initiative on Goebbels's part and had come as a surprise to him.

All he would say about the Germanizing racial theory was that he himself could not espouse it because Germany's central position on the continent had generated a racial mixture from which our real cultural manifestations derived. To cite a contrary example, he pointed disparagingly to the Norwegians, whom he accused of living on herrings and looking and speaking like them as well. He also poked fun at Hermann Göring's game reserve in the Schorfheide, claiming that he had stocked it for breeding purposes, not only with wisent and bison but also with one or two human specimens, Germanic aborigines intended to revitalize the ancient German race.

The artists' parties he gave while staying at Bayreuth between 1936 and 1939 were extremely popular, the more so because, although he himself was a non-smoker and teetotaller, his guests could partake of everything including alcohol. They were usually held in the guest-house or, if it was fine, outside in the grounds. No one was debarred from attending, not even people like Max Lorenz, who had 'Jewish connections' or could then have been prosecuted under Paragraph 175 of the penal code [relating to homosexuals].

Hitler's party in 1938 was marked by a grotesque incident. The major-domo had arranged a particularly ingenious entertainment in the garden behind Wahnfried, only a few yards from the grave of Richard Wagner, whose 125th birthday it was: a pyrotechnical set piece in honour of the occasion. As bad luck would have it, he had inadvertently mounted the figure 2 upside down, so that it resembled a 7 when ignited and altered the total to '175'. Worse still, wind and a light drizzle carried all the smoke and stench towards the guests and engulfed them in it. Hitler, who was not at all amused, upbraided the luckless master of ceremonies for his stupidity in jeopardizing the singers scheduled to appear in the following day's performance.

Another memorable incident occurred at one of these parties. Hermann Göring and his wife had come to Bayreuth at the same time as Hitler – an exception to the usual rule, because they tended to travel separately for security reasons. I wanted to take a photograph of the Reich Marshal, who obligingly struck a decorative pose in a wing chair, but the bulb in my flashgun – a big contraption in those days – exploded, showering him with fragments of glass. 'Anyone would think you were trying to assassinate me,' he snapped, to which I retorted: 'It would take more than a little flash like that to knock you over.' When he tried to get up and brush the splinters of glass off his suit, the wing chair proved too small for his baroque frame: it stuck to him and he to it, so I was obliged to pull it off his backside by main force.

In autumn 1938 Hitler delivered an unusually belligerent speech, although he had just scored a foreign policy success by concluding the Munich Agreement. This prompted us to inquire his reasons. He told us that he had received details of a secret session of the British parliament from which it emerged that Churchill had said that, unless Germany was taught a military lesson by 1940 at the latest, he, Hitler, would do with Europe as he pleased.

Although I was a far from reclusive and unsociable person, I largely refrained – unlike my brother and sisters – from cultivating the official connections that could undoubtedly have been mine as well. The festival situation inevitably brought me into contact with those who wielded power and influence in the Third Reich, in art as well as politics, but I never consciously or deliberately sought their company and steered clear of all the dazzlingly tempting offers and opportunities that came my way. This was because I had no wish to achieve anything by the convenient if dangerous route known as 'connections', whether their effect was benign or questionable. I never, despite numerous invitations to do so, accepted Hitler's or Goebbels's hospitality in Berlin, nor – once again, despite an invitation from Hitler – did I attend the 1936 Berlin Olympics or any artists' gatherings, either there or in Munich. It was my mother's habit, when seeking help on behalf of persons in trouble, to approach Dr Brand,

Hitler's personal physician, rather than Martin Bormann, who was really responsible for handling such requests. Later on, when she was worried that I might be killed in an air raid on the capital, she asked Brand if he would find me a safe billet in the Chancellery. I declined the offer and, for that reason among others, survived the war.

In January 1934, after only three months in the organization, I was able to terminate my membership of the Hitler Youth thanks to an accident – a fortunate accident, because it exempted me from having to waste any more of the time I so much preferred to devote to my own interests. Although I had told the troop leader that, after my afternoon's exertions, I was physically incapable of obeying his order to perform on the rings, I was hoisted up and set in motion by him and one or two other 'comrades'. My strength gave out, as I knew it would: I fell from a height of approximately eight feet, landed on my right arm, and broke it. Since we all paid premiums to the Hitler Youth insurance scheme, I put in a claim for medical repairs. It then transpired that our contributions had been embezzled. Disciplinary proceedings were instituted against the embezzler, or so I was told, but I never discovered their outcome and resigned in any case. My response to the Hitler Youth authorities' protests, which included a threat to call in Baldur von Schirach, the 'Reich Youth Leader', was: 'If he covers up for you swindlers, he's as big a swindler as you are.'

My brother had Hitler himself to 'thank' for his membership of the Nazi Party, though he almost failed to get in. While chatting to us one morning, Hitler asked Wieland if he was a Party member. Promptly scenting trouble, I made myself scarce before he could ask me the same question. Wieland told me later what happened. In order to join the Party he had, willy-nilly, to report to the *Kreisleiter* [district director], who asked him to name his sponsors. When he replied that Adolf Hitler himself was his sponsor, the hidebound bureaucrat told him: 'One isn't enough.' Friedelind and I never joined the Party, nor did Verena, though she had to become a member of the National Socialist Students' League when, after belatedly matriculating, she embarked on her medical studies at Easter 1942. She did not pursue those studies for long, however, because she gave birth to her first daughter, Amelie, on 5 June 1944.

Unlike Wieland and me, our sisters were sent on lengthy educational trips abroad, mainly in order to learn or perfect their knowledge of foreign languages. Friedelind had gone to England and France, as I have already said. Verena went off to Rome, where she remained from January 1939 until the festival opened. In consequence of lingering ailments, my brother and I were granted almost a year's convalescent leave. Wieland had already done his military service; I wanted to get mine over as soon as I completed my year in the labour corps, during which I contracted a severe case of pleurisy, but the effects of the illness were such that I had to postpone my induction until autumn 1938. We decided to employ this unforeseen respite for our own purposes, educational as well as recuperative. Early in 1938 we began by staying at a resort hotel in Bordighera.

The time and leisure available to us imparted a sense of absolute freedom. Between mid-April and June 1938 we undertook a joint tour of Italy, the traditional destination of all travellers seeking to broaden their minds, and travelled as far afield as Sicily.

Our mother, who had often visited Italy with our father and knew the country well, had organized everything in her inimitable way. She provided us with petrol and hotel vouchers and had prudently sought out places that offered half-board accommodation. This was very important because our financial resources were limited by the prevailing foreign exchange regulations, so we naturally had to make the most of them.

Although we found it impossible to assimilate and marshal all our varied impressions until we returned home, a mechanical breakdown afforded us a brief pause for reflection on the outward journey. Our car's camshaft spur gear had worn out and could not be immediately replaced. For one thing, it could not be identified beyond doubt on the available list of spare parts; for another, it had to be ordered from Germany. This unpropitious circumstance compelled us to visit Rome straight away instead of on the return journey, as planned, but Hitler was just about to arrive there on a state visit to the king and Mussolini. To spare our budget we called our mother collect, and she, thanks to her connections and organizing skill, managed to get the requisite spare parts sent to us from Untertürkheim by the quickest possible route. Some deft Fiat mechanics repaired our Mercedes in double-quick time – Mercedes did not at that time have any service stations in Italy, only sale rooms – and we were able to leave the Eternal City on the eve of Hitler's arrival.

Meantime, at the Hippodrome near the Villa Borghese, we saw a gigantic set under construction for Act II of *Lohengrin*. Mussolini had commissioned a performance of this work, in which six hundred people were to take part, as a special Wagnerian treat for his exalted visitor from Germany. Another curiosity that lingers in my memory was an espresso bar for the Vatican's most senior dignitaries, the court of cardinals, in the immediate proximity of the high altar at St Peter's.

Having visited the principal ancient Roman monuments and the papal reception rooms, we discovered – like our father before us – that the finest view of Rome was to be had while enjoying an ice cream on the terrace of a Monte Pincio café. If we had waited to 'do' Rome until after our visit to Paestum and fascinating, Greco-Normannico-Arabico-Hispanic Sicily, we should probably have missed out on that experience.

In Palermo we stayed at the venerable Hôtel des Palmes, where Wagner had spent some time in 1881. A large framed photograph of our grandfather reposed on a chest of drawers in the Salon Riccardo Wagner. Catching sight of it, I said to my brother: 'Let's hope they don't recognize us as Wagner's grandsons, or we may have to settle some of the old man's debts.'

We heard an invisible flautist playing in the temple precincts at Segesta. The peaceful vista and the gentle strains of the flute seemed to transport us back in time to the ancient world – until the air was suddenly rent by raucous, disembodied voices speaking broad Saxonian dialect: 'The white bread they make here! Our stuff's not a patch on it.'

We had the beach at Agrigento all to ourselves. It was wonderfully peaceful and deserted, and we had a long, enjoyable swim. In the hotel that evening we rhapsodized to the head waiter about the beauty and tranquillity of the seashore. Hardly surprising, he said, because it was the only beach in Sicily frequented by sharks...

5

A FICTION

Where plans to develop and modify the Festspielhaus were concerned, the following details merit some attention.

In June 1939, when rehearsals were already under way, the theatre was hit by an exceptionally violent thunderstorm – indeed, many claimed to have seen some globe lightning, a very rare phenomenon. This ripped open a large section of the roof above the stage, which projected beyond the walls and was adorned with a palmette surmounting the gable-end. The building was severely damaged, the electric cables had been ruptured, and the orchestra pit was under water. It at first seemed unlikely that rehearsals for the festival, which was imminent, could proceed in view of the hole in the roof and the considerable amount of damage sustained by the gridiron. That they did so at all was attributable mainly to the enthusiastic and unsparing efforts of the festival technicians, who did their best to limit the damage while the storm was still raging and tackled the repairs as soon as it was over. The roof could only be resecured flush with the masonry and the palmette could not be replaced, so the characteristic features of the original building had to remain unrestored for the time being. It did not prove possible to renovate the frontage and re-create its original appearance, projecting roof and all, until the festival season of 1993.

Because of this unfortunate incident, consideration was given to whether the Festspielhaus, which had been built as a stopgap, could at last be converted into a permanent and 'gradually self-monumentalizing' form (Richard Wagner). Although certain parts of the building had been enlarged in 1924/5 and 1931 to facilitate the introduction of scenery in the round and the reconstruction of the rehearsal rooms and dressing-rooms beside and behind the stage in a relatively more permanent form, the theatre still lacked the rehearsal rooms, workshops and, above all, the scene docks that would have fulfilled the artistic, technical and administrative requirements of a modern festival.

My brother and I were very surprised and dismayed when, at the 'Gauforum' site office in 1939, the architect Hans Reissinger, who had worked for our mother since 1932, showed Hitler the model for a new festival theatre complex to be erected at the village of Theta. Although not originally a Nazi, Reissinger had risen to become the designer of the monumental Gauforum. He had demonstrated his special talents at Bayreuth in 1933/4 by constructing the 'Haus der Erziehung' [House of Education], in which there was a 'dedicatory hall' containing a monument to mother and child. This project had been commissioned by Gauleiter Hans Schemm, president of the National Socialist Teachers' Association. It was also Reissinger who in 1934 designed Bayreuth's first National Socialist monument, a recumbent swastika. Hitler, spotting this on his way up the festival hill in 1934, ordained that it should be removed forthwith. Reissinger's architectural experience included some work on the Festspielhaus in 1933, when the staircases and lobbies had to be moved as a fire precaution. Unfortunately, he executed it without due deference to the building's special features.

Having familiarized ourselves with the architect's plans for Theta, I and my brother and mother agreed that Hitler must be persuaded to reject them in favour of reconstructing the building as Wagner had hoped to, in other words, by preserving all its time-honoured features.

Albert Speer then arranged for a survey to be conducted by Professor Esterer, a widely respected authority.

On 31 August 1939, on the very eve of the outbreak of war, Professor Esterer's report arrived from Munich. He wrote: 'Having thoroughly inspected the structure and checked its existing industrial safety status and road traffic requirements, I can state that, as things stand, it would be possible, without having to destroy or substantially alter the building's valuable core, to eliminate all its present shortcomings and create a festival theatre that fulfils all modern theatrical requirements and is aesthetically pleasing.'

Professor Esterer enjoyed a great reputation during the Third Reich, and it was he who supervised the restoration of Bayreuth's opera house in 1936. After the war he became head of the Bavarian Castles and Lakes Administration and played a leading part in various reconstruction and restoration projects, notably those relating to the famous, or notorious, castles of King Ludwig of Bavaria. His last commission was the Hercules Room in the Residenz at Munich.

Professor Esterer's report formed the basis of our scheme to renovate and enlarge the Festspielhaus. My brother and I proposed to Albert Speer that the design should be entrusted to the Cologne architect and cathedral supervisor Emil Mewes, also internationally known as an industrial architect whose buildings included the Volkswagen works. We suggested Mewes although, or precisely because, he was not a Party member, and our recommendation was accepted.

Owing to the Nazi period's penchant for Herculean monumentality, but also to the effects of the storm and the technical refinements and additional functions to be incorporated, Mewes designed a vast, monumental building whose conformation was far from exclusively determined by that of the existing structure. In addition to stabilizing and enlarging the stage area and adding side and rear rehearsal stages, workshops, store-rooms, and choral and orchestral rehearsal rooms, the plans envisaged a projecting west wing intended to accommodate, among other things, an amalgamation of the Wahnfried archive and the town's Richard Wagner Memorial collection, the budding Richard Wagner Research Centre, and conference and exhibition rooms. It was further envisaged that an east wing of symmetrical design would house, in addition to some of the aforesaid facilities, a restaurant open to visitors and available for functions throughout the year, not during the festival season alone. In order to realize this overall project, the family was to contribute the Richard Wagner archive to it. Even at this stage, consideration was given to the legal form of a public foundation that would – as eventually laid down in the articles of the Richard Wagner Foundation of 1973 – assign the direction of the festival to whichever member or members of the Wagner family qualified for the post in traditional line of descent.

When the Hofgarten and the Gauforum were redesigned, the grounds of Wahnfried were to be enlarged to provide the family with a communal home, and the plans allowed for a small house in which my mother could spend her declining years.

If I have gone into such detail, it is because the subject continually recurs in debates about the Third Reich's architectural mania.

Mewes's plans, together with a large model, were submitted on 15 December 1940. They were overtaken by events.

6

SOLDIERING AND STUDYING

On 18 November 1938 I embarked perforce and with no great patriotic fervour on my spell of military service as a rifleman in the 42nd Infantry Regiment, as eager to be rid of that burdensome imposition as I had been to leave school. I was temporarily released from duty in the summer of 1939 to enable me to participate in the festival. Like my brother and sisters in previous years, I did not remain at Bayreuth throughout the season but spent part of my allotted leave at my mother's holiday home at Nussdorf on Lake Constance, which she had acquired soon after my father's death. My few days at the house were not, however, as carefree as usual because of something in the air, some impending upheaval of vast and ominous dimensions. Even on the lowest rung of the military ladder assigned me by my junior rank, I was aware of certain vague but steadily accumulating indications that a war would very probably break out in the near future. I still had no conception of its extent and effects, of course. My feeling that some grave or even catastrophic turn of events lay ahead was intuitive rather than positive, and conflicted with the authorities' verbose statements to the contrary. Given such an atmosphere, it was almost inevitable that discussion should have been devoted to aspects of our personal future and that of the festival as well.

My brother Wieland had been granted special status. Although two years' military service was the general rule, he had spent only six months in the labour corps and one in the army before being permanently released from active duty. In that respect he resembled another twenty-four young men whom Adolf Hitler was anxious to preserve from the possibility of a hero's death and had personally exempted from conscription. Wieland had undoubtedly been granted this privilege to facilitate his uninterrupted acquisition of the skills he needed to do justice to his role as 'heir'. Hitler and his entourage were fond of thinking and planning along such patriarchal, indeed, positively archaic lines. Wieland had hitherto devoted himself primarily to his first love, painting, and, where the theatre was concerned, to stage design, so I was far from convinced of his willingness to acquire a knowledge of all the other ramifications in which any theatrical administrator must be versed. I therefore told him that I intended to equip myself with all these basic skills so that, if I survived the more than uncertain outcome of the war in one piece, I would if necessary work together with him at Bayreuth.

On 24 August 1939, immediately after my return to Bayreuth, I was recalled to barracks. On 25 and 26 August, having been equipped for combat, my company moved out to Rosenberg in Upper Silesia, its deployment area for the invasion of Poland. Two days before war broke out I celebrated my twentieth birthday with a few Bavarian comrades – an occasion ruined for those inveterate beer-drinkers because stocks of their native beverage were already so depleted that their mood verged on mutiny. Much to their surprise and annoyance, I expressed my conviction that the war would not only last a long time but turn out so disastrously that Germany would be quite incapable of winning it. There was universal consternation at this surprisingly pessimistic forecast, because nearly every-one knew that I was on first-name terms with Adolf Hitler.

By way of Lublinitz [Lubliniec] and Tschenstochow [Czestochowa], home of the Black Madonna, we advanced towards the bend in the Vistula and reached a point just beyond Radom, where a large-scale encircling manœuvre yielded 105,000 prisoners. During this battle one of our outposts was overrun by Poles attempting to break out of the pocket. Our company commander, Oberleutnant Greiner, who thought it a 'disgrace' that German soldiers should have been taken prisoner, mounted an operation designed to locate and release them. I was persuaded to 'volunteer' for this mission, in the course of which we suddenly and unwittingly blundered into the midst of some heavily armed and well-entrenched Polish troops. Although we had often been indoctrinated with the superiority of German military equipment, this availed us little. The scout cars in which we were travelling provided scant protection against a hail of machine-gun fire, and several of my comrades were killed.

Because it would have been quite pointless to offer resistance and, in all probability, die for Führer and Fatherland – a fate I had no wish to undergo – I raised both arms in the so-called German salute. My immediate neighbours followed suit, and the Poles took us prisoner. I had been wounded by a burst of machine-gun fire in the course of the engagement, receiving a bullet through the hand and wrist and a flesh wound in the upper thigh, which looked bad because of the copious bleeding but was luckily not too serious. I had also been hit, boomerang fashion, by one or two splinters from the hand-grenades we had thrown. Less serious, to my mind, was the fact that both my shoulder straps had been shot off. I owed my survival only to our enemies' inadequate equipment, because they were using a German water-cooled machine-gun of First World War vintage, which had a relatively slow rate of fire.

There ensued a series of ticklish and sometimes dramatic situations until I and the other casualties of the above skirmish, including some badly wounded Poles, were loaded on to one-horse carts and, through the good offices of a Polish medical officer, transported to the German lines under a flag of truce.

All the wounded were taken first of all to the field hospital at Radom. A few days later I and some others were flown out to Breslau [Wrocław], whence I was transferred to the base hospital at Liegnitz [Legnica]. I and a soldier from another unit were the hospital's very first casualties, so we received special attention because the other patients were merely sick, and there was still something a trifle sensational about men who had actually been wounded in combat. In the course of treatment I renewed my acquaintance with the much-lauded German talent for organization, which has always struck me as an incomprehensible myth. The medical conscripts at Liegnitz, most of whom hailed from Breslau University, were far from all working in their special fields. They had presumably been assigned in accordance with some higher form of military wisdom, because my own case, which was clearly of a surgical nature, was handled by a dentist. Had the potential consequences of such weird anomalies not been so serious, one could have shaken one's head and laughed at them.

One middle-aged sister was most concerned lest one of the pretty young nurses should have to strip-wash me, an incapacitated twenty-year-old, so she preserved decency and decorum and banished all the temptations of the flesh by helping me to wash myself.

It was pure chance that I managed to keep my arm, which my thirty-six hours in captivity had deprived of treatment for an undue length of time. For one thing, none of the doctors at Radom or Liegnitz decreed that it should be amputated; for another, I was genuinely fortunate in that a senior medical officer of general's rank inspected the X-ray while conducting a tour of inspection and pronounced my arm a suitable case for his friend Ferdinand Sauerbruch of the Charité. At the end of October 1939, therefore, I travelled to Berlin in an ordinary, overcrowded, blacked-out train, having had to pay for my own ticket. My referral to such an eminent surgeon and the excellent treatment I received at his hands were in no way a mark of special favour to a Wagner from Bayreuth. I owed them solely to the unpredictable workings of a kindly providence.

Thanks to my war wound and consequent physical disability, I was officially discharged from the armed forces on 17 June 1940, so Germany's plans for world conquest had to proceed without my assistance. I came out as an NCO of the reserve. This naturally killed my chances of a political career – had I wanted one – because, as everyone knows, the predestined rank for a really successful Third Reich politician was lance-corporal. I was, however, afforded a sooner-than-expected opportunity to do what I had discussed with my brother shortly before the outbreak of war, namely, prepare myself to work at Bayreuth.

Despite the losses Germany was incurring in a war of ever-increasing ferocity and magnitude, it was Adolf Hitler's ambition not to make too many inroads into cultural institutions, and the theatre in particular, by conscripting their personnel. For that reason, neither the Salzburg nor the Bayreuth Festival was discontinued, as they might well have been in the light of the general situation.

Hitler countered my mother's objections and misgivings by declaring that the Bayreuth Festival must remain in being because experience of the ten-year closure occasioned by the First World War showed how greatly this had impaired its artistic continuity, and how laborious and complicated its revival had been. And that, he said, could not be allowed to happen again. It is debatable how far Hitler's decision was influenced by propaganda aims and objectives, but such considerations must secretly have played an important part in it. My mother felt bound to comply with Hitler's wishes. When she pointed to the dearth of visitors from abroad, the travel restrictions to which potential German audiences were subject, and short-ages of technical staff caused by conscription, Hitler promptly disarmed her. Not only were audiences 'organized', but special leave was granted to all the permanent staff who had been called up, together with any additional personnel required for the festival, whatever sector of the front they happened to be serving on. The list included butchers, bakers and kitchen staff as well as administrative personnel such as those responsible for issuing extra ration cards.

The audiences consisted of wounded veterans and munitions workers transported to Bayreuth from all over the Reich by 'Strength through Joy'. All the arrangements, financial included, were handled by that organization, which was also responsible for troops' welfare at home and at the front.

Adolf Hitler attended a performance of *Götterdämmerung* on 23 July 1940. It was the last occasion on which he visited Bayreuth and his last meeting with my mother.

For me this first of the so-called 'wartime festivals' held a special significance because it marked my first really active involvement at Bayreuth. I was able, as a trainee and general factotum, to attend the rehearsals and performances, and thus to acquire my first real knowledge of the theatre. I had sniffed around the place as a child and adolescent, but my interest and enthusiasm were more light-hearted than serious. Although considerable importance undoubtedly attached to this preliminary phase, I now set about developing my practical skills by taking an active part in the work of the festival. I did so in a very modest way, of course, but I was intensely eager to learn and did my best to perform the wide variety of tasks assigned me in a satisfactory manner. I can say without false modesty that I have never minimized the importance of any activity that has devolved on me in the course of my life. I have never tackled any project in a half-hearted way, and have always striven to bring it to a fitting and satisfactory conclusion. Nothing has ever been beneath my dignity, at all events, and I am still grateful to this day that, where my theatrical career is concerned, I started 'at the bottom'. The range and variety of the things I learned and the theoretical and practical knowledge I gained have always constituted a solid foundation on which to build.

There remained the problem of what I should do once the festival ended. Having opted for the theatre, I naturally required a systematic and well co-ordinated training, because I never felt then or later that I possessed the fabulous brilliance and absolute predestination characteristic of many other members of the Wagner family. These qualities, coupled with a surprising sense of vocation, seem to preclude their involvement in subordinate activities but have, on the other hand, often prompted them to lay vehement but unjustified claim to positions of paramount authority.

Having cast around for an arrangement that would suit and benefit me as much as possible, my mother, Heinz Tietjen and I jointly decided that I should undergo my training in Berlin. Bayreuth had to be ruled out in view of the festival's duration, which was normally limited to a few weeks, and of its much reduced wartime programme, which amounted in 1940 to two cycles of *The Ring* and four performances of *Der Fliegende Holländer*, nor could I undertake a university or other academic course because I had precipitately left school with an intermediate certificate only. I did, on the other hand, have excellent and long-standing connections with Berlin and, in particular, the Staatsoper. This was mainly because of Heinz Tietjen, the general administrator of the Prussian State Theatre, who was also artistic director of the Bayreuth Festival and a close family friend. My mother had rented two rooms in his Berlin apartment on a permanent basis, and the premises were spacious enough to house me as well, at least to begin with. I already knew some of the Staatsoper productions – I had often sat in on rehearsals there as soon as I was sufficiently recovered from my war wounds to be allowed out of the Charité Hospital – so I was not a complete stranger to much of what went on there. Accordingly, I negotiated my first proper contract of employment and started earning money, though hardly enough to keep me. The place was Berlin, the date 1 October 1940.

Compared to other, smaller provincial theatres, the Staatsoper was far from badly off in the early 1940s because it enjoyed many exemptions and was at first largely shielded from the effects of the war. Only ten per cent of the staff, at most, had been called up, and many were certified 'Uk', or persons engaged in a reserved occupation. This ensured that the theatre remained fully operative, and it was only in the third year of the war that the possibility of economizing on costumes began to be debated.

There were two initial aspects to my training schedule. In the first place, it was intended that I should acquire practical experience of a well-run theatre with a wide and varied repertoire. I was thrown in at the deep end, so to speak, but I fear that – much to many people's subsequent regret – I immediately felt too much at home there to drown. My official designation was assistant stage manager, then stage manager, which meant that I was responsible for seeing that rehearsals and performances went according to plan. As a job, it was far from always productive of sublime or momentous experiences, because some of what was to be seen on stage was thoroughly inane. I have only to think of Gustav Gründgens's *Zauberflöte*, a truly frightful and vastly expensive production. Having seen it from the auditorium on an earlier occasion, I remember how forcibly it was borne in on me that one's view of the action from the stage is altogether different.

In the second place, I had to school myself in musical theory. My wounds were too severe for me to perfect my piano-playing, a skill not only required by but indispensable to anyone desirous of employment in the musical theatre. I was afraid that my shattered arm would never lose its stiffness. Although this precluded a career as a conductor or any other kind of musician – I felt no inclination to blow the trumpet in any case – I not only wanted but had to master the rudiments of music: harmony, counterpoint, and the analysis of a very wide-ranging musical literature. For this purpose Heinz Tietjen obtained me the services of Rolf Ehrenreich, one of his Staatsoper *répétiteurs*, who also composed in his spare time. Under his expert tuition I managed to master the essentials of musical theory, but not just in the silence of my lonely room. There was a very practical side to my learning process, which required me to attend many rehearsals, both of individual singers and of whole ensembles. These sitting-in sessions were my most valuable source of instruction. To cite one unforgettable example, I followed Maria Cebotari in the part of Salome – her dream role – from the very first run-through, via ensemble, orchestral, and full rehearsals, to the dress rehearsal, première, and all subsequent performances. In addition to Clemens Krauss, who conducted *Salome*, I was able to make a close first-hand study of many other heroes of the baton including the young Herbert von Karajan, whom I saw not only at the Staatsoper but at concerts given by the Prussian State Orchestra, whose conductor he was during the war years. Because Rolf Ehrenreich, like any *répétiteur*, acted as assistant to the conductors of various new productions and made notes for them during orchestral rehearsals, I had ample opportunity to observe the whole range of musical activities in the theatre at first hand, an experience from which I derived considerable benefit. More than that, my learning process led to a growing perception of the way in which great confrères – I am thinking here of Herbert von Karajan and Wilhelm Furtwängler – 'discreetly' conveyed to each other just how important they were. That knowledge was later to prove invaluable.

In addition to this semi-official training course, I doggedly strove to pursue another, extremely relevant course of self-instruction by devoting my leisure hours to reading books on the history of music. All in all, my time was very fully occupied.

My normal working day went more or less as follows. I worked from seven-thirty onwards or studied particular works and prepared myself for the day's rehearsals, which usually began at ten and lasted until one or one-thirty. My journey by underground took between twenty and twenty-five minutes, but I did not find it tedious because I never travelled without a piano score or reading matter of some kind. If, as sometimes happened, I bumped into a colleague or acquaintance on the way to the opera house, I rather resented the encounter because it spoiled my concentration and involved me, willy-nilly, in what I tended to regard as trivial, time-wasting chatter. I went home after lunch. Once I had quit the Tietjen household and moved into a small apartment of my own, I used to do my shopping on the return journey. My purchases were very meagre at this period and called for growing ingenuity, because pretty well everything was in short supply, owing to the war, and could only be had for coupons. Although one could occasionally obtain things off ration, the prime requirement when preparing meals was culinary imagination, because the contents of one's pots and pans were less than scanty. However, since it is well known that a full stomach is not conducive to brainwork, and since mine was often empty, I studied all the harder in the afternoons. My evenings, whenever I was not on duty for a performance, were devoted to more rehearsals. Afterwards I would usually do some more work at home, though I naturally saw friends and acquaintances from time to time.

It was then, at the 'dangerous' age, and because one's yearning for a harmonious relationship is heightened by war, that I got married. Unlike all the outgoing, assertive women in and around my family circle, Ellen Drexel was extremely reserved and self-effacing. I had met her in the course of my work at the Staatsoper, where she was employed as a dancer. We were married at the Siegfried Wagner House in Bayreuth on 11 April 1943. The civil ceremony was conducted by the then mayor, Dr Kempfler, and those members of the family who were present, with the exception of my mother, made a point of behaving like born Wagners. To me, no festivity is complete without roast pork and dumplings, so my wedding menu naturally included that delicacy.

My professional development and advancement had been planned as a gradual process. On 1 September 1941, after completing the 'basic course' designed to familiarize me with every aspect of theatre work, I was promoted to assistant producer with responsibility for directing and stage-managing evening performances. Individual functions were not as strictly segregated in the theatre of those days, so I not only assisted at performances but directed them and conducted post-performance rehearsals on my own. Two years later to the day, in conformity with the extension of my contract, I was engaged as a potential producer. My objective had from the outset been to stage a first production of my own in 1944, provided always that I had, during my training, given evidence of artistically valid and expressive essays in interpretation. It was intended that I should make my début with a work of my father's on the seventy-fifth anniversary of his birth. The following two seasons, 1944/5 and 1945/6, would each feature two non-Wagnerian works produced by me. Having thus attained junior producer's status and divested myself of other activities such as stage management, I would then, in parallel with my work as a producer, be apprenticed to the mighty men of the Prussian State Theatre, there to study the financial and administrative aspects of a complex theatrical enterprise. That would complete my syllabus. What would have become of me then, had all these well-devised and eminently sensible plans come to fruition, remains a big question mark. I recall a vague suggestion that I should be appointed director of a children's and young people's theatre at Tula, some 130 kilometres south of Moscow. Whether this bright idea was seriously intended or just a nebulous notion born of Greater German megalomania, I cannot tell. I would not have objected too strongly, as a matter of fact, if only out of sheer curiosity.

The première of my first independent production took place on 7 June 1944. It was also the last new production to be staged at the Berlin Staatsoper before the closure of all theatres on 31 August of the same year, during the final phase of the 'total war' first proclaimed by Joseph Goebbels at the Sportpalast on 18 February 1943. That this war was already lost must have been obvious to everyone, however obdurate, in view of the fact that all artists were now conscripted and mobilized. For my first work I had chosen my father's opera *Bruder Lustig* [Merry-Andrew], though we agreed in consultation with the production team and the management of the opera house to change the title to *Andreasnacht* [St Andrew's Night], in the first place to convey that it was not in any sense a comic opera, and, secondly, because a bright and breezy title like *Bruder Lustig* would certainly have been inappropriate to the situation prevailing in early summer 1944. Although a beginner, I could call on a really excellent cast that included the Staatsoper's leading lights. Maria Müller, Peter Anders, Margaret Klose, Will Domgraf-Fassbaender, Josef Greindl, Eugen Fuchs – their very names say it all. I soon became aware, while working, that my father's operas should never be performed by any old cast. Their demands on the soloists are so great that they call for voices of the very highest quality.

I had known Maria Müller, who sang the principal female role in my production of *Andreasnacht*, for some time through Bayreuth. During one of the conversations that often arose in the course of our daily rehearsals, I asked about her impressions and experiences of Arturo Toscanini, under whose baton she had sung Elisabeth in my father's new Bayreuth production of *Tannhäuser* in 1930. I found it interesting and instructive to hear how the celebrated maestro had worked with her from the musical standpoint. His German was very poor, and he certainly enjoyed no close or empathetic relationship with what was specifically Wagnerian. He therefore insisted that Maria Müller sing the entire role, notably the so-called 'hall aria' and the 'prayer' from Act III, in accordance with the French translation authorized by Wagner for the Paris production of 1861. In other words, he took his lead from the French libretto and its entirely different phrasing, even though it bore a very peculiar and distorted relationship to the German text used by Maria Müller. Inevitably, this caused him to subject her to some violent and entirely unwarranted outbursts. Since he was also noted and feared for being a conductor who relentlessly imposed his own tempi, took no account of a singer's individuality, and demanded absolute obedience, the day came when Maria Müller ran to my father in tears. He eventually managed, in his sympathetic and conciliatory way, to calm her down and restore her self-confidence by assuring her that her personality and artistry on stage would resolve the problem by themselves.

The circumstances surrounding my first production were unfavourable and at times rather dangerous. On 24 May 1944, while the ensemble and I were rehearsing in the Berliner Schloss, a daylight raid by Allied bombers devastated not only the university and the national library but the cathedral near the Lustgarten. I actually saw the dome collapse, a spectacle as indelibly imprinted on my mind as certain other horrifying memories of those days. Berlin was becoming more and more of a theatre of war on the so-called home front. At the opera this increasingly gave rise to situations in which, if today's multifarious safety regulations and bureaucratic directives had been in force, the curtain would never have gone up under any circumstances. It was different in those days. If only three enemy aircraft were circling the city, for instance, only a 'minor alert' was declared and a performance could proceed without interruption. The sirens could not be heard in the auditorium or on the stage, but this did not apply to the dressing-room area. The singers there were only too aware of the sirens' wailing chorus, and as evening producer I sometimes had to exercise great ingenuity to keep the ensemble in the building at all. It could be quite difficult to restrain some operatic impersonator of a courageous and indomitable hero from making a headlong dash for the air-raid shelter, which was situated outside the opera house, at the very first sign of danger. Despite the genuine gravity of the situation, comical or even grotesque incidents could occur – as, for instance, during a performance of *Die Meistersinger*. The date, I seem to call, was 30 January 1944, the eleventh anniversary of Hitler's accession to power, and a full-scale alert had sounded in the middle of the overture. This was an unmistakable signal for the performance to be discontinued and the auditorium vacated forthwith. The audience used the foyers as a makeshift air-raid shelter because the building was said to have been so stoutly rebuilt by Frederick the Great that it would withstand bombs and provide a secure refuge. The members of the ensemble and other personnel did not subscribe to this reassuring belief, so most of them hurried off to the cellars of the Stadtschloss beside the Lustgarten. Not so the conductor that night, Wilhelm Furtwängler, who flew into a panic. Coat-tails flapping and long legs striding out fast, he made for the Hotel Adlon's air-raid shelter closely followed by a bevy of singers who had not, of course, stopped to remove their *Meistersinger* costumes and make-up. They made a hilarious spectacle despite their understandable trepidation. A somewhat awkward situation arose when the all-clear sounded, because, although the audience resumed their seats soon afterwards, the Adlon fugitives kept them waiting for a considerable time. Being on duty that night, I had a minor argument with Furtwängler, when he finally reappeared, over where to restart the performance: at the very beginning, at the point where the prelude had been interrupted, or at the moment when the curtain rises. Furtwängler doubtless welcomed this debate because it enabled him to catch his breath and regain his composure after such a breakneck long-distance run.

First damaged by an air raid on the night of 10 April 1941, the Staatsoper had been rebuilt at such incredible speed, all wartime difficulties notwithstanding, that it was back in business by 12 December 1942. Langhan's restrained décor had been replaced, under Hermann Göring's supreme command, with a Knobelsdorffian, entirely colour-co-ordinated rococo theatre. The work performed to mark the building's reinauguration was *Die Meistersinger*, with which it also reopened its doors after the war, but the activities of the Staatsoper's ensemble were not appreciably restricted in the interim. During the company's 'homeless' period it began by spending a few days at the Gendarmenmarkt Theatre, where I assisted Wolf Völker with his première of *Cosi fan tutte*. From the Gendarmenmarkt we moved to the former Krolloper, which had acquired a great reputation in the 1920s. When the Reichstag was set ablaze on 27 February 1933 and put out of commission, but was neither restored nor renovated, its functions were transferred to the Kroll. Thus it was there, in an opera house, that Hitler announced the invasion of Poland on 1 September 1939. The National Socialist deputies who assembled there were aptly referred to by irreverent Berliners as 'the world's most expensive choral society' because the building was dedicated to unanimity, not democratic parliamentary debates. The Führer and Reich Chancellor would simply deliver periodic situation reports on such matters as he deemed important, to be greeted by Party members with dutiful ovations and renderings of their anthem, the *Horst-Wessel-Lied*, and *Deutschland über alles*. There was a certain irony – or, rather, a certain all too rare element of justice – in the fact that the Kroll had become a theatre once more, thereby regaining its proper function and identity and enabling true singing to reassert its rights at last.

I made particularly thorough preparations for the première of *Rienzi* on 29 October 1941, among them a comparison between the score of the Cosima Wagner–Felix Mottl version, on temporary loan from Karlsruhe, and the Fürstner Verlag material that was then in general use. It became very clear to me, in the process, why my grandfather had not wanted *Rienzi* to be performed at Bayreuth on a par with his later works. For all its youthful verve and musical charm, in which flashes of the strength and grandeur of Wagner's later genius can already be discerned, the opera diverges so considerably from the works he wrote thereafter, if only in dramatic conception, that he could not fit it into the context of his festival idea.

When the Staatsoper closed for the summer I used to go to Bayreuth to assist with the festival. This was how it came about that Wieland and I worked together at Bayreuth for the first time in 1943, when he was designing the sets for *Die Meistersinger*. Performed by varying casts and conducted alternately by Wilhelm Furtwängler and Hermann Abendroth, it was also the only work presented at Bayreuth in 1944.

As an agreement reached between my mother and Kurt Overhoff demonstrates, Wieland's systematic involvement in our grandfather's festival enterprise began on 15 September 1940. Owing in part to our exhaustive discussion of the subject in August 1939, he had evidently realized that he must abandon his hitherto irresolute attitude towards a career and come to terms with the idea that he was *the* 'heir to Bayreuth'.

Just as she had given her extremely individualistic elder son an opportunity to develop his painting talents under a private teacher, Ferdinand Staeger of Munich, and enabled him to make solid progress in the sphere of technical craftsmanship, so our far-sighted mother once more furnished him with all the prerequisites, financial included, for the best available private tuition.

Kurt Overhoff, whom she entrusted with this task, was no stranger to our family. My mother, who often made information-gathering trips to south-west Germany, had long been as impressed as Franz Konwitschny by his musical ability and profound knowledge of Wagner's œuvre. Thus, on 1 September 1940, by agreement with Dr Neinhaus, the mayor of Heidelberg, my mother dissolved Overhoff's lifelong contractual relationship with the Heidelberg theatre and employed him at Bayreuth on the same terms. By so doing she killed two birds with one stone: she not only gave Wieland a private tutor who measured up to his wishes and ideas, but did Overhoff a good turn by relieving him of public commitments which his poor health rendered him almost incapable of meeting in full.

Drawing on his sound classical education and his wealth of experience as a conductor and composer, Overhoff proceeded during September 1940 to draw up a training programme that took full account of my brother's singularly individualistic temperament and accorded with his objectives.

It should be mentioned that, at Heinz Tietjen's suggestion, the tutor Karl Kittel had, on 20 September 1933, submitted a syllabus designed under the terms of Siegfried Wagner's will for all his children, especially the first-born 'heir to Bayreuth'. In the event, it foundered on the non-acceptance of those for whom it was intended.

Wieland cut his teeth in the theatre at Lübeck in 1936, as designer for a production of *Der Bärenhäuter*, our father's extremely successful first opera. In 1937 he did the same for *Parsifal* at Bayreuth, having one year previously redesigned Alfred Roller's 'Good Friday meadow'. There followed, also in 1937, the scenery for *Schwarzschwanenreich* at Antwerp and, in 1938, for *Bärenhäuter* at Cologne and *Sonnenflammen* at Düsseldorf – all of them works by Siegfried Wagner. After his early Bayreuth ventures as co-designer of the scenery for *Parsifal*, which gave an indication of his knowledge and ability, Wieland embarked on his twin courses of instruction in painting and music. The original intention was that, after following up his theoretical studies with some practical training, he should put himself to the test as a conductor. It never came to that, however, because he definitely opted in favour of stage design and production. His first independent production, given at Nuremberg in June 1943, was *Die Walküre*, for which he also designed the scenery, having in 1942 designed a *Holländer* for the same theatre. Summer 1943 saw the beginning of his collaboration at Altenburg with Kurt Overhoff, who had become musical director there and was continuing to monitor his progress. Wieland's principal achievement at

Altenburg was to design and produce the entire *Ring* cycle. His period of tuition under Overhoff outlasted the war and continued, with certain interruptions, until 1951.

Bayreuth's own conception of its existing and future role is apparent from the way in which our courses of training, which embraced the fusion and interaction of theory and practice, were planned and executed.

Albeit at different places and under different circumstances, my brother and I owed the fact that those training plans were only partly successful to the outcome of the war. Very soon overtaken by such sobering realities as the Allied occupation, our mother's denazification, and the placing of the festival under trusteeship, we were inexorably compelled to undertake a complete reappraisal of the situation.

Some of the relevant documents have been published. On Herbert Barth's initiative, a large-scale series of publications marking the centenary of the Bayreuth Festival was financed by the Fritz Thyssen Foundation and appeared in 1976. The preliminary planning began in 1967. Since it was naturally of considerable importance that the documents in the Wahnfried archive should be made available, my mother and I agreed in principle to grant access to them and any other relevant papers.

Gertrud Strobel, who was in charge of the archive during the preparation of this documentary material, clearly demonstrated her singular and strangely warped conception of fair play by making public, without consulting me or my mother, numerous letters, notes and other documents relating to the peculiarly complicated years 1940–50, together with papers of the most private nature including letters expressly marked 'not sent'. It is an established fact that Gertrud Strobel presumptuously and arbitrarily made use of documents, in some cases unlawfully appropriated them, and deliberately rather than inadvertently flouted the protection afforded by copyright and the right of personal privacy. As in this instance, so in connection with the dispute over *The Ring* in 1976, she violated every basic principle governing the relationship between employer and employee. I myself was ignorant of all these strange goings-on until Michael Karbaum, the author of *Studien zur Geschichte der Bayreuther Festspiele*, came – quite innocently and openly – to inform me of its form and contents, and, in particular, of the sources he proposed to quote. I was considerably taken aback, but, not wishing to gain a reputation for the kind of deliberate obscurantism practised at Bayreuth in the decades prior to 1930, I reluctantly agreed that the book should appear in its existing form. This I did in consultation with my mother, who had been the first to break the spell of Bayreuth's Byzantine love of embellishment.

And here I consider it right and necessary to summarize my attitude to the documents transmitted to the public by Karbaum and to some of the interpretations he placed on them.

As everyone knows, it has always been difficult if not utterly impossible to divorce the Wagner family from the Bayreuth Festival and regard them as two entirely separate things. This has applied as much to Siegfried and his successors as to Richard and Cosima. The effect of the testamentary provisions concerned with entailment and reversionary rights jointly signed by Siegfried and Winifred in 1929 has been that Siegfried's family, in particular, is forever regarded as directly and intimately connected with the festival.

The contents of the published documents, the vast majority of which related to family squabbles, would at best have been a nine days' wonder and thus of no further importance had not Adolf Hitler's name kept cropping up in them – something for which Heinz Tietjen was largely responsible. That my brother and I should have followed relatively parallel courses of training was another factor – given the different ideas arising from our different temperaments and our attempts to carry them out – that prompted a number of variously motivated parties to cause friction in the family and, consequently, in the festival.

The war, of course, affected our whole family, and not least my mother. What with its outbreak, the fact that I was wounded right away, and the institution of 'wartime festivals', which in my view altered their purpose and significance, there was a considerable cooling in her relations with Hitler. She no longer approached the Führer direct, but inquired via Heinz Tietjen what form the festival was to take in 1941 – evidently because the subject had not been discussed during Hitler's last visit to Bayreuth. Even on the threshold of war, however, an incident occurred that might have contributed to her subsequent alienation. Hitler had publicly affronted Sir Nevile Henderson, the British ambassador, by excluding him from the official visitors' box at the Bayreuth Festival of 1939, so my mother seated him in the family box instead. Henderson, whose very last chance to preserve the peace this might have been, asked her if she could arrange a meeting between himself and Hitler, who was staying at the guest-house. Her attempt at mediation was icily rebuffed by Hitler, who curtly rejected the proposal. Thereafter he was so preoccupied with his role as supreme warlord that he paid only one more visit to Bayreuth, and my mother never saw him again.

An unprecedented ovation greeted him when he drove up the Hill in 1940, having launched his offensive against France on 10 May and brought it to a victorious conclusion with the signing of the armistice on 22 June. Extolled as the conqueror of Germany's 'hereditary foe' and the man who had driven the British into the sea at Dunkirk, the commander-in-chief of the Wehrmacht seemed to think that his triumphal reception confirmed the rights of the victor over the vanquished and justified all his people's past and future sacrifices. Those sacrifices and the impositions they had undergone in Poland and France were dismissed and forgotten in a frenzy of jubilation, and Adolf Hitler, who believed himself to be the chosen instrument of providence and felt that his racial and military policies had been vindicated, continued to pursue them with disastrous results.

It should be mentioned that Heinz Tietjen had been general administrator of the Berlin's Prussian State Theatre since 1927, and that his subsidiary activities as artistic adviser to the Bayreuth Festival from 1931 onwards had required the official approval of the Prussian minister of culture. When his Bayreuth appointment was made public, my mother became embroiled in a correspondence with Alfred Rosenberg, then editor of the *Völkischer Beobachter*. Rosenberg, who found Wagner's music disturbing and had admitted in his *Mythos des 20. Jahrhunderts* that *The Ring* defeated him, complained that Heinz Tietjen was a 'Social Democrat' and an unacceptable addition to Bayreuth. My mother's reply of 29 April 1931 put Rosenberg firmly in his place: 'I am much obliged to you for acquainting me with the Städtische Oper-Tietjen affair. Please don't misunderstand me. If the NSDAP [Nazi Party] feels bound to level criticism at me and/or Bayreuth, it should and must do so. I simply think it a mistake to attack Tietjen *because* he is alleged to be a member of the SPD. In so doing, our Party would be espousing the view of those who say, "First get your Party membership book and then you'll land a job." I did not, of course, choose Tietjen because he is an SPD man – which I still don't believe, by the way – but because I think he possesses the right human and artistic qualities to assist me in my duties.'

In order to clarify the position of the 1941 festival, my mother asked Tietjen to go to Hitler, who was still the Third Reich's cultural as well as military supremo, and ask him what preparations should be made. Tietjen, in his turn, thought that the best way of carrying out this reconnaissance mission would be to entrust it to my twenty-one-year-old self. Three alternative proposals had been worked out for 1941: the so-called 'big plan', which envisaged that the programme would comprise a new production of *Tannhäuser* and the *Parsifal* designed by Wieland; a repetition of the 1940 programme; or no festival at all, to enable Wagner's festival theatre, originally a temporary expedient, to be reconstructed and, thus, monumentalized.

In view of developments in the military situation, the second suggestion was adopted.

Despite or because of the problems posed by programme selection, the uncertainty surrounding the reconstruction schedule, the geographically separate courses of instruction undertaken by us two brothers, and the permanent feud between Tietjen and Wieland, my mother was compelled to submit the festival to firm co-ordination. In 1943 she managed, partly by appealing to the common sense of the two fighting cocks, to ensure that Wieland designed the sets for *Die Meistersinger*. His greatest stumbling block, Emil Preetorius, whose 'Expressionism' he thoroughly rejected, had at last been squeezed out of his post at Bayreuth. It had also become necessary, in the festival's third wartime year, to present a single work performed by two conductors and two casts, the conductors being Wilhelm Furtwängler and Hermann Abendroth.

Thus, a unique triumvirate came into being in 1943: Heinz Tietjen (producer), Wieland Wagner (designer), and Wolfgang Wagner (assistant producer) worked together – for the first and last time – on *Die Meistersinger*.

For me, too, this collaboration ushered in a kind of 'truce' to which reference has often been made. As for the permanent state of peace that alone could have enabled the plans for rebuilding and enlarging the Festspielhaus to be carried out, that continued to hang fire.

My brother and Heinz Tietjen finally buried the hatchet when Tietjen was directing the Hamburg Staatsoper between 1956 and 1959. The *Lohengrin* he invited Wieland to stage there was premièred in December 1957. In return, Tietjen was invited by both festival directors to conduct two performances of Wieland's *Lohengrin* at Bayreuth in 1959.

It should be mentioned that, even during the closing stages of the war, my brother came to an important conclusion that would later lead him to distance himself, gradually but irrevocably, from the most active trouble-makers and know-it-alls in his circle of advisers and associates. At a chaotic period in which truths and, more especially, half-truths were hopelessly intermingled, he must have sensed the pressure that was being exerted on him and freed himself from it. The persons concerned included Otto Strobel, Strobel's ex-wife Gertrud, Kurt Overhoff, the authors of sundry programme notes, and, last but not least, his own wife, Gertrud Wagner.

7

PICKING UP THE PIECES

As I have already mentioned, all theatres were closed on 31 August 1944, or a few weeks after the unsuccessful attempt on Hitler's life on 20 July. From 1 September onwards, after participating in the last wartime festival and taking a brief vacation, I remained at Bayreuth for good.

From 18 September until the war ended in the following year I was drafted for war service and employed as 'technical assistant' to Florian Rappl, head of the civil engineering department at the municipal surveyor's office. My duties included the construction and supervision of so-called 'temporary homes', which were either prefabricated in wood or built of salvaged stone. The function of these small houses was to accommodate bombed-out evacuees, refugees, or privileged workers such as some Ukrainian physicists who were working locally and had brought a sizeable library with them from their homeland. Another of my responsibilities was to supervise the labourers employed to excavate trenches and air-raid shelters in the urban area. These included Ukrainian and British prisoners of war, who were transported to the construction sites from their respective camps. I was familiar with the digging of trenches and other such operations from my time in the labour corps, so the job presented no difficulty.

Hitherto, Bayreuth's only first-hand experience of the war and its consequences had occurred in 1941, when a few random bombs had unexpectedly fallen on the town, but these caused little damage and had been almost forgotten in the meantime. They were really a kind of show of strength designed to intimidate the civilian population and demonstrate that Allied bombers could operate deep inside German territory, not just against major cities. On 5 April 1945, shortly before the first real air raid on Bayreuth, some prisoners working in Bürgerreuther Strasse, which has since been replaced by the extension of Tristanstrasse and absorbed into the grounds of the Festspielhaus itself, sought refuge from the approaching aircraft beneath the trees that still flank the approaches to the Festspielhaus canteen. The British, taking their lead from a flight engineer whose plane had been shot down over Germany, contemptuously and ostentatiously turned their backs on their Russian and Ukrainian fellow prisoners to show that, even in so potentially lethal a situation, definite differences in status still existed.

After the first air raids on Bayreuth the doors of the overcrowded prison, the St Georgen Penitentiary, were thrown open. It housed such prominent figures as Eugen Gerstenmaier, subsequently president of the Bundestag, and the theologian Dietrich Bonhoeffer, who was executed at Flossenbürg concentration camp on 9 April 1945, only a few days later. A few of the released prisoners, conscripts from Czech industrial concerns, withdrew to the relative safety of the trenches that had been dug around the theatre for the benefit of festival visitors, there to reflect on their chances of survival. From their manner they could best be described, in modern parlance, as industrial managers. While chatting to them on one of my last inspections of the Green Hill and the Festspielhaus before the war ended, I advised them to await the arrival of the Americans, which was clearly imminent. If they risked trying to make their way home, they would be in mortal danger from military policemen and the notorious SS snatch squads.

I watched the first air raid on Bayreuth from a parade-ground on the outskirts, where I was scheduled to take part in a Volkssturm [home guard] exercise. When the pathfinders dropped their marker flares, the dreaded 'Christmas trees', another participant turned to me with an air of helpless incomprehension. 'What are they doing?' he asked, to which I was forced to reply, 'Smashing up our town.' He looked indignant. 'But are they allowed to do that? It's just not on!' However improbable and ludicrous this exchange may sound today, it was typical of the majority of the inhabitants of Bayreuth, who had still to experience a major air raid and were firmly convinced that their native town would be spared such a fate.

Then the bombs came raining down and Bayreuth was, for the first time, subjected to the treatment that had so often been meted out to other German towns and cities.

I myself had never felt entirely sure that Bayreuth, of all places, would be spared. My time in Berlin having acquainted me with the horrific effects of aerial bombing, I had insisted that all Wahnfried's pictures, busts, and precious manuscripts and scores should be removed. At my instigation they were taken to the relative safety of the 'Winifred Wagner Home', then a Red Cross hospital and now the Krankenhaus Hohe Warte. I had also had my grandfather's library specially boxed in its original order and removed to Burg Wiesentfels. But for my precautions, all these treasures would have been destroyed when Haus Wahnfried was bombed the same day.

Some twelve months previously, again at my suggestion, we had transferred our air-raid quarters to the cellars of the Siegfried Wagner House, because at Wahnfried they projected above ground-level and might have been demolished by blast. The bomb that damaged Wahnfried smashed through the roof and intervening ceiling and exploded in the basement itself. If they had been sheltering there, all the occupants of Wahnfried, including my mother and my first wife, who was very pregnant at the time, would undoubtedly have perished. As it was, only the stores in the cellar were destroyed.

As soon as the all-clear sounded I hurried back into town and made my way to Wahnfried, fearing the worst. Once there I found that my eyes had not deceived me: the house and its surroundings had suffered badly. My brother and my brother-in-law, Bodo Lafferentz, turned up a few minutes later. Alarmed by all the devastation they had seen on their way through the town, they were initially reassured and heartened by Wahnfried's superficially undamaged appearance, its frontage having survived intact. They had come from their place of work, the Neue Baumwollspinnerei [New Cotton Mill], one of the numerous enterprises 'managed' by my brother-in-law. It was the home of sundry military research projects, of which I knew little save that they were concerned with a variety of mysterious aids to final victory such as homing bombs. From my brother's point of view, this was naturally just a form of escape from Goebbels's 'total war'. As a matter of interest, he worked almost next door to Ludwig Erhard, the Federal Chancellor-to-be, who ran an economic research institute on the premises. I cannot, however, prove that this was where the author of Germany's post-war 'economic miracle' evolved his grand design for a market economy.

My mother and my wife, who was near her time, were packed off to Oberwarmensteinach, where nothing too dreadful was likely to happen. On the morrow of the air raid, 6 April, Wieland and Bodo Lafferentz boarded a car fuelled by wood gas and took off for Berlin, which was threatened by the Russians. Their mission was to retrieve the Wagner scores presented to Hitler on his fiftieth birthday by the Confederation of German Industrialists and bring them back to Bayreuth. The confederation had previously acquired them from the Wittelsbach Equalization Fund, and they were now stored in the bunker of the Reich Chancellery. Wieland and Bodo failed to gain access to Hitler, who was destined to commit suicide three weeks later. They only got as far as an aide, who assured them that the scores would be safer in the bunker than anywhere else, so they had to leave the next day with their mission unaccomplished. They were forced off the autobahn near Leipzig by American shelling and had to make several detours. Quite obviously, it would not be long before General Patton's troops reached Bayreuth.

On the day when Bayreuth underwent its second major air raid, 8 April 1945, Wieland and Bodo went off to join their families at Nussdorf. I had taken my sister-in-law Gertrud and my sister Verena and their children to Lake Constance in February, and it was there at Überlingen that my brother-in-law continued his Bayreuth activities, mystery-enshrouded ventures designed to produce war-winning weapons. Wieland and Bodo had been very anxious to take my mother with them, but she firmly rejected the suggestion. At a time of all-embracing folly, she considered it essential to stay on and face up to what lay ahead. Only this, she felt, could guarantee her ability to preserve the heritage entrusted to her by Richard Wagner's son and, possibly, to make some contribution to a better future. As for me, no one even suggested that I go south because there was no question of my leaving Bayreuth.

Before setting off for Lake Constance, Wieland and Bodo removed some rare Wagner manuscripts from the archive, not for safety's sake but because of their monetary value, which might help to keep the wolf from the door or provide them with the wherewithal to start a new life. On 27 April, assuming that these venerable documents would be sufficient proof of identity, they and their families crossed Lake Constance and tried to gain the safety of Switzerland. They failed, however, and were obliged to return to their point of departure.

Now that my mother and my wife had gone to Oberwarmensteinach and my brother and brother-in-law and their families to Lake Constance, I was all alone in Bayreuth and left to my own devices.

On 9 April the Festspielhaus and its outbuildings were scheduled to be requisitioned for military purposes. My mother's resolute intervention had previously thwarted various other plans to misappropriate the building, whether as a Luftwaffe depot, an aerial observers' post, or finally – an idea dreamed up by Goebbels and the ill-famed Hans Fritzsche – a communications centre for the Reich broadcasting service. On 9 April, therefore, two requisitioning officers turned up and submitted their demands. I thought it only right and proper, under the circumstances, to take them to call on Gauleiter Fritz Wächtler, who was also the local defence commissioner, at his office. It was, of course, my intention to nip their crazy scheme in the bud, and to my surprise he backed me up. I was positively amazed, because this held out at least a faint hope that the festival complex, which had so far escaped the bombing, might not be damaged by being handed over to the military, as requested, or ultimately destroyed by enemy action. It was planned to turn the Festspielhaus and its outbuildings into a reception centre for soldiers who had become separated from their units. Wächtler expressed the unwontedly defeatist opinion that even the requisitioning of the Festspielhaus would not turn the tide, let alone win the war, and that it would be preferable to allow bombed-out townsfolk to store their remaining possessions there.

After shaking off the requisitioning officers with Wächter's welcome assistance, I asked him to get me some petrol so that I could mobilize the festival theatre's one remaining car. I told him I intended to fetch the Wahnfried papers from the Hohe Warte hospital and store them outside Bayreuth to preserve them from the turmoil – more particularly, the looting – to be expected when the war ended, as it very soon would. Wächter gave me a voucher for thirty litres of petrol to be drawn from the stocks of an industrial concern that had remained in operation at Bayreuth throughout the war, and I began transferring the archive to Oberwarmensteinach the very next day.

I drove back to Bayreuth on 11 April, the day of the third air raid on the town, which was this time attacked by two waves of bombers. The additional damage they inflicted was such that, after this third raid, 36.8 per cent of Bayreuth's houses and forty-three of its eighty-three industrial buildings were more or less reduced to rubble – a total of approximately 52 per cent. I loaded up the remainder of the archive and waited until nightfall so as to escape the attentions of low-flying aircraft on my way back into the Fichtelgebirge. I left as soon as it was dark, only to be stopped by a combined patrol of soldiers and SS men who proposed to impound the car – and, possibly, me into the bargain. As luck would have it, the patrol included an SS officer from Bayreuth who recognized me and proved reasonable when I revealed the exceptional nature of what I had on board. I was eventually allowed to proceed on my way, so the archive was at least temporarily safe.

By the time I drove back to Bayreuth from Oberwarmensteinach on 13 April, the townsfolk had been warned that enemy tanks were in the vicinity. I parked the car beneath some trees in Friedrichsthal and made my way to the Festspielhaus on foot, accompanied by American machine-gun fire and hedge-hoppers. The same day I contacted the mayor of Bayreuth, Dr Kempfler, whom I found at the St Georgen command post of civil defence area No. 3. While I was there, a man who had been sent off in search of food returned to the command post in high excitement. Having encountered some American tanks on the far side of Thurnau, he had turned back and come to inform the mayor without delay. Clearly, it would not be long before the Americans entered the town.

In view of this obvious fact, and because there was nothing more I could usefully do in Bayreuth, I thought it best to return to my parked car as quickly as possible and drive back to Oberwarmensteinach. I paid a last brief visit to the festival hall, where I showed the constables and auxiliaries at the police station west of the Festspielhaus how best to signal their uncon-ditional surrender – without being shot as deserters and traitors by some rabid last-ditch fanatic – by displaying white cloths and stacking their rifles in the roadway. I myself had in recent weeks served as one of the municipal auxiliaries recruited as an aid to crime prevention, especially after dark.

I remained at Oberwarmensteinach from the night of 13/14 April onwards. Bayreuth itself was occupied on 14 April. There were no foolish heroics, no valiant attempts at defence or martial stupidities of that kind. Precisely what happened is still in dispute. My own impressions and recollections of those turbulent days may differ a little from the published accounts of others who lived through them, which vary considerably.

On 14 April my daughter Eva was born by flickering candlelight. It was a far from easy birth from my wife's point of view, not least because of recent experiences such as the bombing of Wahnfried. The obstetrician in attendance was a Slovenian-German refugee who clearly thought it essential to point out, with a stolid regard for detail, that the Americans were rumoured to treat civilians even more brutally than the Russians. His stories made a deep impression on us, and we awaited developments with varying degrees of apprehension.

On 19 April, the house being situated on a hillside, we had a good view of the Americans advancing up the Mausbach valley in open order, just as I myself had once learned to do on the parade-ground. SS snatch squads were continuing to operate here and there, and might still be lurking in the nearby woods on the lookout for stragglers to enrol in last-ditch formations, so it was essential to wait until the Americans actually arrived before hoisting white sheets in token of one's peaceful intentions; in other words, we could not afford to signal our unarmed state and unconditional surrender too soon. I still admire the fearless and thoroughly practical way in which local matrons dismantled the road-blocks of felled timber erected by their menfolk, whether in a superabundance of fighting spirit or under duress. This task, performed with the two-handed saws which, being good mountain folk, the women wielded with natural dexterity, not only demonstrated their desire for peace but yielded a useful byproduct in the shape of large quantities of fuel.

Much to our relief, the American combat troops who occupied the village were thoroughly humane and impeccably correct in their treatment of the civilian inhabitants. My mother's house and grounds were searched by a small squad of soldiers, but without incident.

Just before the Americans arrived my mother was suddenly seized with panic and thought she would be safer in the surrounding woods, whither she proposed to take my five-day-old daughter. Adopting an extremely loud and aggressive tone towards her for what was probably the very first time, I promptly knocked this hare-brained 'kidnapping' scheme on the head.

On 3 May 1945 my mother received a visit from Klaus Mann and Curt Riess, both of whom were then employed as war correspondents for Allied publications, notably *Stars and Stripes*. I was present at the interview, and I still recall the words with which my mother greeted Thomas Mann's son: 'There's one question you've no need to ask me, Herr Mann: I never slept with Adolf Hitler.' Klaus Mann's report on his meeting with Winifred Wagner noted with a touch of respect that he had just encountered his first self-confessed member of the Nazi Party – and she was British-born!

Germany's unconditional surrender on 8 May 1945 marked the official end of the war in Europe. The skies brightened again, and not only in a figurative sense, because the black-out that had been in force since 1939 was lifted at last. The Allied occupation, during which the Germans were to be thoroughly re-educated, was ushered in by the festive sound of church bells.

The population's basic supplies of foodstuffs and electricity were extremely patchy, and the situation would have been still worse but for the exercise of elementary skills and human ingenuity. Refugees from Silesia, for example, were noted for distilling a potato brandy so potent that it induced vertigo in someone as unused to hard liquor as I, who only took an occasional drink so as not to seem unsociable.

The steam locomotive of the local train that plied between Bayreuth and Warmensteinach had been strafed and badly damaged, but it was repaired and back in commission by 27 June 1945. Thereafter I travelled to Bayreuth every morning to assist in healing the terrible wounds it had sustained. Mountains of rubble had to be cleared away and bomb-damaged buildings made secure before the work of reconstruction could begin. We drew reassurance from the tone of a proclamation by General Dwight D. Eisenhower, which was displayed throughout the American Zone and made us feel that, after a process of clarification, of gradual transition from the afterpains of war to a state of peace, the general turmoil would subside. It allowed me to hope that at some point in time, however remote, I would, as a legitimate heir, be able to speak about Wagner's bequest to the world and its supranational aspects in particular.

For the present, however, there could be absolutely no question of this because I had my hands full in the most literal sense. I began by helping to clear the station precincts, which were badly damaged, but after a few days the authorities permitted me to instil at least some sort of order into the ruins of the house which my grandfather had built at Bayreuth and, in the hope that it would bring him final peace, had christened 'Wahnfried' [translatable only by some such approximation as 'Illusion's Repose', though *Frieden* means peace or tranquillity and *Wahn* can connote delusion or even madness]. The main aim was to ascertain the extent of the damage, salvage whatever remained of the contents, and check the fabric for any components that could be reused. In other words, the object was to shore up the remains of Wahnfried and, at the same time, to discover whether and how the house could be rebuilt. Many objects were buried beneath debris and rubble, for instance several pairs of my grandfather's glasses, some of the original furnishings, the big chandelier, which was completely smashed, and various papers including letters to my mother from Hitler. These contained no sensational disclosures about their relationship and did not seem to merit evaluation, being of a purely personal and unremarkable nature. It was later expressly confirmed that the letters were 'not politically compromising'.

I had prefaced my rubble-clearing activities by trying my hand at carpentry, goat-milking, and agriculture. This was at Oberwarmensteinach, where I single-handedly built a wooden stable with a small hayloft. Some well-disposed neighbours, whom I had known for years, lent me a field. Although it was rather neglected and situated on a north-facing slope, the times were so hard that I resolved to restore it to agricultural use, and I succeeded. The caretaker who looked after my mother's property led our borrowed cow while I guided the plough, so the poor soil eventually made a contribution to our subsistence, albeit a meagre one. A friend had presented us with a goat which I put on a leash, like a dog, and took for walks along the verges and in the woods. I could not let it graze freely, or it would have been stolen at once. Another of our assets was a spring of our own, and the weather was generally very good.

Even before I moved back to Bayreuth, my mother and I were often taken by jeep to be separately interrogated by members of the CIC (Counter-Intelligence Corps) or the military government. These interrogations took place either at the Hotel Anker or in the Reichsbank building. How well prepared my mother was, and what a realistic view she took of the whole situation, is apparent from what she did prior to an interrogation on 31 August 1945: she left me written instructions detailing exactly what I had to do on her behalf if the Americans arrested her. Unwilling to be surprised by the turn of events, she preferred to allow for all contingencies and take due precautions. Our interrogators seemed peculiarly concerned to discover if we knew where Hitler might still be hiding. I remember retorting, when asked this question for the umpteenth time, 'I'm afraid I can't tell you what you want to know, and you don't want to know what I *can* tell you.' I got the impression that the local CIC chief, Lieutenant Lichtblau, who spoke excellent German, did not grasp the sarcasm latent in my response, because he persisted in questioning me along the same old lines.

The US authorities and their German appointees, in other words, all who were empowered to shape the course of future developments, made no bones about their special interest in the estate of Richard Wagner and his family, which was obvious from the outset. One of my first official duties in that connection, performed in the presence of Lieutenant Lichtblau, was to ascertain whether the papers, busts and pictures that had been evacuated to the Hohe Warte hospital, which was also occupied by the Americans, were complete and in good condition; in other words, I had to check that everything I had not already removed was still there. In fact, all the steel cabinets had been broken open and some of their contents stolen. One or two pictures were missing, too, among them *The Holy Family*, an occasional painting by the Russian painter and *Parsifal* designer Paul von Joukovsky, and Hubert von Herkomer's portrait of Wagner painted in London in 1877. The latter was undoubtedly the most valuable item lost. Like the orchestral scores in Hitler's Berlin bunker, none of the missing pictures has ever come to light. I became more and more convinced, during our inspection of the papers and other things, that Lieutenant Lichtblau was planning to ship them back to the States as spoils of war. Being anxious to prevent this at all costs, I kept a wary eye on any developments that seemed suggestive of such a move.

The Festspielhaus had also been looted, like the remains of the archive, but it was not long before the many people who had regarded it as a looter's cornucopia were firmly excluded by an 'Off Limits' sign. Their main focus of attention had, of course, been the costume store. Apart from replenishing many a foreign worker's shabby, threadbare wardrobe, this had helped many a self-appointed camp follower to enhance the charms of her 'eternal femininity' and render them more immediately saleable.

From 31 May 1945 onwards, performances and church services were held in the requisitioned Festspielhaus under the auspices of the US Army. On 24 May a 'Bayreuth Symphony Orchestra' made up of refugees or displaced persons from Germany's eastern territories had been formed under the baton of Erich Bohner, a former soloists' coach and confrère of Rolf Ehrenreich's in Berlin, whom the tide of war had washed up in Bayreuth. It gave its first concert on 24 June, only one month later, and from 26 September onwards the Festspielhaus became a venue for performances jointly given and attended by Germans and Americans.

The completely undamaged Siegfried Wagner House, which had been enlarged after my father's death and had served to accommodate Hitler during his visits to the festival, becoming popularly if bombastically known as the '*Führerbau*' [Führer Building], was confiscated by the Americans and used for a wide variety of purposes in the ensuing years. It was occupied by the CIC, functioned as an interrogation centre, and became, among other things, a brothel. An officers' club from 1946 onwards, it was finally vacated at the end of May 1954, or shortly before the fourth post-war festival opened. This meant that it was once more available for occupation by the family. My mother, whose state of health rendered it inadvisable for her to remain at Oberwarmensteinach after 1956, moved into the house on 23 June 1957. She had always felt like an exile at Oberwarmensteinach, and had never abandoned hope of returning home. Meantime, Wahnfried had been occupied by my brother Wieland and his family since 21 April 1949, when they moved there from Nussdorf, the remains of the house having been restored and made habitable with the aid of a mortgage. In 1956, when it was considered certain that Winifred would move into the Siegfried Wagner House, Wieland and his family had ostentatiously cut themselves and their residence off from her by erecting a wall on top of Wahnfried's old boundary wall. Clearly intended to be symbolic, this barrier came into being five years before the Berlin Wall. It was not demolished until Wahnfried was rebuilt in 1976.

To return to the immediately post-war period, I continued to live at Oberwarmensteinach and work in Bayreuth. It took me three-quarters of an hour to walk to the station, so I had to leave the house at 5 a.m. and seldom got back before half-past ten at night. The return journey took even longer because the locomotive usually had insufficient steam up and found it hard to take the gradients. This daily shuttling to and fro was very time-consuming and became more and more wearisome, especially during the winter months. I duly cast around for a way of moving to Bayreuth, not least because it was desirable and advisable for me to uphold the family's interests by establishing a permanent presence there. Being entirely devoid of political encumbrances from the Nazi era, I was a legal and fully competent reversionary heir. In the spring of 1946 I moved with my wife and daughter into four small rooms on the upper floor of the gardener's house at Wahnfried, which had formerly housed the maidservants. Our numbers were augmented on 13 April 1947 by the birth of my son Gottfried. I did not, however, officially register our change of abode with the police until 3 September 1948 because this omission lent my status a certain obscurity and allowed me greater freedom of movement. Given the very peculiar conditions in which we were living at the time, I thought it would be useful to be able to escape the authorities' clutches and slip away if need arose.

With the exception of the Markgräfliches Opernhaus, which was relatively small, all Bayreuth's cultural centres had been destroyed. Consequently, even discounting the American takeover of the Festspielhaus under a requisitioning order which was not submitted to my mother, as its owner, until 8 September 1945, I and my family thought it altogether natural that the building should be used for functions of an appropriate kind. We neither balked at such requests nor complained about them. My mother and I were equally out of sympathy with those hypersensitive Wagnerians who raised their habitual cry of sacrilege when, for instance, a Stravinsky concert was given at the Festspielhaus.

The representatives of the American military government differed from many Germans, then as now, in bearing absolutely no resentment towards Wagner and his music. This being so, preliminary negotiations of a constructive nature took place over the period 9/15 June 1945 between the military governor of Bayreuth, Captain Miller, his 'subvisor' Mr Lutz, my mother, myself, and the auditor, Wilhelm Hieber. Hieber's report dated 26 November 1945 to Bayreuth's internal revenue office stated: 'On behalf of the United States, Mr Lutz demanded that Haus Wahnfried be restored to its original condition regardless of expense. The USA considers it most important that the festival resume its worldwide cultural function as speedily as possible, but believes that Haus Wahnfried, having been the workplace of the genius Richard Wagner, constitutes the heart of the festival, and that it is indispensable to a resumption of the festival on its former, international scale. Mr Lutz further stated that the Bayreuth Festival is now and will for a long time to come be the *only* means of building a bridge of trust between the United Nations and Germany, and of paving the way to a mutual understanding that will enable Germany's nationhood to be recognized once more.'

All the participants in these talks concluded them by signing a declaration that embodied this binding rider: '... that the rebuilding of Haus Wahnfried be initiated forthwith. This declaration endorses Mr Lutz's demand that all the costs of rebuilding be defrayed out of the resources of the festival administration and the personal estate of Frau Winifred Wagner.'

Given that the bomb-damaged town was bulging with some eight thousand refugees and evacuees, almost all of whom were squeezed into temporary accommodation so overcrowded that it could scarcely contain them, my mother and I considered this plan absolutely unwarrantable and impracticable. We therefore had no hesitation in putting our names to such a noble and magnanimous impulse on the part of the victorious power. This was not, however, the only bubble that burst during the post-war years.

Those who devised activities and plans for the world-renowned home of Richard Wagner, and his festival in particular, were not restricted to culturally interested persons living elsewhere in Germany or abroad. Similar initiatives originated in the town itself. Then the mayor, Oskar Meyer, tried to get in touch with my sister Friedelind, who had been an expatriate since 1939, in the hope of persuading her to return to her home town and carry on 'the Bayreuth idea'.

He also, from 28 August 1946 onwards, made vigorous efforts to cultivate Franz Wilhelm Beidler, who was the son of Isolde, Richard and Cosima Wagner's first natural daughter and, thus, their grandson and my first cousin. A Swiss citizen, Beidler was unobjectionable in every respect and could not be accused of having been close, let alone 'devoted', to Adolf Hitler. In the ensuing period, Meyer and Beidler developed an exchange of ideas on the future of the Bayreuth Festival. These reposed primarily on a distortion of Wagner's original idea and culminated in a scheme for a grand international foundation whose basis, albeit considerably enlarged, was a false interpretation of Wagner's central artistic and theatrical concept. On 31 December 1946, having travelled to Bayreuth from Switzerland the week before, Beidler submitted the document he had drafted for Mayor Meyer. Entitled 'Guidelines for the Reorganization of the Bayreuth Festival', it was far from intended as a New Year's Eve firework (though it fizzled out like one). It envisaged, for example, the appointment of a board of trustees to which the following more or less illustrious persons would belong: Thomas Mann (honorary chairman), the mayor of Bayreuth (chairman), and an unnamed vice-chairman to be elected by the board, of which Franz Beidler and Anneliese Landau were to be first and second secretaries respectively. Also included were official representatives of various social groups and, as ever in such cases, sundry experts whose advice and opinions were considered indispensable.

The new year had scarcely begun when, at three o'clock on the afternoon of 3 January 1947, I and the custodian of the Richard Wagner archive, Dr Otto Strobel, were summoned to Oskar Meyer's mayoral office in the Altes Rathaus for a discussion. I had assumed that the point at issue would be Cousin Franz's grandiose plans and their prospects of success. To my surprise, however, he made absolutely no mention of his scheme for the future of the Bayreuth Festival. He merely expressed a wish – though the discussion's semi-official character and the mayor's supportive presence made it sound more like a demand – to be given access to the Wahnfried archive, the better to fulfil his long-cherished plan for a book on Cosima Wagner, our common grandmother. He was particularly anxious to get a sight of Cosima's diaries. Dr Strobel informed him of their fate in the course of conversation. He also told him of our Aunt Eva's special testamentary provisions and her outrageous machinations in respect of the archive (the largely inexplicable appropriation of her mother's diaries in 1911, the obliteration of certain passages distasteful to her, and the almost total destruction of the correspondence between Richard and Cosima Wagner). Meyer, too, was now acquainted with Eva's stipulation that, after a lapse of thirty years reckoned from her own death, Cosima's diaries should pass to the municipality of Bayreuth for inclusion in the Richard Wagner Memorial Collection, but only – among other things – if Dr Otto Strobel never took charge of it. On the same occasion Cousin Franz expressed his scholarly approval of the publication of the correspondence between Wagner and King Ludwig (Vols 1–4, 1936; Vol 5, 1939), and, in particular, of Dr Strobel's commentaries on the same. He also said that my mother deserved great credit for having brought out such an admirably authentic publication. By contrast, Adolf Hitler and my aunts had failed to appreciate her reasons for doing so, and had consequently disapproved. Winifred had insisted that all the letters be published unabridged and had refused to embellish them in any way.

I had been included in the above meeting only because the US military authorities, who had benevolently sponsored Beidler's visit and activities, knew from Lieutenant Lichtblau that I was very well informed about the Wagner archive. They tried to subject me to moral and even legal pressure by charging that my family had forfeited all further right to that archive because of their conduct under the Third Reich. It was argued that, pursuant to the US military government's Law 52 relating to 'Blocking and Control of Property', the archive had already been transferred to the administration of the trusteeship office with effect from 7 November 1946. In this connection I had written to my brother on 9 November: 'The mayor's influence on the trusteeship office is not what it was until recently. Now, he can advance interests only in his role as head of the municipality – and that alone will dispose of many of his ambitions and claims to authority.' Before Law 52 came into force the mayor had also been a trustee; that is to say, he had assumed the office himself after the Festspielhaus was vacated by American troops on 11 February 1946, though he claimed to have been appointed by Governor Reilly.

I bluntly and firmly informed those who were hanging on my lips, especially Cousin Franz, that I could not, either now or in the foreseeable future, grant them access to any of the documents they had requested because my wartime experiences had persuaded me to store them elsewhere for safety's sake. Their removal to places in all four occupied zones had been carried out by certain trusted persons, some of whom I had no news of or could not get in touch with because they had been interned. I wound up by saying that, quite frankly, I had never expected the division of Germany into zones of occupation to be as rigid as it now was. This concluded the meeting, which had fortunately turned out to be flop, and we went our separate ways in peace.

I had several more meetings with Beidler and his daughter in 1947 – on 11, 14, 16, and 22 January, to be precise. Their relative frequency was naturally a product of his wide-ranging plans for the festival, of which I had since been told by persons who were seriously involved in them and thought it only natural and necessary – unlike Cousin Franz – to put me in the picture. Through them I obtained precise details of all I needed to know, even photocopies of the latest draft. Without revealing all the trumps in my hand, I used my knowledge of Beidler's plans to urge him, most forcefully, to consider the legal position created by my father and mother's joint testament, which had never been contested. Above all, I said, he would have to await the denazification court's legally binding verdict on my mother, who was, after all, the heir in tail. I made it clear that, where Bayreuth was concerned, I could not – contrary to widespread rumours – imagine the American authorities proceeding in the arbitrary and non-judicial manner characteristic of the 'people's courts' of the Nazi era. I also expressed the hope that, if he had not already done so, my cousin would speedily and clearly expound his plans to all who were involved in them or might eventually be so. I have no detailed knowledge of the reactions of those concerned, but Thomas Mann's *Entstehung des Doktor Faustus* contains the following allusion to the undisguised amazement and uneasiness he felt: '... for a hundred reasons, spiritual, political and material, I could not but regard the whole idea as utopian, unrealistic and dangerous, partly premature, partly obsolete and overtaken by time and history. I was incapable of taking it seriously.' This aptly summarizes the prevailing sentiment.

Until my mother's first denazification hearing, which opened on 25 June 1947 and ended three days later, my time was taken up with other activities and proposals, as well as with a variety of grand schemes not dissimilar to Beidler's. It was like counting one's eggs, not just before they were hatched, but before the chicken had even laid them.

On 1 April 1947 public trusteeship of the festival was replaced by individual trusteeship. This was important to the extent that the authorities had yielded to my own and my mother's insistence and paid due regard to the fact that the object in trust was private property and could not be treated as public until it had been formally expropriated. Whether the appointed trustee was the right man for the job is debatable. He was Edgar Richter, the son of Hans Richter, who had conducted the Bayreuth première of *The Ring* and was a close friend of my grandfather's. He was certainly clever enough to maintain and cultivate a sufficient measure of contact with me and my mother to react as the situation demanded and avert trouble. In other respects, being largely ignorant of legal and financial matters, he relied for the most part on Hieber's trusteeship office.

April and May 1947 saw the appearance in Bayreuth of a certain Herr Theodor Kiendl, who, ostensibly with the enthusiastic support and encouragement of the American military authorities in Berlin, offered to reopen the festival by presenting *Parsifal* at the Festspielhaus in 1948. But Bayreuth, according to this megalomaniac, would in future become nothing more nor less than an 'international première theatre' for the cream of new operatic creations from all over the world. More than that, he prophesied that the Markgräfliches Opernhaus would be the medium of a 'unique Mozart renaissance'. Where prospective trustees were concerned, he seasoned his proposal by pulling some influential names out of his hat, e.g. Ernst Legal, general administrator of the Berlin Staatsoper, and Hanns Heinz Stuckenschmidt, the well-known musicologist. Like sundry others, Herr Kiendl clearly felt that he had a vocation. The hubbub he caused, albeit temporarily, was audible as far afield as Munich, where State Secretary Dr Sattler not only responded favourably but added to the general commotion. Because the town would have been quite unable to accommodate any festival visitors – the number of refugees and evacuees had since risen to 16,000 – it was planned to enlarge the Hohe Warte hospital and convert it into an 'international grand hotel' with a capacity of 1800 beds.

Although Beidler's plan for a foundation was obviously doomed to failure, he and the mayor maintained a brisk correspondence after his departure. On 15 May 1947 he wrote to inform Meyer that Thomas Mann, after some initial hesitation, had decided to accept the post offered him. The military authorities approved of all his plans in principle and viewed them with sympathy, said Beidler, but they wanted everything necessary to their fulfilment to be initiated and executed by the municipality of Bayreuth itself. Their approval of any steps to this end could be taken for granted.

Five days later a local newspaper published an interview with my sister Friedelind. The timing was deliberate, first because there were so many different plans afoot, and secondly because everyone was awaiting the start of the denazification proceedings against my mother, who had received her copy of the indictment dated 14 May on 17 May 1947.

Friedelind had given the interview because she obviously regarded her book, *Heritage of Fire*, of which my mother and I had been presented with an original edition by Colonel Fiori, an American, on 31 October of the previous year, as a threat to her own festival ambitions. Considering that all four of us – Wieland, Friedelind, Verena, and I – had been named joint heirs in our parents' will, she must have been afraid of prejudicing her position, so her language was suitably cautious and restrained. She confirmed that Mayor Meyer had invited her to reopen the festival at the end of 1945, but felt that this would not be possible for another ten years. Besides, she

ve left: Siegfried and Winifred Wagner with their children: (from left) Friedelind, Verena,
land, Wolfgang (1924). *Above right:* Wolfgang Wagner on the garden steps at Wahnfried (1924).

nework time at Wahnfried. Richard Wagner's four grandchildren at their desks in the play-
m: (from left) Friedelind, Wieland, Wolfgang, Verena (1932). This room was occupied by
Cosima Wagner for twenty-three years before her death.

Above left: Adolf Hitler, Führer and Reich Chancellor, being escorted to the guest-house Wahnfried by the festival director and her sons prior to the opening of the Bayreuth Festival 1936. *Above right:* Winifred Wagner in conversation with Wilhelm Furtwängler, Heinz Tietjen Arturo Toscanini, 1931.

The model designed by the architect Emil-Rudolf Mewes for a redevelopment, or 'monumentalization', of the Festspielhaus, 1940.

Preliminary clearance work in progress on the ruins of Wahnfried, almost two-thirds of which was destroyed by the air raid of 5 April 1945.

Winifred Wagner leaves the courthouse at Bayreuth after her denazification appeal hearing on 8 February 1948, accompanied by Wolfgang and his wife Ellen (left) and Wieland and his wife Gertrud (right).

Wieland and Wolfgang Wagner outside their bomb-damaged parental home, from which debris has been removed, 1948.

Below left: Wieland and Wolfgang Wagner with the Bayreuth Festival poster for 1951, the year when the Festival recommenced after the Second World War. *Below right:* The last official photograph of Wieland and Wolfgang Wagner in conference at the Festspielhaus, 1965.

pplause for Wilhelm Furtwängler and the Festival Orchestra and soloists after performing
ɛethoven's Ninth Symphony at the Festspielhaus on 9 August 1954. In the foreground, Wolfgang
Wagner presents a bouquet to the bass, Ludwig Weber.

ⁱolfgang Wagner with Paul Hindemith after rehearsing Beethoven's Ninth Symphony for a
ⁱrformance at the Festspielhaus on 11 August 1953. Between them are Horst Stein, the future
ₛtival conductor, then a musical assistant, and Walter Born, musical assistant (with glasses).

Left: 'A curious case!' Wolfgang Wagner as 'festival clerk' on the set of his brother Wieland's *Meistersinger* in 1958.

Below: The dragon in Wieland Wagner's production of *The Ring* (1953) is evidently suffering from toothache. Wolfgang examines the patient while Wieland and a Festival associate watch the dentist attentively.

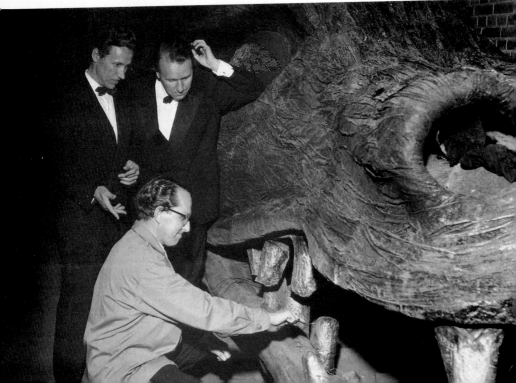

Right: Birgit Nilsson rehearses Isolde with producer Wolfgang Wagner standing in for Tristan, 1957.

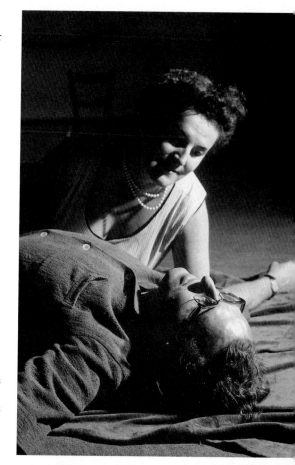

Below: Wolfgang Wagner takes a curtain call after the première of his first Bayreuth production, *Lohengrin,* on 23 July 1953. With him are Joseph Keilberth (conductor), Eleanor Steber (Elsa), Wilhelm Pitz (chorus master), Astrid Varnay (Ortrud), Hermann Uhde (Telramund), and Wolfgang Windgassen (Lohengrin).

Hans Knappertsbusch and Wolfgang Wagner on the stage of the Festspielhaus in 1951. In the background, Elisabeth Höngen (Fricka) and Sigurd Björling (Wotan).

Below left: Wolfgang Wagner in conversation with Karl Böhm on the stage of the Festspielhaus 1963. *Below right:* Herbert von Karajan on the terrace at Wahnfried, discussing with Wolfgang Wagner his rearrangement of the orchestra before the première of *Tristan* (23 July 1952).

was currently engaged in founding an opera company in the States with a view to organizing Wagner tours.

My mother's denazification hearing opened on 25 June 1947 in a handsome art nouveau chamber once exhibited at the St Louis World's Fair in 1904 and now in the Upper Franconian seat of government. My mother's chosen defence counsel was Erich Ebermayer, who, in addition to being a lawyer, was an author celebrated for his somewhat voyeuristic novel about a girls' boarding school. I and my brother and sisters thought him quite the wrong person to represent our mother. As luck would have it, we managed at the last minute to get hold of our long-time family lawyer, Dr Fritz Meyer, whose own denazification hearing had turned out favourably a short while before.

The prosecution had originally intended to cite Friedelind's book as its main incriminating evidence, special weight being attached to her account of the time our mother visited her in Switzerland and tried to persuade her to return to Germany. Friedelind claimed that, when she refused, Winifred made the following monstrous threat: 'If you don't obey, orders will be given to annihilate and exterminate you at the earliest opportunity.' My mother, who had never uttered such an anathema, which was worthy of the Old Testament, protested against this absurd fiction. Dr Fritz Meyer and I did our best to impress upon the court that a subjective and fanciful book like my sister's was of purely psychological interest and should on no account be used in evidence either for or against my mother. Prompted in part by my sister herself, the public prosecutor eventually decided not to offer the book in evidence and thus invalidated it. However, many quotations from it took effect in the course of the hearing because they appeared in the report of the chairman of the 'Cultural Activities Committee of the Bavarian Minister of Education and Culture', Dr Albert Stenzel, which neatly interwove them with erroneous incriminatory conjectures relating to, among other things, the wrongful withdrawal of diplomatic ration cards. Another rather grotesque feature of this report was its hope that Franz Beidler would, with no Winifred Wagner around, make 'the Nazi circus of the Festspielhaus a true temple of Wagnerian art once more'.

Although my mother submitted a detailed memorandum in German and English in which she frankly admitted and described her attitude under the Third Reich without attempting to trivialize it, as the court formally acknowledged, and although her counsel presented authenticated evidence for the defence with great cogency, the final verdict was as follows:

The person concerned is classified, pursuant to Article 4/2 of the law, in Group II of incriminated persons (activists).

The following expiatory penalties are imposed upon her:

(1) She is liable to special community work for a period of 450 days.

(2) Sixty per cent of her assets are to be confiscated as a contribution to the reparations fund.

(3) She is permanently disqualified from holding public office, the functions of notary and advocate included.

(4) She is deprived of her right to a pension or annuity paid out of public funds.

(5) She is disenfranchised, declared ineligible for election, and deprived of the right to engage in any form of political activity or to be a member of a political party.

(6) She may not be a member of a trade union or an industrial or professional association.

(7) She is prohibited for a period of five years:

(a) from pursuing a profession or independently participating in a business enterprise or commercial concern of any kind, and from exercising supervision or control of the same;

(b) from engaging, in a non-independent capacity, in anything other than ordinary work;

(c) from working as a teacher, preacher, editor, author, or radio commentator.

(8) She is subject to domiciliary and residential restrictions.

(9) She is deprived of all the licences, concessions and rights assigned her, and of the right to keep a motor car.

In addition, the person concerned must meet the costs of the hearing. These are set at RM228,694.

Because the court's verdict did nothing to settle the future of the Bayreuth Festival, which remained as nebulous as ever, my mother lodged an appeal. So did the public prosecutor, who was naturally dissatisfied with the outcome of the hearing. This entailed a further wait for all who were prowling around and weighing up the value of their prospective haul.

The US authorities' attitude towards the festival was wholly uprejudiced, as I have already said. In all the legal proceedings undertaken – with varying degrees of relevance and competence – in connection with Richard Wagner's estate, I was repeatedly struck by the way in which they eschewed covert interference of any kind and insisted that Bayreuth's future be shaped by the Germans themselves. My own experience has since been confirmed by Sabine Döhring's study on the subject.

It was not until 8 December 1948, or well over a year later, that the denazification tribunal passed judgement on the appeals lodged against my mother's sentence. The principal points were these:

(1) The public prosecutor's appeal is dismissed.

(2) The verdict of Court II, Bayreuth-Stadt, of 2 July 1947 is revoked at the request of the appellant.

(3) The appellant is classified as a minor misdemeanant.

(4) Her term of probation is set at two years six months.

[...]

(6) Should the minor misdemeanant be involved in a business enterprise as owner or shareholder at the time of her incorporation in the probationary group, she is debarred from participation in the said enterprise for the term of her probation...

[...]

(8) It is directed that DM6ooo (six thousand) be payable as a special, lump-sum contribution to the reparations fund. In the event of non-payment, one day's labour will be substituted for each DM35.

[...]

Given our precise knowledge of Siegfried and Winifred Wagner's joint will, my mother and I felt that every effort must be made to ensure that, by virtue of her rights as the heir in tail, she would be free to entrust the management of the festival to my brother and myself. Were some appropriate ruling to deprive her of those rights, the reversionary heirs would step in and each of her four children would assume the status of a reversionary heir invested with equal rights. I believed then, as I still do, that this would inevitably have spelled the end of the festival as a family-run enterprise. Its demise would doubtless have been hastened by the immense financial burdens imposed by the inheritance tax to which all four of us would even then have been liable, and also, of course, by our extremely divergent ambitions and conceptions of how to run the festival, a task for which none of us had yet demonstrated the requisite degree of competence. It was a probability verging on certainty that circumstances would sooner or later activate that passage in the oft-cited will of 8 March 1929 which stipulated that, should the reversionary heirs drop out, the festival was to pass to the municipality of Bayreuth – and that, of course, could not be allowed to happen. Accordingly, everything was done to render my mother's declaration of assignment legally valid and binding so that it would be possible for my brother and me to be appointed in her stead. Not unnaturally, years of effort and persuasion were needed to induce my mother to renounce in our favour. The outcome of the denazification tribunal's appeal hearing paved the way for this. At Warmensteinach on 21 January 1949, my mother made the following written declaration: 'I hereby solemnly undertake to abstain from any part in the organization, administration and management of the Bayreuth Festival. In accordance with my long-cherished intention, I shall entrust my sons Wieland and

Wolfgang Wagner with the aforesaid functions and assign them the relevant powers.'

Thanks to Hans Rollwagen, who became mayor of Bayreuth on 1 July 1948, and to Dr Karl Würzburger, who had been the town's cultural adviser since June of that year, the debate over the future of the festival was at last submitted to the objective appraisal it so badly needed but had generally lacked. Dr Würzburger, who came from a respected Jewish family long resident in Bayreuth, had emigrated to Switzerland during the Nazi era. On returning home, he was naturally quick to acquaint himself with the festival's situation and prospects and, more particularly, with my parents' will. If he had previously entertained any doubts or misgivings about the festival's continuance, they were promptly dispelled, as he himself stated: 'From that moment on, I was confronted by an entirely new situation. The will is so unambiguous that I cannot understand how Dr Meyer could have tinkered with the festival at all ... Whether the reversionary heirs of Frau Winifred (who seems to have no ambitions to take over the festival) enter upon their inheritance (and of them Wolfgang, at least, should not be legally disqualified in any way), or whether the municipality of Bayreuth inherits, which seems to be precluded as things stand, the position will *always* be such that, in compliance with the will, only Richard Wagner's works will be performed at the Festspielhaus and nothing else, because the will states that nothing else may be performed!' This fundamental, down-to-earth acknowledgement promptly and effectively put an end to all the chatter about the festival and its transformation, likewise to Cousin Franz's scheme for a foundation. They soon evaporated, once and for all.

In Munich on 22 July 1948, quite independently of the outcome of the first denazification hearing and long before the second, my mother and I had a meeting with the American music officer for Bavaria, Mr Mosseley, in the presence of Dr Sattler. Mosseley, speaking on behalf of General Lucius D. Clay, head of the US military government in Germany, asked us if the festival could be held in 1949. Our response was a definite no, and we backed it up by citing our numerous misgivings and objections: an irremediable lack of accommodation for performers and visitors, far too little time in which to engage a cast and make artistic and administrative preparations, and, last but not least, the status of the new D-Mark. No foreigners could visit Bayreuth while the D-Mark was still unquoted on the international money market, and it would be quite impossible to hold the festival, especially after such a terrible war, unless foreigners participated both as artists and visitors. I replied that 1950 was the earliest possible date for a resumption of the festival. Dr Sattler could not forbear to suggest that we, Richard Wagner's inexperienced grandsons, might if necessary be assisted by a veteran of the theatre like Heinz Tietjen, since the two new potential directors were completely devoid of the reputation indispensable to their office.

Before there was even the remotest question of tackling the practical work entailed by a resumption of the festival, it was essential to secure the release of the Festspielhaus – a possibility alluded to by Otto Glück, who had presided over the second denazification hearing. This meant that my mother must consent to renounce the festival and couch her renunciation in a legally irrevocable form. Thereafter, as Glück put it, the way would be open for Winifred Wagner to apply for her term of probation to be prematurely terminated under Article 54, because she would have not only demonstrated her good behaviour but proved it beyond doubt. As I have said, my mother formally signed her declaration of assignment dated 21 January 1949, thereby granting me and my brother the freedom of action we needed. The impasse had been disposed of at last. Only four days later, on 25 January, Bayreuth town council declared its unqualified solidarity with the house of Wagner, acknowledged the family's responsibility for the festival, and resolved to do all in its power to facilitate a resumption of the festival in 1950.

Neither Wieland nor I was motivated by vanity or a desire for self-aggrandizement. All our endeavours were governed by devotion to the festival itself. No other sensible means of resuming and perpetuating it was available to us. Now that we had been legally entrusted with its management we were free to negotiate on an official basis with the municipal and provincial authorities.

Mayor Rollwagen and his cultural adviser, Dr Würzburger, expressed their approval of the new directors, of whom Wieland was then thirty-two and I thirty. At a civic gathering on 13 December 1948, Dr Würzburger had warmly welcomed us both in the following terms: 'We also greet Richard Wagner's grandsons as the future upholders of the Bayreuth enterprise, and we do so all the more joyfully because we not only hope but know for certain that they, who belong to a level-headed generation, are resolved to serve, not a cult of any kind, but the work of Richard Wagner alone.'

Even after the above events, the provincial authorities in Munich continued to have misgivings and create difficulties. Thanks to the firm and unwavering attitude of the town and its representatives, however, the trusteeship office formally handed over the Festspielhaus to Wieland and me on 28 February 1949. Just as in 1876, when the first festival was initiated, the far-sighted attitude of Bayreuth's city fathers had created a durable foundation on which Wagner's grand design could unfold and consolidate itself despite all the crises that arose in later years, some of them genuinely threatening, so 20th-century Bayreuth's wholehearted dedication to *its* festival played a crucial part in the latter's successful resumption.

I have already attempted to describe the general direction of my own and my mother's actions and reactions by citing salient events and facts. I hoped and was, indeed, convinced that my mother would have enough inner strength, not only to survive those difficult times and their great concomitant changes, but to master them for her own sake. But what were the other members of the family doing and planning in the meantime? What of those who lived on Lake Constance, 400 kilometres from Bayreuth? What of my sister Friedelind in her transatlantic stamping-ground?

Post-war living conditions in the French Zone, in which Nussdorf was situated, were even worse than in the American. My brother was therefore obliged, like me, to engage in gardening and, to a limited extent, in farming. There is no doubt that fresh air, and agricultural activities in particular, are aids to concentrated thought, so Wieland must have been granted a certain amount of leisure, as I was, in which to reflect in detail on what we had discussed years before: the festival and our preparations to take it over, which had been interrupted by the war and its consequences. Each in his own way, we had devoted this enforced break to the process of reflection which is commonly referred to in post-war Germany as 'overcoming the past'.

Fortunately, neither my brother nor I had any reason to put on sackcloth or beat our breasts in remorse – our past was too short and insignificant for that. We had not done anything criminal and had no need to seek justification for any actions or sins of omission. How to work in a productive and creative manner – that was our preoccupation, just as our own means of 'overcoming the past' was the Bayreuth Festival, which has manifested itself to an international public in all its freshness and vitality, continuity and change, each year since 1951. At that time, however, our central concern and object of independent study was the acquisition and development of those skills and talents which a vigilant and relentlessly critical outside world would certainly expect of us – and rightly so. Our different characters and temperaments were matched by the difference between our respective routes to Bayreuth and the Green Hill. Unlike me, who always had to deal with legal and financial matters, Wieland's predominant concerns were exclusively artistic and intellectual, and very little else existed for him. He must, therefore, have been quite glad to be far from the centre of events in Bayreuth, at least to begin with, because it gave him an uninterrupted opportunity to indulge in painting, reading, an ample and intensive study of our grandfather's works, and stage design. Besides, my letters kept him abreast of any developments affecting the family and the festival.

As an emigrant and an antifascist, my sister Friedelind needed to worry about the festival less than any of us, particularly since – as her book made clear – she was manifestly endowed with every conceivable qualification for taking it over. This, it seemed, had been additionally and effectively confirmed by Mayor Meyer's invitation to her in 1945, of which I have already spoken.

Friedelind's autobiographical memoirs disclosed the almost preternatural extent to which she had been preordained from childhood to direct the festival. This came as a revelation to an astonished and, in part, awestruck public, not to mention her utterly bewildered family, who had never dreamed what an exceptionally brilliant person she had developed into. For instance: 'I was old enough to understand and share Father's dreams,' she wrote of a time when she was all of six years old. Unlike other children, her siblings included, she was equipped with amazing talents that should naturally have accorded her exceptional status. *Heritage of Fire* also contained various references to the festival functions and activities she had performed before quitting Germany. With the best will in the world, neither I nor anyone else could recollect these, and the whole book struck me as more and more questionable in respect of its veracity and sense of reality. Whose memory was at fault? In view of the sheer abundance of Friedelind's contributions to Bayreuth, which should have made me hang my head in shame, anyone ignorant of the facts found it superfluous to question her aptitude and professional training. How absurdly mean and petty it seemed to cast doubt on this splendid testimonial, in book form, to her supreme competence to direct the Bayreuth Festival!

Those members of the family still living beside Lake Constance had far from abandoned their abortive plan to take refuge in Switzerland. They wanted to bring about a kind of gentlemen's agreement aimed at establishing a new family business that would stage Richard Wagner festivals abroad on the basis of an independent financial set-up similar to Bayreuth's. Should Bayreuth be taken over by the family or individual members thereof, the new enterprise would be brought into line with the Bayreuth interests. Prompt and detailed consideration was devoted to the most expedient way of delimiting the respective functions of those involved, and of obtaining the requisite consent of every member of the family. Irrespective of function, all were to participate and be included in the new enterprise on an equal basis. Wieland and Verena tried to establish contact with Friedelind as soon as possible. This they succeeded in doing, to my knowledge, but their main focus of attention in the course of this exchange, apart from her comments on their exceedingly peculiar scheme, was a number of life-sustaining 'Care' parcels from America. The vision of a 'foreign Bayreuth' could never, in fact, have become a reality, either with Friedelind or through her, because of the arbitrary and eccentric ideas she advanced. These were exemplified by an article she published on 25 April 1947, in which she mooted the bizarre notion of touring the United States with no less than 100 performances of *Tristan* sung in English or German as required. This was yet another regrettable demonstration of her inability, either to draw a precise distinction between an ideal utopia and what was actually feasible, or to place them in their correct relationship. Her audacious project foundered even before it left harbour.

Communications were very poor after the war, and I was unwilling and unable to be absolutely explicit in my letters, so a certain importance attached to my first visit to Nussdorf, where I turned up on 22 March 1946 after a somewhat adventurous journey by way of Stuttgart. I was now able to present a frank and detailed account of all that had happened at Bayreuth since the end of the war. My brother had not been there in the interim, so his knowledge of local developments was only fragmentary. I informed him that Governor Reilly had transferred the confiscated Fest-spielhaus to the trusteeship of the municipal authorities; that the press had lately, since February, begun to exploit our sister's book with a mixture of relish and indignation; and that we could expect a great deal of mud to be slung at our mother and the rest of us. We could only speculate about the actual contents of the book because we had yet to obtain a copy. One important topic of conversation was the law of 5 March 1946 regarding liberation from National Socialism and militarism, its potential relevance to and consequences for our family, and what course of action it might be tactically advisable to pursue in the future. Many other subjects were discussed, too, and by 3 April I was back in Nussdorf to report on further developments. On 2 June my mother visited her children there for the first time. What primarily occasioned all these arduous and circuitous journeys was not so much fraternal or maternal concern as critical events and problems relating to the festival and the rest of the Wagner estate, whose preservation and maintenance was our first concern. Heaven alone knows what would have become of everything if we had simply sat there and fatalistically twiddled our thumbs.

To shorten my journeys to Nussdorf and elsewhere and regain my mobility in general, I applied for a driver's licence. I had had one for years, but the authorities in the American Zone, unlike the British, had declared German licences invalid. In order to acquire one of these coveted pieces of paper, I was obliged – even before it became compulsory for every adult inhabitant of the American Zone – to complete the most minutely detailed questionnaire I have ever set eyes on. All the US military government's 131 questions had to be accurately and exhaustively answered. I handed in the forms on 24 April 1946 and was granted a new driver's licence by the municipality of Bayreuth on 14 August. This episode would have merited little attention in itself. In addition to being authorized to drive a motor vehicle, however, I was entitled to feel relieved and reassured that, although I bore the notorious and highly suspect name Wagner and was, into the bargain, a clan member of the Wagners of Bayreuth, a conscientious examination of all my particulars had ultimately proved favourable and effectively confirmed my political virginity.

The law regarding liberation from National Socialism and militarism prompted me, among others, to try to procure authentic and, where obtainable, notarized documents for use in my mother's defence at her denazification hearing. To this end, before paying another visit to Lake Constance, I called on a number of eminent and influential figures in south-west Germany who were well acquainted with my mother and her conduct under the Third Reich. Many victims of Nazi persecution, whom my mother had helped in her straightforward, even-handed way, spontaneously undertook to give evidence in her favour if she were brought to trial. They included people from all parts of Germany and elsewhere.

My Nussdorf discussions with Wieland were particularly opportune because Mayor Meyer's activities in regard to the festival and the Festspielhaus were beginning to assume ominous dimensions. He based them more on his own wishful thinking and powers of imagination than on the legally sanctioned position. Deliberately underestimating the legal realities, and pinning his hopes on the hopeless confusion that prevailed immediately after the war, he did his utmost to suggest that the Wagner family would soon be dispossessed – indeed, he sometimes behaved as if the Festspielhaus had already been expropriated. He also, needless to say, made strenuous efforts to put his malign and fanciful schemes into effect. It would doubtless have given him supreme satisfaction to go down in German cultural history as the over-life-size reformer and illustrious reinaugurator of a Bayreuth Festival previously founded on family tradition. It was not until November 1946 that these peculiar dreams and fancies received a painful setback and came to grief when the trusteeship office, not the mayor, was assigned to administer the Wagner estate until the position was clarified. This transfer of authority represented a very significant turning-point in the festival's fortunes, and one whose importance cannot be overestimated. Thereafter the situation seemed more or less to have stabilized itself, but it was then that the aforementioned 'Beidleriade' began, a tragicomic stroke of misfortune perfectly in keeping with Bayreuth and the festival.

The archive, which was as fiercely coveted as the hoard of the Nibelungs, continued to excite unwelcome agitation, so I decided to transfer some of the objects and documents to Nussdorf from their hiding-places in Oberwarmensteinach. I had dispersed them with some ingenuity. They

were stored partly in the loft of the parsonage and partly at my mother's
house, in a kind of box-room and behind the bed occupied by Emma, our
former nursemaid. It seems amazing in retrospect that nothing disappeared,
given that the house, which had been built to accommodate a maximum
of eight people, was then occupied by eighteen.

My departure for Nussdorf from Bayreuth on 11 March was preceded
by a grotesque incident. Just as I had loaded the two bulging rucksacks
containing my grandfather's scores on to an iron-wheeled trailer and was
about to cycle to the station with them, I was treated to the unexpected
and highly undesirable sight of Mayor Meyer and an American officer
walking towards me along Wahnfried's tree-lined drive. As if that were not
enough, they interrupted their peaceful but watchful stroll to question me,
then of all times, as to the whereabouts of the archive. Annoyed and
perturbed by this delay, I hurriedly regretted that I had to catch a train and
couldn't stop to talk. So saying, I pedalled past the pair with my load of
scores and made good my escape. I got to Nussdorf safe and sound,
fiendishly delighted to have removed some of the items they coveted from
under their very noses.

My impressions of that visit to Lake Constance were very mixed. My
brother and brother-in-law were busy planning to set up a family council
designed to pave the way for the festival's temporary transfer abroad,
whence it was proposed to reconquer Bayreuth. I found this idea strange
and unrealistic enough, but their assumption that they could fund the new
enterprise out of their own resources struck me as wholly absurd. Their ill-
omened foreign festivals were to be financed by the sale of one or more
original Wagner scores, which would, they believed, raise enough money
to enable the entire family to live in carefree comfort. I rebutted this and
the other wildly fanciful notions to which I was treated beside Lake
Constance by pointing out what I knew for a certainty, namely, that the
political charges which were (and still are) levelled at our family would have
to be disposed of before there could be any question of our relaunching
the festival. Furthermore, we had yet to become accomplished theatre folk
and would be better advised to spend some more time maturing for our
potential roles. My arguments and my doubts about the feasibility of the
aforesaid scheme fell on deaf ears, of course, because the denizens of
Nussdorf either could not or would not grasp the realities of the situation
and considered themselves above such supposed trifles. None of them had
any real conception of the widespread public prejudice against our family,
which had been additionally fuelled by Friedelind's book.

I should mention that my mother, in a mood of euphoric exaltation,
tended to believe that her own past and that of Bayreuth would soon cease
to matter. We had been fortunate enough to survive the recent débâcle in

fair shape, she felt, so an independent 'Bayreuth Festival' would in due course arise like a phoenix from the ashes. She, too, flirted for a while with the idea of an 'alternative Bayreuth' based abroad, naïvely believing that it would be entirely exempt from the burdens of tradition and history, and that Friedelind's charges would be nullified. Hardly anyone in the family realized how ill-founded such ideas and schemes were, and how remote from the rather bleak reality.

Wahnfried was badly damaged and the Festspielhaus so dilapidated, even though it had escaped the bombing, that I requested the trusteeship office to restrict its use to concerts for safety's sake. If the authorities had closed it down completely on those grounds, which was well within the realms of possibility, all plans for the future would have been stillborn.

I conveyed my resigned attitude to the whole situation in a letter to Wieland dated 5 April 1947: 'I very much hope that you [plural] have made some kind of progress. At all events, it became very clear to me during my stay beside Lake Constance that our family is no longer capable of staging the festival on its own ... What is more, I myself am completely indifferent to the effect this may have on our family's relationship to the house up there, because I ... consider our family incapable of this task ...' Obviously upset by this letter, my brother arranged to meet me at a neutral rendezvous where no other member of the family would be present. We duly converged on Richard Strauss's home in Garmisch, our purpose being to air all the irksome and unpleasant subjects that were worrying us. At this distance in time, Wieland's attitude strikes me as unusually ambivalent. On the one hand he was naturally very concerned about Bayreuth, which was, after all, the reason for our meeting; on the other, he displayed a lively interest in our sister Friedelind and was busy designing sets and costumes for her projected American tour. The situation could hardly have been more absurd. I had no idea what he wanted or where he was headed. His sudden affection for Friedelind and his participation in her work might have been understandable from the aspect of pure self-interest, but not when one considered her behaviour towards the family, the non-emigrants who had remained in Europe and whom she despised with all her heart. Selling himself to her in that way was tantamount to betraying the rest of us, who were doing our best to preserve Bayreuth.

Organized by dint of her personality and name and financed with the aid of backers, as was customary in the States, Friedelind's American Wagner tour was intended to enlighten and enrapture the world of art. It was also the means by which she hoped, with Wieland's help, to conquer Bayreuth from outside. Its failure brought Wieland, her clandestine accomplice, down to earth with a bump, and he had to manage without her support. From then on, for good or ill, he was compelled to walk the precarious tightrope of Bayreuth's realities in company with me, his brother.

Immediately after the denazification tribunal sentenced my mother on 2 July 1947 I applied for another interzonal pass to Nussdorf. Having finally got there on 25 July, I presented the others with a detailed account of the proceedings and discussed its possible effects on our future existence. It was even possible, in view of the prevailing situation, that we should have to take our cue from *Die Meistersinger* and say, 'Farewell, then, art and master-tone!'

With the help of Lady Dunn, a rather mysterious, art-loving English-woman who often lobbied the American authorities on Bayreuth's behalf, I managed to get into Austria, which was then completely inaccessible to Germans. From Berchtesgaden, camouflaged as a US citizen, I took a shuttle bus to Salzburg, where I stayed for three days with Gottfried von Einem. This trip was undertaken more for the sake of cultural self-indulgence than with a specific end in view, so I was able to attend a performance of his opera *Dantons Tod*, which had been premièred at Salzburg. I also met Carl Orff, who had likewise travelled to Salzburg by devious means. Being on good terms with the CIC, Gottfried von Einem had managed to get Orff smuggled in and out. The purpose of this cloak-and-dagger operation was to enable the composer to play the piano score of his opera *Antigone*, which was premièred at Salzburg two years later, in the presence of several members of the Salzburg Festival directorate, among them Helene Thimig. I was also able to be present at this performance, after which Orff and I spent the night on the floor of Gottfried von Einem's apartment.

During the autumn I made my abode on the first floor of the gardener's house at Wahnfried somewhat more comfortable and improved the modest sanitary installations. At this period my home was becoming more and more of a rendezvous for all who were in any way connected with the festival, and, at the same time, a kind of 'resistance centre' for the Wagner family.

At around the same time I received a first letter from my sister in America, who seemed to have recognized that her book was having unpleasant repercussions on the family and herself.

Facilities for exchanging information in the years immediately after the war were very poor, and it was an eternal problem even to correspond by post. In August 1947 the Nussdorfers obtained a telephone, which enabled us to communicate with somewhat greater ease. Because my brother-in-law Bodo Lafferentz not only managed a firm whose products were of interest to the French occupation authorities but kept in constant touch with a similar concern in Switzerland, the military government granted him a line. Not so my mother, whose request for a telephone was flatly rejected.

The grounds for her application – that she was 'a person of the twentieth century' and, as such, entitled to a telephone – did not find favour. If we wanted to call each other we had to go to the post office and wait patiently in a long queue.

My brother paid his first post-war visit to Bayreuth between 13 November and 2 December 1947, over four months after our mother's first denazification hearing. He promptly got in touch with the people to whom he was particularly close at that time. That is to say, he conferred with those whose professional competence he then esteemed, among them Otto and Gertrud Strobel, his wife's uncle, Christian Ebersberger, and the architect Hans Reissinger.

At family conferences held on 24, 26, and 27 November we took stock of the past, both recent and more remote, and applied our minds to the immediate present. We asked ourselves how the current situation had arisen and what inferences should be drawn from it. We also tried to size up our chances of taking an active part in the festival and weigh them against our disabilities. The future, uncertain as it seemed, formed the natural focus of our debates, and we recorded our conclusions in writing. It was, for the first time, stipulated in one such minute 'that Wieland and Wolf shall assume responsibility for reconstructing the festival. The facts being what they are, Winifred renounces its management.' A rider noted that 'Winifred Wagner and Wieland acknowledge that Wolf has, under the circumstances, done everything possible to preserve the estate. In this connection, Wieland renews Wolf's authority to take decisions in his absence.' A third section related to our discussions on finance, in the course of which it was again suggested that the score of *Tristan* be sold, and to what effect it might have on Bayreuth should my mother reacquire dual nationality. (The British occupation authorities had offered to grant British people resident in Germany their former nationality.) The fourth point drew attention to 'the potential dangers arising from dualism in the future management'.

We took advantage of Wieland's presence in Bayreuth to voice all the hopes, desires and demands that awaited fulfilment. Like it or not, we all acknowledged that these were still utopian and bound to remain so for some time to come, one of them being the partial reconstruction of Wahnfried and the possibility of moving back into our old family home. Because licences to hold cultural events had to be obtained from the military government, we debated whether it would be possible for Wieland and me to apply for and secure such a licence – or, better still, for me alone, since I was totally unincriminated – so as to prevent it from being granted to some outsider.

On 19 January 1948 my mother, Wieland, Verena and I signed an agreement under which my brother and I were expressly authorized to act on our own. We were empowered 'to speak and act in the family's name'. Only if we failed to agree was the issue to be decided by a 'family council', or, if that reached no conclusion, by 'Mama's vote'.

Even before the festival estate was finally released, it was apparent from Wieland's further visits to Bayreuth prior to moving there permanently, as well as from ongoing negotiations with all the relevant authorities, that everyone was making strenuous efforts to solve current problems in a manner beneficial and appropriate to the Bayreuth Festival's importance, which transcended that of the town and region. This had an effect on the SPD's approach to the municipal elections of 6/7 March 1948, but it also found expression in the speech delivered at the Festspielhaus by Dr Hundhammer, the Bavarian minister of culture, to mark the 135th anniversary of Richard Wagner's birth.

The currency reform of 20 June 1948 brought everyone down to earth and caused many an ambitious project to collapse like a house of cards. Cultural activities at the Festspielhaus, which were largely funded out of confiscated festival assets, lost their financial underpinning overnight and came to a halt. Neither the municipality of Bayreuth nor the *Land* of Bavaria was in a position to offer the Bayreuth Festival financial backing, by whomever and in whatever form it might be held. Even the most interesting schemes were abruptly reduced to waste paper, and all that X or Y had alluringly if self-servingly offered in the way of lucrative temptations and international renown dissolved like a mirage. Inside the family, opposition was necessarily and inevitably replaced by co-operation, though we had already drawn a little closer when Cousin Franz's bright ideas were bruited about.

On 7 October 1948 I drafted a memorandum on an interview at 'Bayreuth Government'. Especially intended for members of the family, this was a frank and down-to-earth situation report in which I listed our outstanding problems.

As I have already said, the revision of my mother's sentence on appeal was like a final chord that resolved the dissonances preceding it and largely dispelled the controversy surrounding her. On 10 December 1948, two days after the tribunal's welcome decision, my brother was formally classified by the denazification commission as a *Mitläufer* [Nazi Party member in name only], which entitled him to resume his active participation in the festival. In other words, he was granted the status that I had enjoyed from the first, and could pursue a profession without let or hindrance.

Now, our most urgent task was to secure the release of the festival property: real estate, capital assets, and financial resources. A ruling by the Bavarian ministry of special affairs dated 28 February 1949 and signed by the minister, Dr Hagenauer, stated that 'pursuant to Article 53 of the

Exemption Law, the embargo on assets imposed by Subparagraph VI of the Bayreuth Appeal Court's judgement dated 8 December 1949, particularly where it relates to the assets of the Bayreuth Festival and the appointment of a trustee, is hereby revoked.' We owed the speed with which this decision was reached to those who had argued our case with the Bavarian premier, Dr Hans Ehard: Mayor Rollwagen, Deputies Pitroff and Hauss-leiter, and, last but far from least, Senator Dr Pöhner, deputy mayor of Bayreuth and my mother's architect since 1932. She had been able to help him when he was in trouble during the Nazi period, and he, in turn, had lent us his unflagging and disinterested assistance ever since the war ended.

In the course of his meeting with the Bavarian premier, Dr Pöhner had urged that a study be made of all those provisions in the denazification law that could help to release the assets prematurely. After some initial opposition, Dr Ehard eventually sanctioned an attempt to release them 'subject to an avoidance of this political-seeming decision [the premature lifting of the embargo]'. State Secretary Camille Sachs was thereupon presented with all the requisite documents, notably my mother's declaration of assignment, and in spring 1949 the festival was at last exempted from trusteeship. Once this exemption became legally valid, my brother and I were at long last able to set about reviving it in an altogether official capacity as well.

8

A NEW START

On 21 April 1949 Wieland moved to Bayreuth and temporarily installed himself in a small studio which our mother had built for him over the greenhouse. We all led a makeshift existence in those days, so he was provisionally obliged to avail himself of my sanitary facilities, my own abode being somewhat better equipped in that respect.

We had, of course, already begun some realistic planning for the better times we hoped lay ahead. My sister Verena and her husband, Bodo Lafferentz, travelled from Nussdorf to Bayreuth on 3 March 1948. We devoted this three-day visit, their first since the war, to a concentrated quest for ways of reviving the festival – or, more precisely, of conjuring something workable and artistically worthwhile out of next to nothing.

To this end we set up a working party consisting of Dr Meyer, Wilhelm Hieber, Heinrich Sesselmann (lawyer, auditor and financial expert respectively), my brother-in-law, and me. Our purpose in holding this conference before calling in the rest of the family was to define immediate administrative and financial requirements. The usual practice in the past had been for members of the family to deliver high-flown speeches and outline grandiose plans. They would now have to be persuaded that solid foundations were essential to the fulfilment of what was best from the artistic point of view. Nothing had come of all their airy talk and nebulous schemes, so these were to be replaced by businesslike, carefully considered action. The outcome of our deliberations was a list of problems to be solved. We would have to:

(1) finance the festival;
(2) create its artistic prerequisites;
(3) resume and maintain the old and well-tried system of co-operation with the muncipality of Bayreuth;

(4) solve the accommodation problem for artists, staff, and visitors – a very tall order, given the disastrous housing shortage;

(5) acquire the type of staff who would be prepared to collaborate in building up an enterprise whose financial resources would remain slender until Germany's budding 'economic miracle' bore fruit;

(6) launch a publicity campaign appropriate to the current situation; and

(7) restore the Festspielhaus and its annexes to the fully functional condition that would secure them the approval of the supervisory authorities.

From the artistic aspect, the logical course was to make it plain to the world at large that we had resolutely turned our backs on all forms of historicism and nationalism, and that our concern was to resurrect the Festspielhaus and Wagner's works in conformity with the one, true tradition that underlay them.

Above all, it had to be made clear, publicly and beyond the shadow of a doubt, that only my brother and I – not the Wagner family – were responsible for running the festival.

How were we to get hold of the money we needed? Thanks to the commendable efforts of a number of townsfolk, we received enough financial support to enable us at least to exist and start work on the festival.

Detailed discussions were held with representatives of the former or reconstituted Richard Wagner Societies as to whether the existing funds of the Richard Wagner bursary foundation could be used to kick-start the festival financially, although these had been considerably depreciated by the currency reform.

In view of our predicament, the proposal to sell one or more original Wagner scores was naturally debated with renewed vehemence, but nothing came of it because Friedelind's consent was far from certain. I still beg leave to doubt if it would have been sensible to touch the archive and scores, and if their sale would really, as the family expected, have rendered the festival completely independent and self-sufficient. Friedelind had reason enough to say no, given her announcement that the Bayreuth Festival would reopen at a much later date. Besides, she inevitably found our activities disruptive of her own plans and could have had no particular interest in allowing the festival to resume so soon and without her direct involvement.

Thanks to the paradoxical fact that Gerhard Rossbach, one of two 'principals', as defined by the denazification law, should have issued the other (my mother) with a 'Persil certificate' [denazification clearance, so called because it certified a person's 'whiteness'], an old and almost vanished connection was re-established and invested with new life. It was a connection whose previous highlight had been my mother's treat for my father's sixtieth birthday on 6 June 1929, when Gerhard Rossbach's artistically active and vital youth group, the 'Ekkehard der Schilljugend' company, gave a performance at Wahnfried. In response to Winifred's appeal for help in solving our financial problems, Rossbach returned to Bayreuth for the first time on 11 May 1949. Of the six different proposals he submitted for our consideration, it was the fifth, I remember, which seemed to offer the greatest prospect of success: 'Rossbach suggests an industrial contribution of DM100 per firm and believes that he can approach people through the chambers of industry and commerce and by means of personal connections. He says that, although it is unlikely that anyone would give more than DM100, that sum should be easy enough to find.' He proved right, because his characteristic mixture of brisk activity and wily ingenuity succeeded in winning over so many individuals, firms and authorities that we and Bayreuth were soon in excellent shape. Meantime, he naturally remained in constant touch with us and consulted my mother on how best to co-ordinate their respective campaigns.

The patronage society that was to prove so important to 'New Bayreuth', the 'Gesellschaft der Freunde von Bayreuth e.V.' [Incorporated Association of Friends of Bayreuth], was founded on 22 September 1949. Present at the founders' meeting in addition to Wieland, me, and our prospective business administrator, Heinrich Sesselmann, were Lotte Albrecht-Potonié, president of the Richard Wagner Society, Dr Hans Bahlsen of Hanover, Consul Dr Franz Hilger of Düsseldorf and his son Ewald, Dr Moritz Klönne of Dortmund, Dr C. A. Schleussner of Frankfurt, Martin Schwab of Telefunken GmbH, Stuttgart, Joachim Vielmetter of Knorrbremse, Munich, our family friend Dr August Roesener of Usingen, and the Frankfurt attorney and notary Dr Hugo Eckert. Representatives were sent by Dr Konrad Pöhner, deputy mayor of Bayreuth and a member of the Bavarian senate, Berthold Beitz, then of Hamburg and later of Essen, and Dr Otto Springorum of Essen.

On the eve of founders' day a few of us met for a preliminary talk with Dr Schleussner, who was hosting the occasion, in a side room in 'Schumanns Säle' opposite Frankfurt's main-line station, an area still displaying considerable signs of bomb damage. Although everything had been settled in advance, near disaster struck at the eleventh hour when a heated argument broke out between Dr Schleussner and Wieland, who was largely ignorant of business jargon and had only the vaguest notion of the meaning of terms such as mortgages, securities, short- and long-term loans, etc. Fortunately, the rest of us managed to avert a major altercation. At the meeting next day, however, the financial schemes and requests that Herr Sesselmann and I had carefully worked out were presented by me, and not, as originally planned, by my brother. Wieland's remarks were wholly confined to his artistic objectives and various matters arising therefrom.

Among other things, I informed those present that, when the trustee handed back the Festspielhaus, we had been obliged to assume additional responsibility for a debt of DM17,000. There were, however, no liquid assets available to cover this, and our other assets consisted of dead stock. No help could be expected from the Bavarian government because my brother and I had categorically declined the Bavarian premier's suggestion that a 'supervisory administrator' be appointed to breathe down our necks. I also took advantage of the occasion to go into the tangled story of the proposal to sell original scores. As if that were not enough, our hopes had been dashed in another respect because UNESCO, on which we had counted to guarantee a bank loan, was pulling out. Thus, we gratefully accepted Gerhard Rossbach's far-reaching assistance, which could, in our opinion, provide a secure and sufficient guarantee of overall financing and liquidity. On the basis of our calculations, which were debated by all concerned, we approved a starting capital of DM400,000, this to be increased to the requisite DM700,000 by drawing on the resources of the festival, ticket sales, and so forth. I expressly emphasized to those present that the resumption of the Bayreuth Festival under the joint management of my brother and me, being uninfluenced by the Bavarian government, would be solely dependent on this financial basis, not only from my own angle as business manager, but artistically from both our points of view. We could not, of course, engage any artists or sign any contracts until it was absolutely certain that we could honour our obligations.

The founding of the Association of Friends and its first successful endeavours acted as a booster to our further attempts to raise money. With its backing we were able to enter into negotiations with other sources of finance, foremost among them the broadcasting networks. We were also guaranteed a subsidy by the Bavarian government, though we accepted this only on condition that it exerted no influence on artistic policy. We could offer the broadcasting networks a genuinely interesting quid pro quo, the right to transmit from the Festspielhaus, but we had nothing comparable to tender in return for a government subsidy.

Accordingly, because the brothers Wagner had yet to win their artistic spurs and were regarded with doubt and suspicion, the Munich authorities appointed a species of committee composed of experts and advisers such as the managers of various theatres and members of the German Stage Association. They did so in the secret and seemingly unconquerable hope that an official investigation would reveal us to be sufficiently inadequate or incompetent to enable them to transform their half-overt, half-latent opposition to a largely independent Bayreuth into direct supervisory control.

Shortly after holding out the prospect of a state subsidy of DM 50,000 for the years 1950 and 1951, which was in itself the product of interminable negotiations, they played their last trump card: no funds would be allocated unless the thoroughly inexperienced brothers Wagner agreed to accept the help (alias tutelage) of an expert (alias watchdog). Not for the first time, Heinz Tietjen's name was mentioned in this connection.

Wieland and I flatly rejected this renewed attempt at supervision, arguing that it would be wrong, now that our mother had bowed out completely, for her erstwhile closest associate to enter Bayreuth by the back door, as it were, and assume a position of some responsibility. We also pointed out, with a touch of pride, that men of the calibre of Hans Knappertsbusch, Herbert von Karajan and Rudolf Hartmann, whose professionalism was undisputed in theatrical circles, were sufficiently confident of our abilities to have faithfully promised to work with us at Bayreuth. As so often happens, matters were clinched by a relatively minor incident. We had submitted our preliminary estimates and schedules for the festival, and for rehearsals and performances in particular, to the board of the Bavarian State Theatre, which still existed at that time. After our plans had been discussed, Bertha Buchenberger, secretary to the board, told the chairman, Dr Diess, that they seemed quite reasonable and merited acceptance. In any case, she added tersely, all the risks of the venture would be borne by Messrs Wagner, 'So let them get on with it.' This evidently proved enough to tip the scales in our favour. However, many of those who were jointly responsible for this state subsidy coupled their approval of it with a fervent desire to see us fall flat on our faces and come to grief.

Our no less nerve-racking arguments with the director-general of the Bavarian broadcasting service, Dr Scholtz, led on 18 September 1950 to our being promised a subsidy of DM 50,000 from the cultural assistance fund. The trade union representative on the board, Max Wönner, who came out strongly in favour of Bayreuth, did a great deal to overcome the director-general's initial resistance.

In order to reassure all those who were afraid that we might, like the managers of some travelling circus, carry the money around in our trouser pockets and squander it as we pleased, Berthold Beitz, acting on behalf of the Association of Friends, sent the trustee of the Iduna-Germania insurance company to Bayreuth to check that we were making responsible and legitimate use of the funds accruing to us. An extremely shrewd and competent man, he took far less than the estimated time to satisfy himself and everyone else that our staff's financial transactions were thoroughly irreproachable.

It had been argued that the original score of *Lohengrin* and various other Wagner manuscripts should be deposited as security with the Karl Schmidt

Bank at Bayreuth. Only private banks could undertake this form of transaction under the laws then in force, so the Bayreuth Festival was unable to make use of its old banking connections. In order to make funds available to us, Iduna granted the Schmidt Bank a cash advance.

The date finally set for the reopening of the Bayreuth Festival in 1951, together with the original programme and its subsequent enlargement, precisely reflected what was, and was not, possible under prevailing circumstances. We were guided not by subjective wishes alone, but by objective factors.

Prior to 1949 it had been optimistically planned to reopen the festival in 1950 with a programme comprising several performances of *Parsifal* and four symphony concerts. Since the Vatican had designated 1950 'Holy Year' and the Oberammergau Passion Play was to be revived, Germany was counting on a big influx of foreign and overseas visitors for whom the Bayreuth Festival could be a further incentive to travel. At the inaugural meeting of the Association of Friends, discussion had been devoted to a programme based on two of my grandfather's works: *Parsifal* and either *Tristan* or *Die Meistersinger*. The question of a conductor was also mooted on the same occasion. Hans Knappertsbusch was our almost unanimous choice, and we also resolved to get in touch with Victor de Sabata and Bruno Walter as soon as the financial situation seemed reasonably secure. Because Wilhelm Furtwängler's Salzburg commitments ruled him out for Bayreuth, Herbert von Karajan's name cropped up. On 22 March 1950, when it transpired soon afterwards that the festival would not, for a variety of reasons, be revived until 1951, we drew up an entirely new financial plan based on our ideas for a different and wider-ranging programme. There was to be an inaugural concert including Beethoven's Ninth Symphony, in memory of the occasion when the foundation stone of the House on the Green Hill was laid on 22 May 1872, followed by five performances each of *Parsifal* and *Die Meistersinger* and two complete *Ring* cycles. The total outlay was put at DM1,483,157.50.

We managed to get Wilhelm Furtwängler for the inaugural concert. He had requested us to engage him for 1951 back in 1949, when the date of the reopening had still to be settled beyond doubt, so we had naturally been unable to give him a firm and binding answer. I believe I am correct in assuming that this was the occasion for certain intrigues in and around Salzburg which Herbert von Karajan, that adept in such matters, was quick to exploit.

The execution of this enlarged plan entailed that I – and, of course, my brother – had to put a great deal more effort into every aspect of the preparations. From my own point of view, it also meant that I had to abandon my intention of producing *Die Meistersinger*.

In an interview on 10 May 1950 we publicly commented on our aims and activities for the first time. At another meeting of the Association of Friends held on 27 May we presented a situation report in which we were able, among other things, to name the artistic participants in the forthcoming festival. Wilhelm Furtwängler would be the conductor of the inaugural concert. Hans Knappertsbusch had been engaged for *Parsifal*, and we had made another important contract with Herbert von Karajan, who was to handle all the *Meistersinger* performances and the musical rehearsals for *The Ring*, the second cycle of which he would also conduct in alternation with Knappertsbusch. Furtwängler's presence at the opening was ultimately motivated by a belief that he had to prevent Karajan from taking over Bayreuth, lock, stock and barrel. The following statement by Dr Pöhner is recorded in the minutes of the Association of Friends: 'Wieland has again been negotiating with Furtwängler, who, after saying "yes" three times and "no" five times, has finally said "yes" on condition that 1951 turns into a Richard Wagner's Bayreuth, not a Herr von Karajan's Bayreuth...'

I had also negotiated in Hamburg with a view to engaging Joseph Keilberth to conduct in 1951, but he was unable to participate in the festival until 1952 because of commitments elsewhere.

Rudolf Hartmann was engaged to produce *Die Meistersinger*, the sets for which my brother entrusted to his wife Gertrud's uncle, the architect Hans Reissinger. We were obliged by financial constraints to borrow the costumes from Nuremberg. It was hoped at the above meeting of the Association of Friends that the inaugural sets would not be purely avant-garde, and the *Meistersinger* team bore out these misgivings to the full.

In addition to conductors, of course, we had to obtain the requisite singers. There was a widespread view even then, and it was often voiced subsequently, that the war and the six-year interval since the last wartime festival had created a dearth of Wagnerian singers. In searching for artists who might fill the bill, we naturally entertained the possibility of falling back on one or two successful names from former years.

On 1 August I attended a Salzburg recital by Edwin Fischer, the Swiss pianist, whom I had last heard in Berlin during the war. The same day I met with Furtwängler and discussed the possibility of a concert at Bayreuth. On 2 August I broached the same subject at an interview with the board of the Vienna Philharmonic. My brother and I always made the most of any opportunity to attract attention by holding such functions at the Festspielhaus. On 22 May 1949, the 136th anniversary of Richard Wagner's birth, Hans Knappertsbusch conducted the Munich Philharmonic there, and on 9 September 1949, after the death of Richard Strauss, there was a memorial concert by the Dresden State Orchestra under Joseph Keilberth. On the following day I was able to speak with Kirsten Flagstad, who was singing Leonora in *Fidelio* that night. I asked if we could count on her participation when the festival reopened, but she declined on the grounds that it would be better for us to mark such an important break and fresh start by engaging some entirely new young singers. When I asked if she could suggest a suitable soloist in her own category she recommended Astrid Varnay, whose unprecedentedly meteoric career at the New York Met had taken off on 6 December 1941, when none of the greats in her field was available and she stepped into the role of Sieglinde at the age of twenty-two. She even sang Brünnhilde precisely one week later, having mastered both roles without a rehearsal. We engaged Astrid Varnay for 1951 without an audition. In her and Martha Mödl we had a highly dramatic pair of sisters whose quality invalidated the question of whether or not Wagnerian singers still existed.

The prelude to Martha Mödl's audition at Bayreuth on 10 September 1950 was as follows. A Belgian singer had failed to fulfil my brother's expectations in the role of Kundry, so he travelled to Hamburg to hear Mödl as Venus in *Tannhäuser*. She was very indisposed on the night in question, so he could not form a definite opinion. I had also heard her in the meantime, even before she came to Bayreuth to audition, and was very impressed. We thereupon engaged her, and her success vindicated our decision.

I cannot forbear to mention one episode connected with the recruitment of singers. Wieland and I once attended a performance of *Die Meistersinger* conducted by Hans Knappertsbusch at Munich's Prinzregententheater. The tenor August Seider was ill and had been replaced by a young tenor named Wolfgang Windgassen, then known only as the son of Fritz. When we visited Knappertsbusch in his dressing-room afterwards, he said, 'Gentlemen, I hope you don't take it into your heads to engage that *Krawattltenor* [a tenor whose tie is more impressive than his voice].' Wieland gave me a sheepish look, because we had already approached the young man with a view to signing him for *Parsifal*, which Knappertsbusch himself was to conduct. We thought it wiser to depart in silence.

Leo Blech, who had been compelled to give up the musical directorship of the Berlin Staatsoper in 1937, had never lost his regard for my mother. Writing to her on 22 October 1948, he said that, since her sons intended to build up a new ensemble – indeed, would have to do so – he wanted to draw their attention to two young singers named Birgit Nilsson and Sigurd Björling. Knappertsbusch made their acquaintance at a guest performance in Stockholm.

We managed to sign Sigurd Björling as Wotan for 1951, but Birgit Nilsson, whom we wanted to sing Sieglinde twice, could not accept our initial offer because of a prior engagement at Glyndebourne. I made her acquaintance at a concert performance of Act I of *Die Walküre* conducted by Leo Blech at the Titania Palast in Berlin. It was there that Siegmund was first sung by Hans Beirer and Hunding by Joseph Greindl, who had appeared as Pogner in *Die Meistersinger* at Bayreuth in 1943 and in my own first production at the Berlin Staatsoper in 1944.

Meeting Leo Blech again after a lapse of thirteen years was a memorable experience. Despite having been forced to emigrate because he was a Jew, he bore no resentment towards Bayreuth and looked upon my grandfather's works as artistic utterances in their own right, not misappropriated aids to political manipulation.

Nothing came of our further negotiations with Birgit Nilsson until 1953, when she took the stage at Bayreuth in Beethoven's Ninth Symphony conducted by Paul Hindemith, whom we had invited to open the third post-war festival in token of our veneration for a composer whom the Third Reich had branded 'degenerate'.

In 1954, the second year of my first Bayreuth production, *Lohengrin*, I was particularly pleased to be able to cast Birgit Nilsson as Elsa, my brother having chosen Gré Brouwenstijn for Elsa in his new production of *Tannhäuser*. As an 'encore' Birgit Nilsson sang the short role of Ortlinde in my brother's *Valkyrie*, which had been entrusted to Kirsten Flagstad at pre-war Bayreuth in addition to Gutrune, the Third Norn, and, in 1934, Sieglinde. In 1955 and 1956 Birgit Nilsson turned her back on Bayreuth because I failed to persuade my brother to give her Sieglinde, which she wanted, in addition to Senta in my new production of *Der Fliegende Holländer* (a role in which she alternated with Astrid Varnay for scheduling reasons). She returned in 1957 as Isolde in my new production of *Tristan* and was also cast by Wieland as the Third Norn. In 1958 and 1959, over the undisguised opposition of the established conductors, I engaged Wolfgang Sawallisch, then musical director at Aachen.

It was I who had some years earlier paved the way for Birgit Nilsson and Wolfgang Windgassen to become the eponymous dream couple in Karl Böhm and Wieland's *Tristan* team from 1962 onwards, so I was delighted to have 'broken in' those two great artists. Nilsson sang all three Brünnhildes in my first *Ring* production in 1960, but only the *Siegfried* and *Götterdämmerung* Brünnhildes in the following year – the first time this three-day role had been shared between two singers. The *Valkyrie* Brünnhilde was sung by Astrid Varnay, who, as ever when presented with an exceptional challenge, rose to it with the unstinted and straightforward enthusiasm so characteristic of her. Since Karl Böhm insisted on having Birgit Nilsson as Isolde in the new production of *Tristan* mentioned above, I naturally consented, and the team enjoyed a predictable success. In 1962 she again sang Brünnhilde in *Siegfried* and *Götterdämmerung* in the first *Ring* cycle, while

Astrid Varnay, in addition to singing all the *Valkyrie* Brünnhildes in the first cycle, took over the role in all three works in the second.

Whenever *The Ring* and *Tristan* appear in the same season's programme, it is understandable that a soprano would rather soar into the immortal songstresses' heaven with the 'love-death' rather than immolate herself with the 'fire-death' that concludes *Götterdämmerung*, especially as it is preceded by another two works, *Die Walküre* and *Siegfried*.

These few examples demonstrate, and our further collaboration with them confirmed, that in women such as these, who were totally dedicated to the peculiarities of working at Bayreuth, we had found persons with whom we could mount authentic 'festival' productions. Wieland's subsequent flirtation with the idea of bringing Maria Callas to Bayreuth would have signified the exact opposite, and would certainly not have accorded with our continuous process of development and our workshop approach, which was based on team spirit.

The tenor problem, which always proves troublesome, especially at Bayreuth, was solved in 1951 by engaging Bernd Aldenhoff, Hans Hopf, and Wolfgang Windgassen, with whom Hans Knappertsbusch had finally come to terms.

The recruitment of associates, and singers in particular, was then and still is dependent on the following: (1) recommendations from conductors, fellow artists, singing teachers, and members of the public; (2) auditions conducted at one's own request; (3) suggestions from agents and record company executives; (4) reports in the trade press; (5) fact-finding trips such as Wagner undertook in preparation for his festivals. Today, audiovisual techniques afford an additional source of advance information, but modern recordings are the least informative of all 'auditions', for our purposes, because they often employ a variety of ingenious tricks, and the possibility of such artifices can never be excluded.

Bearing all these points in mind, my brother and I travelled widely and held numerous auditions at Bayreuth itself. We finally succeeded in assembling a cast of singers who seemed, all prophecies of doom notwithstanding, to justify the resumption of the festival in the eyes of public and critics alike. As subsequent years proved, the artists we had engaged for 'minor roles' would later fulfil the hopes we pinned on their future development. For example, the singers who played the so-called 'minor mastersingers' included Gerhard Stolze, Werner Faulhaber, and Theo Adam, who matured from the noble young knight in *Lohengrin* into Wotan in *The Ring* and Hans Sachs in *Die Meistersinger*.

As if to demonstrate that promising young singers still existed, we discovered Leonie Rysanek, then a novice of twenty-four. On 25 April 1951, when it was certain that we could not count on casting Birgit Nilsson as Sieglinde, we auditioned the young Austrian from Saarbrücken and were highly impressed by her. We thus cast Günther Treptow, who had already proved an experienced Siegmund prior to Bayreuth, alongside a far from experienced twin sister. In the event, Leonie Rysanek's Bayreuth début was a sensational success and, from our point of view, a great stroke of luck because it justified our faith in her. My brother offered her the role of Brangäne in 1952. She did not consider it important enough after the success of her début as Sieglinde, however, and came to the conclusion that it would not be the best way of furthering her international career. The result was that, although she returned to us again and again, she did not contribute to New Bayreuth's ongoing process of artistic stabilization in the way we had hoped. It is not uninteresting to list the sopranos who took over the role of Sieglinde until Leonie Rysanek returned in 1958: Inge Borkh (1952), Regine Resnik (1953), Martha Mödl and Astrid Varnay (1954 and 1955), Gré Brouwenstijn (1956), and Birgit Nilsson (1957). Leonie Rysanek sang Senta in Wieland's new production of *Der Fliegende Holländer* in 1959. In contrast to her first year at Bayreuth, she turned up for rehearsals in skin-tight stretch jeans and sweaters reminiscent of Marilyn Monroe. My brother failed to recognize her at first. Remembering that she had been one of the less punctual members of the cast in 1951, he gave vent to the memorable remark: 'That slovenly bitch Rysanek is late again!' Rather surprised and dismayed, a young woman who looked like a pin-up girl retorted: 'The slovenly bitch is here, Herr Wagner.'

It soon became clear that Herbert von Karajan was determined to enforce his casting suggestions and his other wishes and ideas at all costs, not least with the aid of Walter Legge. The pair had joined forces in 1946, and from then on, just as Alberich obtained the ring and the *Tarnhelm*, they combined art and business in a 'world-inheriting' way, though without having to forgo 'the power of courtly love'. Protected by the glittering magic helmet, they hoped at Bayreuth to hitch the world's best artists to their wagon.

It was only right and proper, during the reinaugural phase, to consider whether the production and worldwide distribution of gramophone records might generate the fresh publicity Bayreuth needed and induce certain artists to participate, quite apart from yielding additional revenue with which to finance the festival's future.

However, my brother and I sought to make it clear from the outset that we would never contemplate granting one record company a monopoly. That was why we had planned to make contracts not only with Legge's Columbia but also with Teldec, which had since the 1930s been issuing records of Bayreuth under its former name, Telefunken. Sales were dependent solely on the quality of the black disks. Live recordings of orchestral and dress rehearsals, as of almost all performances, had to be rendered marketable by editing the tapes with extreme precision. This applied particularly, for example, to the 'cudgel scene' and the 'Awake!' chorus from *Die Meistersinger*, recordings of which repeatedly displayed inconsistencies and discrepancies. Nevertheless, the artists under contract to Legge, notably Elisabeth Schwarzkopf, had to spearhead the attempt to make casts conform as closely as possible to the record producer's ideas.

Rudolf Hartmann and my brother thought it particularly inappropriate and unworthy of Bayreuth that, because microphones were still technically inefficient, singers should have to comply with Legge's ideas by adapting their movements on stage to the recording engineer's requirements. As for Herbert von Karajan, who habitually neglected to bring singers in on cue, he sought to achieve the requisite precision with the aid of an assistant conductor in the prompt box.

Legge employed another devious means of making *The Ring* recordable or unrecordable with the aid of his exclusive seven-year contract. He managed to talk my brother into a most peculiar concession, namely, that a lone recording be issued of Act III of Karajan's *Valkyrie* from the second *Ring* cycle, the first cycle having been conducted by Knappertsbusch. Although an equal partner in law, I was not consulted about this piece of horse-trading. Having failed to nip it in the bud and prevent Wieland from consenting to an arrangement whose disastrous repercussions were lost on him, and not wishing to stab my brother in the back by disavowing him, I reluctantly let matters rest.

Wieland held 'fireside chats' at Wahnfried – occasions on which he evidently felt he could achieve better results by dispensing with my presence and my potential objections – which often provoked certain differences between us, though other people deliberately construed them as irreconcilable antagonisms. The situations provoked by such 'chats' frequently arose from subjective and purely personal motives and were not always compatible with the objective, overall interests of our joint enterprise.

It was no accident that my mother did not sign the tenancy agreement between her and us brothers until Wieland's demand that he should be *primus inter pares* had been deleted from the agenda. Although my mother owned the Festspielhaus, she had renounced all involvement in the festival. Consequently, she was obliged to rent it to us and live on the proceeds. Her declaration of assignment left her free to entrust us equally with the management of the festival. Believing that Wieland was incapable of handling financial matters properly, she took the view that we should make all decisions and sign all documents on a joint and equal basis, and that the substitution of fraternal concord and harmony for one-sided authoritarianism would enable any outstanding problems to be solved in concert. She trusted that intelligence and common sense would always prompt us to reach agreements consistent with the importance of the task we had undertaken.

From 1876 until the end of my mother's era, the festival's assets and management had been a single entity. Now for the first time, thanks to the well-devised arrangement that had separated them, the risks attendant on organizing the festival were divorced from the liability of the estate as a whole, which encompassed its land and buildings and the Richard Wagner archive. Because the liabilities of a *Gesellschaft des bürgerlichen Rechts* [partnership under the civil code] affected neither prior nor reversionary heirs, this precluded the dominance accorded to a family council, which, in view of my family's structure, would have led to predictable squabbles and complications.

This new arrangement was prompted by the specific situation I have already described, which was ultimately governed by the sober realization that the festival could only be carried on by members of the Wagner family, in the longer term as well, if the task were undertaken by those who had best prepared themselves for the task and were likely to perform it diligently.

The scepticism inspired in me by Gertrud Reissinger, who had married my brother on 12 September 1941, had steadily intensified in the meantime. Born of my numerous and sometimes disagreeable arguments with Wieland between 1940 and 1945, it had temporarily culminated when I was telephoning him from Berlin in 1941 and she snatched the receiver in the middle of our conversation. I inferred, even at that stage, that my brother could no longer be regarded as his own man, and this was proving more and more to be the case.

I had to be careful to forestall any development that would have enabled my sister-in-law to acquire a predominant say in the running of the festival. Legally, no one apart from Wieland and me was entitled to exert a direct influence on it: neither my mother, nor my sisters – of whom Verena had never cherished any ambition to take an active part in festival business – nor Verena's husband. This being so, it would have been quite absurd to employ either my wife or Wieland's in an active capacity of any kind. We agreed on this point, but only orally. Although Wieland observed our agreement in 1951, his wife was credited as choreographer on the following year's programme and thereafter.

There is no truth in Gertrud Wagner's recurrent assertion that she made an indispensible contribution to Wieland's productions. As I have said, he did not enlist her services for his second Bayreuth *Ring* production from 1965 onwards, and he had previously engaged other choreographers of international repute, e.g. Maurice Béjart in 1961 and 1962 for *Tannhäuser*, on which Birgit Cullberg also worked from 1965 to 1967. If I acknowledged my sister-in-law's contribution at all, it was by voluntarily remunerating her for it. A purely personal gesture on my part, this was intended to help balance Wieland's budget, on which his financial requirements were already imposing a considerable strain.

Audiences and insiders – with the exception of Frau Ebermann – found Gertrud Wagner's choreographic treatment of the Venusberg in the 1954 *Tannhäuser* a 'rhythmical and gymnastic' portrayal of sex, and, as such, aesthetically hard to accept. It was inspired by her own first experience of *Tannhäuser*, my father's 1931 production with choreography by Rudolf Laban. This sowed the seeds of a dream, which Wieland shared, that she might some day stage a *Tannhäuser* of her own. Still obsessed with that dream twenty-three years later, they were finally in a position to realize it in accordance with their own fanciful ideas.

The reason why their subsequent estrangement almost exactly coincided with my brother's affair with the soprano Anja Silja may not have been simply that their marriage had gone stale. Everyone knew that, although Wieland was no saint, his attachment to Anja Silja had sprung from her artistic and instinctive grasp of his intentions, and that this was what ultimately sustained it.

Despite her rather dynastic cast of mind, my mother declared in her characteristically forthright way that Gertrud had never shown any artistic understanding of her husband, whereas Anja Silja's unerring feel for his theatrical ideas had enabled her to put them into practice promptly and fully.

Anja Silja had come to Bayreuth because we could not afford to pay the exorbitant fee demanded by Leonie Rysanek for the 1961 repeat of *Der Fliegende Holländer*, and because we did not wish to create a precedent. This meant that we had to find another Senta, a role that has always presented casting problems. After some discussion I mooted the possibility of engaging the 'auditioner' Anja Silja, then only nineteen years old, because I felt it would be preferable to use a young unknown rather than an established singer whose relations with Leonie Rysanek would inevitably be soured. My brother was extremely dubious about this proposal and said that he had no idea what he would do with such a 'young thing' on stage. Wolfgang Sawallisch, conductor of *Holländer* and currently musical director at Wiesbaden, sent for Silja, who was then singing minor roles at Frankfurt, and worked on the role with her. This finally clinched his and Wieland's decision to engage her as the new Senta. As everyone knows, their gamble paid off.

It was none the less curious that a few years later, when Wieland's *Ring* was in preparation at Cologne in 1964, Silja provoked such altercations between conductor Sawallisch and designer Wieland that the former declined to conduct *Die Meistersinger* at Bayreuth if she was cast as Eva.

I had already earmarked Wolfgang Sawallisch as musical director of my own *Ring* production in 1960, and had secured his agreement, when I was suddenly deprived of his services. This was yet another of the accomplished facts with which I was presented by those 'fireside chats' conducted in the seclusion of Wahnfried. I was not a little surprised to be informed by my brother that he wanted Wolfgang Sawallisch to conduct *Der Fliegende Holländer* in 1960 as well. It transpired that Sawallisch had been induced to renege on his firm undertaking to me at a meeting with Wieland on 2 August 1959. This development was not only disappointing but serious, because we had already worked with some of the singers and co-ordinated our ideas during the rehearsals and the festival season itself. Having already learned what was brewing on 3 August, even before Sawallisch brought me the bad news, I had sent for my senior musical assistant, Paul Zelter, and asked him, after lengthy deliberations with him and the chorus master Wilhelm Pitz, to make immediate inquiries about the availability of Rudolf Kempe. On 8 August my representative, Dr Andreas Wirz, was able to inform me that he had definitely engaged Kempe to forge a new *Ring* with me.

Sawallisch found his work on *Holländer* in 1959 harder than he had expected. Once, when rehearsals were in progress, he came to me and let off steam, mainly about my sister-in-law's insistence on the tempi she needed for her choreographic extravaganzas – tempi so excessively fast that he thought them quite unwarrantable. 'I never knew my sister-in-law was a conductor as well,' I told him. 'Please don't be governed by your choreographer.'

Between the beginning of 1950 and the reopening of the festival, the rehearsal period being its most outstanding feature, we succeeded in augmenting the few remaining members of my mother's artistic and administrative staff with other personnel whose practical concerns were scenery, costumes and make-up, and their redesigning. Since my brother thought more of Paul Eberhardt's abilities as a lighting engineer and technician than as a designer – Wieland felt that his execution of sets was far too technical and failed to bring out the artistic side sufficiently – a division of responsibilities was instituted. Walter Bornemann and his assistant took over the construction and painting of the *Ring* scenery, while Otto Wissner, who handled all our model construction and projection painting until he left in 1957, handled the scenery for *Parsifal* and *Die Meistersinger*.

The design of the *Parsifal* models, on which work had started during Wieland's visit to Bayreuth in 1948, had undergone considerable changes at the very beginning of their translation to the stage, and important modifications were introduced in the course of construction. What audiences finally got to see was the only production that showed, in that reinaugural year, how my brother intended to interpret his grandfather's works – and that, as everyone knows, provoked some initial turbulence among members of the public and critics alike. In retrospect I am bound to say that neither *Die Meistersinger* nor the *Ring* of 1951 could be described as forward-looking. Professor Walter Erich Schäfer wrote of *The Ring* that it was manifestly an offspring of Leopold Jessner's productions in the 1920s. As for *Die Meistersinger*, audiences revelled in it precisely because it contained nothing that might have inflamed their passions.

One difficult problem was how to procure gauze drops for the stage, because the celebrated sixteen-metre loom at Luckenwalde had been smashed by invading Russian soldiers. The only materials then available in Germany came from abroad, so we had to try to purchase some from a Frankfurt importer, a gentleman who supplied all the Americans' favourite night-spots in Kaiserstrasse and its environs. Among the tools of the trade used by the ladies commonly employed in such establishments was a 'more artistically demanding' form of veiling. When I was eventually able to examine a sample of this material in Frankfurt, I found that it met our requirements admirably. The only trouble was, it was a mere three metres wide and had to be imported from Belgium. Noticing that the edges of the material had no selvage, however, I asked what width it could be supplied in and received the welcome information that the original weave was twelve metres wide. Three metres might have been on the wide side for the dance of the seven veils, but it was too narrow for our purposes, so I ordered a consignment in the original width. It was then sewn together without the seams being unduly visible.

Although the sets for *The Ring*, to which my brother attached such importance, were visually satisfactory from the auditorium side, their invisible 'innards' consisted of rough battens crudely nailed together. Problems inevitably arose every time they were transported from the store to the stage, because the battens and nails worked loose and the rickety structures were constantly in need of repair. Wieland favoured this form of set construction, which conflicted with traditional techniques, not only in the hope that it would be quicker and cheaper, but because he wanted to demonstrate that the traditional method of construction was outmoded.

In the case of *Das Rheingold*, for example, it emerged in the course of lighting experiments and artists' rehearsals that the Rhine Maidens' original swimming-machines were to be re-employed. Highly dissatisfied with these old contraptions, Wieland abandoned them after a few rehearsals, with the result that an entirely different scenic solution had to be found – and this, in turn, entailed major changes to the set. The other sets for *Das Rheingold*, which were already finished, suffered the same fate and had to be completely rebuilt while rehearsals were in progress.

Because Wieland was quick to recognize that his designs for the 1951 *Ring*, when translated into stage terms, fell short of his original conception and did not measure up to what he had achieved in *Parsifal*, he later forbade any photographs of them to be published. It was not until the publication of a historical survey such as Dietrich Mack's *Der Bayreuther Inszenierungsstil*, which appeared in the *100 Jahre Bayreuther Festspiele* series, or of Walter Erich Schäfer's book, that their documentary evidence of my brother's gradual development as a stage designer became accessible.

Because of financial constraints and the renewed public irritation it would inevitably have provoked, there was, of course, no immediate prospect of Wieland's staging an entirely new and appropriately avant-garde production of *The Ring* based on the lessons he had learned in 1951. He therefore resolved that the programme for 1952 should include a third production of his *Tristan*, in addition to *The Ring* and *Parsifal*. *Tristan* had always been regarded as technically easy and inexpensive to stage, discounting the difficulty of casting the title roles. I was thus taken unawares by the result of yet another plan concocted in the seclusion of Wahnfried when Wieland flatly informed me that he intended to mount a new production of *Tristan* with Herbert von Karajan conducting.

Although I might reasonably have expected that, having forgone a production of my own in 1951, I would be granted one in the following year, I concurred with his plan because I thought it desirable to allow him to express himself better through the medium of another work than he had managed to do in 1951. I did not, however, conceal my misgivings.

For one thing, engaging Karajan to conduct yet another new production would appreciably complicate our plan to enlist Furtwängler. For another, being convinced that Karajan would inevitably break with Bayreuth, I preferred him to do so in the already 'proven' Wieland/Karajan context rather than in collaboration with me – not that I ever sought such a collaboration – because the blame would automatically have been laid at my door. When conducting the second *Ring* cycle in 1951, Karajan had achieved only a limited degree of co-operation with Wieland. The breach I feared seemed unavoidable because, on the one hand, neither Karajan nor Walter Legge could be granted primacy in the matter of casting, and, on the other, the festival's singular structure made it impossible for Karajan ever to dominate the management as he subsequently did at Salzburg. I later found tangible evidence of my supposition that this was his secret aim. We could not afford to give our leading associates secretaries of their own, so Karajan's correspondence was handled by my secretarial staff. He not only used the Bayreuth Festival letterhead but inserted the word

'Management' at the top. I made this remarkable discovery when the festival was over because he had left all the file copies behind.

Because of our experiences with conductors in 1951 and the fact that *Tristan* had already been assigned to Karajan, which was a handicap, the second post-war festival was subject to several changes. Although Hans Knappertsbusch had declined to participate in a letter dated 30 August 1951, immediately after the first festival ended, Wieland, the 'desecrator' of the Grail forest, managed to re-enlist him early in December, not only for the 1952 *Parsifal* but also, as a kind of sop, for *Die Meistersinger*. Karajan had not conducted the last performance of that work in 1951, even though he had contracted to do so, claiming that he had to attend a festival concert in Lucerne. It was strange that this had occurred to him so suddenly and belatedly, the more so since it transpired that he was not even in Lucerne at the time in question.

The last performance was given for the trade union federation, which was accorded one closed performance in 1951 and two from 1952 onwards, a tradition that survives to this day. This idea, which had played a major role in our deliberations prior to reopening the festival, for instance at the inaugural meeting of the 'Association of Friends', was an integral part of our plans. Apart from the beneficiaries of the bursary foundation co-founded by Richard Wagner, other, broader sections of the population were to be afforded an opportunity to attend the festival in accordance with its original conception.

As previously mentioned, the production of a worthy recording of *Die Meistersinger* was presenting problems. Knappertsbusch, who had conducted the last performance of the work in 1951 and knew that there had been a lack of co-ordination between the stage and the orchestra, particularly in the 'Awake!' chorus, was moved to make the following suggestion: 'Legge can now do what he couldn't do before and incorporate the recording of my performance in Karajan's record.'

Knappertsbusch and Karajan ... I am reminded of a bizarre little incident that occurred in 1951 and perfectly exemplifies the mordant humour and sarcasm so characteristic of 'Kna'. Karajan and Maximilian Kojetinsky were down in the orchestra pit, playing four-handed for a *Ring* rehearsal. Knappertsbusch was conducting – an exceptional circumstance in itself, given his dislike of rehearsing. The rehearsal ended and the maestro made his way down to the third level of our pit, which descends in tiers. Karajan, one hand on the piano, stood looking up at his considerably taller confrère in the expectation that he would say something appreciative to the two pianists. Knappertsbusch merely gave his fellow *Ring* conductor an appreciative pat on the back and said, 'If there's a coach's job going begging somewhere, I'll put in a good word for you.'

Another minor recollection: Knappertsbusch, whom someone had irritated by remarking that Herr von Karajan conducted without a score, snapped, '*I* can read music.'

Because exalted personages do not feel that their status has been properly acknowledged unless they are assigned a WC of their own, it went without saying that Herbert von Karajan coveted one all to himself. One of my responsibilities was the allocation of quarters to festival participants, but in those days we could provide a sitting-room with separate WC for only *one* conductor. My brother, to whom Karajan had made several representations on the subject, urged me to find an appropriate solution. In the end I had to give way and devise an arrangement that would fittingly acknowledge Herr von Karajan's importance, above and beyond his artistic status, by investing him with the distinction of a separate WC in which to relieve himself in undisturbed seclusion. I could only grant his wish by reserving him one of the few WCs near the musicians' room on the first floor, or immediately above our office. I had his name put on the door, installed a new lock, and gave him the only key to it. Knappertsbusch, who was always well informed despite his air of detachment, one day deemed it necessary to make a detour on the way to his ground-floor room in the Festspielhaus. Instead of entering by the garden door as usual, he led his retinue past the porter, up the stairs, through the musicians' room, and past the said WCs. There he briefly paused for thought before commenting on the festival management's 'WC policy' as follows: 'Ah, so this is Herbert von Karajan's WC.' Then, indicating the other WCs, he added, 'And those are for the other arseholes.'

Knappertsbusch again, to an assistant of my brother's, who had worn a conspicuously garish checked flannel shirt for so many days on end that even the maestro could not fail to notice: 'Tell me, Hager, who's wearing your *clean* shirts?'

Sharing *The Ring* between two conductors did not have a very salutary effect, particularly on the singers, although, according to a *bon mot* that went the rounds at the time, the best performances were obtained when Karajan rehearsed and Knappertsbusch conducted in the evening. A conductor had therefore to be found for *The Ring* in 1952, and we managed to get Joseph Keilberth.

On the recommendation of Astrid Varnay, whose artistry had won our complete confidence, and who was fully aware of her responsibility in putting his name forward, we engaged Ramon Vinay to sing Tristan. Our ensemble was also joined by Hans Hotter and Gustav Neidlinger in the role of Kurwenal. We had two highly dramatic Isoldes at our disposal in the persons of Astrid Varnay and Martha Mödl, and since Leonie Rysanek had turned down Wieland's offer of Brangäne, as I have already mentioned, her place was taken by Ira Malaniuk, who had already proved herself at Bayreuth in 1951. The above singers were joined in the role of King Marke by Ludwig Weber, who had sung Hagen, Gurnemanz and Fasolt in the opening year.

Much ill feeling arose during the rehearsals for *Tristan*, notably between Karajan and Ramon Vinay, because of the former's rehearsal technique. Unbridled in later years, Karajan's predilection for conducting even stage rehearsals with the aid of recordings was already assuming absurd dimensions. In order to rehearse the soloist and impart a musical message that accorded with his own ideas, Karajan would interrupt him after the second or third bar, not just at the end of a phrase. Vinay's nerves became so frayed that he begged us to persuade Karajan to abandon this procedure. Things reached such a pass during one of the orchestra stage rehearsals that Vinay fled from Karajan's baneful presence by scrambling through a window and vaulting a fence. It took a great deal of laborious diplomacy to establish at least a tolerable working relationship between Vinay and Karajan and enable *Tristan* to be premièred as originally cast. However, the maestro's decision to turn his back on Bayreuth for ever was undoubtedly triggered by our injunction to desist from rehearsing singers with the aid of recordings, and also by his realization that he would never attain the omnipotence to which he aspired.

The infallible Karajan sustained his deepest wound and most manifest defeat in the orchestra pit itself. Having abandoned the long-established seating plan based on Wagner's practical experience and rearranged the musicians to suit himself, he was compelled to retract this decision in time for the première. As is often done in opera houses with open pits, he had put all the strings on the right and all the wind instruments on the left. Although this produced a terrible travesty of the celebrated Bayreuth sound, he flatly refused to accept that his seating arrangements were a failure and retained them for the dress rehearsal itself.

A conference took place at Wahnfried on the morning of the première, and for once – I suppose because there were chestnuts to be extracted from the fire – it was held in my presence and with my participation. My brother expected me to ward off the threat of disaster by doing what it was not my place to do: deliver the judgement of Solomon that would restrain Karajan from ruining the whole performance by persisting with his experiment. Although my arguments did not immediately fall on fertile ground and elicit an admission of failure, we were reassured to note, an hour and a half before curtain-up, that the orchestra attendants were restoring the music stands to the places they had occupied when Wilhelm Furtwängler or Victor de Sabata was conducting. This time, at least, Karajan had been compelled to acknowledge that he was not infallible after all.

Karajan had agreed to return in 1953 after his last *Tristan* performance in 1952, but I mistrusted this specious truce – and rightly so, because the very next day, 26 August 1952, a message from Munich transformed his acceptance into a refusal. He had doubtless conferred in the meantime with his public relations and financial adviser, Walter Legge.

For all that, the *Tristan* had achieved something. Better than the preceding *Ring*, it conveyed my brother's innovative intentions with regard to Bayreuth and lent them visible expression on the stage.

However, this production attained its true effect by degrees, after the requisite changes had been effected on a materially sustainable basis. His two guest presentations of *The Ring* at Naples in March 1952 and April 1953 afforded him another excellent opportunity to try out various experiments, and it was the lessons he learned from these that enabled him to evolve his own form of interpretative stage design at Bayreuth. From 1954 onwards there emerged into full view that which has since become thought of, and rooted in the consciousness of the world at large, as Wieland Wagner's interpretation of *The Ring*.

On 13 April 1953, immediately after the second Naples guest appearance ended with *Siegfried* and *Götterdämmerung*, Knappertsbusch sent Wieland a letter revoking his agreement to conduct the two *Ring* cycles and *Parsifal* in 1953. This move was obviously prompted by Wieland's progressive abandonment of *Ring* traditionalisms, and by a continuing inability to appreciate his scenic interpretation of *Parsifal*. My brother tried to talk him round, but on 1 May 1953 he received the following telegram: 'Dear Wieland, I want to take all the sting out of our split-up, which I hope is only temporary, so I beg you to come to terms with the step I have taken. As soon as the spirit of Richard Wagner moves back into the Festspielhaus, I shall be the first to return.'

Joseph Keilberth was the only one of the previous year's conductors who mounted the podium in 1953. Karajan was replaced as the conductor of *Tristan* by Eugen Jochum. Keilberth not only collaborated with me on my first new production at Bayreuth, *Lohengrin*, but, being an experienced *Ring* conductor, undertook the first cycle of the tetralogy. For the second cycle and *Parsifal* my brother engaged Clemens Krauss, whom he had known and heard while studying painting and music in Munich during the war, and whom he considered a worthy replacement for Knappertsbusch. Krauss conducted at Bayreuth only once, as it turned out, because any more permanent connection with the festival was precluded by his untimely death in Mexico City on 16 May 1954. It was, however, abundantly clear from Krauss's behaviour in 1953 that his Karajanesque claims to omnipotence would have made his collaboration with my brother an awkward one.

My brother had engaged Igor Markevitch to conduct the new production of *Tannhäuser* in 1954. The reason why his name appeared in the brochure for that year but not on the programme itself was as follows. The positions imposed by the producer and choreographer in regard to the pilgrims' choruses, which are notoriously difficult to handle, and, more importantly, when the guests enter the Wartburg, introduced complications that not only hindered smooth co-ordination between stage and orchestra but rendered it quite impossible. One piano rehearsal – which is always easier for the chorus master and his assistants to direct on stage than an orchestral rehearsal – lasted from 3 p.m. until 2 a.m., with only two one-hour breaks, and was predominantly devoted to working with the chorus, who had already spent over two hours rehearsing on their own that morning. The timing of their movements, as my brother envisioned them, was incompatible with the musical tempi favoured by Markevitch, who kept demanding that Wieland respect his judgement. In view of the fact that Knappertsbusch had been persuaded to return in 1954, and that Knappertsbusch was just as widely respected, it seemed quite absurd that Markevitch, a man esteemed and famed for his accurate renditions of the most difficult modern music, should have been unable to cope with his allotted task.

It finally emerged in the course of an orchestra rehearsal on 16 July 1954 that the stage/orchestra problems were insurmountable. A mood of increasing depression, indeed, total resignation, descended on all concerned: Markevitch, Wieland, the soloists, and – most of all – Wilhelm Pitz, who was responsible for *Tannhäuser*'s exceedingly difficult choruses. Something had to be done. In the end we thought it opportune to enlist the help of Markevitch's wife in finding him a way out that would be universally acceptable and, thus, honourable. A slipped disk seemed an adequate reason for him to stand down, so the conflict was solved both plausibly and contractually.

That left us with the problem of who was to conduct *Tannhäuser* in Markevitch's place. Very little time remained before the première, which was scheduled for 22 July 1954, and the production, sets and costumes could not, of course, be modified at this late stage, so who would take over this 'finished article'? Knappertsbusch, who had just been wooed back for *Parsifal,* was a non-starter as far as *Tannhäuser* was concerned. So was Furtwängler, who had been heartened by Karajan's departure and enticed into contemplating a genuine, long-term commitment to Bayreuth by being invited to conduct a recent performance of Beethoven's Ninth. As things stood, the only two possible candidates were Joseph Keilberth and Eugen Jochum. Wieland was very anxious to engage Keilberth, but without, of course, offending Jochum. Negotiations between the four of us – Wieland, Keilberth, Jochum, and me – got nowhere at first because the two conductors persisted in exchanging compliments and urging each other to take the job. As so often in awkward situations of this type, Wieland suddenly excused himself on the grounds that he was late for a rehearsal, leaving me to settle the matter. Fortunately, things turned out as Wieland hoped.

Fifteen minutes after the meeting had broken up Keilberth came and informed me that he would be unable to conduct the last performance of *Tannhäuser* because of an absolutely irrefrangible engagement in Lucerne. Being as reluctant as Jochum to take on an additional work, he doubtless hoped to wriggle out of it altogether, but his final attempt failed. I asked him to let our agreement stand until shortly before the last performance, when I was sure that a *deus ex machina* would appear in the nick of time. And so it did – in the person of Eugen Jochum.

I should mention, while on the subject of musical directors and our turbulent dealings with them, that we engaged André Cluytens as well as Joseph Keilberth for *Tannhäuser* in 1955. This was to prepare him to conduct the new production of *Die Meistersinger* planned for 1956 by familiarizing him with the theatre's peculiar acoustics.

There was a curious prelude to my new *Holländer* production in 1955, the six performances of which were shared between Knappertsbusch and Keilberth. A rumour was circulating in the theatre that I intended to engage an entirely new young conductor who had been unaffected by the way in which the ball had been batted to and fro by the others. One day during the festival season of 1954 there came a knock at my office door and a peculiar duo filed in: big, burly Knappertsbusch, wearing his usual broad-brimmed *borsalino*, followed by the thickset and considerably shorter figure of Keilberth. In view of the above rumour, Knappertsbusch felt called upon to make the following announcement: 'I'll conduct *Holländer* for you next year. Keilberth will handle all the musical rehearsals and the last three performances, I'll take the dress rehearsal and the first three. *Auf wiedersehen,* Herr Wagner.' And out they strode.

Their combined operation was all the more remarkable because they had no great love for each other. Knappertsbusch used to refer to Keilberth as 'Keilberg' and pronounce that misnomer as if it were hyphenated ['Wedge-Mountain']. As for Keilberth, many was the hour I had to spend with him after evening rehearsals, helping him to recover from 'Knappertsbusch cramp'. Once, when I had unsuccessfully tried to relieve him of his car keys after he had not only consumed seven consoling *Bocksbeutel* – almost five litres of white wine – but proposed to have a nightcap at *Die Eule*, a musicians' favourite haunt, I telephoned the police. Instead of formally confiscating his keys, they sandwiched his Volkswagen between two patrol cars with flashing blue lights and guided him to the nearest parking lot.

(One looks back regretfully on the days when the arm of the law extended a helping hand instead of a breathalyser!) The proprietress of the *Eule* was obviously more persuasive than I, because I later learned that she had managed to take Keilberth's keys into safe keeping.

In spite of his initially harsh and critical remarks about Wieland, Knappertsbusch returned to Bayreuth every year except 1953, prompted in the main by his extreme veneration for Richard Wagner's synthesis of the arts. He last conducted there in 1964. Ill health compelled him to stand down in 1965, and he died in October of that year.

We did not find it easy to re-enlist him as the conductor of *Parsifal* in 1954. His minimum demand was that Wieland comply with our grandfather's original intention and show the dove hovering above the Grail at the conclusion of Act III. My brother was at first in two minds whether to adopt this suggestion, which went against the grain with him, or to dispense with Knappertsbusch's services. Eventually, after much deliberation, we hit on an ingenious solution to this ornithological problem: the dove was lowered from the gridiron just far enough for Knappertsbusch to see it from the podium but not far enough for it to be visible from the auditorium. After the performance Knappertsbusch and his wife celebrated his return to Bayreuth with some friends. 'So Wieland showed the dove again at last!' he said contentedly. His wife, who always sat in the front row of the stalls when he was conducting, looked puzzled. 'But Hans,' she said, '*I* didn't see any dove.' The maestro shook his head impatiently. 'You women are always so damned unobservant,' he growled. His suspicions must have been aroused, however, because subsequent inquiries confirmed that he had been the victim of a deception. Thereafter, 'that scoundrel Wieland' resumed its place among his stock phrases.

To begin with, however, Joseph Keilberth was our 'anchor man' for 1954. In spite of the strained relations between him and Knappertsbusch, we had somehow to persuade the former that the latter was needed again. The unexpected death of Clemens Krauss in May left us little time, so we quickly arranged a meeting at which Keilberth would, so I prophesied to Wieland just beforehand, broach the subject himself and say, 'Gentlemen, you have no choice but to recall Knappertsbusch.' Before he came to Bayreuth on 24 May 1954 we privately discussed how best to coax him into suggesting the Knappertsbusch solution, and our powers of persuasion must have been pretty effective. After only a few minutes, Keilberth said (and I quote his exact words), 'Gentlemen, you have no choice but to recall Knappertsbusch.' Temporarily suppressing the delight of a prophet whose prediction has been fulfilled to the letter, I suggested that the simplest course would be to call Knappertsbusch right away. I got through at once, almost as if my call had been expected. Although the phone was answered by Marion, the maestro's wife, I could tell that he was right beside her because I heard him grumble that he wanted nothing more to do with Bayreuth, least of all with Wieland. Marion, who did her best to mediate, kept insisting that it was Wolfgang on the phone, not Wieland, and that what was at stake was Richard Wagner's Bayreuth. After growling a while longer, Knappertsbusch took the receiver from her, and the upshot was that he agreed to meet us in Munich that same evening. It proved to be a typically Knappertsbuschian occasion.

I drove to Munich without Wieland, to be on the safe side, and turned up at our rendezvous, Walterspiel's restaurant in the Hotel Vier Jahreszeiten, where I found the maestro at his favourite corner table with a boyhood friend whom he introduced as a complete dunce, but one who was now General Motors' sole distributor for New York City and State and a millionaire to boot. Then, despite his wife's attempts to restrain him, he proceeded to attack my brother for his sins of commission and omission in respect of Richard Wagner, a stream of invective that culminated in his condemning 'that scoundrel Wieland' for having engaged 'that arch-Nazi Clemens Krauss'. Although I succeeded, with the help of his wife and his schoolfriend, in mollifying him sufficiently to extract an undertaking that he would return to Bayreuth, he kept on blurting out how weak-minded it was of him to go back there.

In the end, being a great devotee of champagne and caviare, he decided to extend a visible token of his personal goodwill by ordering me a large helping of caviare in addition to the liquid refreshment already on the table. I tried to reduce this to a small helping, but he wouldn't hear of it. 'No, make it a large one,' he called after the waiter in a voice so stentorian that no one in the restaurant could have failed to hear. 'At Walterspiel's the large ones are small ones anyway!' I could not, unfortunately, do as much justice to the vintage champagne as I should have liked because I had to drive back to Bayreuth the same night.

Knappertsbusch continued to conduct there without further interruption until 1964, as I have already said. The only year in which he did not conduct every *Parsifal* was 1957, when, being preoccupied with several cycles of *The Ring*, among other things, he relinquished a few performances to André Cluytens. The latter was universally liked for his amiable, open-minded attitude, and Knappertsbusch was visibly delighted when Cluytens asked him to introduce him to *Parsifal*. The outcome was a *Parsifal* of even longer duration than Knappertsbusch's.

Wieland collaborated so smoothly with Cluytens that he invited him to conduct the new, 1958 production of *Lohengrin* in the celebrated blue setting with the swan by Ewald Mataré. It was for personal reasons that Cluytens left Bayreuth thereafter and returned only once more, in 1965, to conduct *Parsifal* and *Tannhäuser*.

The reason why my brother changed conductors so often was, I think, that he was always hoping to find – and settle permanently on – *the* conductor who would measure up to his scenic ideas. In 1959 he entrusted *Die Meistersinger* to Erich Leinsdorf and *Lohengrin* to Lovro von Matacic. The following year he gave renewed proof of his motivation by splitting *Lohengrin* between Ferdinand Leitner and Lorin Maazel, and in 1961 Josef Krips took over *Die Meistersinger*.

From festival conductors to the festival chorus. We first considered appointing Hermann Lüddecke of Berlin to the important post of chorus master, but failed to conclude a contract with him. In the course of a business conference with Herbert von Karajan, the latter recommended Wilhelm Pitz, with whom he had worked very closely during his seven years at Aachen. Before we ourselves got in touch with him, we asked Karajan to give him some indication of what we had in mind. This he did by telegram on 30 January 1950. The same day, on my own and my brother's behalf, I wrote to Pitz and inquired if he would be willing to take charge of the festival chorus. He came to see us in Bayreuth on 4 February, only a few days later, and our rapport was so immediate and so spontaneous that we signed him at once. Owing to the time that had elapsed since the last festival, and to the fact that the German population had been scattered and dispersed by the ravages of war, we had no reservoir of proven choral singers to draw on. Our new chorus master had therefore to pick out a number of singers, male and female, from which we could jointly make our final selection.

Erna and Wilhelm Pitz auditioned no less than 900 singers from forty theatres in East and West Germany and travelled 9000 kilometres by train in the process – an average of ten kilometres per singer. We eventually exchanged contracts with a hundred of these aspirants, and our new chorus master led them on to heights that were to earn the Bayreuth Festival chorus a legendary reputation. Because our hundred singers had, by general request, to be augmented for the festival meadow scene in *Die Meistersinger*, the male chorus in *Götterdämmerung*, and the performance of Beethoven's Ninth Symphony, Wilhelm Pitz and his wife visited Bayreuth on 3 and 4 March 1951 and held a mass audition in the parish hall. Such was the response to an appeal we had issued on 24 February that all of 458 eager Bayreuthers were auditioned with Pitz himself at the piano. It was a very gratifying mark of the local inhabitants' interest in the reopening of the festival, and competition was so intense that membership of the requisite choruses could be determined on a highly selective basis.

We discovered when the festival chorus first assembled in the shored-up wooden hall known as the 'Rüdelheim', so called after the celebrated chorus master Hugo Rüdel, who had worked at Bayreuth from 1906 to 1934, that some ten per cent of those present were known to us from earlier years. We were also pleased to note, when they first rehearsed on stage, that they had a firm grasp of what was required of them visually and histrionically.

This method of choral recruitment, though innovative at the time, is now current practice where scouting trips are concerned. The task is somewhat easier today, of course, because we have an existing foundation on which to build and no longer have to start almost from scratch.

Immediately after the inaugural concert in 1951, Wilhelm Pitz was glowingly complimented on his singers' performance by Furtwängler, who said that such a highly qualified ensemble ought really to work together all year round. This, of course, was a utopian suggestion. Hans Knappertsbusch always addressed Pitz as 'Hugo' – a special token of regard, because he considered Hugo Rüdel the greatest chorus master ever.

Among the many applicants for a place in the revived festival, when it began to take shape, were 519 orchestral musicians. The exceptional circumstances of the time meant that continuity had also been lost where the composition of the festival orchestra was concerned, and one of my allotted tasks, in accordance with the division of labour between Wieland and me, was to assemble it. The majority of the new applicants were unknown to me, of course, so I had to find some way of solving this problem. I duly consulted various conductors and musicians of my acquaintance and asked them to brief me on individual applicants or suggest instrumentalists who might be suitable candidates for Bayreuth. The sixty-one musicians from earlier festival years were relatively easy to select; the remaining ninety I found through Bernhard Hübner, who had recruited the RIAS Light Orchestra [in the American sector of Berlin] and was experienced in this form of activity. Hübner had been recommended to me as an orchestral director by Professor Jakobs, the trombonist and bass trumpeter. I trusted the latter's judgement because I had often observed an orchestra at work by sitting beside him in the 'mystic abyss', armed with a score, during my apprenticeship in Berlin, and, above all, during the phase when I was eager to learn about the musician's place in the Bayreuth scheme of things. His ability as a wind instrumentalist and the relaxed, unschoolmasterish way in which he imparted the valuable fruits of his experience were sufficient reason, from my point of view, to accept his recommendation and engage Bernhard Hübner. It very soon became clear to me, as he gradually put the festival orchestra together, that Hübner possessed all the skill and mental agility his task demanded. I had no hesitation, as time went by, in leaving it more and more to him to examine the qualifications of individual musicians and consult conductors on the suitability of the instrumentalists recommended by them. He managed to fill all the positions and submit his own recommendations in good time, so that Wieland and I could sign final contracts with each individual musician. The Bayreuth Festival orchestra, which was specifically composed of willing volunteers, had thus been resurrected.

Furtwängler was as satisfied with the quality of the orchestra as he had been with that of the singers, and Knappertsbusch solemnly pronounced it 'miraculous'. After the first festival, when we were discussing what had been achieved and where room for improvement remained, he made the following appreciative and illuminating remark: 'All the musicians you engaged were excellent, but next year you'd better drop the ones I recommended.' Karajan, on the other hand, was careful not to express an opinion because he could not make up his mind whether it would be good policy for him, as the would-be 'boss' of the whole enterprise, to stress its special or unique qualities before he took it over. This reticence was rather uncharacteristic of him, as one of his favourite sayings demonstrates: 'If *we* don't tell people we're good, who will?'

In conclusion, I must say at least a few words about Bayreuth's own contribution to the festival.

Germany's so-called economic miracle was a consequence of several things: the Marshall Plan, the integration of the three western zones of occupation into the Federal Republic in 1949, and the deterioration in East-West relations that led to the Cold War. In my view, therefore, we paradoxically owed our sometimes over-affluent existence to communism.

The municipality of Bayreuth was confronted by some extremely grave problems prior to the reopening of the festival. With more than one-third of its residential and commercial buildings in ruins, it had somehow to house up to 16,000 refugees and displaced persons in addition to the townsfolk themselves. It was only thanks to the inhabitants' determination to rebuild their town, the gradual upturn in business activity associated with it, and the growth of economic stability promoted by the currency reform, that Bayreuth was able to accommodate festival participants and visitors within its walls. My brother and I were delighted to find, having conducted a private and confidential poll of our own, that Bayreuthers were as willing as ever to accommodate visitors to 'their' festival. The municipality and its citizens gave us a vote of confidence wholly comparable with the one that Wagner had been privileged to receive from them in the 1870s. The question of accommodation presented immense problems, almost unimaginable today, which could only be surmounted by the closest co-operation between the festival management and the municipal authorities. Even the occupants of the restaurant and chorus buildings, which had been requisitioned as refugee and transit camps, were housed elsewhere to enable those premises to be restored to their original use. Without ignoring the problems of the post-war period, we and the town succeeded in doing a great deal to make our festival visitors feel at home once more.

Conscious of our entire responsibility for what lay ahead, we waited for an international public to confirm that any suspicion of Bayreuth's re-establishment as a chauvinistic 'hoard' à la Alberich should be dismissed out of hand.

9

TWO RINGS

In 1958, when it was still possible to make detailed plans for the next year's festival during the current season, something novel and – to me, at least – unexpected happened: my brother felt that his creative development of *The Ring* had spent itself, and that he could not undertake the cast changes he had desired and intended. I was therefore expected to conjure a complete new *Ring* into existence in less than a year.

There was an agreement between us that, before enlisting the services of other producers, each of us should express his artistic ideas by staging two new Bayreuth productions of our grandfather's works. I had not, however, expected such an abrupt and unheralded confrontation with *The Ring*, which came like a bolt from the blue. It was quite impossible for me to meet the practical and administrative demands of such a project or put a new cast together in barely ten months, let alone evolve the different interpretations that were expected of me where stage design and artistic approach were concerned, so I not unnaturally requested another twelve months in which to prepare. Wieland had, after all, had eight evolutionary years in which to educate the public in his ideas, which were now regarded as exemplary.

We agreed to rest *The Ring* for a year. Wieland would be represented in 1959 by *Parsifal, Die Meistersinger, Lohengrin,* and a new production of *Der Fliegende Holländer*, while I would present my *Tristan*. By repeating the latter I would be breaking the biennial cycle that had obtained hitherto, but this was justified by public interest in the work – and anyway, the pattern had already been disrupted by Wieland's repetition of his 1956 *Meistersinger*.

I had produced *The Ring* in Venice in 1957, but conditions at La Fenice were so entirely different that the experience I had gained there furnished no grounds for agreeing to stage a Bayreuth production at such short notice. The Fenice is not a *Ring* theatre in the Wagnerian sense, so I was governed by a set of rules that had nothing in common with the ideals and practicalities of scenic reproduction to which my grandfather had aspired at Bayreuth. For my own production there I naturally hoped to make use of facilities far more extensive than those available in Venice. The Fenice's practical, technical and artistic limitations had not been such as to remind me of Bayreuth or awaken any ambition to produce something Bayreuthian, nor had I been able, for want of time, to try out the soloists. That I nevertheless succeeded in staging *The Ring* for an appreciative Venetian audience was due in large measure to the co-operation of the general administrator, Virgilio Mortare, and the conductor, Franz Konwitschny. I was also assisted by one or two experienced technicians whom I had brought with me from Bayreuth to ensure that things went smoothly, and, last but not least, by an excellent cast whose selection had owed nothing to my influence. All else apart, the canals, palaces and inhabitants of tourist-free, out-of-season Venice combined to make my stay there a great and memorable experience.

The cultural history of the West has known nothing comparable in scale to *Der Ring des Nibelungen* since the heyday of Attic tragedy. It heaps one drama on another to produce a world tragedy that unfolds, with the inexorability ordained by fate, on three levels of creation. At Bayreuth I endeavoured with the aid of modern technology, and of lighting in particular, to render its symbolism intelligible and bring it into the domain of human reality.

The symbolic shape underlying my interpretation of *The Ring* at Bayreuth in 1960 was a concave disk representing the world in its intact state: the divine sphere as opposed to the convex, repellent world of Alberich.

These initially abstract considerations helped me to arrive at a stage design. I got a joiner to turn me a concave-convex disk whose dimensions were almost proportionate to those of the finished steel structure on a scale of 1:50. This I cut into three sectors and two segments so that I could, while retaining the circular shape, experiment with an infinite number of juxtapositions, varying the components' height and angle of inclination to create areas of activity that would correspond to the course of the action. In addition, a mobile ram or piston beneath the central point, which necessitated the installation of special machinery in the trap room, made it possible still further to vary the relative positions of the five components, which, when fitted together, summoned up a picture of the earth floating above a dark void. By juxtaposing them in different ways I was able to create formations analogous to the development of the plot. Breaks between them signified rock scenes and spaces were bounded by vertical architectonic elements, as for instance in Hunding's hut, Mime's cave, and the scene between Siegfried and the Wanderer. At the end of *Götterdämmerung* the terrestrial disk closed again and regained its original integrity. I had intended, during the final bars, to show a young, naked couple lying on it, but this idea was considered too audacious by contemporary standards and had to be abandoned.

The lighting accorded with my structural arrangement of surfaces. I had already pressed on with the development and application of large-scale lighting equipment and experimented with the projection of chromatically intense shadows in *Lohengrin, Holländer*, and *Tristan*, my previous Bayreuth productions. This enabled me to use the cyclorama and lighting in an interpretative manner, so that in the 'false Gunther' and 'spear oath' scenes, for instance, their element of drama and brutality was visually expressed by the projection of a jagged black structure on a sulphur-yellow background.

The xenon lamp came closest to the sunlight spectrum at this period, and did not, like halogen or incandescent lamps, shed a warmer light when turned down, but merely dimmed without any alteration in chromatic values. (The final ten per cent can only be mechanically controlled, unfortunately, even today.) This also made it possible to convey an entirely different message in terms of the colour of costumes and make-up.

Kurt Palm and I collaborated closely on the costumes, which, like the surface area and lighting, accorded with my strongly outlined and geometrical scheme of things. The figures, down to their make-up and foam plastic wigs, designed by Willi Klose, were synchro-optically adapted to the lighting, and their colour corresponded to their status in the overall proceedings, Siegfried and Brünnhilde being the palest couple. Side lighting had often been used to excess in the past. I myself could not employ it because of the way the acting area was structured, nor did I wish to because, in my opinion, it robs the singers of three-dimensionality.

Models scaled up to twice the original size enabled my intentions and needs to be discerned in ever greater detail, so the customary technical rehearsals could begin in the autumn of 1959. Because the individual components were marked, these tests helped to preclude the modifications that so often occasioned unwelcome additional costs when scenery came to be built in the workshops.

As I envisaged it, the set could only be constructed of steel. Since the Festspielhaus did not at this time possess the requisite workshops, machinery and craftsmen, we employed a firm that had moved to Bayreuth's new industrial estate and was able, after taking account of all the set's static specifications, to weld it together out of structural steel. Paul Eberhardt, who was then in charge of all our technical operations, showed a regrettable disregard of my wishes and requirements, with the result that grave and unforeseen problems arose when the structure was installed. The mobility I had been promised, in particular, was not only less than satisfactory – as Eberhardt himself saw during a rehearsal – but downright dangerous.

As so often when the unforeseen happens, chance came to the rescue – this time in the person of a garage owner who had heard of my problem. One day, while I was filling my car, he mentioned a builder of fairground rides whose products, which incorporated hydraulic systems, were widely admired. I at once got in touch with this man, whose name was Völker, and he managed to solve all my mobility problems in a remarkably short space of time, despite the difficulty of procuring the special hydraulic systems required. Herr Völker not only took charge of all disk-moving operations during the three weeks preceding the première but operated the controls at every performance. This made a theatrical reality out of what many of the Festspielhaus staff had dismissed as a crackpot idea.

Early in May 1960 I was able, with the aid of sketches and photographs of models, to expound my ideas to a meeting of the Association of Friends of Bayreuth. My work was bound to be regarded with considerable scepticism by them in particular, not least because I planned to replace many of the artists whom they had come to know and like.

Because there were eleven singers available whom Sawallisch and I considered engaging for our 1960 *Ring* – soloists who had not appeared in my brother's *Ring* in recent years but had sung other roles at Bayreuth – we were able to try them out in 1959. Whenever I was present I discussed with them the content of the work and how I conceived it. That is to say, I did so until 4 August 1959, the day on which the man in charge of musical study abandoned *The Ring*'s hard labour in favour of his next year's engagement to conduct *Der Fliegende Holländer*, which was certainly a far easier task.

During my *Ring* production's five-year run I was able, with the active assistance of Herr Völker, to introduce many technical refinements and thereby augment my artistic vocabulary. Further improvements were also made to the new lighting installations.

Years of confrontation with *The Ring* have made me increasingly aware of what Richard Wagner meant to express through the medium of that 'world myth', and, more particularly, of the abiding impression which he, as a 'mythographer' or 'mythopoet', wished to leave on his audiences through the transitory art of the theatre. The meaning and content of his festivals were communicated largely by the peculiar layout of the Festspielhaus itself. He deliberately assigned the role of the ancient Greek chorus, which was drawn up in the circular *orchestra*, to those who performed his symphonic music; in other words, everything that had served to supplement the principal players on the *skene* was transferred to the pit. But, because he did not regard the musicians' visual dimension as part of his *Gesamtkunstwerk* and was solely concerned with what was seen on stage, he took another crucial step. The *orchestra* was the 'technical seat' of the drama. That was why he hid the conductor, the tail-coated, white-tied 'high priest of music', from the audience's view and thereby imbued him with the aura of an unseen demiurge. He was privileged, as it were, to take the elements that develop from *Das Rheingold*'s long, opening E flat, and are subsequently allied with the most varied harmonies, and unite them into something from which could spring the emotional understanding to which Richard Wagner attached so much importance.

The linguistic conformation of *The Ring*'s text, which has been unjustly derided, is an inseparable part of the tetralogy and, in a sense, its intellectually appealing aspect. Though often ridiculed, its alliterative structure was not an eccentric's whim but an artistic aid employed for a specific purpose. It promoted the operatic text or libretto, which had hitherto been pedestrian, even in Richard Wagner's case, to the status of pure poetry, divorcing it from the humdrum and elevating it to a plane on which it acquired new, mythical significance. It was the combination of poetry and music that produced the Wagnerian drama known as *The Ring*, which is not merely a series of four works. It obeyed its own laws from the very first, and the interpreter's task has always been to heed those laws and do justice to them.

It was vividly brought home to me while visiting the magnificent ancient theatre at Epidaurus in 1958 that the shape of an amphitheatre united the audience and eliminated all hierarchical distinctions between them. The special architectonic solution devised for Bayreuth took the form of echeloned proscenium arches which are, so to speak, carried over into the auditorium by the pillared buttresses that flank it. This format, together with the sunken, invisible orchestra, focuses all attention on the stage and sets up an interaction between it and the audience which cannot, in my opinion, be compared with the effect produced by any place of worship or conventional theatre. Thanks not only to the internal arrangement of the Festspielhaus but to the festival hill itself, Bayreuth remains a meeting-place of a very exceptional, if not unique, kind.

On 15 September 1877, or about a year after the first festival, Richard Wagner presented his Bayreuth sponsors with a résumé that still holds good today: 'We have demonstrated our firm resolve to everyone; we have shown what concerns us, why our theatre had to be built like this one, why everything had to be arranged as it is here, why the scene of our activities could not be a centre devoted to modern artistic luxury. Everyone here has felt this, even if he has had objections to contend with. Here we are free to breathe and collect our thoughts.'

In my opinion, one of the reasons why Wagner took so long to carry out his festival scheme at Bayreuth, which he had chosen in conformity with his ideas, was that an artistic statement like *The Ring*, which required the presence of an audience on four successive evenings, necessarily presupposed the willing and enthusiastic participation of the members of that audience. The rhythm of their fourfold experience, which they underwent of their own free will, was determined by its temporal sequence. The conditions imposed by Wagner still exert the same effect today, generating what is specific to Bayreuth. The Bayreuth experience is not compulsory; it does not depend on the prestige of the individual or yield any material benefit. This should be the essence of what is known as the Bayreuth atmosphere, and it is by being in places and buildings that are the visible expressions of an artist's ideas that one truly encounters the Bayreuth phenomenon.

My task, as I have often made clear, has been to preserve Bayreuth's vitality, and it is a task that naturally involves one in reflecting on the nature of its founder, who is commonly described as a monomaniac.

The unique and categorical objective of all Wagner's actions and creative endeavours after the success of his conventional *Rienzi* is indicated not only by his abandonment of that form of operatic expression but by the ever more personal character of his works. He had gained a wealth of experience at Würzburg, Magdeburg, Riga, Königsberg, and Paris, that theatrical Mecca, before settling in Dresden. Thereafter, having taken part in the insurrection of May 1849, he fled into exile in Switzerland, where he shook off his wearisome and debilitating theatrical commitments. It was those periods of artistic reflection that shaped his very personal ideas and visions of what the musical theatre should convey. By October 1851 he had evolved his quadripartite conception of *The Ring*'s poetic text, which he completed on 15 December 1852. Being a practical man of the theatre, he did not tackle such a massive work with the intention that it should be discovered aeons hence, a dusty relic of his secret life's work. He was dominated from the outset by a determination to present it to an audience in keeping with his idea of a 'theatrical mission'. Realizing at the same time that prevailing conditions in the theatre would make it impossible to stage a work lasting fourteen and a half hours – different interpreters have varied its length from 13 hours 39 minutes (Boulez) to 15 hours 20 minutes (Knappertsbusch) – he very soon hit on 'his' festival idea. It was inevitable, given his ever more decisive break with theatrical conventions and his rejection of the generally accepted operatic approach, that he had to take this road alone.

King Ludwig's summons to Munich presented Wagner with an opportunity to complete the tetralogy and have his works performed as he intended. Despite Ludwig's exceptional tokens of friendship, however, it was his almost absolutist attitude – exemplified by his insistence on premièring *Das Rheingold* on 22 September 1869 and *Die Walküre* on 26

June 1870 in defiance of Wagner's wishes – that largely contributed to the collapse of plans for a Munich festival theatre designed by Gottfried Semper in close consultation with Wagner himself. Other factors were the numerous intrigues of the court camarilla and, to a certain extent, Wagner's unbourgeois way of life, which rendered him vulnerable in many ways.

In addition to the first performances of *Tristan und Isolde* on 10 June 1865 and *Die Meistersinger* on 21 June 1868, the following works were performed in Munich: *Der Fliegende Holländer* in 1864 and *Lohengrin* and *Tannhäuser* in 1867. In view of the sets and costumes that dominated these performances, Wagner realized that he would require artistic resources of a different kind to lend his ideas adequate visual expression. Ludwig cultivated Wagner's world of myth and legend in his own way, mainly by building the castles and other edifices so beloved of modern tourists. These 'interpretations', which in my view attain or even transcend the frontiers of kitsch, still distort Wagner's image to this day.

It is likely that the results of the Munich performances were also responsible for Wagner's wish to stage 'exemplary performances' of his works, from *Der Fliegende Holländer* onwards, at Bayreuth, though Cosima's subsequent interpretation of this desire prompted her to employ the Munich productions as her 'models'. Just how harmonious an atmosphere prevailed at the *Lohengrin* performance of 1867 can be inferred from the following description by Oswald G. Bauer: 'The king left! Tikhachek (who sang Lohengrin) left! Wagner left!'

In the case of *The Ring*, that very special work, Wagner wanted to preserve the latitude which only complete freedom could bestow, and that he only attained at Bayreuth in later years. His experience of the first festival in 1876 convinced him that *Parsifal* should not be performed elsewhere, an understandable wish that ultimately confirmed all his theatrical hopes and intentions.

As so often when the true meaning of an artistic statement becomes obscured by tradition or ephemeral value judgements, one has to rediscover its roots. Only thus can its inherent timelessness be restored to life – in my case, visually and acoustically – by means of artistic heightening.

No element of pure theatrical routine must enter into a production of *The Ring*, even today, because its content and message are chronologically and historically indeterminate and cannot, therefore, be pinned down. What matters, as I see it, is to express what is timeless in the work in a way that is intelligible to a modern audience. A painter or sculptor can capture a momentary image, whereas the three-dimensionality of the stage and the additional dimension of sound call for an interplay of movements determined by the work's dramatic, vocal and temporal structure.

The founder of the festival endowed it and his theatre with certain unique peculiarities. In addition to providing scope for individual interpretations, specific forms of rehearsal and experimentation, and a limited programme, these enable one to make the fullest and most effective use of sets, technical aids and materials, and to employ the personnel best suited to fulfilling one's intentions. The results obtained continue to attract enthusiastic and receptive audiences from all over the world. This is another aspect of what I mean by Bayreuth's vitality: it does not 'deliver' evenings at the theatre based on norms laid down by business executives and financial backers.

My brother had hoped, under the wing of Baldur von Schirach, the Nazi governor of Vienna, to pave the way for a Bayreuth *Ring* by staging one with Karl Böhm at the Vienna State Opera in 1945. This collaboration did not materialize until 1965, or twenty years later, Böhm's only previous Bayreuth involvement having been to conduct *Tristan* from 1962 onwards. Wieland's illness and his death in 1966 raised the question of whether Böhm would be willing and able to conduct *The Ring* for another four years in addition to his other, international commitments, and whether he could give the work the continuous and concentrated attention to detail it required from the artistic aspect. It is apparent from a letter Wieland wrote in hospital on 14 July 1966 that he was planning to collaborate with Böhm on another *Tristan* and a film of *Tannhäuser*, plus a recording of the same, and that Böhm was also, if he so desired, to conduct *Die Meistersinger* or at least some performances thereof.

Wieland found it particularly depressing that George London could not be cast as Wotan. He had worked with him on his Cologne *Ring* in 1962 and 1963, which he regarded as a preliminary study for his next production at Bayreuth. London had sung and set standards at Bayreuth since 1951, initially in the role of Amfortas and later in that of the Dutchman as well. My brother, who had made generous cuts for his sake at Cologne, at first cherished the overambitious belief that he could do the same at Bayreuth. He was ultimately compelled to yield to the objections of Karl Böhm, who declared that festival audiences would be outraged by such a proceeding. Despite this, the producer and conductor did agree to make one cut in the new *Ring* of 1965. In its first year the Gutrune scene after the heroic dirge in Act III of *Götterdämmerung* was dropped and Hagen entered immediately, the hiatus being bridged by a drum roll.

It became clear after the first orchestral rehearsal of Act II of *Die Walküre* on 30 June 1965 that George London would have to be replaced. That night, after a full day of rehearsals, I drove to Munich and called on London at his hotel, the Vier Jahreszeiten. He was currently being treated by a well-known ear, nose and throat specialist in the hope that he would recover sufficiently to rejoin the cast. We jointly devised a humane and, from his point of view, innocuous way of explaining to outsiders why he had been dropped.

Because of London's indisposition, Theo Adam took over the role of Wotan four days after his last rehearsal on 30 June, though with the proviso that he could not insist on retaining it if London returned. The possibility of casting another singer in the role of the Wanderer in *Siegfried* had been entertained from the outset, so this was sung by Joseph Greindl.

I set to work on my second *Ring* in 1970 fortified by the experience I had gained while producing my first *Ring* between 1960 and 1964, as well as by some invaluable lessons derived from my brother's production of 1965. I did so in the knowledge that it would mark the end of our own interpretations of the tetralogy, because a fresh start and an entirely novel interpretative approach would be required once my latest production had completed its run.

I acquired a fruitful collaborator in Horst Stein, who had conducted *Parsifal* in 1969 and had worked at Bayreuth between 1952 and 1954. He knew the work well, having assisted Hans Knappertsbusch and Clemens Krauss, and was also familiar with the theatre's peculiarities. Above all, he would be available to work with me continuously throughout my second *Ring*'s six-year run. In 1975 he collaborated with me on my new *Parsifal*, which replaced my brother's. I had resolved in 1973 to drop Wieland's production, which had remained in the repertoire, albeit with modifications, since 1951, and which he had anyway intended to remodel with Pierre Boulez from 1966 onwards. I did so in order to nip the threat of a sterile new 'cult tradition' in the bud.

I felt that certain features of my first *Ring* had not, or not entirely, translated my ideas into an appropriate form. These I now endeavoured to rectify by making substantial changes, particularly of a scenic nature, with the aid of the much improved technical facilities installed between the 1964 and 1965 festivals. During this so-called 'rest' period I put in a new gridiron complete with brail lines, and the stage area, hitherto 20.5 × 20.5 metres, was enlarged to 20.5 × 27 metres; in other words, I gained nearly 3.5 metres on either side. In addition to an acoustically excellent plywood cyclorama, which could be either shifted in its entirety or swivelled in sections to form wings, the enlargement brought considerably improved lighting conditions. The removable cycloramas, which were three-centred, not semicircular, afforded different and better modes of artistic expression. The chief lighting technician, Kurt Winter, had built and experimented with new lighting equipment in our own workshops. These new developments, which I used in my *Ring* from the third year onwards, were subsequently perfected and mass-produced by the Viennese firm of Pani.

Thanks to its lack of colour distortion and with the aid of appropriate lens systems, the HMI (gaseous discharge) lamp facilitated large-scale projections of a luminous efficiency hitherto unattainable. Since the theatre had enough space available in all positions, even for back-lighting from the gridiron, the big apparatus and the mechanical dimmer it required could both be installed. The HMI lamp is non-adjustable, so it still has, even now, to be dimmed with the aid of an elongated sensitometric wedge.

Back-projections from the gridiron yielded lighting of a very different kind. The surface lighting I achieved was as expressive as the most vividly coloured of Emil Nolde's paintings, and performers could be lit by follow spots from the appropriate angle of incidence so that they stood out independently against coloured backgrounds. For the seven-part surface area I had xenon spotlights built which made it possible to achieve special lighting effects. This they did in isolation for the first three years of my *Ring* production and in conjunction with the Pani projectors for the last three.

Walter Huneke, who took over as technical director in 1966, proved a

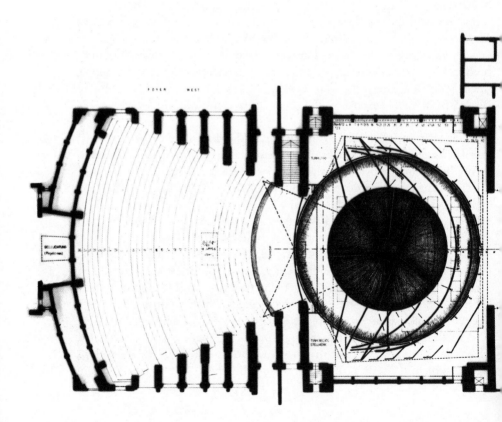

resourceful and energetic collaborator, and an aid to the solution of some interesting and unusual problems.

In rendering my new production of the *Ring* tetralogy and the resumption of my *Meistersinger* artistically valid, I enjoyed the support of Steffen Tiggeler, not only as an assistant producer but as an aid to the fulfilment of all my other functions. He worked for the festival for twenty years.

Once again, I employed a circular disk. Centred on an irregular pentagon, the six sectors into which I divided it differed in shape and dimensions. All of them were mounted on wagons and could be hydraulically rearranged and juxtaposed at a wide variety of heights and angles. I could thus achieve fluctuations in mood by recombining them into a circle or creating more diverse and expressive gaps between them than had been possible in my first *Ring*. The pentagon, a shape possessed of worldwide symbolic significance, formed the centre of the disk, whatever position the outer sectors were in, and provided the area in which the principal action of a scene or act took

Auditorium, orchestra, stage: the components and their planned scenic relationship.

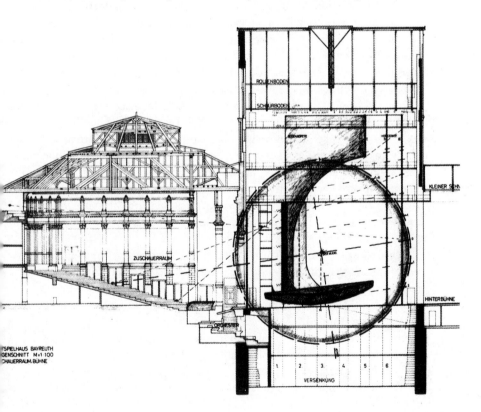

place. Inspired by the echeloned proscenia, I had special shutters built to take the place of the usual curtain. When in the zero position they enabled the disk to float in the dark; when moved simultaneously they faded the stage in and out in a special way. I employed them, for example, for Brünnhilde's concluding moments in *Götterdämmerung* by closing them to such an extent, when the hall of the Gibichungs 'collapsed', that the three-dimensional elements of the set could be removed, unseen by the audience, and all that was visible between the upper and lower shutters was the element of fire. Thereafter they opened fully to reveal – in addition to the flood, the Rhine Maidens regaining the ring, and Hagen drowning – the downfall of Valhalla and the disk's reintegration, symbolizing the dawn of a new and better age.

The genesis and history of *The Ring*, as I have said, are indeterminate. This is a problem, but it also presents an opportunity and incentive to interpret the work into something above and beyond an unquestionably mythical occurrence. The fate of the gods is already sealed in *Das Rheingold*; all that remains to be determined is the timing and magnitude of the disaster to come. It is not Alberich's theft of the Rhine gold that provokes it, but Wotan's offence against Nature. Whether one construes Wotan as the contemporary 'sum of intelligence', a tragic hero, a model of repressive behaviour, or a weary provincial attorney, he is certainly no exalted deity. Wotan represents a world that bears the impress of his own essentially morbid ideology. The music does not run counter to this. Wotan is on the defensive from the first, and his resignation springs from circumstances of his own making. His situation dawns on him in three stages: first in his argument with Fricka, then in his farewell to Brünnhilde, when he renounces his claims to power and pins his hopes on a new era of human love, and finally in his prophecy as the Wanderer. In the end he makes one more attempt to hold back the world with his spear, knowing at the same time that this spear, whose point he does not aim at Siegfried, must be shattered because, being the symbol of a bankrupt system, it may not be handed down to posterity. There is no smooth transition from one generation to the next, only a radical break and a fresh start.

Regrettably, it became more and more customary – even for us of festival management – to supply exegeses and interpretations of *The Ring*. Foremost among these, because it pointed the way and exerted a con-siderable influence on later performances, elsewhere as well, was Hans Mayer's essay entitled '*The Ring* as a bourgeois parable-play', which appeared in our brochure for 1966. Against my better judgement, therefore, I too was compelled to yield to the insistence of everyone, especially the press, and put into words what was visually and musically expressed on the stage.

My brother and I found it increasingly easy, from 1958 onwards, to recruit new interpreters for our Bayreuth productions. When it came to casting *The Ring*, in particular, all the prerequisites existed for introducing singers to new roles, though our unremitting efforts to select interpreters according to their specific aptitudes were not invariably as successful as we would have wished. On the whole, however, we were fortunate in engaging one or two artists who supplemented our ensemble and were worthy of a place alongside its tried and tested members. There was no deliberate attempt to stabilize the *Ring* casts until 1976 and thereafter. It was intended, for instance, that the Boulez/Chéreau/Peduzzi/Schmidt team should be able to work with singers regularly available to them. This would enable the artists to concentrate on their roles and do justice to them without being exposed to a mixture of styles. A work as demanding as *The Ring* lends itself to continuous development for five successive years at most. The aforesaid team accepted this from the outset, and it precluded them from delegating their responsibilities to assistants.

I had already made a great many variations in the cast of my *Ring* during its fifth year, my object being to try out singers for 1976. To prepare for the great centenary as exhaustively as possible, I had decided to present the work for a sixth time. This enabled me to show my future production team one or two singers on stage, thereby demonstrating their capacity for expression and the potentialities of the stage itself, in the hope that this would stimulate their ideas about the forthcoming production.

Although I might reasonably be expected to detail the casts of my two *Ring* productions, it would be unfair of me to omit even one name while seeming to lay special stress on others. It is obvious, on the other hand, that to list them all would exceed the scope of what are primarily autobiographical reminiscences drawn from almost seventy-five years of life. As a producer, I had dealings with only a limited number of singers; as a festival director jointly responsible for other productions of *The Ring*, I was involved with all who took part in them. A complete enumeration, which would illustrate certain lines of development and embody precise statistics, might be desirable but could only be attempted within the context of a large-scale history of the festival, which would also be a history of the Bayreuth ensemble. I have therefore decided to include an appendix that lists all the casts (arranged according to years and roles) not only of my own *Ring* productions but also of all the works I have produced at Bayreuth since 1953 (Appendix II).

I should also like to include a few basic remarks about the casting of festival works. Limited though it is, my tabular compilation not only affords an overview of the singers who took part in my productions on the stage of the Festspielhaus but points up certain continuities and discontinuities in their ranks.

The engagement of singers for Bayreuth is not determined solely by the demands of particular works, but, above all, by the order in which these appear in the festival programme. And this, in turn, is closely bound up with the extent of the demands to be made on the orchestra and chorus and the technical development and difficulty of the works in question – a factor that also applies to the preparatory, rehearsal period. In framing our programmes and determining the frequency with which works are performed, we also take account of public demand. And, needless to say, the whole process is subject to the pressure of financial feasibility.

The Wagnerian works performed at Bayreuth require the services of one highly dramatic and one heroic tenor almost every day. The structure of the works in our programme is such that they all call for Wagnerian voices, as everyone knows, so the best possible casts can be assembled only by striking a balance between various wishes, requirements, and possible courses of action.

After my brother's death I fulfilled my plan to introduce Bayreuth to a variety of interpretations by enlisting one or more production teams with very different artistic intentions and styles. The result was that artists could be so individually attuned to their roles that consistent performances were assured. This entailed a considerable increase in the number of singers engaged.

In addition to any considerations arising from the production aspect, I tried – successfully, in my opinion – to ensure that the prospective conductor closely familiarized every singer with his or her allotted role before work on a production began in earnest. This helped to create a genuine and lasting rapport between stage and orchestra. In contrast to earlier years, which were characterized by very frequent changes of conductors, I strove for continuity in musical direction because I have always felt that the motto of Goethe's theatrical director, 'He who offers much will offer something to many', is particularly inapplicable to Bayreuth.

It sometimes happened, for a wide variety of reasons, that singers were unable or, more rarely, unwilling to complete the long process of mastering a role. Whether artistic or personal, these obstacles to fulfilment occasioned regrettable but unavoidable breaks in continuity.

If my name is coupled with the term 'overall responsibility', this should be taken literally and applies both to casting and to all Bayreuth productions. In other words, my own interpretations of Richard Wagner's works do not enjoy absolute priority, but fall within the general context of what the Bayreuth Festival represents.

Personally, I have always managed to obtain collaborators and assistants who co-ordinated their plans with mine and developed a complete understanding of the overall scheme of things. Of the few who were egoistic enough to claim that their own contribution should take precedence over all else, most dropped out before they really started work at Bayreuth.

Rehearsal periods at Bayreuth are not subject to the pressure of nightly repertory performances, and there are three rehearsal stages of the same size as the main stage. These exceptional facilities, together with a universally perceptible willingness to learn and work hard, make it possible to accomplish more and achieve a greater concentration of effort at the Festspielhaus, perhaps, than at any other theatre. If ever one encounters an inability or reluctance to accept these preconditions, it generally springs from self-assertive egoism, or, in certain cases and to a certain extent, from an insufficient knowledge of the work, which many artists do not, unfortunately, acquire until they actually start rehearsing it. Prior knowledge of the work is essential, and so is a knowledge of what one wishes to convey. If the intended effect is not achieved right away, the 'Bayreuth workshop' makes it possible, always provided one handles the production oneself, to perfect it when the work is repeated in future years.

I should like to make it absolutely clear at this point that I never engage creative personnel – be they producers, conductors, stage and costume designers, or choreographers – unless I feel I can count on them to produce something genuinely novel, interesting, imaginative, original, and as inherently true to the work and intelligible to a modern audience as the Bayreuth Festival demands. The fact that I gladly offer them help and advice based on my many years' experience of Bayreuth, and that they can, if need be, enlist the services of festival staff, should not be confused with 'censorship' or any other kind of regulatory curb on artistic freedom.

10

SPREADING WORD AND SOUND

The Bayreuth Festival's relations with the press merit a chapter of their own.

Having been institutionalized by Cosima Wagner, the festival remained until 1908 a self-reliant and entirely autonomous enterprise that purveyed the master's works to a large, international Wagner community in an ossified form devoid of any historical basis or definite tradition other than that which had been established by artificial means. Although Wagner was far from satisfied with the artistic results of the first festival, as everyone knows, the deficit of some RM150,000 precluded him from revising *The Ring* and restaging it at the Festspielhaus himself, so his hopes of being able to 'do everything differently next year' remained unfulfilled.

At the end of the 1920s, the very different circumstances prevailing since the First World War rendered it desirable to invite critics to Bayreuth and entertain them there.

After the Second World War, generating publicity *prior to* the festival's resumption was not only essential but easy, because leading journalists themselves approached us and expressed an interest in the subject. To publicize the Bayreuth Festival in general and the festival season in particular, we needed someone who knew how to issue critics with complimentary tickets and handle them in the most appropriate way when they turned up. Even if one avoided being over-familiar with them, one could not afford to ignore their individual peculiarities.

We were right in thinking that young Walter Eichner would prove to be the man for the job of press officer, because he performed his duties to our entire satisfaction from 1951 until 1959. On behalf of the Association of Friends of Bayreuth he produced a brochure, 'Weltdiskussion um Bayreuth', which presented a comprehensive picture of New Bayreuth and how it was regarded. This brochure not only contained some very effective illustrations but, more importantly, reproduced a variety of opinions by established theatrical celebrities. Also included – contrary to my own wishes – was a letter of a private character from Albert Schweitzer, who was not too pleased to see it in print. Eichner's skilful handling of the critics bore fruit, because their understandably subjective attitude to our work went hand in hand with a predominantly receptive and objective approach to the festival as a whole.

The 'official' Bayreuth Festival guide published until 1939 by the local firm of Niehrenheim was revived in a modified form in 1951 and 1952, when a 'Festival Book' appeared.

One genuine innovation and break with tradition was the publication of separate programmes for each of the works presented. This was prompted initially by financial considerations, because numerous commercial firms helped us by taking advertisements. The programme notes afforded an opportunity to acquaint audiences with the history of the festival and reflect on the works and their interpretative content. In the early years some of these notes stemmed from members of the old guard who had analysed Wagner's *œuvre* on paper before the Second World War, among them Zdenko von Kraft, Gertrud and Otto Strobel, Hans Grunsky, Curt von Westernhagen, and Kurt Overhoff. Even at this stage, however, we managed to enlist younger musicologists such as Walter Panofsky, Karl Schumann, and Kurt Honolka. I am bound to say in retrospect that what we now consider interpretatively possible in Richard Wagner's *œuvre* was then governed largely by earlier ideas and patterns of interpretation. Until my brother's death, he and I almost invariably selected the contents of programmes where they related to our own productions.

As the necessity for a change of interpretative approach in programme notes was gradually recognized and deliberately pursued, so a growing need arose for writers whose critical detachment prevented them from being 'pro-festival' or 'Wagner-blind'.

Herbert Barth was no stranger to us. On returning home from prisoner-of-war camp in 1946, he devoted his energies to the cultural events organized by his wife Hanna at Schloss Colmdorf, part of which they occupied. Having been a promoter of cultural activities in former years, especially among the young, he now became – *inter alia* – a co-founder of the German section of 'Jeunesse Musicale'. His talent for organization was such that Edgar Richter, then licence-holder and trustee of the Festspielhaus and wholly inexperienced in such matters, appointed him his concert organizer. Among the concerts arranged with Barth's help was one given by the Bamberg Symphony Orchestra under Hans Knappertsbusch in 1948 and another by the Dresden Staatskapelle under Joseph Keilberth in 1949. Closer links between us were forged by his activities on the trustee's behalf and the other events organized by him, with the result that further concerts were given at the Festspielhaus in line with the intentions of which I have spoken elsewhere. Barth was particularly receptive to modern music, and it was through him that we established contact with Wolfgang Fortner and Hans Rosbaud. The 'Institut für Neue Musik und Musikerziehung', which he founded and created from scratch, later developed into the 'Internationales Jugendfestspieltreffen', and in 1982 he initiated and opened the 'Internationales Jugendkulturzentrum' at Bayreuth.

It was far from certain that the festival would consolidate itself in 1952, and not only because of the loss carried over from 1951, which amounted to DM96,131.76. Many visitors had disliked *Parsifal*, *The Ring* had yet to mature, and there was little public demand for the new production of *Tristan*, which was to be conducted by Herbert von Karajan, not Wilhelm Furtwängler or Victor de Sabata. The result of these teething troubles was that seats for *Tristan*, in particular, were not fully booked. What with the shortfall in our receipts and the previous year's indebtedness, we needed strong nerves to face the coming season. Although friendly industrialists in and around Bayreuth bought up as many of the unsold tickets as they could – to the delight of those who were presented with them – we had somehow to plug the remaining gaps in the auditorium, which would have ruined the atmosphere. The young people whom Herbert Barth mobilized as 'paper' may not have helped to swell the festival's takings, but they did get to attend some Festspielhaus performances free of charge, thereby fulfilling my grandfather's utopian dream.

The difficulties besetting the 1952 season prompted Barth to suggest, in the middle of June, that we should launch an advertising campaign designed to promote public interest in Wagner and Bayreuth and encourage attendance at the festival. We agreed that he should work for us from September 1952 onwards in a free-lance capacity defined as 'publishing and advertising'. Compared to the fees now demanded by public relations or marketing consultants, the DM300 per month he charged for his services seem – even allowing for the ravages of inflation – almost derisory. When Walter Eichner left us in 1959 Barth took over the press office as well, and he continued to run it until 1976.

It was Barth who, in the late 1950s and throughout the 1960s, introduced Bayreuth to the writings of a new generation of musicologists and scholars. To cite only the first year in which they wrote for us, those who contributed to our programmes included Theodor W. Adorno (1957), Ernst Bloch (1960), Hans Mayer (1962), Carl Dahlhaus (1968), and Walter Jens (1970). The 1970s introduced a younger generation of musicologists and students of the theatre, among them Dietrich Mack, Egon Voss, Theo Hirsbrunner, Gernot Gruber, and Oswald Georg Bauer. Contributions to our Bayreuth programmes were also made by Wagner scholars of such subsequent repute is Martin Gregor-Dellin, Dieter Borchmeyer, and Peter Wapnewski. The eminent Catholic theologians Hans Küng and Norbert Greinacher wrote articles for Bayreuth, as did Claude Lévi-Strauss, each from the aspect of his own particular field. Nor must one forget Pierre Boulez and Patrice Chéreau, who also recorded their thoughts on the so-called centenary *Ring*, on which they collaborated. Götz Friedrich was another producer, apart from my brother and me, who analysed his productions in the programmes.

Significantly, the first foreign authors were Frenchmen. Marcel Doisy, who wrote for Bayreuth as early as 1951, was followed by Guy Ferchault, Jacques Feschotte, Antoine Goléa, Jean Mistler, Marcel Beaufils, and Paul André Gaillard. They were later joined, for Britain, by Viviar (V. V. Rosenfeld). Our present contributors hail from a wide range of countries including Britain, the United States, Austria, Italy, Poland, Hungary, Japan, and Israel. In the course of more than four decades, our programmes have developed into one of the foremost outlets for scholarly dissertations on Wagner.

When it became known that the Fritz Thyssen Foundation had initiated a research project into the 19th century, Herbert Barth and I resolved to lay a proposal before the board. This was that, in view of the forthcoming centenary of the laying of the Festspielhaus's foundation stone in 1972 and the ensuing centenary of the first Bayreuth Festival in 1976, they should commission a project devoted to the phenomenon of Wagner's *œuvre* and its realization at Bayreuth, past and present.

Our proposal, made shortly after my brother's death, was soon acted upon. In this we were aided by my mother's continuing friendship with Thyssen himself, and by the fact that the chairman of the board, Hans Sohl, maintained close links with Bayreuth through his membership of the board of the Association of Friends.

Carl Dahlhaus, Heinz Becker and Ernst Coenen assembled a team of young scholars and assigned them their various areas of study. The original intention was to bring out a thirteen-volume work on the Bayreuth Festival in time for the centenary of the stone-laying ceremony, but this plan proved impossible to fulfil by that date. As usual in collective ventures of this kind, the individual contributions became far too independent of each other. Viewing the matter objectively at this distance in time, I feel that it would be desirable to bring out a second, carefully revised edition.

As I have already remarked elsewhere, the unauthorized disclosure of sources led to some grotesque situations. In particular, the researchers were incapable of using financial or common theatrical terms correctly. Moreover, facts were sometimes presented in an unsystematic, pseudo-scholarly manner, with the result that the construction so often placed upon them is suspect.

Like many other things before it, however, this venture ultimately left Bayreuth unscathed. As in the case of every publication dealing with the theatre, what matters most of all is the lively interest and enthusiasm of the public, not the dissection of a non-existent corpse.

Herbert Barth's important position as the Bayreuth Festival's chief press officer and his creation of the 'Internationales Festspieltreffen' enabled him to engage in co-ordinated activities aimed at opening chinks in the Iron Curtain, which was then tightly closed. He not only succeeded in making the Bayreuth Festival accessible to critics, scholars and, above all, young people from the other side, but organized East-West cultural events.

By 1960 the functions of the press, publishing and advertising section had proliferated to such an extent that it could fulfil them only by remaining in operation all year round. We were almost invariably fortunate in obtaining female staff who had the knack of dealing with artists and journalists, critics and authors of programme notes, not to mention interview-hungry representatives of radio and television networks, to which ever greater importance was attached. They were proficient linguists and possessed the special tact and discretion essential to their job.

In 1965, when a vacancy appeared in this section, Gudrun Armann was chosen to fill it by the chief press officer and the head of personnel, who found that she measured up to their stringent standards of selection. My brother being absent, as he so often was except during rehearsal periods and the festival itself, she was formally engaged by me – a fateful step, not that either of us knew it at the time. The young lady soon became acquainted with my brother's working methods. Despite his esteem for Herbert Barth, he expected him to be in constant attendance and took the same for granted of anyone in the section designated 'press'. If the mood took him, Wieland would call for press reports at 7 a.m., before the ink was even dry, and it almost went without saying that Fräulein Armann would have to wait until after midnight to take last-minute amendments to programme illustrations and text or submit photographs of artists and sets, most of which were at that time taken by Siegfried Lauterwasser, for examination and approval. Wieland expected much the same service from the members of other sections, for instance our technical staff.

Herbert Barth was not only recovering from a lengthy illness in 1965 but much occupied with his youth festival commitments, so Gudrun Armann had to take on some important additional duties that were entirely new to her, being inexperienced in theatrical matters. Thanks to her unremitting readiness to carry them out even when Wieland's demands on her time were quite absurd, he found her a satisfactory employee. His office manager, Gerhard Hellwig, had surrounded him with a number of all-embracing, time-consuming rituals and routines, but these the young lady breached and swept aside in her briskly irreverent way. Whenever she thought it essential to contradict him, she did so. Wieland was unaccustomed to such treatment, but this was just what made their work together so constructive.

She protested via his office at the number of memos he sent out, declaring that it would be quicker and more effective if he phoned instead. Knowing my brother's predilection for firing off spontaneous and superfluous memos, I was delighted to hear this baldly stated by a new and unprejudiced employee. Another amusing passage between Gudrun and Wieland occurred at the time of the 1965 premières. One morning, when she brought him his daily batch of newspapers, he berated her because a Munich tabloid was missing. It had come out at 11 p.m. the night before, but the station kiosk at Bayreuth had not yet received a copy. Knowing that an assistant of his had bought one in Munich in the small hours and given it to him, she fended off his accusation of inefficiency by saying that she wasn't a 'cyclist', in other words, someone who bows to the boss up top and bends at the knee below. When Wieland suggested that she hand in her notice, she said she would think it over, if only because she had been engaged by his brother Wolfgang and didn't want to leave him in the lurch at such a busy time. Wieland was amused by this skirmish, and next morning's newspaper delivery was a harmonious affair, with grins on both sides.

Incidents of that kind could only have stemmed from our very different working methods, because in my 'department' rituals of any kind were unknown.

Gudrun Armann's knowledge and ability were such that young scholars like Dietrich Mack were happy to be initiated by her into the tasks I set them. Later on, in 1974, she did the same for Oswald Georg Bauer, whom I appointed chief press officer two years later.

Thanks to the expert knowledge and assistance of Gudrun Armann and Oswald Bauer, I was able to survive spells of exceptional turbulence like those occasioned by the 'centenary *Ring*' and the contents of the programmes I presented in subsequent years. Where public relations were concerned, the period between my brother's death and the centenary was a time of preparation designed to bear fruit in 1976.

I had for many years enjoyed the services of my indispensable secretary and personal assistant Elisabeth Suchanek, a refugee from Karlsbad, who spoke English as well as the Slav and Romance languages. When she left in 1976, I replaced her with Gudrun Mack (as she had since become) because I felt that Gudrun's knowledge of festival routine made her the person best qualified to assist me in such an exceptional year.

There was a hint of Wagnerian drama in the fact that my first wife's petition for a divorce should have been granted at the very time when the Boulez/Chéreau/Peduzzi/Schmidt team and I were struggling to put the finishing touches to the new *Ring* production, or just when the tension of the rehearsal period was at its height. My aim was to première a version of *The Ring* that would gain the public acceptance I hoped for, although I knew that reactions to it would be mixed. Quite apart from these 'minor problems', however, there was the intimate relationship that had developed between Gudrun and me. I was concerned to make the nature of that relationship clear to the outside world, if only to banish the preposterous rumours that were circulating in the press, in theatrical circles, and, above all, among the members of my not invariably well-meaning family. From then on, though not on that account, we were Wolfgang and Gudrun *Wagner*.

At the end of 1985, by mutual agreement and on the friendliest terms, Oswald Bauer gave up his work at Bayreuth to become secretary-general of the Bavarian Academy of Fine Arts in Munich, another post that accorded with his knowledge, ability, and love of the theatre. Even today, however, we are fortunate in being able to call on his scholarly and literary talents in consequence of the long and interesting road we travelled together. Munich University employs his practical experience of the theatre for teaching purposes. He is also much in demand, especially at meetings of Richard Wagner Societies at home and abroad, as a guest speaker noted for his erudite but succinct and intelligible lectures.

A kind of interregnum set in after Bauer's departure from Bayreuth, a term that best describes the period 1985–9 because the 'regent' concentrated more on self-fulfilment than on Bayreuth's needs.

At the end of the year in which the Dresden State Opera reopened I staged *Die Meistersinger* with sets of my own design – the first Western producer to be engaged there. Adapted by request from my Bayreuth production, the work was premièred on 19 December 1985. In 1988, or a year before the Berlin Wall came down, I was employed by Dresden to stage *Der Fliegende Holländer* with new sets, also of my own design. While engaged on this production I came into contact with a large number of theatre folk, young as well as long established, one of the former being Peter Emmerich, who proved an invaluable assistant. Thanks to my activities in Dresden and the efforts of the then general administrator, Gerd Schönfelder, I was able – for the first time in twenty years – to engage East German musicians, stage managers, assistant producers and choral singers for Bayreuth. Discounting one year, singers and producers of the first rank had been subject to an almost total ban on foreign travel.

In the spring of 1989 we managed to persuade the East German authorities to grant Peter Emmerich the unique 'privilege' of a three-year eave of absence from the Dresden Opera so that we could employ him in he Bayreuth press office. My wife, who had shown the ropes to many a 1ewcomer in the past, had been working in Dresden as a production 1ssistant, so she and I were able to have many talks with Emmerich on he subject of his future role and functions, and we were both convinced hat he would fulfil them to our complete satisfaction. At that stage, none)f us dreamed that 9 October 1989 would so radically transform the)olitical climate that, even if he overstayed his leave of absence, he would 1ever be charged with *Republikflucht* [illegal emigration from East Germany].

The turning-point in Germany almost coincided with the development)f a situation in Europe that made certain topics of conversation at 3ayreuth seem outmoded and ushered in discussions of a relevant and 1ppropriate nature.

Federal President Richard von Weizsäcker had suggested that Germany's)rincipal musico-theatrical contribution to the 1992 World Exhibition at 3eville should be a performance of the Bayreuth production of *Parsifal*. Xhen this proved impossible because the Austrian instruments from Vienna 1ad been left at the Teatro de la Maestranza and turned up too late, an all-German' solution was devised: my 1988 *Holländer* production was chosen ·o conclude the music-theatre series, and scored a widely appreciated :ultural success. In preparing and staging these performances I was aided)nce again by my Dresden assistant and Bayreuth press chief.

The Bayreuth Festival's travelling exhibitions, too, were invariably ,mpressive and informative. Carefully geared to the varied requirements of ·he places where they were shown, they reconciled their underlying purpose vith the interests of those who attended them. We always made provision for personal contacts between festival representatives and visitors, whether ;tudents, young people, or culturally interested persons in general. It was ;ratifying, if sometimes rather strange, to hear representatives of the German diplomatic corps or German cultural institutions acknowledging,)r being compelled to acknowledge, the universal importance of Richard Wagner as a manifestation of Germany's accessibility to the world and vice versa. People had not yet forgotten that it was largely the favourable response of foreign visitors which had helped to ensure that the Bayreuth Festival was not – as many Germans hoped – throttled to death.

The first large-scale post-war exhibition devoted to Richard Wagner and Bayreuth was attributable to the initiative of a foreign historian and author who visited us at Bayreuth on 2 September 1949. My brother welcomed him with the words: 'You come to us, when not even a dog will accept a piece of bread from us!' In 1950 we placed an office in the Festspielhaus at his disposal, having jointly planned, at out first encounter, to mount a travelling exhibition entitled 'Wagner in the World', our intention being to show it at major theatres and opera houses in Europe and, if possible, overseas as well. With the backing of our foreign office and of André François-Poncet, the French high commissioner, it opened on 23 April 1951 at a prominent Parisian venue, the Grand Opéra, and proved so successful that it was later transferred to the Bibliothèque Nationale. Among those present at the opening ceremony were my first wife and I and my cousin Blandine Ollivier de Prévaux.

From Paris the exhibition moved on, at the invitation of the US high commissioner, to the Amerika-Haus in Munich, and from there to Bayreuth in time for the 1951 season. Its other ports of call during the decade 1951–61 included Barcelona, Madrid, Bilbao, Florence, Venice, Zurich, and Rome. Well attended and much discussed in all these places, it was accompanied by numerous symposia devoted to Wagner's influence on the culture and art of the relevant countries and their influence on the composer's work.

Thanks to the contacts we made in Barcelona, we concluded a contract for nine Bayreuth guest performances at the Gran Teatro Liceo in 1955. Our success in Spain bore fruit, so we travelled to Buenos Aires to negotiate a guest season at the Teatro Colon, where it was envisaged that four cycles of *The Ring* should be given under our supervision between 24 April and 23 May 1957. The contract was never signed, partly because the laws enacted for the protection of German cultural assets precluded them from being loaned abroad, even if privately owned, and partly because a minor revolution broke out.

Exhibitions have been jointly mounted since 1973 by the Bayerische Vereinsbank and the Bayreuth Festival. This fruitful collaboration was attributable to the initiative and enthusiasm of Rudolf Eberhardt, the former finance minister and Vereinsbank board member, and to vigorous efforts on the part of Elfi Haller, who then headed the bank's cultural section. The themes of these exhibitions have related either to new festival productions such as *Tristan* (1974), *Tannhäuser* (1985), and *Der Fliegende Holländer* (1990), to the centenary of the first performance of *Parsifal* (1982), or to persons who were connected with the festival and left their mark on it, e.g. Richard Strauss (1973), Hans Knappertsbusch (1977), Siegfried Wagner (1980), Max Lorenz (1981), Franz Liszt (1986), Cosima Wagner (1987), Wieland Wagner (1991), and Friedrich Feustel (1993).

Exceptions to the above were the 1988 exhibition devoted to the festival orchestra and the Bayreuth centenary exhibition entitled '1876 Bayreuth 1976'. The latter opened at London's Festival Hall on 21 May 1976, when the BBC documentary of the festival centenary was first televised, and later moved to Bayreuth for the festival season. Thereafter it travelled to Munich, Zurich, Milan, Wiesbaden, Frankfurt, Düsseldorf, the Paris Opéra, Ludwigshafen, the Sydney Opera House, Tokyo, Osaka, Seoul, and São

Paulo. This one exhibition attracted a total of some 1.2 million visitors. The Wieland Wagner Exhibition of 1991, held twenty-five years after my brother's death, was the first comprehensive analysis and acknowledgement of his contribution to the history of the theatre.

On 18 August 1931, when I was just short of my twelfth birthday, I had a memorable experience at my mother's holiday home beside Lake Constance: I heard the first direct, worldwide radio broadcast from the Festspielhaus. This sensational radio première of *Tristan und Isolde* was conducted by Wilhelm Furtwängler with Lauritz Melchior and Nanny Larsén-Todsen in the title roles.

The development of facilities for electronic transmission, and of television technology in particular, enabled a wholly different worldwide broadcast to be made, this time via London. A few minutes' worth of happenings from all parts of the globe were spliced together into a live television programme lasting several hours. Our own TV bosses had originally suggested contributing a *Schnadahüpferl* [humorous vocal] group, but London insisted that Germany would be better represented by Bayreuth. The selected item was part of a rehearsal of Act II of the new production of *Lohengrin*.

The first radio broadcast in 1931 heralded an uninterrupted series of transmissions from Bayreuth. It was the lasting impression made by that broadcast which prompted the general administrator of the ARD [West German public broadcasting corporation], despite the negative attitude of the head of the Bavarian radio network, to resume such transmissions in 1951. Modern recording techniques make it possible, on the basis of contractual agreements, for non-commercial companies to transmit recordings of performances until 31 December of each year in addition to a live transmission of the première broadcast with the aid of a programme exchange. Undiminished public interest in these broadcasts testifies to the continuing vitality of what happens on the festival hill. The intermissions are usually devoted to comments on the continuing relevance of Wagner's works and interviews with artists and members of the festival management.

It should be mentioned, for completeness' sake, that international television networks annually devote coverage to the festival, and to premières in particular.

Two black-and-white television recordings of Act I of *Die Meistersinger* in 1959 and Sachs's workshop in Act III of the same work in 1963, both produced and designed by my brother, were disliked by him because the director had made them in a way that struck him as thoroughly unsatisfactory.

It was many years before a work was recorded in its entirety at the Festspielhaus. The first such occasion was in 1978. Television recordings

have regularly been made since then, depending on the artistic, admir
istrative and financial resources of those concerned. The first was a cc
production between the first and second German TV channels an
UNITEL, which has collaborated with us independently since 1979. Ther
now exists a complete Wagner edition comprising videotapes of all th
festival works recorded live at the Festspielhaus. Their high quality, bot
artistic and technical, has assured them of successful sales all over th
world, but problems still arise in the audio field, where 'black' recording
continue to infiltrate the market despite the laws of copyright.

11

ALONG THE LINE OF CONTINUITY:
(I)

Wieland's death confronted me with the need to find new ways and means, because it was obvious that I would not be capable, if only physically, of staging every new production in addition to shouldering the overall responsibility that was now mine alone. That would have been pointless in any case, because it would inevitably have reduced Bayreuth to a kind of one-man band. Although artistic supervision by a single person may be all right for a normal repertory theatre, which can draw on a wide range of works, the limitations imposed by ten operas and music dramas must sooner or later exhaust the ingenuity of any producer, however creative.

I have already touched on the fact that Wieland and I had already, in earlier years, considered involving other producers in the festival as soon we ourselves had staged two interpretations of each work. Once a rather vague intention, this now became my first priority.

At the same time, I clearly recognized that there must be no undermining of the festival's 'workshop' character, which we had always programmatically emphasized and developed in the course of sixteen years' joint endeavour, and that it must be consistently perpetuated and enhanced by granting new teams opportunities compatible with the festival's specific requirements.

The situation was far from intractable, because I could easily have found a dozen so-called big names who would have graced the festival. I could not, however, afford to be guided by mere reputation or assuage the ambition of this or that person eager to glorify himself by means of the festival and at its expense. I had to find creative individuals who gave promise of an ability to produce expressive and intelligible interpretations faithful to the essence of my grandfather's works. They would also have to align themselves and their work with the continuity which the workshop idea had progressively developed in the Bayreuth treatments of Wagner's *œuvre* since 1951, and to be willing and able to work with me on a regular basis. I was not seeking a swift series of sensations or the dubious glamour emanating from stars and celebrities. My decision to engage someone – or not to do so – has always been governed by the above criteria, whose object is qualitative effect, not quantitative success. As I understand it, Wagner's 'Children, create something new!' does not imply *carte blanche* for everyone to do something 'new' at all costs – something that all too quickly evaporates into superficialities and quite often turns out to be merely another version of 'the old'. The Bayreuth Festival is not a place of pilgrimage or an idolater's temple, but neither is it a playground for egoists nor a self-service stall in vanity fair.

Since I shall be going on to detail the recruitment and activities of the production teams employed at Bayreuth from 1969 onwards, these introductory remarks will doubtless be amplified by the events described and thus need no further comment. It only remains to add that any element of drama was offset by a touch of irony: if something misfired the public tended to lay the blame at my door; if it succeeded, I had no part in its success.

For the 1969 festival season, having staged my own new productions of *Lohengrin* in 1967 and *Die Meistersinger* a year later, I was faced with the task of engaging a producer as well as a conductor and stage and costume designers. My brother's 1959 production of *Der Fliegende Holländer* had last appeared in the programme in 1965, so the present requirement was to stage it afresh. My choice fell on August Everding, the product of a good school, having been assistant to Hans Schweikart and Fritz Kortner. Producer and general administrator of the Munich Kammerspiele since 1963, Everding had made his operatic début at the Munich Staatsoper with *La Traviata* in 1965. In June 1968 we quickly concluded a binding contract and discussed the question of a conductor and cast for *Holländer*, which was to be his fourth opera production and his second venture into Wagner. On 28 August 1969 Silvio Varviso agreed to conduct, and on 19 November contracts were exchanged with the stage designer Josef Svoboda. The costume designer Jörg Zimmermann completed the team. Since the preliminary negotiations had gone so smoothly, these names could be officially announced in the Bayreuth Festival brochure, which was, as usual, circulated at the beginning of October.

The cast for the première year was as follows. Leonie Rysanek and Gwyneth Jones doubled in the role of Senta and Donald McIntyre and Theo Adam in that of the Dutchman. Daland was sung by Martti Talvela, Erik by Jean Cox, who had played the Steersman in 1965, Mary by Unni Rugtvedt, and the Steersman by René Kollo, whose Bayreuth début this was.

This production reinstated the version as originally composed, which was intended to be performed without intervals in conformity with its original subtitle: 'A Romantic Opera in One Act and Three Parts'. The objections of the Berlin management, to whom Wagner had first sent his work, persuaded him to make the necessary concessions before its first performance in Dresden. He separated the 'parts' by inserting definite conclusions and introductions, so the opera was performed with intervals at its première on 2 January 1843 and thereafter. It was not restored to its original form until first presented at Bayreuth by Cosima in 1901, and the continuous version was retained until my brother's 1959 production. Wieland was compelled for technical reasons to insert one longish interval and a brief 'light interval' during which the audience remained in their seats. Despite the dimensions of the Dutchman's exceptionally impressive and convincing ship, Josef Svoboda managed to solve the technical problems in such a way that the work could be performed 'ballad fashion' and without a break, as my grandfather had intended.

Musically, the 1969 production embodied the version of the so-called *Erlösungsschluss* [redemption finale] that invests the end of the overture and that of the third part with a transfiguring, almost apotheosis-like character, not least because of the addition of two harps. This version dated from January 1860, when Wagner wrote it for inclusion in some Paris concerts of fragments of his works. Wieland's production used the original, comparatively 'hard' Dresden version, which is balder and far less forgiving.

Compact and well thought out, with a balanced cast and lighting effects that were interesting, both technically and artistically, the 1969 production also won universal acclaim for its musical quality and provided a good foundation on which to think about the future.

My second *Ring* production followed in 1970, and the programme for 1971, preceded by four years of new productions, consisted entirely of repeats.

The next outside producer to be engaged was Götz Friedrich, who staged a new *Tannhäuser* in 1972. Of the seven performances, the sixth was conducted by Horst Stein and all the rest by Erich Leinsdorf. Jürgen Rose designed the sets and costumes, and the Venusberg choreography was by John Neumeier. Another important feature of this festival was that Norbert Balatsch took over from the legendary Wilhelm Pitz, who could not participate for health reasons. Balatsch, chorus master of the Vienna Opera, had been recommended by Horst Stein, who knew him very well from his own activities there. Stein was convinced that he would do full justice to the demanding job that awaited him at Bayreuth and smoothly perpetuate the tradition established by his long-serving predecessor.

In its first year this production of *Tannhäuser* was cast as follows. Hugh Beresford and Hermin Esser doubled as Tannhäuser and the roles of Venus and Elisabeth were, for the first time at Bayreuth, sung by a single soprano, Gwyneth Jones. Hans Sotin played the Landgrave and Wolfram von

Eschenbach was shared between Ingvar Wixell and Bernd Weikl, making his Bayreuth début. Of the remaining knights and minnesingers, Walter von der Vogelweide was sung by Harald Ek, Biterolf by Franz Mazura, Heinrich der Schreiber by Heribert Steinbach, and Reinmar von Zweter by Heinz Feldhoff.

The very birth of this new production took place under dramatic circumstances. I received Götz Friedrich's agreement to stage a new *Tannhäuser* on 1 July 1971, but the contract proved extremely difficult to finalize. Friedrich's current artistic home was the Komische Oper in East Berlin, which was run by his teacher, Walter Felsenstein. Although the East German authorities made it hard for established, well-known artists to appear at Bayreuth in those days, they did permit Friedrich to pay several visits to Bayreuth to enable all the requisite negotiations and preliminaries to be concluded. The first meeting between the conductor and the producer took place at Bayreuth on 24 August 1971. However, our brochure had to be mailed without naming the new team because, despite Walter Felsenstein's representations to Gysi, the East German minister of culture, it was not until 19 December 1971 that the contract with Götz Friedrich could be signed and sealed.

Bayreuth was unknown territory to Friedrich, because he had never staged a Wagnerian work before. In his own words, he came there neither 'Bayreuth-impaired' nor 'Bayreuth-initiated', and he wanted nothing better than to be a 'Bayreuth go-getter'.

One innovation was that the producer and stage designer had a self-supporting ramp built out over the orchestra pit for the exclusive use of Tannhäuser and the shepherd boy. This and the main acting area, which was heptagonal, consisted of wooden planks. In Act II part of the downstage section was removed and the remaining area hydraulically raised more than three and a half metres and provided with steps on which the singers could be excellently positioned, in particular for the 'entry of the guests'. The result of this appreciable reduction in acting area was that, although it could accommodate the female chorus, it enabled only part of the appreciably larger male chorus to sing and move about. Our new chorus master was understandably dissatisfied with the volume of sound produced by the reduced male chorus once the ladies had made their exit, so it was agreed that the remainder should unobtrusively enter the stage from behind. Because no costumes had been provided for these additional singers, who numbered twenty-four in all, they had to be made at short notice.

No extra money was available for the purchase of more materials, but it fortunately – or, as it later turned out, most unfortunately – transpired that too much imitation leather had been bought in, and that enough of it remained to make the requisite costumes.

The acoustic problems posed by this scene were solved by installing a plywood baffle above the acting area and out of sight of the audience, and this went some way towards producing the Bayreuth sound.

The first-nighters were very disturbed by the sudden appearance on stage of such a preponderance of leather-coated figures because they evidently associated them with members of the Gestapo and Security Service – a possibility that had never entered our heads. But that was not the end of our unintentional provocations.

Götz Friedrich had planned that the work should end with Tannhäuser and Wolfram alone on stage while the whole of the final chorus was sung behind the scenes. This reduced the volume of sound to such an extent that Norbert Balatsch genuinely feared for the success of his Bayreuth début. He succeeded in convincing the producer that his misgivings were well founded, and it was jointly agreed that the pilgrims should enter in the dark, forming a tableau that was steeped in light only when they began to sing.

The first act was generally well received, but the second act provoked a certain amount of unrest in the auditorium and the third brought it to a head. Many of the audience thought they glimpsed undergarments of infamous communist red beneath the chorus's stylized cowls of grey-blue net. Some claimed that the pilgrims had sung the East German anthem, not 'Hail to the miracle of grace!', others that they had heard the strains of the *Internationale*, and still others that they had seen fists raised in the communist salute – a blasphemous accompaniment to the pilgrims' hallelujahs.

A since-deceased politician walked out, protesting vehemently. In a caustic letter to a major Sunday newspaper a few days later he posed the question '*Quo vadis?*' and declared that, despite the excellence of the singing, the final chorus created the impression that it was meant to represent the 'workers' militia choir of the state-owned "Red Locomotive" works at Leipzig'.

There was much rustling of German newsprint. Press notices ranged from fair comment to scathing criticism and virulent abuse. However, even that was mild compared to the raging tempest of disapprobation that swept the auditorium on that first night, which was loud enough, in a theatre not unused to the sound of booing and whistling, to constitute a première of its own. Poor Norbert Balatsch, who was the first dinner-jacketed figure to appear in front of the curtain, bore the brunt of the abuse because the audience was so blind with rage that it mistook him for the largely unknown producer.

The opening performance of every festival had been followed by a reception in honour of the Bavarian premier ever since the mid-1950s –

the first took place on 21 July 1954 – and 1972 was no exception. This time the mood was strangely uneasy, especially when Götz Friedrich, that universal target of merciless vilification, made his appearance. It was as if the guests had just been compelled to witness the swan-song of the civilized world – indeed, the decline of the West. The atmosphere was terribly subdued, the prevailing sentiment a mixture of embarrassment and indignation at the cultural atrocity that had been perpetrated on the Green Hill. It was whispered at one of the numerous tables that, if Wolfgang Wagner chose to employ an arch-Bolshevik like Friedrich at Bayreuth, his public grant should be cut or, better still, revoked at once.

Having already closed ranks with the *Tannhäuser* team by joining them in front of the Festspielhaus curtain *coram populo*, I now did something quite contrary to my usual custom. Together with the 'desecrator', Götz Friedrich, I went the rounds of various Bayreuth restaurants favoured by festival visitors in the hope that this conspicuous display of solidarity would pour a little oil on troubled waters.

At the festival's international press conference next morning I commented on the rumour that our grant might be cut or withdrawn. I demanded that Bayreuth retain its artistic freedom and expressed my incomprehension that a member of the Bavarian government should have threatened to clip our financial wings if we staged any more productions like the previous night's *Tannhäuser*. I further declared that, if the Federal Republic aspired to be a democratic state, threats of that kind were beyond the pale.

The very next day the Bavarian premier denied that any consideration had been given to stopping our grant and gave an assurance that it would be maintained. A member of the parliamentary opposition announced his intention of supporting me and said that anyone who spoke of withdrawing a subsidy because a theatrical production displeased him was employing the very methods he claimed to abhor.

Götz Friedrich firmly disclaimed any wish to stage a politically tendentious production, and one of the soloists wondered aloud if the audience would have reacted differently had Friedrich not come from East Germany. As for me, I vehemently condemned any attempt to make political capital out of the production.

After the second performance we provisionally had the final chorus sung off stage, a change applauded by some but taken by others to mean that the producer had got cold feet. Both schools of thought were clearly wrong, because in 1972 and subsequent years Friedrich learned from these misunderstandings and, without infringing the essence of his interpretation, perseveringly refined and enhanced it. In 1978 his *Tannhäuser* was the first full-length Bayreuth performance to be recorded for television – *with* the final chorus sung on stage – and Wagner-lovers throughout the world are glad to have this version of the production permanently available to them. What was once a scandal has become a milestone.

In furtherance of my efforts to engage new conductors whose interpretations might enrich the festival, I had since late November 1967 been in touch with Leonard Bernstein. My brother had briefly met with him in Vienna two years earlier and discussed the possibility of a Bayreuth engagement. In the course of my own talks with Bernstein it was suggested, among other things, that he might conduct a new production of *Tristan*. Unfortunately, our ideas and wishes could never be reconciled sufficiently to form the basis of a collaborative venture. Bernstein wanted television recordings made of him at work, as well as gramophone records and television recordings of the performance itself. Even discounting the requirements of the other works in the programme, lack of time alone would have rendered this impossible, particularly in the first year of a new production, which always necessitates extensive and intensive rehearsals. If one further takes into account that the première year produces an initial result that very often undergoes development and alteration in subsequent years, to record it audiovisually would have lent it an aura of finality. Bernstein and I failed to reach an accommodation, so contact between us ended on 19 November 1970.

On 6 April 1990, when he was already a dying man, Leonard Bernstein visited Bayreuth after making his last television recording at Waldsassen. Accompanied by my sister Friedelind, he had come to see the Festspielhaus as well as the national archive and the Richard Wagner Museum at Wahnfried. I was not there that day, unfortunately, being absent on a long-prearranged trip, so the last meeting that would surely have resolved our personal differences never took place. I was told that Bernstein understandably showed a special interest in the orchestra pit of the Festspielhaus, and that he lingered for quite some time on the conductor's podium...

Informal and intermittent negotiations with Georg Solti had been going on since the summer of 1953. Although these intensified in respect of *Tristan* between January 1971 and early August 1972, their failure was preordained, as in Bernstein's case, because no reasonable compromise could be attained between the conductor's suggested rehearsal schedules and performance dates on the one hand and his planned leaves of absence on the other.

While rehearsals for the 1971 festival were in progress I received a letter from Carlos Kleiber. 'I should esteem it an honour and a pleasure,' he wrote, to "kibitz" during rehearsals at Bayreuth and also, perhaps, to sit in the orchestra pit (my father trained me to sit *still*!), thereby becoming somewhat more prepared for the possibility of an intimidating persona appearance some day.'

Meantime, I had another fight on my hands with Karl Böhm. After my brother's 1962 production of *Tristan* was dropped in 1970, a new production of the work had been planned for 1974 and discussed with Böhm in 1971, during his brief visit to Bayreuth to conduct a live recording of *Der Fliegende Holländer*. Having learned that I did not plan to entrust him with the new production, he legalistically asserted his claim to it. I put paid to this disagreeable controversy on 3 November 1971 by writing to remind him of the following passage in a letter from my brother dated 29 July 1965. 'For my part,' Wieland had written to Böhm, 'I undertake on behalf of the Bayreuth Festival to offer you all the works that ... are newly produced by me or subsequently appear in the programme as having been produced by me ... Similarly, "our *Tristan*" will remain under your musical direction whenever we can present it. My brother Wolfgang's freedom of choice ... is not affected by our agreement. I shall give you first refusal of any repeats or new productions of mine of *Die Meistersinger, Der Fliegende Holländer* and *Tannhäuser*.' Despite this unequivocal statement of the position, Karl Böhm's wife Thea – and, more especially, his son Karlheinz – neglected no opportunity to accuse me, both privately and in public, of having broken my word to him.

I was all the more delighted when, at the centenary celebrations on 23 July 1976, Karl Böhm conducted the prelude and festival meadow scene from *Die Meistersinger*. The speeches were on the long side, regrettably, but he listened to them as patiently as everyone one else until the moment came when he could pick up his baton.

Radio Bavaria, which was transmitting the ceremony live to numerous countries, got into difficulty because the time allotted to the speeches was exceeded, notably by Federal President Walter Scheel and the Bavarian premier, Dr Alfons Goppel. I became increasingly aware of this situation as one speaker followed another, but I was lucky enough to be last on the list. This enabled me to solve the problem of transmission time by abandoning my prepared speech. 'Enough said,' I told the invited audience. 'Now let Richard Wagner speak!'

On 2 August 1972 I sent Georg Solti a telegram expressing my regret that he could not conduct *Tristan* in 1974. I at once got in touch with Carlos Kleiber, whose keen interest in Bayreuth I have already mentioned, and was pleased to receive his prompt acceptance. On 26 August 1973, after a long series of conversations in which his queries and requests in regard to working with the orchestra had been settled, I sent him the contractual documents embodying the rehearsal and performance schedules agreed between us. August Everding and Josef Svoboda also received their contracts two days later. It had been decided, after joint consultation, to engage Reinard Heinrich as costume designer. Heinrich was already well acquainted with the special features of this domain through his teacher, Kurt Palm, and his work to date.

Although Kleiber was reputed to be a most difficult conductor, he differed from Leonard Bernstein and Georg Solti in being able to reconcile his wishes with the requirements of the Bayreuth management. His three years with us, 1974–6, were almost completely devoid of friction, and his musical achievements were enthusiastically hailed by artists, festival staff, and audiences alike. It was unfortunate that personal reasons prevented him from conducting in 1977, the last year of this *Tristan* production. His place as musical director was taken by Horst Stein, who had conducted the last three of the six 1976 performances because of an injury to Kleiber's wrist.

My relations with Kleiber were of the friendliest, and we kept in touch. It was a matter of regret to us both that we never worked together again. I should add that Kleiber wrote to me on 16 and 17 May 1977, each time in a most original, intimate and charming vein, about his having dropped out. He said that his refusal was being improperly and absurdly attributed to the orchestra's complaints about the new *Ring* in 1976, which had been misrepresented and exaggerated, and that he had a high regard for Boulez and Chéreau.

The cast for the première of *Tristan* in 1974 was as follows: Tristan was sung by Helge Brillioth, King Marke by Kurt Moll, Isolde by Catarina Ligendza, Kurwenal by Donald McIntyre, Brangäne by Yvonne Minton, Melot by Heribert Steinbach, the Sailor and the Shepherd by Heinz Zednik, and the Helmsman by Heinz Feldhoff.

As an important stylistic element, Josef Svoboda used the cyclorama he had successfully used before, which consisted of 122 kilometres of 3.5 mm plastic cord. Suspended in lengths ranging between 15 and 18 metres, this not only formed a backcloth for his varied, three-dimensional treatment of the ground but afforded interesting and diverse opportunities for projections whose effect was vaguely three-dimensional. I still remember Svoboda rummaging in the vast number of boxes he had brought with him and extracting all kinds of projection plates in search of the ones most suitable to the effects he had in mind.

Unlike other interpretations staged since 1952, this production was marked by certain realistic features on the acting area that formed an attractive contrast to the dreamy unreality of the background. The latter was notable for its gradations of colour, ranging from the pointillism of Act II to the finale, which did not, for example, fade to black but was flooded during the '*Liebestod*' with white, all-consuming, incandescent light.

The characterization was firm and concise, its recurrent motif being the way in which the hands of the two principals reached for one another.

As producer of the current *Ring*, I was robbed by this new production of an ideal Brünnhilde and Siegfried in Catarina Ligendza and Jean Cox. As festival director, on the other hand, I gained an ideal Isolde.

Continuously planning ahead with an eye to the new *Ring* in 1976, I took advantage of the fact that Brünnhilde's role was vacant in 1974 to try out three different Brünnhildes (that is to say, one each for *Die Walküre, Siegfried,* and *Götterdämmerung*). Having given Gwyneth Jones a chance to sing all three Brünnhildes in the cycle in 1975, I entrusted her with them in the following year as well.

The 1976 *Ring* has evoked such a flood of diverse publications since its first performance, and every argument for and against it has been so exhaustively documented, that it would be superfluous to recapitulate all the sense and nonsense that has been written about it. The first complete Bayreuth *Ring* to be audiovisually recorded, it is often televised to this day, so all who are interested in the subject can satisfy their curiosity with ease. If I now recall a few aspects of what happened before, during and after this production, which was considered spectacular in its day, I do so after a lapse of almost twenty years, during which the events of the time have naturally undergone a metamorphosis in the public estimation and in my own memory. Many a Saul has since become a Paul, and it would be petty and stupid of me to attempt a full reconstruction of the complaints and conflicts, mistakes and misapprehensions of those days. Their authors, who had a disastrous penchant for publicity, must have besmirched tons of paper over the years. Personally, I seek neither to be spiteful nor to set myself up as a judge whose verdict on the past lays claim to absolute finality.

The 1976 production of *The Ring* was anathematized by its contemporary critics. Over the years the pendulum has swung to the opposite extreme, and it presently occupies a place on the Olympus of classicism. Once abhorred and execrated, it has now – no less grotesquely – been transformed into a cult object by certain reverent Wagnerians. Both extremes are equally foolish. Patrice Chéreau, to whom the 1 August 1976 edition of *Die Welt am Sonntag* attributed the dictum 'I wanted to take Wagner down off his pedestal' was subsequently clothed in the aura of a youthful prodigy and placed on a pedestal himself.

It is not uninteresting to trace the production's prior history. Having conducted my brother's *Parsifal* from 1966 to 1968 and again in 1970, Pierre Boulez asked me to release him from that obligation. We parted in the hope of resuming our collaboration at some future date, and I assured Boulez that I would get in touch in the event of some major new project that might interest him. On 6 June 1972, after sending an associate of mine, Dr Mack, to Strasbourg to sound him out, I wrote and asked if he would be willing to conduct *The Ring* in 1976.

In quest of a suitable producer, we at first considered engaging Ingmar Bergman, but he was reluctant to take on such an undeniably difficult task and declined. We then entered into negotiations with Peter Stein. My first, exploratory letter was dated 14 June 1973, and our first personal encounter took place in Berlin on 7 November – a meeting of which I informed Pierre Boulez on 20 November. As our talks and meetings dragged on, I became increasingly convinced that it would be impossible to reach the sensible and mutually acceptable agreement essential to any productive collaboration. Stein bundled his crude ideas and suggestions into a monstrous parcel whose Gordian knot he eventually severed himself. It might be said that he was like a looter debating the value of something which he clearly felt entitled to take, but which he had no idea how to put to proper use. *The Ring* must have struck him as a theatrical monstrosity, because he seriously proposed that it be cut and shoe-horned into two nights. Intended to convert the bulky into the 'handy', this process would have not only mutilated the entire work but positively castrated it. Stein further suggested that we engage four different producers because he would have his hands full enough with *one* part of the tetralogy. He also aspired to redirect the course of the festival by organizing a variety of fringe activities with a picked team of like-minded cronies, doubtless so as to have at least some subject to flog to death if the festival itself proved too skimpy. Finally, he wanted the stage and auditorium remodelled to suit his own ideas.

Failure was inevitable, given that neither Boulez nor I could ever have reconciled such proposals with our knowledge and understanding of the work and the festival concept, which included the theatre specially designed for it.

Peter Stein finally withdrew from the *Ring* project on 6 September 1974. His letter of resignation was initially sent to Boulez alone and later communicated to me in the form of a copy. He clearly thought it necessary to cover his retreat with due theatrical thunder by roundly abusing me, but Boulez, undeterred by such epithets as stupid, silly, arrogant, mulish, reactionary, tight-fisted, and conniving, kept faith with 'the Bayreuth blockhead', Wolfgang Wagner.

With my approval, Boulez had contacted Patrice Chéreau in Paris as far back as 27 January 1974, when we already thought it unlikely that we would reach a sensible accommodation with Peter Stein and had no wish to waste any more valuable time. On 31 January I sent Chéreau some material on Bayreuth and his prospective duties there. On 22 March Boulez brought Chéreau to see me in Bayreuth so that we could make each other's acquaintance and take preliminary soundings. On 29 May Chéreau sent me an exposé that greatly impressed me and betrayed an amazing knowledge of the sources on which *The Ring* was based. For various reasons, it was not until 4 November, or two months after Peter Stein had dropped out, that I was able to resume negotiations with Chéreau and, in consultation with Boulez, bring them to a successful conclusion. By 8 December it could finally be said that the team for the centenary *Ring* had been found. We settled on most of Chéreau's immediate associates, notably Richard Peduzzi for stage design and Jacques Schmidt for costumes, and worked out a thoroughly realistic mode of procedure. The team attended the first cycle of the current *Ring* in 1975, which helped to crystallize our ideas on casting.

The usual prerequisites of any production – finalizing contractual agreements, laying down deadlines for set construction, technical installations and costumes, casting the roles, engaging musicians, and a multitude of other matters – were completed in time for rehearsals to begin on 1 May 1976, exactly as planned.

It was to be expected that the four prospective cycles of *The Ring* would arouse great public interest. We intended not only to do justice to it but to cast two fully rehearsed singers in some of the named roles. This will be apparent from those instances in the following cast lists where two names are separated by an oblique stroke:

Das Rheingold
Wotan: Donald McIntyre/Hans Sotin; Donner: Jerker Arvidson; Froh: Heribert Steinbach; Loge: Heinz Zednik; Fasolt: Matti Salminen; Fafner: Bengt Rundgren; Alberich: Zoltan Kelemen; Mime: Wolf Appel; Fricka: Eva Randová/Yvonne Minton; Freia: Rachel Yakar; Erda: Ortrun Wenkel/Hanna Schwarz; Woglinde: Yoko Kawahara; Wellgunde: Ilse Gramatzki; Flosshilde: Adelheid Krauss.

Die Walküre
Siegmund: Peter Hofmann; Hunding: Matti Salminen/Karl Ridderbusch; Wotan: Donald McIntyre/Hans Sotin; Sieglinde: Hannelore Bode; Brünnhilde: Gwyneth Jones/Roberta Knie; Fricka: Eva Randová/Yvonne Minton; Gerhilde: Rachel Yakar; Ortlinde: Irja Auroora; Waltraute: Doris Soffel; Schwertleite: Adelheid Krauss; Helmwige: Katie Clark; Siegrune: Alicia Nafé; Grimgerde: Ilse Gramatzki; Rossweisse: Elisabeth Glauser.

Siegfried
Siegfried: René Kollo; Mime: Heinz Zednik; The Wanderer: Donald McIntyre/Hans Sotin; Alberich: Zoltan Kelemen; Fafner: Bengt Rundgren; Erda: Hanna Schwarz/Ortrun Wenkel; Brünnhilde: Gwyneth Jones/Roberta Knie; Forest Bird: Yoko Kawahara.

Götterdämmerung
Siegfried: Jess Thomas; Gunther: Jerker Arvidson; Hagen: Karl Ridderbusch/Bengt Rundgren; Alberich: Zoltan Kelemen; Brünnhilde: Gwyneth Jones/Roberta Knie; Gutrune: Irja Auroora; Waltraute: Yvonne Minton; First Norn: Ortrun Wenkel; Second Norn: Dagma Trabert; Third Norn: Hannelore Bode; Woglinde: Yoko Kawahara; Wellgunde: Ilse Gramatzki; Flosshilde: Adelheid Krauss.

Unfortunately, it emerged from critical analysis of the 1976 festival that the four cycles had not stood the test where double casting was concerned, because the artists who took part had not been granted a fair share, musically speaking, of *The Ring's* thirteen and a half hours.

In 1976 Boulez and I succeeded to only a very limited extent in accomplishing our aim, which was to explore new and different modes of interpretation, musically as well as scenically. Although it would be unjustified and pointless to assign blame after the event, there did exist a group of musicians whose response to the novel and unwonted features of Boulez's interpretation was uncomprehending – indeed, overtly hostile. These malcontents went so far as to declare that Pierre Boulez was a 'modernist' who could not conduct and was totally incapable of reading the score of *The Ring*. So much for his highly acclaimed *Parsifal* début in 1966 and his work in subsequent years, whose excellence is preserved on disk, and so much for his career as a conductor of international repute. His opponents formed a clique that found favour with 'experienced' musicians who should really have known better. This soured his relations with the orchestra, in part because of deliberate provocation.

It was insidiously and maliciously rumoured during the 1976 season itself that seventy-three orchestral players had declined to participate in 1977 on Boulez's account. Whoever that anonymous prophet may have been, he was mistaken, because the final score was seventy-seven. However, their reasons for dropping out were very diverse. Oswald Kästner, their chairman, conducted a poll when the festival ended. Although he found that twenty-nine members of the orchestra were expressly opposed to working with Boulez again, we had known since the spring that we might have to allow for an unusually large turnover of musicians in 1977. Some, who had children of school age, were governed by changes in holiday dates introduced by the Federal *Länder*; others had already notified us that they intended to take at least one summer off after the centenary year. The last two categories amounted to forty-eight, so the total was seventy-seven. How anyone had arrived at the ominous figure of seventy-three remained an unfathomable mystery – but then, what ill-intentioned person has ever given precedence to the sober truth when beguiled by the chance to provoke a sensation that accords with his dubious purposes? This malign fiction proved durable, needless to say, and continued to surface in publications of later date.

As if Bayreuth's cauldron of lies and distortions were not already bubbling sufficiently, it was given an additional stir by the orchestra's unanimous decision to appear on stage during an interval in the first cycle's *Götterdämmerung*, and not, as was customary, at the end. That this was an own goal became apparent early in August, when the press agencies circulated a statement by Boulez and the chairman of the orchestra: 'This year's *Ring* was intensively rehearsed with Pierre Boulez from 22 June onwards, when orchestral rehearsals for *The Ring* began. Pierre Boulez and the chairman of the orchestra state that no differences of any kind arose in the course of this work, and that all rumours of a destructive opposition are false and fabricated. The conductor and the orchestra are fully alive to their mission and are naturally at pains to give of their best.' After all that had gone before, the public was only half inclined to take such a display of harmony at face value.

All this juggling with numbers proved ultimately pointless, because Pierre Boulez not only conducted *The Ring* at Bayreuth in 1977 but did so with an orchestra of the size prescribed by the composer, not an attenuated chamber orchestra. Rehearsals for the three cycles of *The Ring* gave a foretaste of what Boulez was to achieve, thanks to the receptiveness of all concerned, in subsequent years. We noted with pleasure that in 1979 and 1980 – when the television and gramophone recordings were made – many of the erstwhile protesters applied to rejoin the orchestra so as to document their own achievements and share in a certain 'immortality'. It should be added that the twenty per cent turnover in orchestral players, which was in any case attributable to a variety of factors, dwindled after 1978 to an average of ten per cent per annum.

The Bayreuth Festival has always been subject to opposition, both external and internal. Just as its originator once hurled a blazing torch into the world of 'modern artistic luxury', so opposing forces of every description have appeared on the scene: on the one hand, volunteer firefighters eager to stamp out every spark; on the other, self-appointed guardians of the blaze. Nor should one forget all those who like to warm themselves at another's fire in the hope that they may be illuminated, if only briefly, by the glow from its flames. Sadly, spells of concentrated, uninterrupted work are thus a rare and enjoyable phenomenon.

Our opponents not only regrouped in 1976 but deemed it essential to articulate their opposition in public. Instead of rendering unto the theatre that which is the theatre's, they sensed a threat to their cultural assets and feared lest the hoard of the Wagnerian Nibelungs be purloined (and I quote) by a French 'Beelzebub'. They girded themselves for a last-ditch struggle under the experienced leadership of Gertrud Strobel, who presided over the Wagner archive like some goddess out of Norse mythology. In addition to her other activities, of which I have already spoken, she saw fit to present the journalistic authors of books and articles who came to her for authentic information with material that would lend their effusions spice and credibility. It was a new way of disseminating 'revelations' about the irresponsible activities on the Green Hill.

Rehearsals for *The Ring* began on 1 May, as I have said, the first work on the agenda being *Die Walküre*. I was reassured to find that Chéreau and the singers got to know and respect each other in a remarkably short time. He was adept at explaining his ideas and putting them over, so their work together was not hampered by any time-wasting impediments, either interpretative or – incidentally – linguistic. Pierre Boulez, who arrived on 22 May, had been admirably represented until then by Jeffrey Tate, his first assistant and head coach for *The Ring*, so work on the musical side was also progressing well. Lighting rehearsals got under way on 1 June 1976, in addition to scenery rehearsals, and Pierre Boulez started orchestral rehearsals on 22 June. Double casting meant that these rehearsals had to be conducted, not with the orchestra alone, but as *Sitzproben* [rehearsals including soloists]. Despite the multifarious problems that inevitably beset any performance of this immensely demanding tetralogy in any theatre, everyone worked with unflagging diligence and enthusiasm.

The beginning of dress rehearsals at Bayreuth always represents a watershed, in a sense, because that which has hitherto matured in private must now be exposed to the eyes and ears of people who, if not complete outsiders, are not directly involved in a production. They are not an audience of the kind that streams into the Festspielhaus on first nights, but they do constitute a limited form of public. Although artists and interpreters are naturally aware that all their activities at the theatre are intended primarily for the spectators whose presence invests those activities with true significance, the advent of full rehearsals often inspires a sense of dissatisfaction with what has been achieved hitherto. I know from experience how crucial this juncture can be, and how it can threaten to shatter a performer's nerve. Being in overall charge of the Festspielhaus, I always have to exert a particular influence at such times, so as to maintain or even heighten the tension essential to a first night proper. Anyone who has ever worked in a theatre and faced a first night will know how everything inside one rebels at the prospect of having to surrender the product of weeks of concentrated effort – a process interspersed with moments of fulfilment and failure, delight and discouragement – to the judgement of the outside world. Hans Richter, the great conductor of Bayreuth's early days, once told my grandmother Cosima: 'When the curtain goes up, my pleasure ceases.' This was not, of course, an aspersion on the public whose approval any theatrical performer seeks and needs, merely an apt description of the feelings that can possess a highly motivated artist who has, up to now, been closeted with his own kind.

The *Ring* of 1976 unleashed a storm of agitation and argument. The waves beat high – just how high I propose to illustrate by citing a few incidents which, although they may well read like exaggerations or figments of the imagination, are absolutely true.

The festival's opening day, 24 July, began on a serious, dignified note far removed from the cacophony that replaced it some hours later. The morning of the *Rheingold* première was devoted to a memorable event: the reinauguration of Haus Wahnfried, now restored to its original dimensions. Rebuilt in a remarkably short space of time thanks to the Foundation, of which I shall have more to say later, the Richard Wagner Museum and the National Archive were formally handed over to the public.

Federal President Walter Scheel's speech at the previous day's ceremony had rather puzzled some of the numerous guests of honour from Germany and abroad. Indeed, one or two fanatical Wagnerians found it 'shameful' and 'reprehensible' that he should have brought out Wagner's ambivalence instead of fervently glorifying him as an artistic nonpareil, as they had clearly expected him to do, quite apart from placing the Master in the same historical context as other European composers. In short, our head of state's exposition of the 'Wagner case' and the aberrations and confusions of German history provoked a great deal of controversy. This was successfully allayed at the reinauguration of Wahnfried by Werner Maihofer, the minister of the interior, whose shrewd and tactful speech admirably defined the significance of the festival and the term 'Bayreuth' in relation to the rest of the civilized world.

I had been prevailed on to open the proceedings with a wholly unscheduled speech in which I uttered the sentence that proved so inflammatory – 'I think that bomb *had* to fall on Wahnfried' – and expressed my special thanks to Walter Scheel for having spoken as he did. I was followed by Hans Walter Wild, the mayor of Bayreuth, Hans Maier, the Bavarian minister of culture, the minister of the interior, and Alfons Goppel, the Bavarian premier. The ceremony's musical setting was supplied by the festival choir under the direction of Norbert Balatsch.

On this occasion, the official reception that normally followed the festival's opening performance was held at the Neues Schloss, not far from Haus Wahnfried, and hosted by Alfons Goppel, who had always been a true friend to Bayreuth. Because it took place at lunchtime, immediately after the museum's inauguration, we were fortunately spared the kind of embarrassment and annoyance that had ensued on the première of

Tannhäuser. Had it been held that night, the storm of indignation and disapprobation which *Das Rheingold* provoked in the auditorium would doubtless have continued to rage in the sumptuous, candlelit reception rooms of the Neues Schloss. What seemed a wise precaution had come about for various logistical reasons. As it was, the interpreters of *The Ring* and the invited guests did not come face to face, so no unpleasant or awkward scenes arose. The artists and I were also exempted from having to brave the photographers' flashguns after such a 'scandal' and feed sensation-hungry journalists with interviews and statements.

As usual when some long-established cultural possession is felt to have been dishonoured, the audience benevolently applauded the singers as they took their curtain calls, alone or in groups, but as soon as one of the dinner-jacketed 'chief culprits' appeared – *morituri te salutant* – he was assailed with unbridled fury by a many-throated chorus in which scattered 'bravos' were effectively drowned by the boos of the vast majority, who seemed to have succumbed to atavistic, inarticulate rage. My one regret is that there was no way of measuring the decibels they produced, because I doubt if any theatre in the world has heard the like.

Not wanting to throw Pierre Boulez to the lions alone, I grabbed Patrice Chéreau and sent the pair of them out in front of the curtain together. Boulez was in formal attire, but it was not customary for the producer to take a bow until the end of *Götterdämmerung*, so Chéreau was wearing jeans. These were naturally construed as an additional insult and provocation. I would not have thought it possible for such an earsplitting din to increase in volume, but I was wrong. Chéreau was in his working clothes, because he insisted on supervising the numerous steam effects in person.

I not only felt at one with *The Ring*'s new interpreters but gave a visible demonstration of my solidarity by joining them in front of the curtain – not my usual practice. Already at fever pitch, the atmosphere became more hectic still and more dominated by the thrill of the chase. From the threatening letters I received, I suspect that many members of that frenzied mob discovered that they possessed murderous proclivities. On 22 July 1976 the municipality of Bayreuth had elected me its forty-second freeman since 1851. It was later intimated to me that I was fortunate to have received that honour *before* the new *Ring* because it would have been very hard, if not impossible, for me to have done so *after* it.

Bayreuth-inured artists and I, whose long experience of violently hostile demonstrations in the Festspielhaus left us relatively unmoved, knew that success or failure at Bayreuth is far from determined by those who are loudest in their denunciations. My paramount concern, however, was to ensure that the audience's reaction did not destroy the confidence, drive and enthusiasm of those involved in the latest production, because we all had three big nights ahead of us.

For my 1976 Christmas card I had chosen a quotation from *Der Fliegende Holländer* reproduced in Richard Wagner's own handwriting: 'Patience, the storm abates. If it rages thus, it will not long endure.'

Our 1977 Siegfried, René Kollo, insisted on devoting the interval between two cycles of *The Ring* to sailing his new yacht, which was berthed at Travemünde. As bad luck would have it, he tripped over a railway line near the berth and broke his leg. His sister Marguerite, who acted as his agent, informed us that he would be unable to sing Siegfried on 20 August. We failed to find a substitute anywhere – it would have been difficult enough, in any case, to recast the role at such short notice in a production as complex as Chéreau's – so I had to persuade Chéreau himself to mime the role on stage while Kollo sang. First seated in the orchestra pit for acoustic reasons, Kollo was thereafter concealed behind a screen on stage. A similar situation occurred in *Siegfried* on 12 August 1978, or almost exactly one year later, except that this time Kollo mimed the role, being vocally indisposed, while Jean Cox sang.

Gwyneth Jones, the Brünnhilde, offered some initial resistance to this solution but was ultimately persuaded to go along with it, especially as it was her hundredth performance at Bayreuth. I was told that she soothed her agitation by gathering mushrooms.

Even when the audience is notified of a cast change in advance by leaflet or notice-board, I usually go out in front of the curtain before the performance or act, whichever, and explain the circumstances in person. In the case of the *Siegfried* on 20 August 1977, of course, it was particularly necessary to advise the audience of the curious fact that the title role would be played by the producer and sung by the soloist. I gained the auditorium via the left-hand side of the curtain, a less conspicuous way of eating humble pie than if I had emerged dead centre.

Now that Chéreau's *Ring* was in its second year, press and public resistance to it had been steadily diminishing. As soon as I announced what lay in store for the audience that night, however, the cauldron started bubbling again and I was bombarded with abuse. On diving back into my hole I encountered the blond-wigged figure of Chéreau, alias Siegfried, standing apprehensively at the stage manager's desk. He looked anything but the 'laughing hero'. 'Patrice,' I reassured him, 'they've already taken it out on me. Nothing can happen to you.'

Today, many an eye grows moist when that night is mentioned. Those who were present feel proud *à la* Goethe – 'And you can say you were there!' – and revel in the memory of a very special Bayreuth experience rendered fascinating by Chéreau's consummate acting and the precision with which he synchronized his lip movements with the singer's voice. He was not only warmly applauded, like all the singers, but acquired a different status in general. When he was standing behind the curtain after the performance, so drained and exhausted that he could hardly stand, I told him, 'You've now experienced at first hand what you demand of the singers – and you didn't even have to sing.'

When Jess Thomas became unavailable in 1977, Manfred Jung took over the role of Siegfried in *Götterdämmerung*. He had auditioned for me and Boulez just after Christmas 1976, and we engaged him on the spot. He also sang the title role in *Siegfried* from 1979 onwards, because Boulez felt that Kollo had failed to stabilize *The Ring* and round it off artistically.

The 1976 *Ring* 'made a lot of noise in the street'. I personally investigated the negative and positive response it attracted by referring to the many letters sent me. It was noticeable that, just as sound of the night watchman's horn sets the seal on the commotion in *Die Meistersinger*, the ultimate effect of the noisy whistling in the Festspielhaus was to herald the end of all the organized tumult. Though seemingly cognizant of the Paris production of *Tannhäuser* in 1861, which had been killed off by the same blunt instrument after only three performances, the industrious instigator of that whistling must have been disappointed that its effect on this production did not match that of trumpets on the walls of Jericho.

The members of the *Ring* team responded to censure, criticism and vicious tirades – for instance during interviews or at the press conference – by putting up a calm defence. They realized, even in 1976, that the production and interpretation would require further work in subsequent years, because no four-part work of so profound a nature could receive its final polish within a few short months. Changes were introduced in 1977, to the extent that our circumstances permitted, and these were appreciated by the public. In particular, 'Valhalla' and, thus, the conclusion of *Das Rheingold* were entirely refashioned, likewise all the rock scenes. The Valkyrie rock, too, was completely redesigned to make the 'fire magic' more convincing. When Boulez and Chéreau left Bayreuth at the end of that eventful 1976 season, they and I were fully satisfied that the new *Ring* must be retained at all costs, and we agreed, after conducting an objective review of the difficulties that had arisen, that we must overcome them and steadfastly maintain the course on which we had embarked. Boulez wrote me a letter on 12 October 1976 in which he described the outcome of a meeting with Chéreau and set out exactly what had to be done. From this I inferred what I myself would have to do in my own sphere of responsibility.

Chéreau and I received no more threats to murder us in 1977, and my wife was free to show her face in public without, as in 1976, having one sleeve and half the bodice of her evening gown torn off. Police protection, a temporary necessity, could be discontinued. No woman in the audience had an earring ripped out of her ear by a next-door neighbour who disagreed with her verdict on the performance, and no one in the gallery lowered a banner reading 'Boulez and Chéreau – Chéreau and Boulez: If only they would kill each other!' Repeats of *The Ring* continued until 1980, even though a party of French visitors offered to cover all my costs if I took Chéreau's production off the programme and substituted another – a suggestion I declined with thanks. There were also fewer of the nationalistic outbursts whose abstruse but sinister tone had not amused us. I was reproved for having entrusted Frenchmen with 'the most German of all works'. One person wrote that the portrayal of Sieglinde was 'an insult to German motherhood', another that his 'most profound, sacred sentiments' and 'religious and theological [*sic*] feelings' had been wounded and derided – by *The Ring*, be it noted! But to accuse the team of having 'desecrated a German cultural asset' was pretty innocuous compared to this execrable comment by an anonymous letter-writer on the Federal President's address: 'His hostility to Wagner is the work of Judas! Zion is opposed to everything German.' Another, who signed himself 'a sincere German', spat out the following, unpleasant combination of *lingua tertii imperii* and the arch-enemy legend *redivivus*: 'Since the Bayreuth *Ring* of 1976 I have learned once more to hate the French nation and the French!' Together with other brutal utterances made in public, remarks like these constituted an overt and extremist threat to freedom of expression.

On the other hand, I cannot help wondering, ironically, if there is any country where a theatre and the interpretations of Wagner's works are taken more seriously. It all depends, of course, on the motives that underlie such an attitude.

All in all, I felt it was a good and necessary thing, on the centenary of a festival often regarded – inadmissibly and stereotypically, in my opinion – as the embodiment of some kind of 'German ethos', that *The Ring*, which is likewise claimed to be 'quintessentially German', should be staged by a youthful French team. It was the turn of another mentality and another generation to submit their experiences, attitudes and hopes for discussion – a generation that construed *The Ring* as a timeless European work, pointed up its timeless remoteness and topical relevance, and endeavoured to portray its mythical core by means of symbols drawn from various periods of European cultural history. For all the chauvinistic aberrations and artistic resentment that greeted this production, a great deal of approval and enthusiasm was also perceptible, and it ultimately predominated. This provided outside confirmation of my belief that I was not guilty of a deliberate artistic breach with Bayreuth, as originally charged, but that I had preserved the essential continuity of our work and consistently developed it by means of the acoustic and visual modifications that continued to be made thereafter.

12

ALONG THE LINE OF CONTINUITY:
(2)

If the centenary *Ring* made as much 'noise in the street' as the mob in *Die Meistersinger*, I can justifiably claim that this applied to my private life as well. I granted my wife a divorce and remarried soon afterwards. To make it absolutely clear, once and for all: I regard my wife neither as an ornamental appendage, nor as a species of agent, nor as an extension of my arm. Just as I am not my grandfather – however much I owe him – so my wife is in no way a 'Cosima III', neither from the purely superficial aspect nor in terms of character. If she enjoys respect and authority both inside and outside the festival, she owes this first and foremost to her long and arduous work at Bayreuth, not to any kind of pose. It would take a sewage farm of substantial capacity to dispose of all the lies and distortions, verbal abuse and abject filth that have been heaped on us both since our marriage, both publicly and semi-publicly, and even that would leave a residue of mendacious slime. I can only regret that a reputable German news magazine should recently have seen fit to plunge into the turbid stream and swim with the current. If I do not explore this vileness in greater detail here, it should not be taken to imply that I am cloaking it a mantle of Christian charity. It simply means that I have no wish to soil myself by coming into contact with it and prefer to write without wearing a gas mask.

My two children, Eva and Gottfried, have unfortunately been prompted by their father's divorce and remarriage to give increasing rein to their aversions as the years go by. They also committed the fatal error of confusing their private life and my own with the festival happenings on the Green Hill, so it was inevitable that we should drift apart. My son, then studying for his doctorate of music, assisted Chéreau for a time in 1976; my daughter acted as 'production assistant' during the rehearsals and festival seasons from 1968 to 1973, and was an assistant producer in 1974 and 1975. She also undertook certain business trips for me, gathering information and arranging schedules. I do not propose to enumerate all the exchanges between us that began in 1976 and have continued ever since, most of them regrettably polemical in tone and often sustained by illusory pretensions. I make no charges and rebut none, though I have ample reason to do both. Also worthy of mention here is a somewhat different incident dating from 1976. My nephew Wolf-Siegfried, Wieland's son, sounded the charge against me in the press. 'One thing is certain,' he trumpeted. 'I shall fight for Bayreuth!' Only five days later he sang a different song elsewhere: 'Now is definitely not the time for a change. For me, at any rate, the moment has not yet come to assume a position of responsibility here. I believe I am not yet mature enough to feel capable of securing a foothold at Bayreuth overnight, so to speak.'

Since then, several younger members of the extensive Wagner clan have formed a kind of 'succession syndicate' (thus a recent newspaper) dedicated to hammering the festival in its present form and me as its director. Unfortunately, they do so mainly in statements and interviews that display little of their great-grandfather's vigour and confine themselves to looking backwards and conjuring up 'the voice of Nature' in the shape of an adamantine blood brotherhood. My niece Nike Wagner warned against this back in 1976, when she proclaimed, Cassandra-like: 'He's a pitfall for apprentices' feet as they totter dynastically along!'

The first volume of my grandmother Cosima's diaries was unveiled to the national and international press in the festival restaurant on 27 July 1976. Published only after lengthy legal battles had been fought on its behalf by Martin Gregor-Dellin and Dietrich Mack, it was regarded by me as a deliberate contribution to the full disclosure of all documentary material. 'This book belongs to my children,' Cosima had prefaced her notes. Several of her great-grandchildren were sitting almost opposite me. I have in front of me a press photograph that shows them all. It brings me, logically, to the Norns' question, which can never be definitively answered because their thread snapped: 'Know ye what is to come?'

On 1 December 1976 I wired Harry Kupfer, the next in the chronological sequence of producers who have worked at Bayreuth, and offered him the new production of *Der Fliegende Holländer* scheduled for 1978. His work had long been familiar to me, of course, and I settled on him after my wife and I had seen and assessed his Dresden production of *Tristan* on 28 November – not as yet in Gottfried Semper's opera house but in the Grosses Haus, which has since then reverted entirely to the theatre. Kupfer, who had been a visiting student at Bayreuth in the 1950s, wired me his acceptance on 2 December. Being an East German producer, he could not at that time work in West Germany without the say-so of a government agency, so I promptly – still in December – got in touch with the GDR's artists' agency in East Berlin, which controlled all guest artists' contracts. Its general manager, Herr Falk, issued permits for Harry Kupfer and his stage designer, Peter Sykora, on 19 May 1977. They both paid a preliminary working visit to Bayreuth on 22/3 May, in the course of which we jointly debated possible casts and, with gratifying speed, mapped out the entire production schedule and its preliminaries. The start of production rehearsals, for instance, was scheduled for 22 May 1978. Kupfer and Sykora then attended the 1977 festival's first cycle of performances, and we took the opportunity to discuss and settle other aspects of our forthcoming collaboration.

By the time the 1977 festival ended, the new, 1978 *Holländer* production had been cast in its entirety. Daland was to be sung by Matti Salminen, Senta by Lisbeth Balslev, Erik by Robert Schunk, Mary by Anny Schlem, the Steersman by Francisco Araiza, and the Dutchman by Simon Estes. No changes occurred thereafter, so these names were identical with those of the first-night cast.

Reinhard Heinrich was engaged as costume designer. The conductor I had in mind was Dennis Russell Davies, whom I engaged for *Der Fliegende Holländer* after hearing him conduct Hans Werner Henze's *Wir erreichen den Fluss* [*We Come to the River*] in Stuttgart on 8 June 1977.

That autumn I went to Amsterdam to confer with Harry Kupfer on the preliminary work in progress. A few days later, on 2 November 1977, I agreed to engage Peter Sykora as stage designer, having obtained a variety of information about him in the interim. In the event, he and our team of technicians admirably fulfilled the technical requirements of the production, which necessitated major alterations in the structure of the stage.

At my suggestion, Russell Davies and Kupfer chose the original, Dresden version of *Der Fliegende Holländer*. This meant that it was performed without intervals and with the 'hard finale', in which the scoring, particularly of the wind section, differs in some respects from the version that became established later on.

The performance was a breathtaking experience, and fascinatingly consistent in its emphases, which laid most stress on the figure of Senta. The overture itself was incorporated in the action. Senta was on stage from the beginning of the opera to the end, witnessing the whole story like a dream or a vision. Her character was dominated by elements of a psychopathological nature, and she displayed unmistakably hysterical traits. Anything overtly or latently banal was demonically heightened, as in the spinning sequence in the second act and the sailors' chorus at the beginning of the third. Because the team portrayed the Dutchman as an 'idea' in Senta's head, he could not die at the end and was unredeemed. The curtain fell on enta lying dead in a street, having jumped out of the window: suicide as he gateway to freedom. Taken as a whole, this was a psychological nterpretation that hovered midway between fantasy and reality. The opening nd closing of the walls of Daland's house were intended to convey the fluctuations between illusory, dreamlike fantasy and down-to-earth, mundane reality. Kupfer, who cited Ibsen in this connection, said that he wanted to portray 'a banal world in which no one can really live because one stifles in it'. Although the press made much of the fact that Grace Bumbry's 'black Venus' in the 1961 *Tristan* had now been matched by a black Dutchman', this was absolutely irrelevant to Kupfer's conception of he work and the way he produced it.

The first-night audience applauded wildly, drowning a smattering of boos, and nothing came of the leaflets distributed in advance by our inveterately conservative foes, who appealed to everyone not to allow Bayreuth to degenerate into an 'experimental workshop'. (Their very steadfastness has almost transmuted them into faithful old friends.) Russell Davies's very fast tempi were all that failed to appeal to his listeners, many of whom found them extreme.

Kupfer, already regarded as a potential producer of *The Ring* at the Vienna Opera, firmly espoused the Bayreuth workshop concept at the post-première press conference. He also drew attention to the paradoxical fact that no one would every dream of condemning or opposing a new interpretation of Goethe's *Faust*, as opposed to a work by Wagner, merely because it was new.

Kupfer's production of *Der Fliegende Holländer* remained on the Bayreuth programme, with one interruption, for seven years. It was recorded on disk and for television transmission or videotape distribution in 1985, its last year. Dennis Russell Davies conducted it until 1980, Peter Schneider took over from him in 1981 and 1982, and the last two years were entrusted to Woldemar Nelsson, under whose baton the recording was made.

When questioned about future programmes at the 1978 press conference, denied the rumour that Kupfer was to produce a new *Parsifal* in 1982, the hundredth anniversary of its first performance, and announced the names of the producer and stage designer for the new production of *Lohengrin* in 1979. I had yet to settle on a conductor, however. Since the conductor problem had not been satisfactorily resolved during the 1978 festival, I sought the good offices of Dr Hans Hirsch, then with Deutsche Grammophon, and asked him to find out if his current recording artist Daniel Barenboim would be interested in conducting *Lohengrin*. Barenboim could not accept my offer because of existing recording commitments, unfortunately, but he did express his general willingness to participate at

Bayreuth. I was informed of this on 28 August 1978, and we remained in
touch thereafter.

On 19 October 1978, after the usual tussle over a conductor for *Lohengrin*,
and after weighing up the various candidates' ideas and conditions, we
finally signed Edo de Waart to conduct the new production.

Götz Friedrich had agreed to take on this *Lohengrin* in the summer of
1977, when his *Tannhäuser* was being repeated. Like the latter, the *Lohengrin*
was to be his first production of the work. On 29 April 1978, having failed
to get the stage designer recommended by Friedrich, I engaged Günther
Uecker, who had caused a furore and become celebrated in the 1960s as
'Nail Uecker'. The recruitment of a costume designer proved equally
laborious, but by 18 December 1978 we could at last feel assured of Frieda
Parmeggiani's collaboration.

Our ideas on casting differed appreciably. However, since all that really
matters in the end is who sang at the première on 25 July 1979, the cast
was as follows:

King Henry: Hans Sotin; Lohengrin: Peter Hofmann; Elsa: Karan
Armstrong; Telramund: Leif Roar; Ortrud: Ruth Hesse; King's Herald:
Bernd Weikl; First Nobleman: Toni Krämer; Second Nobleman: Helmut
Pampuch; Third Nobleman: Martin Egel; Fourth Nobleman: Karl Schreiber.

The set design, which was jointly evolved by Uecker and Friedrich, and
the preliminary technical rehearsals on 6 and 8 October 1978, made it clear
that the perspectivally foreshortening platforms to left and right would
entail a relatively statuesque arrangement of the chorus, with the result that
its movements would have to be directed quite differently from those of
the *Tannhäuser* chorus. Having seen the designs for the swan and the
backstage wall, I was in no doubt that Uecker intended to do justice to his
nickname and trademark in Bayreuth, too. We had constructed an inex-
pressive disk with nails crudely and inartistically hammered into it. Once
he himself had studded this with nails in his own artistically discriminating
way, thereby achieving the iridescent swan effect he wanted, I saw how
simple materials in everyday use can be transformed into a work of art.

The première caused no offence, nor did it arouse any great enthusiasm.
The general verdict was subdued and hesitant. Not having expected
Friedrich to indulge in symbolism and stylization, people were surprised to
see him suddenly harking back to the earlier post-war productions. Friedrich
himself said: 'Wherever the meditative character manifests itself, the scenery
must hold back. That's where one has to depend on imagery and sound.'
Lohengrin did, in a sense, set the seal on Wagner's romantic operas, as
everyone knows, and was largely responsible for propelling him in the
direction of other forms of musico-theatrical expression. It is surely not
fortuitous that performances of the work are in general measured by its

ve left: Wolfgang Wagner rehearses Act I of *Die Walküre* with Gwyneth Jones, 1973. *Above*
: Donald McIntyre is congratulated by Wolfgang Wagner after his hundredth Bayreuth
formance (in *Die Walküre*) on 6 August 1977. Looking on are (from left) Pierre Boulez, Patrice
Chéreau, Jill McIntyre and Gwyneth Jones.

rearsing Parsifal in 1993: (from left) Placido Domingo (Parsifal), Deborah Polaski (Kundry),
Wolfgang Wagner (producer), and James Levine (conductor).

Pierre Boulez, Wolfgang
Wagner and Patrice Chére
announce details of the
centenary *Ring* production
1976.

The team that staged the
production of *The Ring* in
1983: (from left) Peter Ha
Georg Solti and William
Dudley at the production
with Wolfgang Wagner.

Harry Kupfer and Daniel
Barenboim rehearsing a n
production of *The Ring* in 1

The soloists' 'singing school' for the Bayreuth Festival première of *Die Meistersinger* in 1981: (from left) Siegfried Jerusalem (Walther von Stolzing), Bernd Weikl (Hans Sachs), Graham Clark (David), Hermann Prey (Beckmesser), Wolfgang Wagner (producer), Steffen Tiggeler (assistant producer), Mari Anne Häggander (Eva) and Mark Elder (conductor).

New production of *Die Meistersinger* (Act III, festival meadow), 1981. Production and stage design: Wolfgang Wagner.

New production of *Parsifal* (Act I, Scene 2), 1975. Production and stage design: Wolfgang Wagner

New production of *Lohengrin* (Act I), 1967. Production and stage design: Wolfgang Wagner.

production of *Parsifal* (Act I, Scene 2), 1989. Production and stage design: Wolfgang Wagner.

production of *The Ring* (*Götterdämmerung*, Act I, Scene 2), 1960. Production and stage design: Wolfgang Wagner.

New production of *The R*
(*Das Rheingold*, Scene 4),
1970. Production and sta
design: Wolfgang Wagner

New production of *The R*
(*Die Walküre*, Act II), 19
Production and stage des
Wolfgang Wagner.

New production of *The R*
(*Siegfried*, Act II), 1970.
Production and stage des
Wolfgang Wagner.

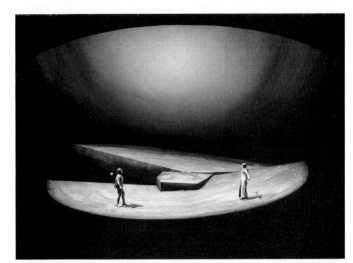

v production of *The Ring*
fried, Act III, Scene 2),
ɔ. Production and stage
ɡn: Wolfgang Wagner.

v production of *The Ring*
terdämmerung, Act II),
ɔ. Production and stage
ɡn: Wolfgang Wagner.

v production of *The Ring*
terdämmerung, finale),
ɔ. Production and stage
gn: Wolfgang Wagner.

This last photograph of Winifred Wagner with her surviving childre was taken in May 1979, on the occasion of the Richard Wagner Society's conference at Saarbrücke In front: Friedelind, Winifred, Ver Behind: Wolfgang and his wife Gudrun.

Gudrun and Wolfgang Wagner wi their daughter Katharina, watchin football match between 'Valhalla and Bayreuth Town on 20 Augus 1984. On the left is substitute Man Jung (Siegfried).

Gudrun and Wolfgang Wagner at opening of Bayreuth's Franz Liszt Museum in Haus Wahnfried on 2 October 1993. A bust of the composer can be seen in the background.

choruses and the Grail story (though I myself regard the bridal chamber scene as an important yardstick). The chorus is omnipresent, the action descriptive and ever-responsive to all that occurs – a function assigned by Wagner to the orchestra in *Das Rheingold*. The work's conspicuously choral structure and the need to present the 'miracle' in a credible manner are perhaps the main difficulties besetting any stage interpretation, and it requires a complicated balancing act to avoid that step from the sublime to the ridiculous against which Napoleon warned. Unless one means to stage something utterly preposterous – like the recent production with Bavarian highlanders in lederhosen – *Lohengrin* lends itself least of all to spectacular treatment.

I became increasingly fascinated by the leaden floor covering, which calls to mind a particular episode. Our technical director, Walter Huneke, was justifiably averse to people who had no business on stage walking around on the soft metal, especially if they were women in high heels. As it turned out, the unintended effect of these unwelcome intrusions was to enhance the beauty of the floor by adorning it with an ever-increasing number of indistinct little indentations.

When a worried patron wondered if the lead floor was a justifiable expense, and if it could not have been replaced with a conventional stage imitation, I was able to reassure him that its subsequent resale as scrap metal would actually benefit the festival budget.

No new production was staged on the Green Hill in the following year, 1980, largely because of the time it took to record *The Ring*. *Götterdämmerung* had been recorded in 1979, and it was now the turn of the remaining three parts of the tetralogy. Bayreuth was to compensate for this by presenting two new productions in 1981.

By late January 1979 my exchange of ideas with Daniel Barenboim had progressed sufficiently for us both to assume that he would conduct *Tristan* in 1981. Patrice Chéreau was scheduled to produce it, and he and Barenboim had already been in touch. We were all the more disappointed, of course, when Chéreau withdrew from the project on 18 October 1979. On 17 November Barenboim and I met at a Berlin hotel in the presence of his agent for Germany, Witiko Adler, to confer on the subject of another producer. We also, even at that stage, had a thorough discussion about possible soloists. Before we eventually settled on Barenboim's first choice, consideration was given to the following producers: he suggested Harry Kupfer, Franco Zeffirelli and the John Cox/David Hockney team; my nominations were Kurt Horres, Robert Wilson, Adolf Dresen, Göran Järvefelt, and Peter Brenner. We finally chose Jean-Pierre Ponnelle.

On 10 January 1980 my wife and I attended a concert performance of the second act of *Tristan* at the Salle Pleyel in Paris. Daniel Barenboim was conducting, and I was reassured to find that he possessed the quality that predestined him to conduct the work at Bayreuth. After the concert Barenboim invited us to dine at his apartment. Also present was Jean-Pierre Ponnelle, *Tristan*'s producer, stage designer and costume designer all rolled into one. We devoted detailed discussion to the forthcoming project and the casting of the soloists. However, so many imponderables arose before the première on 25 July 1981 that we seriously began to doubt if anyone was capable of staging a production under such chaotic conditions.

The first-night cast eventually crystallized as follows: Tristan: René Kollo; King Marke: Matti Salminen; Isolde: Johanna Meier; Kurwenal: Hermann Becht; Melot: Robert Schunk; Brangäne: Hanna Schwarz; Young Sailor: Graham Clark; Shepherd: Helmut Pampuch; Helmsmann: Martin Egel.

The production was so universally acclaimed and rapturously admired that it seems downright sacrilegious to say another word about it. I must, however, add one comment that will doubtless fall like wormwood into a cup of lasting joy: even allowing for inflation, Ponnelle's *Tristan* was the most expensive in the entire history of the Bayreuth Festival.

Ponnelle's original intention was to banish Isolde from the stage during the '*Liebestod*' and have her transfigure herself invisibly in the pit. It required some pretty tough talking by Barenboim and me to dissuade him from such an acoustic as well as visual monstrosity. At the end of her song she disappeared like Daphne behind a big tree trunk. Ponnelle also lowered the curtain *after* the B major chord, which Richard Strauss called 'most beautifully scored', had died away. This prompted me to remark that he seemed to consider his arrangement of the three remaining figures – Tristan, Kurwenal, and the Shepherd – even better than what the composer had managed to express in music.

Audiences were wildly enthusiastic nevertheless, presumably because their desire for sublime aestheticism had been so amply fulfilled.

In a departure from the usual Bayreuth practice, the production was recorded for television in its third year, 1983, and in the autumn rather than during the rehearsal period. This had previously applied only to the Venusberg scenes of the *Tannhäuser* filmed in 1978, which were done by John Neumeier and his Hamburg Ballet in a version that differed from the original and was filmed under completely different visual conditions. These scenes were recorded playback, a procedure now employed for the third act of *Tristan*. Ponnelle, who always used playback for his numerous television recordings elsewhere, had repeatedly interrupted the first and second acts and insisted on additional camera positions. This conflicted with the practice that had served us hitherto, which was to record an entire act, or at least a self-contained scene, straight through, thus preserving its theatrical flavour and vitality. The result was that in the third act, which was demanding enough already, René Kollo found himself vocally over-taxed.

Tristan was restored to the festival programme in 1986 and 1987, after a two-year break, but with different principals. Tristan was sung by Peter Hofmann, Isolde by Jeannine Altmeyer in the first performance in 1986, by Ingrid Bjoner in the second, and by Catarina Ligendza from the third onwards.

Tristan was not the only new production staged in 1981, the other being a *Meistersinger* produced and designed by me. Since the funds available for the two productions were limited, I had perforce to economize for *Tristan*'s benefit. Our technical director put all his love of botany and horticulture into the sumptuous tree in the second act of *Tristan* and the other trees in that production, so my own lime-tree in the festival meadow suffered badly: it looked from the first as if it were diseased and dying.

Carlos Kleiber's refusal of an engagement in 1977 was irrevocable, so on 19 August 1976 I got in touch with James Levine and inquired if he would be able to conduct *Tristan* the following year. His prior commitments ruled this out, as bad luck would have it. He was also unable, for similar reasons, to conduct *Lohengrin* in 1979 or the new production of *Die Meistersinger* originally scheduled for 1980 but postponed for a year because of the elaborate *Ring* recordings. However, I learned on 25 April 1979 that he could arrange his schedule for 1982 in such a way as to enable him to conduct the centenary *Parsifal*, and that he would be happy to do so.

Levine had known Bayreuth since 1962, when he first visited the town in connection with the 'master classes' run by my sister Friedelind.

And here I take the liberty of inserting a brief digression on the subject of Friedelind's master classes, their prior history and consequences. On 21 July 1953, when she set foot in Bayreuth for the first time since the festival season of 1938, my brother was at pains to avoid doing anything that might encourage her to take a personal hand – more precisely, to meddle – in the festival and festival business. Like me before him, he had come to see that she showed little capacity for systematic development or realistic effort, and that her participation would only add to our troubles. At the same time, we wanted to defuse her relations with us. Because she was currently in financial difficulties and, as ever when money matters cropped up, claimed that it would be child's play to mobilize audiences and sponsors for the Bayreuth Festival, we granted her the requisite authority to act on our behalf and agreed, in return, to pay her a certain percentage of the money she brought in. Unhappily, this venture only confirmed my scepticism in her regard. Her legal representative, Robert M. W. Kempner of Frankfurt, formerly US deputy chief prosecutor at the Nuremberg War Crimes

Tribunal, had written my mother a letter on 13 May 1953 in which he endeavoured to assert Friedelind's rights to Bayreuth and suggested that her claims as a disadvantaged daughter might be settled out of court. On 16 June our own legal adviser, Dr Gottfried Breit, drew Kempner's attention to the fact that my brother and I had been legally and unobjectionably entrusted with the management of the festival, and that our status — particularly since it had been conferred under the new legal provisions by the prior heir, Winifred Wagner — was incontestable. In consequence, Dr Breit pronounced Friedelind's claim to be disadvantaged erroneous and firmly rejected it. Having ascertained the legal position, Kempner accepted our point of view but reserved the right to take further steps in regard to the enforcement of certain demands. Friedelind was naturally anxious to operate not only under the name Wagner but under the Bayreuth Festival label as well, so her efforts to satisfy her itch for activity merely increased the strain on Bayreuth's financial resources. Such was her addiction to helping and instructing young people, especially in the theatrical sphere, that she developed a deep-seated ambition to found the 'Bayreuth Festival Master Classes, Inc.' or 'Bayreuther Festspiele Meisterklassen e. V.' My brother and I felt compelled to yield to her unbridled love of activity, albeit with the express proviso that this institution should not be an appendage of the Bayreuth Festival itself, and that she alone must be financially and legally responsible for its management. The first of these master classes was held at Bayreuth in 1959, the last in 1967. My sister certainly contrived — let it not be forgotten — to attract some distinguished, interesting and eloquent speakers. They included Walter Felsenstein, Astrid Varnay, Pierre Boulez, Gian Carlo Menotti, Maximilian Kojetinsky, Hanne-Lore Kuhse, Kurt Winter, Willi Klose, and the acoustician Werner Gabler. My brother and I also made ourselves available from time to time.

On 28 February 1964, five years after this enterprise was founded, its precarious financial position made it necessary for us to examine whether the master classes could justifiably be continued. By 1967 so many debts had accumulated, and I had privately stood guarantor for Friedelind on so many occasions, that the master classes were faced with financial ruin and ingloriously sank without trace. Friedelind naturally found it easiest to explain their demise by saying that her master class pupils had lost interest in Bayreuth once our brother was dead. That tone and that line of argument were all of a piece with those that are still adopted by other members of my family when something in and around Bayreuth fails to match their intentions.

In July and August 1976, during my sister's period of residence in England from 1972 to 1981, she held master classes at 'Southlands', the house she had acquired there. These helped to provide her with a financial basis, now that she had paid off her debts and obtained her reversionary share in the proceeds of the sale of the Wagner archive to the Richard Wagner Foundation in 1973.

So much for the master classes, and back to 1979.

On 28 August of that year I met and talked with James Levine for the first time. We parted having resolved to settle all questions relating to the stage design and casting of *Parsifal* by means of regular exchanges of information. Meantime, I was not to announce his commitment to Bayreuth before the 1980 press conference, and not without his prior consent. On 16 August 1980 Levine returned to Bayreuth for an on-the-spot attempt to resolve the many problems that remained. We clarified a certain number of them, but further problems arose concerning all those – apart from the conductor – who were to work on the centenary *Parsifal*. Finally, on 10 August 1981, I was able to announce that the team of James Levine and Götz Friedrich – whose work at Bayreuth was thus a genealogical ascent from son to father – had become constant fixed stars (note the pleonasm!) in my *Parsifal* firmament. On 27 May 1982, after seeing some photographs of the sets sent to him by Levine, his brother Tom informed me and Götz Friedrich that they looked 'fabulous'. The designer was Andreas Reinhardt, who also designed the costumes and thus became, in a sense, my third fixed star.

As producer, Friedrich made it an almost inviolable rule to have the curtain open during the prelude or overture to a first act, and he proposed to follow it in the case of *Parsifal* as well. As the conductor, James Levine was absolutely opposed to this, and a heated argument ensued. In the end the pair of them came to me, stated their points of view in forceful terms, and asked me to decide. Being highly reluctant to intervene in artistic matters *à la* Beckmesser, I ruled that, in case of doubt, the author of the work should be the supreme authority. I wanted to keep this production in the repertoire for as long as possible, but not to accord it the status of earlier *Parsifal* curiosities – in other words, not to promote it into a cult object, as had happened with the very first interpretation and, to some extent, with my brother's. That was why I had dropped my 1975 production of *Parsifal* in 1981, because I did not wish to create another 'hallowed' norm. Similarly, the centenary *Parsifal* was presented only from 1982 until 1988, with a one-year break in 1986.

The first-night cast was as follows. Amfortas: Simon Estes; Titurel: Matti Salminen; Gurnemanz: Hans Sotin; Parsifal: Peter Hofmann/Siegfried Jerusalem; Klingsor: Franz Mazura; Kundry: Leonie Rysanek; First Knight: Toni Krämer; Second Knight: Matthias Hölle; First Esquire: Ruthild Engert; Second Esquire: Sabine Fues; Third Esquire: Helmut Pampuch; Fourth Esquire: Peter Maus; Flower Maidens: Monika Schmidt, Anita Soldh, Hanna

Schwarz, Francine Laurent-Gérimont, Deborah Sasson, Margit Neubauer; contralto solo: Hanna Schwarz.

In 1983 the role of Kundry was double-cast at Leonie Rysanek's request. On the recommendation of Hans Wallat, I signed Waltraud Meier. Although the conductor and producer did not at first share my confidence in that young artist, they were very soon compelled to acknowledge that her engagement was more than justified.

The production, which was very well received on the whole, could unquestionably be described as a success. The basic structure on stage was a fallen tower into the base of which the audience could see. In the second temple scene at the end of Act III, light streamed down from above and the stage was additionally lit from upstage. This seemed to convey that day was breaking as the work drew to a close. For the first time, the redeemed knights of the Grail were joined on stage by a group of women. To Friedrich this symbolized the dawn of a new society that might possibly put an end to *Parsifal*'s inherent conflict between the sexes. Although he drew on symbols and rituals of Christian origin, he was more concerned to symbolize a utopia than to stress the Christian aspects of the work. Encased in dreams and illusions, his utopia contained no recipes for fulfilment and ended inconclusively. He defined the concept of redemption as contemplation, as a new sense of values and a summons to individual responsibility. The onlooker's imagination was stimulated because the range of potential associations seemed so wide.

In August 1978 I received from the festival press office the text of a curious interview with Georg Solti in the August issue of the magazine *Orpheus*. I was not a little puzzled by his remarks about Bayreuth and *The Ring*, remembering our numerous negotiations since 1953, the failure of our plans for *Tristan* in 1972, and the series of complete *Ring* cycles under his direction. Remembering, too, the summer holiday plans which he also restated in the interview, and which had, as I have already said, proved decisive in respect of *Tristan*, I was convinced that the customary, cyclical succession of performances was a discreet and effective allusion to his *Ring* recording sessions of 1962–4 rather than a realistic prerequisite of his participation in the festival. There was also his two-night *Ring* in Paris in 1976, conducted in collaboration with Peter Stein and Klaus Michael Grüber, who had realized their bipartite conception of *The Ring* by presenting *Das Rheingold* and *Die Walküre* in isolation, thereby eliminating *Götterdämmerung*, investing Wotan's farewell to Brünnhilde with finality, and depriving her of a chance to reawaken. Those performances, too, gave no indication of whether Solti would be able to measure up to Bayreuth's prescriptive presentation of *The Ring* as a complete cycle.

Sir Georg's interest in Bayreuth was conveyed to me by Hans Ulrich Schmid of Hanover, his local agent, in a letter dated 1 December 1979. My first meeting with the maestro had taken place in Berlin on 1 February of that year.

If I now recapitulate the singular experiences I have undergone in connection with my work at Bayreuth, and if I look back, as I inevitably must while writing these lines, on all the associated correspondence, memos, business trips, auditions, orchestral and technical conferences, rehearsal schedules, reports of performances, and countless incidents during rehearsals and performances, I realize more and more clearly that the 1983 *Ring* could not have been less typical of Bayreuth. That it ever came about at all was attributable to my having been repeatedly urged by a wide variety of people, members of the festival orchestra included, to engage a conductor of such international repute.

A major advertising campaign launched by DECCA during the 1982 festival proclaimed Solti to be 'The *Ring* conductor of our age'. This extravagant slogan made me uneasy, not only because it was based largely on his reputation as a recording artist, but also because it naturally committed him in advance to achieving superhuman feats on which, from past experience, I could not count with absolute certainty. If one extols some proprietary brand as the best on the market, one has to reiterate that claim daily, exerting immense pressure on the manufacturer to succeed and, where the public are concerned, generating vast expectations which only the sensational and unprecedented can satisfy. Much the same applied to Solti's first press conference in July 1961, when he assumed the musical directorship of Covent Garden and undertook to make that opera house nothing more nor less than 'the best in the world'. A similarly ominous pattern was followed by most of the assurances he gave to interviewers, even before the curtain went up, that his *Ring* would do full justice to each and every one of the composer's ideas. Last but not least, producer Peter Hall's 'romantic *Ring*' formula, which inevitably meant different things to different people, also helped in its maladroit way to provoke disastrous repercussions. All my warnings to that effect were carelessly brushed aside.

In mid-February 1983 I was further disquieted by Georg Solti's suggestions as to the form our programmes should take. He planned to include interviews with himself. Personally, I have always felt that the proper place for a production is on the stage, not in a programme, and it would hardly have done for the conductor to proclaim, in print: 'I'm not interested in performing a centenary *Ring*; I wanted for once to see a *Ring* I like.' (Presumably, one like those conducted by Solti elsewhere.) At the same time, there were telephone calls with his secretary, Charles Kaye, about *The Ring*, a prospective book by Stephen Fay and Roger Wood. This had been taking shape in the conductor's London studio ever since the first stage design conference on 7 December 1981, because Peter Hall had brought the two authors along without notifying me or Solti in advance.

William Dudley, the stage designer, showed his models for the first time. These could initially be demonstrated only with the aid of an engineer named Barnett. I very soon realized that the 'romantic' treatment was going to entail incredible expense and a vast amount of imagination. An engineering firm supplied special 'scenery machines' for this production. The technical literature described these as follows: 'The multifunctional scenery machine, employed in all performances as a platform with a convex and concave acting area. It generates very special scenic effects, because the platform can be rotated 360 degrees on its longitudinal axis (turning speed: 60 seconds per rotation). The specifications are impressive: platform 10,000 × 15,000 m, vertical lift 9,000 mm, infinitely variable. In spite of these dimensions the structure is assembly-friendly and extremely light-weight (may be assembled or dismantled in 2.5 hours). In addition to rotating, the platform can travel along the longitudinal axis of the stage (extent of travel 9,000 mm, speed 0.2 metres per second). Hydraulic motor rating 100 kW, cylinder strength 300,000 N/Cyl.'

When I wrily suggested that a set's main purpose should be to solve the problem of how actors enter the stage and leave it again, I inadvertently touched a sore nerve. This simple but central problem was later to rob Peter Hall of a great deal of time that could otherwise have been spent on artistic refinements, precisely because the numerous entrances and exits had not been sufficiently thought out in advance. I also objected that the big hydraulic structure left no cycloramic surfaces free for artistic purposes. My misgivings were not taken seriously until lighting rehearsals confronted the team with the realities of the situation. Peter Hall then asked me to procure him a curved, quadrangular sheet, similar in size to the platform, which could be suspended behind it and adorned with a representation of the sky. It was made within two days, cost DM 32,000, and – after Hall had experimented with its artistic possibilities for half an hour – proved to be utterly useless. In the autumn of 1983 we converted it into a canopy for the garden of the Festspielhaus canteen. Nicknamed 'Dudley's Hall', it continues to shield hungry patrons of the canteen from inclement weather to this day – unlike all the other scenery, which was dismantled once The Ring had run its course. The production's much-vaunted 'romanticism' was engendered on the cyclorama by diffuse lighting. Three times more mist, vapour and dry ice were expended than in the time of Chéreau, the 'mist champion'. The more romantic the intention, the greater the use of unromantic technology.

Rehearsals began on 18 April 1983. Regrettably, Peter Hall's knowledge of German was almost nil, despite his promise to learn some, so he worked with Andrew Porter's translation of the Ring text. Though good in itself, this was geared to its singability in English, with the result that many levels of meaning and many obvious points were lost, and this, in turn, had an effect on Hall's direction. Because he achieved some excellent and promising results at the very outset of his rehearsals of the first scene of *Das Rheingold*, he came to believe that he had virtually forged the entire *Ring* already.

The planning and implementation of the rehearsal schedule soon ran into trouble because the rhythm of rehearsals was governed, not by the task in hand, but by the manifold limitations imposed on themselves and us by Georg Solti and Peter Hall. Even discounting the effect of this on stage rehearsals, far more time than usual was taken up by the technical installations, and the hydraulics in particular. On the few occasions when I urged him to rationalize his working methods and refrain from attaching too much importance to what to us were technical trivia, Hall promptly took umbrage because he felt that I was criticizing him and restricting his artistic freedom. To cite one record that had never been surpassed at Bayreuth (and probably never will be), 145.5 hours of lighting rehearsals were required for *Götterdämmerung*.

I could never understand why the producer and stage designer, to the extent that the latter was present, hardly ever left the production desk to check lines of sight and scenic effects from other parts of the auditorium. Whenever they were not working with the singers or technicians on the stage itself, they seemed to be glued to it.

The 1983 premières were cast as follows:

Das Rheingold
Wotan: Siegmund Nimsgern; Donner: Heinz-Jürgen Demitz; Froh: Maldwyn Davies; Loge: Manfred Jung; Fasolt: Manfred Schenk; Fafner: Dieter Schweikart; Alberich: Hermann Becht; Mime: Peter Haage; Fricka: Doris Soffel; Freia: Anita Soldh; Erda: Anne Gjevang; Woglinde: Agnes Habereder; Wellgunde: Diana Montague; Flosshilde: Birgitta Svendén.

Die Walküre
Siegmund: Siegfried Jerusalem; Hunding: Matthias Hölle; Wotan: Sieg-mund Nimsgern; Sieglinde: Jeannine Altmeyer; Brünnhilde: Hildegard Behrens; Fricka: Doris Soffel; Gerhilde: Anita Soldh; Ortlinde: Anne Evans; Waltraute: Ingrid Karrasch; Schwertleite: Anne Wilkens; Helmwige: Agnes Habereder; Siegrune: Diana Montague; Grimgerde: Ruthild Engert-Ely; Rossweisse: Anne Gjevang.

Siegfried
Siegfried: Manfred Jung; Mime: Peter Haage; The Wanderer: Siegmund Nimsgern; Alberich: Hermann Becht; Fafner: Dieter Schweikart; Erda:

Anne Gjevang; Brünnhilde: Hildegard Behrens; Forest Bird: Sylvia Green-
berg.

Götterdämmerung
Siegfried: Manfred Jung; Gunther: Bent Norup; Hagen: Aage Haugland;
Alberich: Hermann Becht; Brünnhilde: Hildegard Behrens; Gutrune:
Josephine Barstow; Waltraute: Brigitte Fassbaender; First Norn: Anne
Gjevang; Second Norn: Anne Wilkens; Third Norn: Anne Evans;
Woglinde: Agnes Habereder; Wellgunde: Diana Montague; Flosshilde:
Birgitta Svendén.

I was permanently mystified by Solti's manner of conducting the huge,
four-part work. All the other *Ring* conductors I had observed at Bayreuth
employed a technique carefully calculated to ward off physical exhaustion.
The purpose of rehearsing the orchestra on its own, as everyone knows, is
to enable the conductor to work out what he can achieve with the musicians
from the interpretative aspect. He can then, during full rehearsals and,
above all, during performances proper, calmly and self-assuredly conduct
the singers without having to exert much of a controlling influence on the
orchestra. Solti's downright aggressive manner during rehearsals, which was
often accompanied by the habitual if unconscious whistling and discordant
singing with which he hoped to spur the singers on to even greater heights,
was extraordinarily impressive but never allowed a balanced performance
to emerge, even when the makings of one were there. I became aware that,
because of the 'doctoring' made possible by recording techniques, notably
in his highly acclaimed *Ring* recording of the 1960s, this undeniably great
conductor lost a great deal when it came to bringing music to life in a
theatre. I am bound to say, with genuine regret, that Solti's wish to achieve
something truly great and important at Bayreuth, the very home of *The
Ring*, remained unfulfilled. During our preliminary discussions he had made
the quite unacceptable request that only *Das Rheingold* and *Die Walküre* be
performed in the first year. This resulted from an unconscious recognition,
which dawned on him later, that there was an appreciable difference
between his aspirations and reality – more precisely, between the demands
of *The Ring* and the limits of his physical strength. The miracle he
prophesied – a reproduction of the work that would, for the first time,
measure up to Wagner's ideas and requirements – did not come to pass.

The choice of Peter Hall as producer and William Dudley as stage
designer was not an immediate one. We had previously discussed the
possibility of engaging Rudolf Noelte, Franco Zeffirelli, Peter Bauvais, Boy
Gobert, and sundry others. If only because of the artistic antitheses latent
in those names, it was apparent that Solti had no clear idea of what he

expected from a producer, and that, as I have already said, he wished to assert the conductor's absolute primacy – something he had clearly failed to do in Paris with Peter Stein and Michael Grüber. It was very soon borne in on me, even during the first scenery conference, that he would fare no better in this respect with Peter Hall. He devoted so much time to auditioning the cast that he had too little to spare for intensive preliminary work with them prior to the production rehearsals, and the resulting situation could only have been remedied by persevering and continuous work throughout *The Ring*'s customary five-year run. The plan to exploit the production commercially and bring out a video in the very first year was not in Bayreuth's best interests at that stage, experience having taught me that no interpretation should be released to the media until it has matured for a certain length of time. There is no denying that the hoped-for pecuniary rewards were disappointing – wholly proportionate to the 'miracle' that had been proclaimed but not yet accomplished.

While I was visiting London on 5 March 1984, Solti handed me a letter dated 2 March which now reposes in my files. Its gist, as he informed me in the course of conversation, was as follows: on medical advice, he proposed to conduct all the rehearsals and the first cycle in 1984, but to delegate the second and third cycles to another conductor. I asked for time to consider.

Unable to sanction such a division of responsibilities, I entrusted *The Ring* to Peter Schneider, who had proved himself at Bayreuth by conducting the *Der Fliegende Holländer*. On 19 May 1984 we put out a press release announcing the change of conductors in such a tactful manner that on 31 May Sir Georg wrote me a letter expressing his thanks for my sympathetic understanding and the way in which I had dealt with the problems that had arisen in recent months. Despite these, he looked back on our collaboration with pleasure and trusted that I shared his sentiments.

There was, of course, a faintly humorous sequel to these events: not long before the festival opened, the DECCA posters were quietly pasted over.

Peter Hall fulfilled his contractual obligations in 1984 by developing his interpretation and conducting an appreciable number of rehearsals. In the third and fourth years he handed over to his second assistant, Michael McCaffery, and to Dorothea Glatt, whose many modifications to the sets and production were, in my opinion, both valuable and appropriate.

It is taken for granted at Bayreuth that a producer has a continuing commitment to his production. I still regret that Peter Hall should have felt compelled to withdraw from that obligation, whereas Solti had expressly stated before the 1983 premières that the results he hoped for would not be attainable until the third year. In the event, Solti was not missed. Peter

Schneider's familiarity with the Festspielhaus enabled him to win his fight with *The Ring* – and not only on points.

This *Ring* drew a very mixed response from audiences and critics in 1983, but their differences of opinion lacked the electric intensity so often generated by the live theatre. Many features of the production were inchoate. They aroused expectations that remained unfulfilled, as did the watchword 'romantic', which had been publicized in advance and proved very influential. Being irreducible to a common denominator and associated with different things by different people, however, it only provoked an even wider divergence of view after the event. For all its discrepancies and its partly truncated character, and although the above circumstances render it impossible to draw up a true balance sheet, the production was none the less necessary and useful to Bayreuth in a general context.

To conclude with a curiosity, I should mention that, after the very last *Götterdämmerung* in 1986, those who would once have gladly tarred and feathered Chéreau proceeded to surpass the sensational record for applause set in 1980. Chéreau's *Ring* had received 101 curtain calls in 85 minutes; Hall's score was 128 in 77.

On 17 April 1985 I had sent Werner Herzog a telegram asking if he would be interested in working at Bayreuth, and our first meeting took place in Munich on 24 April. Oswald Georg Bauer had given me a detailed account of his production of Ferruccio Busoni's *Faust* in Bologna, and I was anxious to confirm my impression that he might be the person to evolve a new and entirely different interpretation of *Lohengrin* that would contrast with its predecessors. Only two days later, on 26 April, we met again at Bayreuth so that he and the stage and costume designer of his choice, Henning von Gierke, could acquaint themselves with the peculiarities and potentialities of the Bayreuth stage and the Festspielhaus in general. Meantime, consideration was given to the question of a conductor. To my delight, I was immediately able to fulfil my promise to Peter Schneider to entrust him with a new production. At a conference in Mannheim on 21 October 1985, detailed discussion was devoted to casting and cuts, for instance the so-called '*O Luft*' cut in Act III, Scene 2, and the longer version of the Grail story. The second part, which Richard Wagner himself had cut, had been given at Bayreuth only once: in 1936, with Franz Völker in the role of Lohengrin. We agreed that the conductor and producer should remain in close touch.

A laser was to be installed at Bayreuth for the first time, and this was tested at the Festspielhaus on 3 June 1986. The following day the producer and stage designer were joined by the conductor and the chorus master, Norbert Balatsch, for a joint inspection of the models and a discussion of the practical problems posed by various scenic ideas. Schneider and Balatsch expressed certain misgivings about the positioning of the chorus. In the last week of August 1986 we conducted some more technical experiments, one of them concerning the snowfall with which it was planned to conclude the opera. My main task was to ensure that the work would be performed at all by putting a brake on von Gierke's extravagant ideas.

On 25 May 1987, or only a few weeks before rehearsals began, I was compelled to apply the brake even harder. Herzog and von Gierke had dreamed up a peculiar 'external installation'. They proposed to surround the Festspielhaus with a ring of seven huge, monolithic blocks of stone designed to serve as an *al fresco* extension of the stage design and create a kind of mythical zone. An eighth monolith was to be erected on the stage at the point where Lohengrin appeared. It was envisaged that the stones should be arranged around the judgement oak that stood in the notional centre of the auditorium, more or less where the production desk was situated. There would also be a circle of small stones on stage, forming a counterpart to the big ones outside. The laser used for Lohengrin's apparition would have shone out over the roof of the Festspielhaus and across the world, evoking speechless amazement at this magical production from people at least as far distant as Palermo (the curvature of the earth, etc., being grandly disregarded).

I argued that it would be obstructive to have seven huge granite monoliths standing around (Henning von Gierke had pronounced a lighter substitute inappropriate), and that it would cost a fortune to transport the stones, install them securely, and take them down after each performance. Apart from that, however, I objected to the scheme on principle and for quite a different reason. My brother and I had striven hard and successfully to divest Bayreuth of its aura of sanctity: we had re-created a theatre out of a temple devoted to esoteric rituals. Von Gierke's proposal would have nullified a reform that had been in progress for over thirty years by sneaking a new superstition in through the back door, so I firmly rejected it. I did, however, permit him to outline his ideas on the subject in our brochure entitled 'Retrospect and Preview – Bayreuth 1988'.

Our technical director, Walter Huneke, expressed his own views on the absurdity of this plan for *Lohengrin* cult monoliths in a memorandum dated 26 February 1987. The whole affair not only confirmed my aversion to this type of exaggerated theatricality but made me realize, yet again, that it is the fulfilment of such unrealistic demands in many productions that helps to bring our medium into general disrepute. In this particular instance it had been suggested that the scheme be promoted by asking quarrymen to sponsor it. I could only shake my head at this. Was the requisite mythico-transcendental aura to be achieved by adorning each monolith with an eye-catching plaque advertising the services of the firm that had donated it?

If I have gone into some detail about a plan that never materialized, I do so only to show that my function as the ultimate authority at Bayreuth is not confined to insisting on the observance of financial and material guidelines. I also have to ensure that the urge for self-fulfilment and interpretation indispensable to any artist does not assume lunatic forms, and that subjectivist egomania does not impose it on us as the *ne plus ultra* of theatrical wisdom. The Festspielhaus is not a place of worship, nor are our stage props devotional objects or sacred relics. Just as audiences are not religious communities at prayer, so producers and stage designers wield no priestly authority and fulfil no mystagogic function. A performance at Bayreuth should not be confused, far less equated, with the administering of a sacrament. Ideally, the stage designer should create images true to a particular work. If the former dominate the latter, however, it is as well to recall Wagner's own dictum that scenery must be a 'silently-enabling background to the action'.

Lohengrin was a great and enduring success, even without the mystic circle.

The use of the laser was not an unalloyed delight, admittedly, because the beam did not have its hoped-for effect unless sufficient vapour was blown on to the stage when the lights were dimmed. The stage area being aerodynamically quite unpredictable, the luminous hero had to make his appearance in darkness, not that this detracted from the enchantment of the spectacle. In the first two scenes of Act II the moon was reflected in a lake of real water, and wavelets could be heard lapping against its banks from time to time. The water had to drain away between the second and third scenes to make room for the choruses. The incurable gurgling sound it made as it flowed down the pipe was particularly audible during the piano passages of the intermezzo, but no one minded. Similarly, no one inveighed against the production team because of other features such as the Gothic architectural relics reminiscent of well-known paintings, or the bridal chamber situated on an island of steppe grass in the midst of an icy waste surrounded by wolves with glowing eyes, or the violent onset of winter at the end. Contented audiences were left smiling a trifle nostalgically at the memory of the meteorological stage effects, which were magically successful. After so many festival seasons littered with bones of contention, they fell under the gentle and beguiling spell of this visually and musically enchanting production. There was nothing to take offence at, for once, and all could once more devote themselves in peace to the captivating, 'silvery-blue beauty' of wonderful music combined with images familiar to them, perhaps, from childhood.

Werner Herzog was a very popular producer and, from my own point of view, an extremely pleasant associate. His *Lohengrin* remained in the repertoire from 1987 until 1993, with a single break in 1991, and was recorded on CD and video. I should add that, where the latter recording was concerned, our make-up department under Inge Landgraf and Hans-Rudolf Müller achieved the impossible in fulfilling Henning von Giercke's inordinate requirements in regard to make-up.

Nadine Secunde, who had been cast as Elsa, fell ill before the dress rehearsal in 1987, so we were compelled to ask Catarina Ligendza, who was due to sing Isolde in the *Tristan* première two days later, to step in at the last moment, which she did without hesitation. Nadine Secunde had recovered by the second performance. King Henry was sung by Manfred Schenck, Lohengrin by Paul Frey, Ortrud by Gabriele Schnaut, Telramund by Ekkehard Wlaschiha, and the Herald by James Johnson. The four noblemen were Clemens Bieber, Helmut Pampuch, Manfred Hemm, and Heinz Klaus Ecker.

On 29 March 1985 I wrote to Dr Claus Helmut Dreese in Vienna and thanked him for enabling me to entrust Harry Kupfer with the new production of *The Ring* scheduled for 1988, Dr Dreese having generously released him from his Vienna commitments in June of that year. Hans Schavernoch agreed to handle the stage design on 24 May, and the costume designer's place in the team was filled by Reinhard Heinrich. I had taken advantage of every meeting with Daniel Barenboim since October 1983 to raise the subject of the new *Ring*, and on 7 February 1984 a more definite prospect of discussing the project and his part in it arose because there was a possibility of his conducting a concert version of the work before the relevant festival.

As soon as the whole team had been decided upon, we engaged in the preliminary activities essential to any fruitful discussion of conceptual and vocal matters, as well as to the co-ordination of the sequence in which rehearsals and performances are to occur. We also debated how the seventh Bayreuth *Ring* since 1951 could be fitted into the festival context in terms of its overall conception. Harry Kupfer, in particular, wanted the periodic and cyclical nature of the Bayreuth *Ring* to form a conceptual link between his own *Ring* and previous productions.

Minutes dated 18 October 1986 record that the dimensions of the 'street of history', which ran off into 'infinity', had been finally determined, and that laser experiments had been conducted to ascertain the extent to which that technique could be used in the first scene of *Das Rheingold*, in the 'fire magic' of *Die Walküre*, and the finale of *Götterdämmerung*. Meantime, we had finalized the casting of some major roles in the première year. John Tomlinson was to sing Wotan in *Das Rheingold* and *Die Walküre*, Reiner Goldberg was a certainty for one of the two Siegfrieds (the role was to be shared by two singers, as on previous occasions, because of its vocal demands), and the three Brünnhildes were to be sung by Deborah Polaski. Graham Clark, originally cast as Mime in both *Siegfried* and *Das Rheingold*, later sang Loge in the latter work instead, while Alberich went to Günter von Kannen and Gutrune to Eva-Maria Bundschuh. Siegfried Jerusalem was studying the name part in *Siegfried* with Daniel Barenboim and his chief assistants, Antonio Pappano and John Fiore, in the hope that he could be correctly and successfully coached in the role. By the end of the 1986 season it had been agreed that, in addition to musical rehearsals with the soloists, preliminary scenic rehearsals of *Die Walküre* (omitting the Valkyrie scene in Act III) and *Siegfried* (omitting Act II) would be held on the rehearsal stage, complete with original sets, from 25 July 1987 until the festival ended on 27 August. The only roles still to be cast on 9 December 1986 were those of Donner, Fasolt, Helmwige, and the Third Norn.

At the scenic rehearsals and conferences on 5 and 6 October 1987, it became clear to the 'treasurer', i.e. Wolfgang Wagner, that the latest estimates of expenditure on scenery and costumes had already overrun the total budget by some DM250,000. I consequently requested all concerned, not to be unimaginative, but at least to restrain their flights of fancy sufficiently to keep within our means. At the next scenery rehearsal and meeting for demonstration purposes, held on 16 November 1987 in the presence of Kupfer, Schavernoch, and Heinrich, it was established with the Bayreuth technicians that the laser had been tested and modified sufficiently to be regarded as a definite adjunct to Scene One of *Das Rheingold* as well as to all fire effects and the 'water-road' at the end of *Götterdämmerung*. A minute dated 22 March 1988 stated that all the proposed effects, including that of the 'funeral procession' in Act III of *Die Walküre*, had been determined or already developed to the extent that they could be technically perfected at rehearsals from 18 April 1988 onwards, and that production rehearsals could begin on 23 April.

Thanks to Daniel Barenboim and his outstanding musical assistants, and also to Harry Kupfer and his staff, who were headed by Peter Ehrlich, it was possible to conduct repeat rehearsals with the singers from a certain stage in rehearsals onwards. I must again point out in this connection that the limited casting of *The Ring* (discounting certain scenes in *Götterdämmerung*, the Valkyrie scene, and parts of *Das Rheingold*) enables a sensible and well-devised rehearsal schedule to make use of the time available in an intensive and productive manner. This prevents some of the singers from having to stand around – as so often happens – in idleness. One eminent producer's engagement at Bayreuth came to grief on another occasion because he deemed it necessary to keep all concerned (in 1988, for example, *The Ring* employed twenty-eight soloists) waiting on the benches outside the rehearsal room, where they would be readily available whenever he deigned to work with one or another of them. Harry Kupfer is the exact opposite. He embarks on rehearsals with everything precisely mapped out in his head beforehand, and his long experience, which never lapses into pure routine, is universally perceptible. He grasps at once how best to realize his ideas with each singer individually. He also knows precisely how and by what means his technical requirements can be fulfilled, thereby avoiding the needless tension and altercations that so often arise. I never heard him – unlike certain other leading artistic associates of mine – complain that time was too short to produce a polished *Ring*. It should nevertheless be emphasized that forging a *Ring* sometimes necessitates the use of a blacksmith's hammer!

Although *The Ring* is a work whose demands can never be met in full, it is only natural that every interpreter should take any opportunity, especially here at Bayreuth, to develop the accomplishments of the past in his own way. This was particularly true of Kupfer, whose interpretation of the work was uncompromising in its clarity and consistency. He developed the tetralogy in an overwhelmingly logical manner, casting it in a single mould and never allowing it to disintegrate into separate parts or particles. His was not *the* definitive interpretation of *The Ring*, but only, as he himself repeatedly stressed, one of perhaps two hundred and fifty possible interpretations. Many people were disturbed by his stringent consistency, many others found it impressive. Audiences being more accustomed to inconsistency in everyday life, it may have been precisely this aspect of Kupfer's *Ring* that moved them to approbation or condemnation.

I much admired Daniel Barenboim's empathetic grasp of *The Ring* and the congruence he established between music and stage, bringing the orchestra and the cast into harmony without sacrificing or subordinating the purely musical constituents of Wagner's work. His own, individual way of working with the singers and musicians, and also of consorting with them on an everyday level in the atmosphere peculiar to Bayreuth, bred a sense of security and a mood of communal artistic endeavour.

Although CD and video recordings of this *Ring* were made in the fourth and fifth years of its run, 1991 and 1992, these are only partly successful in conveying the lively interaction between stage and audience. It has been the subject of a lengthy book, and the articles and reviews devoted to it are legion. I do not propose to amplify or comment on all that has been said or written about it. I shall simply conclude by appending the cast lists of the four works when they were premièred in 1988:

Das Rheingold
Wotan: John Tomlinson; Donner: Bodo Brinkmann; Froh: Kurz Schreibmayer; Loge: Graham Clark; Fasolt: Matthias Hölle; Fafner: Philip

Kang; Alberich: Günter von Kannen; Mime: Helmut Pampuch; Fricka: Linda Finnie; Freia: Eva Johansson; Erda: Anne Gjevang; Woglinde: Hilde Leidland; Wellgunde: Annette Küttenbaum; Flosshilde: Jane Turner.

Die Walküre
Siegmund: Peter Hofmann; Hunding: Matthias Hölle; Wotan: John Tomlinson; Sieglinde: Nadine Secunde; Brünnhilde: Deborah Polaski; Fricka: Linda Finnie; Gerhilde: Eva Johansson; Ortlinde: Lia Frey-Rabine; Waltraute: Silvia Herman; Schwertleite: Hitomi Katagiri; Helmwige: Eva-Maria Bundschuh; Siegrune: Linda Finnie; Grimgerde: Uta Priew; Rossweisse: Hebe Dijkstra.

Siegfried
Siegfried: Siegfried Jerusalem; Mime: Graham Clark; The Wanderer: Franz Mazura; Alberich: Günter von Kannen; Fafner: Philip Kang; Erda: Anne Gjevang; Brünnhilde: Deborah Polaski; Forest Bird: Hilde Leidland.

Götterdämmerung
Siegfried: Reiner Goldberg; Gunther: Bodo Brinkmann; Hagen: Philip Kang; Alberich: Günter von Kannen; Brünnhilde: Deborah Polaski; Gutrune: Eva-Maria Bundschuh; Waltraute: Waltraud Meier; First Norn: Anne Gjevang; Second Norn: Linda Finnie; Third Norn: Lia Frey-Rabine; Wogline: Hilde Leidland; Wellgunde: Annette Küttenbaum; Flosshilde: Jane Turner.

Towards the end of May 1987 I received Dieter Dorn's agreement in principle to produce *Der Fliegende Holländer* at Bayreuth in 1990. Giuseppe Sinopoli had already been engaged to conduct, and in August of the same year I managed to obtain a stage and costume designer in Jürgen Rose, whom I had known since his setting of *Tannhäuser* in 1972. Because I was as closely acquainted with his working methods as he with mine, the prospect of needless mutual friction was precluded from the first.

On 15 January 1989 a meeting took place at Dieter Dorn's current sphere of operations, the Munich Kammerspiele. In addition to purely artistic and administrative matters, we discussed casting problems, one of which had arisen because Cheryl Studer was unavailable. Having sung Elisabeth in my 1985 *Tannhäuser* under Sinopoli's direction, she had been the conductor's first choice, together with Bernd Weikl, for the new *Holländer* production.

After many such meetings, in the course of which Sinopoli and the chorus master, Norbert Balatsch, expressed misgivings about certain proposed chorus positions, agreement was finally reached, though various production-governed problems continue to affect the musical flow of the work and preserve their complexity to this day.

By mid-December 1989 we had also succeeded in finding a financially warrantable and acceptable solution for the technical effect whereby the spinning-room in Act II rises and rotates 360 degrees. This not only enabled Senta to subside into her 'wonderful dreams', but fulfilled the dreams of the producer and stage designer. As originally estimated, the cost of this would have swallowed up three-quarters of the entire scenery budget.

We resolved all the problems that arose by discussing them in a sympathetic manner. As the ultimate authority, I eventually agreed, despite my personal dislike of it, to the solo pantomime during the overture. Although I yielded to the producer's request, I remain immutably opposed on principle to overloading a production with apparent profundities whose interchangeable and, thus, noncommittal symbolism merely illustrates but fails to interpret a piece of music – in this case, music which Wagner, the dramaturgical musician, certainly did not conceive of in visual terms but intended simply to attune the audience's ears to the ensuing work.

The pantomime shows a man, a 'stranger', attempting to scale a triangular white mountain but continually slipping and falling: a Sisyphus who, though not identical with the Dutchman, closely resembles him. He is striving to reach some red ropes strung diagonally so that they intersect just above the summit of the triangular mountain, but he also has designs on a sphere (the world?) apparently rotating in the distance. He manages to gain the summit but snaps the ropes of destiny and sinks back. The curtain closes before the redemption motif rings out at the end of the overture. This is obviously a parable, not a mountaineering scene with musical accompaniment, but its disadvantage, in my opinion, is that it pre-empts the plot of *Holländer* and makes the opening of the curtain after the overture seem almost superfluous. To me this visual representation of the overture is a definite pleonasm that can weaken, if not almost nullify, the story of the ensuing opera.

The producer thought it appropriate to develop a further dimension in the story by making lemur-like creatures of the ghost-ship's crew (who only play a really active part in Act III) and bringing them into play, whenever he considered it dramatically relevant, from Act I onwards.

After Kupfer's psychological interpretation of the work as Senta's personal tragedy, Dieter Dorn's unpretentious reading yielded a no less highly-charged production whose simple but potent imagery lingered in the mind and found almost universal favour with a public responsive to post-Modernism. As Dorn himself put it, he was aiming for 'sensory enlightenment' as to who man is and what he is capable of, but he did not necessarily want to shed light on his motivation because 'psychology has no place on the stage' and the characters should be allowed to preserve their secret. Thus, symbolic shades and shapes were the production's most impressive feature, though its luminous colours and aesthetic harmony tended to soften and sometimes stylize much of *Holländer*'s rigour. On his own submission, Dorn's aim was 'to capture the story behind the story' and seek out its inherent mysticism. Magical and poetic effects emanated from a carefully-devised and thoroughly tasteful composition in which the dominant colours were red (the ingenious sail of the Dutchman's ship), yellow (the stage and Daland's tiny, medieval-looking ship in Act I, the spinning-room in Act II), blue (Act III), and black (the universal background and base colour). When combined with the formal tension existing between symbolic geometrical figures – triangles, spheres, and rectangles – these were probably more productive of intellectual fascination than of emotional involvement in a rich, full-blooded theatrical experience.

In the great Senta–Dutchman duet in Act II, the moon and stars shone in a dark infinity of cosmic space with the spinning-room standing forlornly and unrealistically in the centre foreground, a little, yellow, thin-walled hut of pentagonal shape. Emerging from it for their duet, the singers seemed almost to be floating in space – an impression heightened when the building rose and slowly rotated on its axis. As Dorn put it, this was 'a sop to the imagination' designed to convey that, for Senta and the Dutchman, the world had turned upside down. That, of course, was an extremely tense moment, and what added to its tension was that most of the audience were staring – like birds mesmerized by a snake – at the Dutchman's hat. Although he had left this behind on a chair, it did not fall off when the hut rotated. Many members of the audience were so enthralled by this seeming suspension of the force of gravity that they ceased to concentrate on the duet, which became no more than the musical accompaniment to a technological feat. Not so at the dress rehearsal, when the hat became detached and fell to the floor as the hut canted over. Not realizing that it was meant to stay put, everyone watched with amusement as it tumbled inexorably from the first surface to the fifth and back to the first. That hat became a favourite topic of conversation, and, needless to say, the invited guests at the dress rehearsal were quick to pass on this outstandingly interesting feature of the new production to those who were due to attend subsequent performances. Thus do artistic ideas sometimes beget comical results.

'Anyone who flies a kite wants it to take off,' Dieter Dorn remarked in an interview. 'It's a shame when there's no wind, that's all.' Generally speaking, however, there was no lack of wind in this *Holländer*'s sails, and the whole production was a concerted and harmonious team effort on the part of Giuseppe Sinopoli, Dieter Dorn, and Jürgen Rose. The version chosen was the continuous one of 1860, complete with 'redemption finale'.

Except in the second part, the scenery's numerous set drops produced a curiously muted and un-Bayreuthian sound, not that this worried anyone, because the tonal inadequacies were offset by what was happening on stage. For me, however, experience of this particular combination of the visual and the aural raised the question, yet again, of where the ideal balance lies. Does visual fascination betoken a loss of tonal beauty? Is this acceptable? From the musical aspect, is a CD the only guarantee of perfection where an opera or a music drama is concerned? Or, to be more specific, should more importance be attached to what happens on stage than to a tonal effect diminished by the nature of the production? These are open questions of abiding relevance and concern.

The cast for the première was as follows: Daland was sung by Hans Sotin, Senta by Elizabeth Connell, Erik by Reiner Goldberg, Mary by Barbara Bornemann, the Steersman by Clemens Bieber, and the Dutchman by Bernd Weikl. From 1991 onwards Senta was sung by Sabine Hass and May by Hebe Dijkstra.

The prior history of the new *Tristan* production of 1993 was a long one. Before opening formal negotiations with Heiner Müller, the *Tristan* producer-designate, my wife and I had visited Berlin at Daniel Barenboim's suggestion and met with Müller for a first, exploratory talk. On 10 July 1990, while rehearsals were in progress at Bayreuth, Barenboim, Müller and Erich Wonder, the stage designer, met there to discuss all the requisite details of casting, assistants, and so forth, and to clarify certain terms of employment. This was the occasion on which it was first proposed to engage a Japanese costume designer, as yet unnamed. Erich Wonder showed my wife and me his set models in Vienna on 8 April 1991. A few days later, on 15 April, they were brought to Berlin, where we discussed them with Wonder, Heiner Müller, and Daniel Barenboim. The first technical rehearsals took place in Bayreuth on 22 and 23 May.

On 19/20 October 1991 the costume designer Yohji Yamamoto, better known as a couturier, visited Bayreuth to discuss the costumes with Heiner Müller and Erich Wonder. It was agreed that these should be available for the preliminary rehearsals in August 1992, because the singers' movements would be appreciably influenced – indeed, governed – by their special design. It was also arranged to meet again early the following year. This meeting, which took place in Munich on 21 March 1992, was attended not only by Heiner Müller, Erich Wonder and Yohji Yamamoto, but by the heads of the Bayreuth costume department, Heike Ammer and Renate Stoiber, who had come bringing numerous bolts of materials from friendly suppliers of our acquaintance – materials that might possibly accord with the costume designer's previously expressed ideas and requirements. Between 11 and 14 July 1992, fittings and walk-on trials were carried out on the main stage of the Festspielhaus with the singers of Tristan and Isolde, and also with supernumeraries. One side of the stage was devoted to an accurate mock-up of the set for Act I and the other to that for Act II, each in its own particular colours, so that simultaneous lighting tests could determine their effect on the coloration of the costumes.

Preliminary rehearsals for this new *Tristan* were held between 9 and 23 August 1992, as arranged. Heiner Müller, actively and effectively assisted by Daniel Barenboim, worked with the singers of Tristan, Isolde, Brangäne, Kurwenal, and Melot on Rehearsal Stage IV, a nearby dustbin depot having been removed for the occasion. Rehearsal Stage IV was exclusively reserved for the members of the *Tristan* team, and it was not long before they all felt very much at home there. Continuity breeds solidarity, and the immediate proximity of the Festspielhaus canteen, which they jointly patronized, played a not important part in cementing their *esprit de corps*.

I was delighted to note, even during the earliest preliminary rehearsals, that Heiner Müller's long experience as a stage director stood him in good stead when it came to working with singers. To the great amusement of all present, he used to preface every rehearsal by reading out the day's horoscope in *Bildzeitung*, to which, as a 'disaster-lover', he was much addicted. It soon emerged in the course of these preliminary rehearsals that the costumes made for them could not be used because they were incompatible with the producer's intentions. Yohji Yamamoto's appointments in Bayreuth were always arranged so as to coincide with his visits to Europe, so all he had to bear was the expense of the journey to and from Paris. He would come either before or after presenting his collections there, for instance between 17 and 19 October 1992, when some new ideas were broached and tried out in consultation with Heiner Müller. On that occasion Yamamoto brought along – at his own expense – three female assistants who diligently collaborated with our own wardrobe and make-up staff in improving the costumes. Although these continued to make waves because everyone, including the singers, had very different ideas on the subject, they were all stage-worthy by 9 July 1993. As for the 'objects' that formed an integral part of the costumes, these were individually moulded in Plexiglas by a skilled associate of Yamamoto's, a true master of his craft, who completed them by 15 July (four days before the dress rehearsal and ten days before the première). Yamamoto displayed unvarying Japanese courtesy and composure throughout, coupled with a marked feeling for essentials, and there was no doubting the pleasure it gave him, as an artist working at the seat of a long tradition, to participate in Richard Wagner's festival.

Heiner Müller's work at Bayreuth confirmed the special esteem in which I had held him since attending a performance of *Die Hamletmaschine* and conversing with him afterwards. Once attuned to his often sarcastic, sometimes almost cynical way of talking, one learns through him to appreciate 'disasters' because they can shed a different light on many things and lead one to revise one's opinions. Where Erich Wonder was concerned, I greatly valued the harmonious and creative way in which he brought his knowledge of the theatre to bear, not only when collaborating with Heiner Müller but later on, when his designs were being executed by my staff. As musical director, Daniel Barenboim enjoyed the support of his assistants, notably Simone Young. Heiner Müller brought Stephan Suschke with him and 'inherited' Isao Takashima, already a veteran of Bayreuth.

For Gero Zimmermann, who had been employed as a technical assistant during the 1969–73 seasons and was appointed assistant to our technical director in 1990, this *Tristan* was the first new production he handled in his capacity as technical director, a post he has held since 1 October 1990.

The achievements of this international team, as of the cast, were greeted by the first-night audience in summer 1993 with that mixture of enthusiastic approbation and predictable condemnation which in my view makes it highly probable that this production has many years ahead of it. A *Tristan* in which almost all the singers were new to their roles is exceptional enough in itself, and gives the lie to those who hold that Wagnerian voices no longer exist. My assessment of the first year is wholly favourable, and Heiner Müller was quite correct in his self-derisive quip: 'Anyone who doesn't commit himself becomes committed anyway – sometimes against his will.'

Here, in conclusion, is the première cast list. King Marke: John Tomlinson; Tristan: Siegfried Jerusalem; Isolde: Waltraud Meier; Kurwenal: Falk Struckmann; Brangäne: Uta Priew; Young Sailor and Melot: Poul Elming; Helmsman: Sándor Sólyom-Nagy; Shepherd: Peter Maus.

13

WAGNER & WAGNER

I do not propose to give a detailed account of my first three Bayreuth productions (*Lohengrin* in 1953, *Der Fliegende Holländer* in 1955, and *Tristan und Isolde* in 1957). Although their results were interesting from my own point of view and had an enduring effect on the public, they could only be discussed in the same context as my brother's productions, and that would involve me in drawing needless comparisons. I shall therefore confine myself to my subsequent interpretations – works infused with the knowledge and experience I had gained in earlier years.

Wieland's death put an end to the tried and tested continuity that had marked the alternation of our new productions at Bayreuth. It meant that I would have to decide which of his interpretations in the 1966 programme should remain in the repertoire.

It was intended that his *Ring* production should run for five years, or until 1969, and that the *Tristan* should be repeated after a one-year break. To enable a suitable programme to be drawn up for 1967, his *Tannhäuser* was retained for that year. The *Parsifal* could with some justification be presented until 1973, but the absence of the *genuine* collaboration Wieland had hoped for between himself as producer and Pierre Boulez as conductor had made it impossible to develop that production in an evolutionary manner.

I discussed my technical and dramatic conception of *Lohengrin* when interviewed on the subject by a Munich newspaper in 1967. My concern was to preserve the acting area as a field of tension and human conflict clearly distinguishable from the external power that invades it in the person of Lohengrin. The true conflict inherent in the work does not, after all, occur on the personal plane – e.g. between Elsa and Ortrud or Elsa and Telramund (King Henry is neutralized in any case) – but consists in Lohengrin's clash with the world he aspires to join. This desire to descend from on high, this 'yearning to be overcome with happiness', was regarded by my grandfather as 'the most profound, tragic situation of the present day'. Logically, therefore, every detail of my production had to flow from a recognition of that conflict. My stage design was naturally influenced by certain architectonic ideas. I used it to define a human field of action that would set off the 'apparition' of the Knight of the Grail. I also tried to carry the architecture over into the characters by means of their costumes. Where scenic representation was concerned, it seemed to me that Roman-esque stylistic elements, with their earth-bound flavour, would be the most suitable. Thus the décor was governed by the octagon, which also formed my acting area. Here, as in my *Ring*, I wanted the stage to abandon its tendency towards abstraction and reacquire three-dimensionality. This was achieved not only by incorporating architectural borrowings and remi-niscences but also by means of lighting, because visual factors can never be excluded from consideration. I was constantly at pains to find symbols adequate and appropriate to the mythopoetic kernel of the work. One or two critics condemned my stylized treatment of trees and creepers, calling them a poor imitation of art nouveau. The same 'connoisseurs' were rather discomfited when I published my references in the programme for 1968: they were the bronze doors of St Zeno's at Verona.

Nineteen-sixty-eight was the hundredth anniversary of the first per-formance of Richard Wagner's *Meistersinger* in Munich. It had long been envisaged by my brother that Karl Böhm would conduct the production planned to mark this occasion, and some of the roles had already been cast. Although Wieland had already staged two productions of his own after Rudolf Hartmann's (1951 and 1952), it had been his express wish, after the first repeat (from 1956 to 1961) and the second approximation with the celebrated Shakespearian stage (1963 and 1964 only), to mount a third new production that would synthesize the experience gained from the two that preceded it. This could only have denoted a feeling that he had still not fully come to terms with the work. Tragically, he was denied another opportunity to do so. It was an inevitable consequence of his death that my wish to stage *Die Meistersinger* at Bayreuth was fulfilled so soon. At the same time, of course, I inherited a mortgage with it. The production was preceded by an expectant murmur. Everyone wondered what *I* would make of *Die Meistersinger* after Wieland's two productions of 1956 and 1963, the more so since widely differing opinions had been voiced about my guest production of the work in Rome on 22 March 1956.

The Rome Opera had firmly insisted on a conservative treatment. Together with Otto Wissner, the Bayreuth Festival's head of stage equip-ment, I produced some very accurate models. The naturalistic elements were to be eliminated by means of perspectival foreshortening, notably of the street in Act II, and by graphically dissolving the architectural components *à la* Buffet. When I first saw this particular set in Rome, I found that the technicians responsible had reduced everything to right angles and inserted every detail with meticulous care. Rather than hurt their feelings, I decided to swallow my displeasure and undertake no corrections. I also had to restrain myself with the man responsible for the lighting, whose treatment of the moon in Act II was in line with decades-old tradition but not, unfortunately, with my own ideas. Discounting the solo costumes, which Kurt Palm had most skilfully and imaginatively designed to accord with the original conception mentioned above, I was compelled to make do with what I could find in the 'Old German' section of a rental agency near the Forum. All in all, my task was not an easy one.

Oreste, the property master, was the pleasantest person to deal with on a human level. The collection of props over which he presided in the catacombs of the theatre was so vast that it encompassed items from every conceivable historical and stylistic period. Strange to relate, however, it could not produce an 'Italian' elder tree for Act II. Fortunately for me, Oreste did not offer me an eight-foot olive tree in lieu: he betook himself to a little public park in the neighbourhood, cut down an oleander of the appropriate size, and erected it outside Sachs's house. He did so with such delight and alacrity that I had no choice but to accept this ultra-Mediterranean shrub, even though it has nothing in common with the German elder, either in shape or in the colour of its flowers.

I discovered one important source of inspiration for my first Bayreuth *Meistersinger* in the woodcut technique of the illustrations in Hartmann Schedel's world chronicle, published at Nuremberg in 1493. The half-timbered structure I used on the stage was neither Alemannic nor Frankish – not an exact historical reconstruction, in other words – but thoroughly irregular. To me this seemed to convey the order of things prevailing in a late medieval municipality, with its guild and class hierarchies, as well as in the mastersingers' domain. At the same time, the scope for an individual to question that system and move freely within it was expressed by the dramatic development of the story, which culminates in a conflict between legitimate, traditional form and free, creative imagination. This interpretation was underpinned by variegated translucent surfaces within the half-timbered structure. With the aid of coloured xenon back-projections and filters, which produced diffuse effects and softened outlines, the walls of painted film stiffened with wire netting and applied joints managed to convey something of the transparency required to divest the action of its 'solidity' and dematerialize the space within which it unfolded. I made particular use of this effect to conjure up the atmosphere of a midsummer's eve heavy with the scent of elderflower.

The brightest and most confined space was the cobbler's workshop in

Act III, a place of mental concentration and enlightenment – less a cobbler's workshop, in fact, than a workshop of the mind. Last of all came the outdoor scene set in the festival meadow, with its purely temporary appurtenances. The factor that primarily governed my design of the festival meadow set was the build-up from the simple, robust, cheerful guild choruses, to Beckmesser's 'professional' but meaningless and futile efforts, to Walther von Stolzing's prize song and the utopian idealization of art, which is democratically acclaimed by the populace: in sociological terms, the involvement and participation of ordinary folk whose artistic receptivity and discrimination entitles them to deliver a verdict of which the 'masters' clique' has proved incapable. This finale was yet another manifestation of Wagner's utopian conception of a *demos* that constitutes itself by participating in art and artistic expression, discovers its identity, and thereby comes of age from a more than merely artistic point of view. His concern was with an artistic ideal communicated by art itself, not with any form of Teutomania or chauvinistic nationalism. Hans Sachs's concluding words, which are taken up by the crowd, are quite unequivocal: come what may, art transcends the nation and national sentiment.

I am often asked why I never staged *Parsifal* until I was fifty-six. The answer is that, although I had many opportunities to do so, I wanted my first production of the work to be at Bayreuth – not out of any false piety, but because the special characteristics of the Festspielhaus fulfil Richard Wagner's acoustic intentions and have a unique ability to bring out the fascination inherent in the sound of voices issuing from above. Given the programme sequence described above, I had no opportunity to stage *Parsifal* at Bayreuth until relatively late in my career.

By the time I undertook my first Bayreuth production of *Parsifal* in 1975, my knowledge of the work stemmed from more or less active involvement in rehearsals and performances stretching back for almost half a century. I had quite a vivid recollection of the *Parsifal* performances in 1927, so forty-eight years had passed since I first became acquainted with the work – initially in my father's interpretation, which was based on the original production but had been modified by him since 1911, especially in regard to Act II. Wagner intended the design of the Festspielhaus, with its unconventional stage area and sunken, invisible orchestra pit, to effect a transition from reality to dramatic 'ideality'. The scenic modifications introduced by Alfred Roller (in 1934 and 1936) and by my twenty-year-old brother soon thereafter were in line of descent from Wagner's aesthetic conceptions and requirements. In redesigning and reinterpreting the work in 1951, Wieland was doubtless guided by the following ideas: 'The visible manifestations of this mystery are only parables, and the agents are not specific individuals ... but symbols of humanity in general.'

What concerned me quite as much as the visual element was the wide variety of musical interpretations to which *Parsifal* had been subjected at Bayreuth by conductors as diverse as Karl Muck, Arturo Toscanini, Richard Strauss, Wilhelm Furtwängler, Franz von Hoesslin, Hans Knappertsbusch, Clemens Krauss, André Cluytens, Pierre Boulez, Horst Stein, and Eugen Jochum. Their readings of the work differed considerably in respect of tonal quality as well as tempo. The profundity of the first transfiguration music, for example, regularly reduced Richard Strauss to tears at certain points, despite his seemingly down-to-earth and uncomplicated nature. In me, especially during and after my training period, it engendered a desire to grapple more closely with the musical messages and structure of the work, thereby enhancing my insight into their ambiguities in relation to the principal characters. My first Bayreuth production of this work could thus be conceived of only as an attempt to analogize the abolition of space and time on the stage with the content of the music.

After many exhaustive discussions – dialogues in the true sense of the word – I asked Oswald Georg Bauer to make a written record of the aims and basic ideas underlying my *Parsifal* productions of 1975 and 1989. In my view, communal discussion is one of the special characteristics of the Bayreuth 'workshop'.

'It recently dawned on me again that this is bound to be another thoroughly unpleasant task,' Richard Wagner wrote of his future *Parsifal* to Mathilde Wesendonck in 1859. What is 'thoroughly unpleasant' about it, beyond doubt, is its critical view of the world of the Grail and its antipole, the world of Klingsor. The Grail knighthood should be an ideal community centred on those two symbols of compassion, the Grail and the Spear. On the stage it is portrayed as humanly inadequate – indeed, positively decrepit. Titurel has built a 'shrine' in which to safeguard the Grail and reserve it for the egoistic 'self-intoxication' of an élite band of men who have misappropriated that symbol of compassion and turned it into a fetish. The institutionalization, petrifaction and dogmatization of the original Grail idea has imparted a sense of élitism and exclusivity. Instead of judging the world around them on its merits, the knights take a purely subjective view of it. The social functions of their brotherhood have taken second place to a striving for personal perfection that finds its clearest expression in Titurel's advocacy of asceticism. The guardians of the symbols of compassion are devoid of compassion themselves and incapable of healing or redeeming Amfortas. Their estrangement from the original Grail ideal is clearly demonstrated by Titurel's contemptuous spurning of Klingsor and the arrogance of a band of men who set themselves above the dualism of male and female. The evil in Klingsor is not primordial; it stems from the lack of goodness in Titurel. The terms good and evil, which *The Ring* clearly differentiates, are sceptically presented as relative values. Parsifal receives no clear-cut answer to his questions: 'Were they evil? Who is good?' Klingsor's exploitation of sexuality, for which the knights of the Grail condemn and reproach him, is nothing more nor less than the ultimate consequence of Titurel's call for asceticism. His original hankering after the Grail becomes transmuted into a perverted imitation of the world of the Grail by the theft of the Spear, the seduction of the knights, and his hopes of acquiring the sacred chalice. None of the knights (except Gurnemanz and Amfortas) recognizes Kundry's longing to be disburdened of her curse or her efforts to that end. The problems and conflicts inherent in every character and at every level cannot be resolved into a 'state of redemption' until all concerned experience a change of heart and attain a degree of self-knowledge that makes it possible for them to understand and feel for one another.

The terms 'redemption' and 'redeemer' are not peculiar to Christianity, but are common to various cultures and myths. In the latter, a redeemer is generally someone who ends a chaotic, pernicious, or oppressive situation. In a broader sense, he also has a socially regulating function. To Richard Wagner, myth was 'the poetic expression of a common outlook on life' (*Oper und Drama*). Here, he sought the mythical element in Christianity. To him, the Christian myth was only one of many. He declared, albeit regretfully, 'that all our Christian myths have an extraneous, pagan origin', and believed that the Grail idea, born of the 'early Christian era's enthusiasm for relics', represented the ideal of early Christianity: compassion in a complex, not an ecclesiastically dogmatic sense. Amfortas realizes that a change in his personal fortunes, and in those of the Grail community as a whole, can be effected only by someone who is free from all constraints, but whom shared experience of suffering has rendered sufficiently mature to perceive the nature of things – someone who must personally travel the road of human error and suffering in order to attain maturity on another's behalf. Within this process of comprehension, Kundry's kiss is a release mechanism that enables Parsifal to grasp those manifestations of suffering in others which he has hitherto failed to comprehend. That process is initiated by the great struggle between Parsifal and Kundry in Act II, a conflict that cannot be resolved because neither of them is yet mature enough: he spurns her, she curses him. Parsifal has to tread 'the paths of error and suffering' before his eyes are opened by manifold experiences. In the Good Friday scene the balance is restored, visually in the serene natural beauty of the Good Friday meadow and also – in modern parlance – in Kundry's acquisition of 'equal rights': she is not only released from her curse and baptized but brought to the Grail.

The structural symmetry of *Parsifal*'s three acts possesses a dramaturgical function: Acts I and III each contain one 'natural' and one architectural scene, Act II embodies a combination of both. Klingsor's sorcery misuses Nature and constructs a counterpart to the world of the Grail. In presenting an image of Nature both suffering and redeemed, Wagner translated his demand that 'the purely human' be kept in harmony with 'the eternally natural' into the visual language of the theatre.

The last scene set in the castle of the Grail differs fundamentally from the first. Act I presents us with the ritual of an esoteric male society at pains to disguise its decrepitude in traditional conventions. The finale is not a restoration of its original state. The antithesis between Titurel's and Klingsor's worlds, which are mutually determinative in their petrifaction and distortion, is removed by Parsifal. His redemptive act possesses the power, not to decide the contest in favour of the Grail community in its existing form, but to eliminate 'thesis' and 'antithesis' in favour of a utopian hope. The knighthood's regulatory function, which had been forsaken for an élitist way of life, is reinstated. Parsifal endeavours to make his own realization that each should respect and sympathize with the other a universal possession. Openly displayed in a bright, open space, the Grail and the Spear, those symbols of compassion, are now available to and at the service of all. Compassion has become a social quality.

As I have already said, 1981 was the first year since 1951 in which two new productions were premièred on successive days. Another Bayreuth rarity was that two press conferences were held. *Tristan und Isolde* was followed on 26 July 1981 by my second production of *Die Meistersinger*, which remained in the festival repertoire until 1988, with a one-year break in 1985. Rather than describe what was to be seen on the stage, I propose to shed a little light on the main factors governing my dramatic and musical conception of the work. I shall not try to enumerate every last detail, nor to marshal the results I obtained into an analytical compendium, because that would be tantamount to canonizing my views. Derived from many years' preoccupation with the work, the particles of knowledge that follow are merely those which I myself consider important and relevant.

On 18 July 1868 Wagner wrote to Heinrich Esser, conductor of the Vienna Opera: 'Beckmesser is no comic; he is quite as serious as all the other masters. It is only his position, and the situations into which he gets himself, that make him seem ludicrous. The direct contrast between his impatience, rage and despair, and his intended lyrical courtship – that is what makes him seem comical.' I never had any doubt that Beckmesser should be portrayed as an educated man. He is, after all, the town clerk of Nuremberg. In that capacity he also superintends the municipal guard, and this invests him with a certain status relative to other citizens including his fellow mastersingers. In deference to his superiority as a theorist he was elected 'marker', or custodian of its traditional code of rules, by the mastersingers' guild. He has evidently been too preoccupied with intellectual conceit and the dignity of his office to dream for one moment that life may have something more to offer, e.g. marriage, and now it is almost too late. But even this confirmed bachelor yields to 'spring's command' and experiences the 'sweet necessity' with which he has no idea how to cope. Trapped in a thicket of rules, Beckmesser is lured into an abortive courtship display. He is the first to learn of Veit Pogner's self-seeking plan to marry off his only child, Eva, by offering her, 'with all my goods', to the winner of the song contest on midsummer's day. However, Pogner quickly gathers from Beckmesser's reaction – the town clerk promptly tries to take out an option on Eva – that the outcome of his bright idea may be unacceptable to her. He grows even more uneasy when, after he has formally promised to give Eva to whomsoever wins the contest in the presence of all the masters of the guild including Sachs, who turns up last, the masters roundly applaud his gesture in anticipation of a grand public entertainment. Pogner realizes that he has demeaned his daughter by making this pledge designed to boost his own reputation and demonstrate his high regard for art. Because it dawns on him that his announcement has saddled him and the others with an unsuitable mixture of art and emotion, he qualifies his offer: Eva can refuse the man to whom the masters award the prize, but she may 'never desire another', i.e. he must be a mastersinger. This only aggravates the situation. At this point Sachs intervenes for the first time, having realized from the first that Pogner's plan may very well miscarry. He proposes that the verdict on this affair of art and the heart be left to the people, the onlookers and listeners, acting not as a court of last resort, but as a superior authority of democratic complexion.

Whether or not it is in the nature of man to believe that any woman he covets is his for the asking, Beckmesser feels he must seize the chance to get a wife at last, especially as marriage would set the seal on his status. Eva is not just any girl; she is unquestionably the most respected burgher's daughter and the child of one of Nuremberg's wealthiest citizens – and that makes her doubly desirable. Even in the latter years of my first Bayreuth production, I made Beckmesser return to the festival meadow for the finale and exit, reconciled with Sachs, in his company. To me, this is justified by what the music says and avoids any false glorification of the latter. For all his humiliation, Beckmesser has learned that losing a contest need not entail the loss of one's honour or one's life.

The story of the *Die Meistersinger* unfolds within twenty-four hours. This makes it one of Wagner's most compact works, and constructed strictly in accordance with Aristotelian dramatic principles. Since these applied primarily to tragedy, it strikes one almost as a dramatic and structural joke on my grandfather's part that he should have played with such set pieces, blithely taken them apart, and fitted them together again: a metaphor for a topsy-turvy world.

During the final chorale of the afternoon service before the midsummer's day festival, Walther von Stolzing tries to flirt with Eva, whom he has known only since the previous evening, when selling his estate at Pogner's house and with Pogner's assistance. For this pantomimic declaration of love Wagner employs interludes in the chorale, drawing on his knowledge of the work of his Central German compatriot, Johann Sebastian Bach. The congregation has scarcely departed when Eva, that impetuous and headstrong young woman, tells the knight exactly what he wishes to hear: 'You or no one!' This at once makes it clear to them both, if not to the world at large, how their union can come about. Pogner has stipulated that his daughter's future husband must not only be a mastersinger but win the contest, so Magdalene advises David, Sachs's apprentice, to give the knight a crash course in the mastersingers' rules and regulations. One can take it as read, in view of the context, that Eva will not play the 'micro-Isolde' and administer a love- or death-potion to herself and Walther.

While David is trying to school Walther in the mastersingers' musical and linguistic conventions, the other apprentices get everything ready for the singing lesson. David, who prides himself on knowing everything and having everything under control, neglects to supervise the operation and finds that the youngsters have naturally done everything wrong. The occasion turns into a vocal 'trial', not a singing lesson, and this gives Walther, a true high-flier, a chance to be dubbed a master and gain the victor's garland – an outcome of which he is, of course, supremely confident. But the gods have decreed that any success must be earned by the sweat of one's brow, and David warns Walther to refrain from '*Meisterwahn*' [roughly: wild dreams of becoming a master].

Wahn is a word with which Wagner had a very special affinity. Not only does it constantly recur in his works, but he even incorporated it, as I have already mentioned, in the name of his house. To him it possesses a wonderfully wide range of meanings on the most divergent levels. It can connote expectation, hope, folly, suspicion, opinion, vague conjecture, imagination, poetic illusion. In *Die Meistersinger* it occupies a central position and becomes a determinant of action, affecting all the characters without exception. *Wahn* is a fundamental category – indeed, an essential ingredient of the human condition. ''Tis just the old folly [*Wahn*], without which nothing can happen,' Sachs says perceptively in his great philosophical monologue, which ultimately gives perspectives of relativity to all the emotions of love, hatred, passion, despair, vanity, the seemingly sublime and the supposedly banal. This is no denunciation of the infinitely futile and worthless, but a humorous recognition of the imperfect and inadequate – in short, of human nature.

The so-called *Wahn* motif first occurs in the third verse of Sachs's cobbler's song in Act II and runs through the rest of the work. Eva, who at first brushes Sachs's song aside because she already knows it, feels strangely affected after this third verse: 'The song grieves me, I know not why.'

With the exception of *Die Feen*, the earliest of Wagner's works, *Die Meistersinger von Nürnberg* is the only one whose title emphasizes the plural. From the interpretative aspect, this is quite as important as the title's definition of place.

Being unable to deny the wealthy Pogner his request, the other mastersingers agree to give Walther a chance to audition for the mastership. Beckmesser promptly scents danger when Pogner greets Walther in a friendly manner and recognizes the young knight as a rival, his suspicions kindled by jealousy and a deep-seated fear of inferiority. Being unable and unwilling to circumvent the masters' majority decision, he takes advantage of his function as the 'marker' to nip the danger in the bud by putting this blithely singing rival in his place, once and for all, and exposing him to derision. Although he cannot prevail over Walther's youthful freshness, he converts that asset into a liability, for 'admission here is by the rules alone'. He sends the honest mastersingers into an uproar, skilfully manipulates them, and provokes Walther beyond endurance. In Act III he smugly declares: 'We masters are rid of him after all!'

In addition to speaking up on Walther's behalf, Sachs reveals his full character when he earnestly debates how the young knight's rightful claims in respect of life and art can be justly met without entirely discarding long-established traditions. But Sachs is not just a worldly-wise philosopher who steadfastly preserves an aloof or superior stance. Although he likes to conceal his other side – rough-hewn and robust but humorous and boyishly mischievous – behind his 'cobbler and poet' calling card, the cobbler's songs in Act II and his vehement outburst in Act III reveal him to be sensitive as well as mischievous. He is as prone to emotional turmoil as anyone else, the only difference being that his advice is sought on all kinds of problems: 'And a cobbler must know everything and patch every rent; and if he's a poet as well, that side of him, too, is given no peace; and if he's a widower into the bargain, he's considered a fool indeed.'

Thus, uproarious situation comedy is meaningfully contrasted with, and sublimated into, artistic enthusiasm.

Just as – notably in the scene between Walther and Hans Sachs in Act

III – Wagner illustrates his own artistic activity and aesthetic principles, which are born of contradictions, so Sachs's attitude until the end of the opera may be construed as a model of humane emancipation. Sachs listens receptively and attentively, strives to be unbiased but not neutral, and acts and reflects on his actions in order to arrive at conclusions and perceptions that will guide his future conduct in a rational manner. I conceive of Sachs as a regulative force, and also as a teacher who is himself open to instruction. He does not preside at a desk; he teaches from his cobbler's bench, in other words, from the very midst of life. By a gradual process compounded of active intervention and thoughtful contemplation, he progresses from his nocturnal reminiscences beneath the elder tree, to his lucid philosophic reflections early the next morning, to his final, proclamatory appeal to the public at large. Sachs seeks a synthesis between tradition and innovation. Like the music, man and action are contrapuntally opposed so as to produce a harmony that does, admittedly, point the way to a utopia.

Hans Sachs comes to see that individual freedom can be attained only *in* society, not *against* it, and that this presupposes the individual's amenability to social ties and acceptance of rules. Unless these preconditions are met, man behaves antisocially and everything drifts into chaos and anarchy – this, too, being a potential '*Wahn*'. *Die Meistersinger* is an opera of the 19th century, which, following on from the Enlightenment and man's emergence from his self-imposed nonage, was increasingly discovering the individual and demanding that man develop from an object into a subject. The Faustian theme is an eloquent expression of this. 'Self-fulfilment' strikes one today as a thoroughly ambivalent concept, its primary function being to justify ruthless and inconsiderate conduct in an implacably self-seeking society. Far from advocating a utopian return to a patriarchal, hierarchical class system, *Die Meistersinger* sketches its opposite: the establishment of a democratic community that signifies more than merely the sum of its parts because the individual fulfils himself within that community but not at its expense. This is one of the opera's unfulfilled humanistic messages.

The characters are as diverse as their modes of behaviour. They love and contend together, young against old and old against young, but also young and old against old and young. Theirs is a variegated society whose members are neither caricatures nor ideological mouthpieces.

Order and disorder – *Die Meistersinger* deals with them too. That which Sachs characterizes in his '*Wahn*' monologue as 'peaceful in its steadfast customs, content in deed and work' is introduced right at the beginning of the opera and illustrated by the congregation's chorale. All present know that they are under the aegis of a higher order. Walther's mute dialogue with Eva disturbs and disrupts that order. Another regulatory principle is the mastersingers' tablatur. Walther disregards it, and everything goes haywire. Order is vulnerable to disorder.

The so-called cudgel scene, which turns Beckmesser's innocuous seranade into an affray ('riot and uproar', as the frustrated troubadour terms it), is construed by many as an eruption of the deep-seated violence allegedly latent in every human being. Theodor W. Adorno even likened it in his *Versuch über Wagner* to a 'pogrom'. In my opinion, views of that kind completely overlook the theatrical purpose of this skilfully-laid scene. Beckmesser, whose serenade is being rendered progressively more futile, at first tries to drown Sachs's hammerblows by singing louder. Unlike him, David recognizes Magdalene, who is disguised as Eva, and promptly flies at his supposed rival for her affections. The entire neighbourhood is roused by Magdalene's cries for help and the general rumpus, and the outcome is a free-for-all of the kind that was not uncommon in South Germany and Franconia. It is not, however, a deliberately aggressive, still less murderous, proceeding. One has only to refer to the musical treatment and the text. I view the entire scene as the figment of a midsummer night's dream, because a few buckets of water and the night watchman's horn (this, interestingly enough, is scored in the same C major tritone that occurs in the cobbler's workshop quintet) suffice to restore peace at a stroke. One loud blast and order prevails once more: that shows how easy it is to re-establish discipline and decorum.

When the crowd in the festival meadow delightedly and expectantly strike up Sachs's hymn to Martin Luther, the 'Wittenberg Nightingale', this is not simply a tribute to its author. 'Awake! The break of day draws nigh' and 'Night sinks in the west, day rises in the east, dawn's fiery glow shines through the gloomy clouds' indicate a firm belief in a better future, and the hymn to Luther becomes Nuremberg's *Marseillaise*.

I believe that my interpretation of the work is validated by the way in which the finale welds old and young, mastersinger 'art experts' and ordinary folk, into a single entity infused with the spirit of democracy under the auspices of art and its significance as a unifying medium. I also had that in mind when designing my sets for *Die Meistersinger*. They were intended to summon up an urban ideal that finds its ultimate expression in a festival venue for the entire community. The dominant symbol of that venue is the tree of life, a Franconian 'dance linden' such as Walther von Stolzing sings of in his Prize Song. Lime-trees of this kind, complete with dance floors, still exist in Franconia to this day, and all the local inhabitants, young and old, celebrate and dance there on special occasions.

Thanks to my decades-long experience of working with singers, I took particular care to ensure that the sets were 'singer-friendly' in design and materials. The church, the Nuremberg street and the cobbler's workshop functioned as acoustic reflectors, so that the opera's exceptional demands on the human voice could be met more easily.

Where direction was concerned, I deliberately tried to point up the differences between the members of the masculine triangle centred on Eva, i.e. Sachs, Walther, and Beckmesser. As I visualized them, Sachs and Beckmesser were roughly the same age, or not more than forty-five, while Walther was about twenty-two and Eva seventeen or so. This made it possible to portray a male-female relationship imbued with genuine tension.

To me, Sachs is man of the world enough to become immediately aware of the spontaneous bond between Eva and Walther. Although he manages to renounce Eva with deliberate composure, he does not yield to resignation.

In my view, to misuse *Die Meistersinger* as a prop for complacent, arrogant nationalism is to betray the grossest ignorance of its true nature. One would have to be deaf, blind, and utterly unperceptive to take this sublime depiction of human gaiety, with its utopian potential, and read a pogrom or a Party rally into it. Any attempt to force the work into an ideological mould is bound to be a distortion.

Thanks to the uncertainty surrounding the various versions of *Tannhäuser* as conveyed by the traditional production material, and to the inordinate artistic ambitions of those who had choreographed the top-heavy Venusberg scenes, I had no wish to stage the work myself until I found a conductor and a choreographer who agreed with me that the fresh and youthful Dresden version was ripe for production at Bayreuth.

I first met Giuseppe Sinopoli when Götz Friedrich brought him to Bayreuth. He was not at that time an experienced operatic conductor, so my plan to engage him encountered some resistance even from people whose judgement I respected. Apart from watching him at work on one or two operas, I also attended the Munich première of his own opera *Lou Salomé* on 10 May 1981. We kept in touch thereafter, partly through his agent, and contact between us gradually crystallized to such an extent that by 19 July 1983 his collaboration on *Tannhäuser* in 1985 was as good as certain. To seal this new alliance I kept a rendezvous with Sinopoli at Munich airport at 9 a.m. on 16 August 1983, the morning of the fourth festival performance of *Parsifal*. The outcome of our meeting was altogether satisfactory from my point of view, so I returned to my producer's duties at Bayreuth feeling thoroughly reassured. I had an appointment with Daniel Barenboim that afternoon, and James Levine wanted to see me after the performance. Betweentimes, and especially during the intervals, I had to fulfil my obligations in respect of prearranged meetings with sponsors and guests. (I can check on the progress of a performance at any time, thanks to the monitor installed in my office.)

I was able to discuss questions of casting and interpretation with Sinopoli on several occasions between 1983 and 1985. We settled on the Dresden version on 15/16 April 1984, and I greatly welcomed the fact that his views coincided with mine in that respect.

The so-called Dresden version of *Tannhäuser* was the product of two revisions of the finale which Wagner undertook subsequent to the first performance of the work in 1845. I found it particularly interesting that in 1860, shortly before retouching it for the Paris production in 1861 (with the long balletic interlude at the beginning of Act I), he had republished the Dresden version. The Paris version attempted to make a virtue (a chance to make improvements) out of a contractual and financial necessity. The unresolved problems of this work exercised Wagner for most of his life, and as late as 23 January 1883, or some three weeks before his death, he told Cosima that he 'still owed the world a *Tannhäuser*'. My grandfather had every intention of thoroughly revising the work, even then, and would have liked to stage it at Bayreuth, for, as he himself said, *Tannhäuser*, *Tristan* and *Parsifal* 'go together'. Eight days before he died, Cosima recorded him as expressing a wish 'to do *Tannhäuser* at Bayreuth first; if he can arrange that, he will have achieved more than by staging *Tristan*.' From all this I inferred that my grandfather did not consider his Paris version, with its top-heavy ballet, to be the definitive one. *Tannhäuser* was not included in the Bayreuth repertoire until 1891, later than *Tristan* and *Die Meistersinger*. For that production Cosima fell back on the version produced for Vienna in 1875, which in its turn derived from a partial revision for Munich in 1867 and differed in certain respects from the Paris version.

I myself am not in favour of adapting Wagner's earlier works to conform with the Bayreuth treatment of his later ones. To me, such a process of assimilation would introduce a foreign body into the overall structure from the aspect of compositional technique, harmonic treatment, and instrumentation. It remains a noteworthy and interesting fact that Wagner did not change the traditional forms, e.g. the ensembles, and that he devised an entirely novel way of handling and employing the chorus from *Lohengrin* onwards. I consider its youthful spontaneity of expression particularly striking, for any visitor to Bayreuth can rediscover aspects of *Tristan*'s tonal and harmonic coloration in works from different periods of Wagner's life. When he assured King Ludwig II that he would recognize many features of *Lohengrin* and *Tannhäuser* in *Parsifal*, I think he was taking out insurance: he was afraid that this late work would disconcert his royal patron.

In addition to finding a conductor who shared my ideas, I later found a choreographer of the same mind. This was Iván Markó, who devised a dramatic and creative solution for the Venusberg that expressed courtship and loving union in an artistic, aesthetic form. It did not stress the orgiastic, giddy, insensate element so regrettably popular today, which is naturally easier to tie in with the bacchanalian revelry of the expanded Paris ballet version, and which in my opinion wholly fails to motivate the conflict between two such solitary individuals as Tannhäuser and Elisabeth.

It was Robert Schulz, probably the best-informed theatrical agent that ever lived, who drew my attention to the Györ Ballet and its director, Iván Markó. I gained a preliminary impression of the company's work by attending a guest performance in Berlin on 19 October 1984. On 7 November of the same year I travelled by way of Budapest to Györ, my intention being to negotiate a contract with Markó. I was delighted to find that he did not insist on the Paris version or display the balletomane's vanity that had so often given rise to masquerades condemned by Wagner himself. I had previously conducted negotiations with three of the world's most celebrated women choreographers, but they had considered it incompatible with their artistic image to commit themselves to such an 'insignificant' project, which would not have given their egos free rein.

The set for *Tannhäuser* is an imaginary space, a space designed to stimulate the imagination, not restrict it. The basic shape I chose was the circle, symbolizing the life cycle and the terrestrial globe. Ever changing, ever rotating, it affords no firm foothold for the human beings who seek to orient themselves in the conflicts to which they are exposed: they circle in quest of some meaning in a world and a life that are always in a state of flux. Contrapuntally opposed to this set is the singers' hall in Act II, which symbolizes Wartburg society: rigid, immobile and unshakeable, it is bounded by a series of stout columns.

Thanks to the development of electronic linear drives with correspondingly sensitive controls, I was able to have the main acting area constructed in the requisite manner. A central circle with a diametre of 7.5 metres is used as the acting area in Acts I and III, together with a stepped structure consisting of circles that can be moved in parallel and in opposite directions. When the separate elements are moved, a slant of ten per cent produces differences in height whose effect is diffuse and variable.

The centre of the circle may be likened to an ancient place of worship occupied by Venus *and* Mary, just as ancient temples of Venus were converted into churches of Mary in which the heathen, spiritually dangerous element had been banished but the magical properties of the place are retained and turned to good use. Also implicit is a mute accusation that the abolition of such places of worship was accompanied by that of all other, divergent modes of thought and their replacement by an absolute claim to the truth. And this absolutism, the exact opposite of tolerance, together with the negative consequences of such an exclusive spiritual attitude, is another count in *Tannhäuser*'s indictment. Also to be seen in this context is a further characteristic of the work: the superimposition of Christian and pagan motifs, the blurring of outlines between the two spheres, the ambiguity of central concepts in both worlds, the questioning of their incompatibility and, thus, an attempt to eliminate the polarization of the pagan and Christian concepts of love. The direct, sensual depiction of love – in a cultic dance, in Tannhäuser's tribute to Venus, and in his summons to Elisabeth to praise the god of love for his return – is contrasted in the minnesingers' contest with a verbal debate on the nature of love. The conflict first arises when the minnesingers proclaim that their sexually hostile attitude is the only one possible. Tannhäuser's response to these high-minded singers, who pay no more than resigned homage to the 'wondrous fount' of love, is to retort that 'the world would surely run dry' of such languishments. Then, when these same melancholy inquirers into the nature of love and venerators of a sublimated, exalted 'courtly love' express their horrified condemnation of the physical and sexual side of love, he flies into a rage. In Tannhäuser's perception and experience, no conflict arises until an antithesis is deliberately created between 'exalted love' and the so-called lower form of love, condemned as 'the pleasure of hell', the first being visually represented by the image of Mary, the second by Venus. To him, a dichotomy of that kind is contrary to nature – that is why he deserted Venus. Significantly, it is the 'chaste virgin' Elisabeth who makes a move 'to express her approbation' after Tannhäuser has told Wolfram: 'I drink deep of bliss unmingled with hesitation.' Elisabeth's love may be 'chaste', but it none the less springs from 'the soil of utter sensuality', as Wagner said elsewhere. In her prayer she implores Mary, the 'Almighty Virgin', to forgive her 'sinful desire', her 'worldly longing', which she has striven to suppress 'with a thousand pangs': 'But, could I not atone for every fault, receive me mercifully!'

Tannhäuser and Elisabeth find their deathbed on the spot sacred to Venus and Mary. He, who roamed between those two alternatives, comes to rest there; she, who sought to understand him and defended him, is first united with her love in death – a synthesis that appears conciliative only at first sight and goes tragically astray, because the nature of love as a primordial, natural life-element cannot be comprehended dualistically and dialectically. Just as Tannhäuser's road to the Venusberg was a wrong road, so the inhibiting world of the Wartburg did not permit Elisabeth's love to blossom. Far from being conciliative, their union in death is thus profoundly tragic.

The unanswerable inquiry into the nature of love develops into an inquiry into redemption and the ending of love's conflicts and embroilments by death. Wagner used the Pope's refusal of absolution and redemption as an opportunity to analyse the ecclesiastical conception of the latter. He construed it in a way that would now be termed 'early Christian'. What concerned him was a special spiritual disposition, not compliance with rigid, dogmatic conventions, with sin and atonement, guilt and expiation – with submission and dependence on the one hand and the exercise of power on the other. Tannhäuser makes his pilgrimage to Rome out of sympathy for Elisabeth and because of the pain he has inflicted on her; not for his own salvation's sake, but 'to sweeten her tears'. Hence his disgust when he encounters 'lies and heartlessness' in Rome – when he is 'denied the right to exist because of the supreme sincerity of his sentiments'. He is not drawn back to the Venusberg by its sensual delights, but because he hopes for clemency: 'O merciful Lady Venus!' Elisabeth's love for Tannhäuser proves more effective than the whole, scandalized world of the Wartburg and the Papacy itself. In defiance of them, she includes Tannhäuser in her prayer and is thereby able to grant him redemption. Wagner wrote that she acted 'in sacred cognizance of the strength of her death' and thus 'acquitted the unhappy man'. Far from confirming them, the opera's dénouement casts doubt on secular and ecclesiastical institutions and their dogmas.

Wolfram, the 'well-practised singer', witnesses that dénouement. Initially the archetypal virtuoso and courtier, conformist, popular, and urbane, he is disturbed because it calls his whole existence into question. He sympathizes with Tannhäuser's fate. It is borne in on him that one should not condemn a life that sentences the inflexible, erring nonconformist to failure and sorrow, and that a man like Tannhäuser is deserving of tolerance and compassion – of which the latter is well known to have occupied a central position in Wagner's ideas.

From these salient interpretative considerations I shall now turn to the rather more prosaic subject of rehearsals.

The first problem was that Gabriela Benackova-Cap, who had been engaged to sing Elisabeth, sent a message through her agent regretting that she would be unable, because of ill health, to be present when rehearsals began on 23 June 1985. Her continuing absence and a further postponement until 6 July rendered her retention artistically unjustifiable, so her contract had to be declared null and void. Rehearsals for the Valkyries in *The Ring* were to begin on 27 June. Cheryl Studer had been engaged to sing Gerhilde and Freia. Knowing that she was due to arrive in Bayreuth the day before, I asked Giuseppe Sinopoli, who was depressed by the loss of his Elisabeth, if he would be kind enough to give Studer another audition, my hope being that he would come to share my opinion that she would make a very good Elisabeth. Sinopoli agreed to hear her, and we quickly arranged an audition for the evening of 26 June. She sang the 'hall aria' and, after a brief interval, repeated it to enable us to confirm our impressions. Before the next 'round' she ran through Elisabeth's 'prayer', which she had never sung before, with one of our musical assistants. When the audition was over Sinopoli agreed to study the role with her vocally to see if he thought we should engage her for it. Their sessions went so well that we did so. Although she had only studied the 'hall aria' for an audition some time before, she learned the entire role of Elisabeth remarkably quickly, so rehearsals went smoothly and our carefully planned schedule suffered no delays.

The same cannot, I fear, be said of the artist contractually engaged to sing Tannhäuser, René Kollo, for whom the role had been earmarked from the outset. Not for the first time, our negotiations with him took far longer than was customary at Bayreuth. It proved to be a lengthy business, agreeing the dates on which he had to be present, and which were convenient to him. It is particularly disagreeable when performances have to be underwritten by engaging a second singer, because the principal singer can take advantage of this arrangement. Kollo, who had originally intended to sing at all seven performances, proposed to delegate first one of them, then two, and eventually three. This entailed my engaging a second tenor for Tannhäuser from among those who would be present at Bayreuth during the festival but had other commitments. Having heard Richard Versalle sing Tannhäuser at Saarbrücken on 12 March 1983, I already knew him to be a dedicated, accurate and vocally gifted singer.

Tannhäuser being a great ensemble opera, it infuriates the soloists and chorus and verges on the totally unacceptable when a principal as important as Tannhäuser disrupts rehearsals by singing inaccurately or inaudibly, or by being absent altogether. In soloists' passages like the 'Venusberg strophes' or the great duet with Elisabeth in Act II the singer punishes himself if he has mastered the role imperfectly or not at all; in the difficult ensembles he unwarrantably punishes the entire cast.

Although Richard Versalle earned himself a growing reputation by conscientiously and successfully rehearsing his stand-in's role, Giuseppe Sinopoli still hoped that intensive work with Kollo would bring him up to the mark. The result was that all save one of the stage orchestra rehearsals allotted to Versalle were taken away from him and given to Kollo instead.

There were just forty-seven minutes left until curtain-up on 25 July 1985 when René Kollo informed me that he could not, after all, appear in the première – and this although I had asked him, if only out of fairness to Richard Versalle, to give me his decision either way by eleven-thirty that morning.

Two days earlier, on 23 July, I had telephoned Kollo's personal physician and medical specialist in Vienna. He told me not to worry: Kollo was quite fit enough to sing the role of Tannhäuser. Writing to me from Vienna over one month later, the same doctor certified on 27 August 1985 that Kollo could not, in fact, have sung the role – a curiously belated justification of his patient's last-minute withdrawal.

Partly because of Kollo's great popularity and versatility as a television performer, his Bayreuth début as Tannhäuser had been trumpeted and acclaimed in advance, not only by the 'serious' illustrateds but also, of course, by the trashier ones. Irresponsible as all this advance publicity was, in my view, the unexpected turn of events made it thoroughly embarrassing and absurd.

Mindful of Kollo's previous behaviour, I was ready for anything – even some quite unprecedented occurrence – on the day of the première. I told Richard Versalle to be sure to be at the Festspielhaus by 2 p.m. and remain on call in my office. Its seclusion might help to allay his understandable nervousness at the prospect of having to take over from his celebrated fellow tenor, though he would naturally have to be prepared to do just that.

Even prior to Kollo's last-minute cancellation, I had satisfied myself of its extreme likelihood some two hours before curtain-up by taking a good look at the artist's car in the parking lot. It contained a number of suitcases – heavy ones, judging by the weight of the rear wheels. One did not have to be Sherlock Holmes to infer that Kollo was not planning to attend the official first-night reception and celebrate with his fans after the performance. Everything pointed to his imminent departure.

The only artistic mark he left on that season consisted of some handwritten cues on the harp for the 'hymn to Venus'. I was later told by the conductor Horst Stein that Kollo had successfully learned and sung the role of Tannhäuser for a Christmas 1985 performance at Geneva.

I was delighted when Richard Versalle's Bayreuth début turned out to be far more than a *succès d'estime*. As for Giuseppe Sinopoli, that spirited thoroughbred of a musician, he thoroughly fulfilled my expectations and made a valuable addition to Bayreuth.

In accordance with Bayreuth custom, I continued to work hard on this *Tannhäuser* production over the years. Among other things, cast changes proved necessary. Originally recommended by Jean Cox, Donald C. Runnicles had worked for the festival as a musical assistant since 1982. In 1992 and 1993, by which time he had built up an international career as a conductor in his own right, I entrusted him with the musical direction of *Tannhäuser*. Improvements to the sets were deliberately undertaken with new materials whose main advantage was that the cyclorama could be lit to greater effect. The production was taken into the repertoire, and the sets have not yet been dismantled at the time of writing.

Following the 1989 festival, a guest presentation of *Tannhäuser* was given in Tokyo, where Mamoro Miura, head of the Tokyu Department Store, had invited us to open the new Bunkamura cultural centre. For the first time in the history of the Bayreuth Festival, the entire cast and the original scenery (kinetic set props included) were flown in for the occasion. Where the technical equipment of its multipurpose hall was concerned, the Bunkamura centre had been planned and executed in consultation with us, so *Tannhäuser* could be reproduced without modifications or limitations of any kind. Thanks to our hosts' exceptional – indeed, positively unique – readiness to assist and co-operate, working with them was a very special experience, not only for me but for all of us.

Much public speculation was aroused when the *Parsifal* production was postponed from 1988 to 1989. Among other things, the press peddled a rumour that, for the first time in the history of Bayreuth, a programme change had been made in deference to the wishes of an artist, in this case James Levine – in other words, that the festival management had bowed to his insistence and substituted one production for another. I therefore found it necessary to comment on this publicly during the festival season. In the first place, I stated that I had neither been subjected to, nor had yielded to, pressure of any kind. If James Levine disliked the production so much, he would certainly not have returned to the Bayreuth podium, after a two-year break, in order to conduct it again. I was concerned to prevent *Parsifal* from becoming ossified by running it for too long, and pointed out that my own production of that work had been performed at only seven festivals. I also pointed out that new productions are staged in no set rhythm, and that their inclusion and exclusion are governed by administrative and financial as well as artistic considerations.

Experience gained from staging my *Parsifal* production between 1975 and 1981, and subsequently from my *Meistersinger* and *Tannhäuser*, had given me ample reason to reflect on the treatment of space and time on the stage. So had the interpretations of *The Ring* by Patrice Chéreau, Peter Hall and Harry Kupfer, of *Tristan* by August Everding and Jean-Pierre Ponnelle, and of *Lohengrin* by Götz Friedrich and Werner Herzog. This was largely because, despite their very different 'handwriting', they all had one objective in common, namely, to do at Bayreuth what Wagner himself would do today, if we are to believe his own injunction: 'Children, create something new!' If I have only cited the names of producers for simplicity's sake, this is not, of course, to belittle the equally indispensable contribution made by conductors, stage and costume designers, singers, and all the other participants in a production.

I based my approach to *Parsifal* largely on three factors that impelled me to consider how best to stage that ever-special work after so many years' practical experience of the theatre, with all their highs and lows, and how, after treading 'the path of error and suffering', I could present it in a form relevant to the present day.

The first factor was Richard Wagner's oft-cited allusion to the 'invisible theatre', which Cosima recorded in her diary on 23 September 1878. The full quotation expresses more, I feel, than any elaborate commentary: 'How I hate the thought of all those costumes and all that make-up! When I think that these characters will have to be dressed up like Kundry, I'm immediately put in mind of those frightful artists' parties, and having created the invisible orchestra I'd now like to invent the invisible theatre!' ('Concluding his dismal reflections on a humorous note,' as Cosima put it, he promptly added: 'And the inaudible orchestra.')

The other two factors that interest me are Wagner's description of *Parsifal* as a '*Bühnenweihfestspiel*' [stage dedication festival play] and as a '*Weltabschiedswerk*' [world-farewell-work]. Both these terms have long been vitiated by ridiculous clichés and deliberate misunderstandings. They do, however, possess a long tradition, because Cosima's diaries make it very clear that she herself construed *Parsifal* as only quasi-religious from the first, twisting it almost into Catholicism and conceiving of it as a substitute religion. Hans von Wolzogen, editor of the *Bayreuther Blätter*, also helped to foster this idea. Although Wagner was in general very pleased with an essay of his entitled '*Bühnenweihfestspiel*', he was quick to comment that Wolzogen was going too far when he characterized Parsifal as a portrayal of Christ: 'I did not have the Saviour in mind at all.'

As for '*Weltabschieds-Werk*', Wagner employed that striking word formation in his last letter to Ludwig II dated 10 January 1883. He went even further in the same letter, calling *Parsifal* a '*Lebens-Abschieds-Werk*' [life-farewell-work]. In a positively mystifying way, the latter expression became associated with his death a good month later, and the fateful transfiguration of *Parsifal* began. Although Wagner did not intend to write any more works for the theatre, he was planning far ahead: he hoped to mount Festspielhaus productions of all his earlier works from *Der Fliegende Holländer* onwards, partly revise them, and write some plays and one-movement symphonies. The sense in which he meant 'a farewell to the world' is clearly and precisely explained in '*Das Bühnenweihfestspiel in Bayreuth 1882*', a piece to which he referred in his aforesaid letter to the king, and which interprets both '*Bühnenweihfestspiel*' and '*Weltabschied*' with no transcendental obfuscation whatsoever. It may be useful to quote a few passages here, though anyone interested in the subject would be well advised to read the whole piece.

The very first sentence strikes a note which, while seeking detachment from everyday life in conformity with the festival-play idea, in no way aspires to stage a sacred rite: 'Given that our present church-consecration days have remained a popular attraction, mainly because of the so-called

Kirmes-Schmäuse [consecration-day feasts] held on those occasions and named after them, I felt that I should present the mystically significant love-feast of my Knights of the Grail to present-day opera-goers exactly as if I conceived the stage festival theatre to have been specially consecrated for the representation of just such an exalted occurrence.' Wagner goes on: 'Anyone who was able with the right cast of mind and eye to comprehend, in keeping with the character of the productive and receptive activity prevailing there, all that ... occurred on the premises of this stage festival theatre, could not but liken it to the effect of a consecration which, without anyone's instructing it to do so, flowed freely over all present.' Wagner gives an outwardly puzzling response to the question of what 'government authority' had made possible the outstanding organization and 'unerring execution of all scenic, musical and dramatic occurrences' at every stage: '... whereupon I was able good-naturedly to reply that anarchy had achieved this, because each had done what he wanted, to wit, the right thing. That was certainly the case: everyone understood the whole thing and the purpose of the effect to which the whole thing aspired.' It can be said without exaggeration that this, *mutatis mutandis*, still holds good today.

'What seemed magical here,' Wagner wrote, 'and pervaded the entire performance of the stage festival play in a consecrative manner, became everyone's paramount concern in the course of the rehearsals and performances ...' A few lines below once comes to the following, noteworthy passage: 'Our understanding could not yet be hastened by experience; it was enthusiasm – consecration! – that creatively promoted the acquisition of a carefully cultivated awareness of what was right.'

As for the significance of Wagner's 'farewell to the world', this is cogently exemplified by the following words: 'We were thus enabled, partly by the effect on all our faculties of the surrounding acoustic and visual atmosphere, to feel as if we were remote from the accustomed world, and our awareness of this clearly manifested itself in an uneasy exhortation to return to that same world. After all, *Parsifal* itself owed its genesis and development merely to a flight from the same! Who can, with an open mind and an untrammelled heart, spend a lifetime looking upon this world of murder and rapine organized and legalized by falsehood, deception, and hypocrisy, without sometimes having to turn away from it in horrified disgust?'

As in 1975, I got Oswald Georg Bauer to make notes of our exhaustive discussions of the factors that guided and inspired my production of *Parsifal,* and of the ways in which I endeavoured to translate my ideas into scenic, visual terms.

'Here, time becomes space.' One of Wagner's most often quoted statements, enigmatic, baffling. In what space, what time, is *Parsifal* set? In the northern mountains of Gothic Spain, in the chivalric Middle Ages, in Arab Spain? Yes, if we interpret the letter, not the spirit, of the information Wagner gives. *Parsifal*'s space is an imaginary space, the time in which *Parsifal* takes place is an imaginary time. As soon as space appears, past and future time become the present. Light creates space, changing light is changing time.

The scene of events is surrounded and enclosed by vertical objects of a crystalline structure. Crystal, a formation from the dawn of Nature, with its transparent, natural tone, is capable of absorbing light and colour and is brought to life by light. Space is created by light – coloured light. Light is life. This life is brought by light out of the vast, cosmic night of the universe.

The acting area in *Parsifal* is a labyrinth, the basis and bedrock of our existence. The labyrinth neutralizes space and time, and is itself space and time. The problem is to find the right access; then the path leads to the central point, the end of the labyrinth and its new point of departure. Each of us creates that central point or objective as his personal solution. Titurel places the altar in the centre as a sanctum for the Grail, Klingsor creates an imitation of that sanctum, which to him possesses equal significance, for Kundry to appear in. Parsifal picks up the spear, holding it horizontally, i.e. non-aggressively, and thus turns the sacred spear, which has been misused as a weapon, back into a holy relic. That is the form in which he brings it back into the temple.

The sacred spring also flows in the centre, a theatrical translation of what Wagner, in Act II, calls the source of salvation for which Kundry and the Knights of the Grail all yearn: what Friedrich Hölderlin calls the 'sacred, sober water' that not only washes away guilt but soothes, purifies and allays ecstasy and longing.

In contrast to crystal, a changeable material, the temple is rigid and abstract in design, and the light within it is calculated, not natural. The Grail must only shine for an esoteric elect in a confined space. The temple's monumental architecture cites architectonic elements from various cultural epochs: Assyro-Babylonian, the ziggurat motif, echoes of Mexican Aztec cult sites and of post-Modernist architecture. Architectural metaphors are a principle and instrument of authority, also associated with prisons and barracks. Monumental architecture has always been mausoleum and funerary architecture as well: the monument as an expression of the desire for perenniality and eternal life. This is Titurel's original sin, his betrayal of the living Grail idea. He misconstrues his function and guards the Grail by hiding it away, walling it in, reserving it for an élitist clique, appropriating it to himself and legitimizing his claim to God's grace by using the Grail as an adjunct to magical, mysterious ceremonies. The tormented Amfortas longs to die, but Titurel, as ossified as his own conception of the Grail, wishes to obtain eternal life by means of that symbol of life. He creeps around the temple and withdraws to his government bunker. A cruel, unseen giver of orders, he mercilessly compels Amfortas to fulfil his office because he has no wish to renounce his life-prolonging drug, the Grail's 'sacred bliss'. Spatial and ideological limitation go hand in hand, and the final outcome is a demand for asceticism as a principle of hostility to life. This finds metaphorical expression in absolute discipline as the governing principle of the Temple of the Grail, in the paramilitary drill of regimentation, in the apotheosis of depersonalization and deindividualization as an aid to ideological intimidation. Stiff, aloof and unintelligible, remote from life and absolutely unsensual, the knights celebrate their ritual in an ascetic, hermetic manner, without reference to the outside world and life out there, whatever its nature. They are incapable of compassion, of love, of all that the Grail, a symbol of life and salvation, stands for. These Knights of the Grail should really inspire the pity which they themselves can no longer summon up for their king. Obsessed with their ownership of the Grail, they stare 'dully' at the sacred chalice, which glows under their mesmerized, stupefied gaze. Like Titurel, they seek ecstasy and longevity, not salvation.

Klingsor's conduct is the logical and most drastic consequence of Titurel's demand for asceticism, and is, in the latter's view, sacrilegious. His counterpart of the Temple of the Grail, the magic garden, is an imitation of the Titurelian idea of the Grail. In their internal structure, the two antithetical worlds are related and similarly organized. Klingsor performs his seduction magic just as Titurel performs his Grail magic, and the objective in each case is power. Both men seek power, possession, and authority. One misuses asceticism to maintain his absolute authority, the other misuses the sexual urge.

The only character to transcend space and time is Kundry, for whom both are permeable. Past, present and future are embodied in her single person. She was there and 'saw much' before ever Titurel erected his castle for the Grail – she emerged from space on her aerial steed like an Amazon, a Valkyrie. Kundry is accursed because she mocked the sufferer. Imprisoned and obsessed by her notion of the male as a heroic idol, she found the suffering king unmanly and contemptible. Now she must tread her own path of suffering. Although she is not the primordial she-devil by nature, men execrate her as such.

Kundry is the victim of the value which an exclusive, élitist male community places on all women: in the masculine imagination, they are either whores or servants, and Klingsor and the Knights of the Grail misuse her as one or the other. In the 'Heart's Sorrow' story in Act II she is, as a person, wholly in command of herself. As Parsifal's Samaritan of the Grail in Acts I and III, she comprehends the original Grail idea. The last

words Wagner wrote before his death – 'The process of women's emancipation must inevitably be accompanied by ecstatic convulsions. Love –
tragedy . . .' – may be related to Kundry's warring emotions in Act II. She
quickly realizes that Parsifal may be the person for whom she has waited
for an eternity, but her longing to be released from her curse is at this
stage merely a longing for the source of her suffering and, thus, no escape
from the vicious circle of eternal rebirth. In Wagner's poetical phrase, her
senses are still clouded by worldly folly. It is Gurnemanz who breaks the
spell and brings her to life, to her last rebirth, like an embryo. 'Serve, serve'
are her final words. But her days as a servant and seductress are over.
From now on she remains mute but is present and develops a new role –
her own. In the Good Friday scene she is no hair-shirted penitent but a
partner, companion, and beautiful embodiment of eternal womanhood.

In Act II Parsifal recognizes the inherent kinship of Titurel's and
Klingsor's worlds. Wagner told Cosima on 18 September 1878 that Parsifal's
'"*Ein Andres ist's*" [It is another] almost transcends the bounds of what is
didactically permissible'. These verses deliberately accentuate Parsifal's
acknowledgement of the inner relationship between good and evil as he
has come to know them in both their manifestations, in their deformation
and their relativity. On the one hand, the Knights of the Grail, who
'torment and mortify their flesh' in 'dire distress', believing this to be the
source of salvation; on the other, Kundry in her seductress's role, who
pines for the source of her curse in her longing to be released from it. The
'one true source of salvation' could be the symbol of life, redemption and
compassion: the Grail in its original form. After the kiss, Parsifal's eyes are
opened to the world by his recognition of its 'dark folly'. Realizing that
Titurel's and Klingsor's worlds are equally flawed, he renounces them both,
seeks his own way forward, and urges Kundry, the temptress who has been
unleashed on him, to do likewise.

Parsifal may possibly suspect in the temple that something is wrong and
has gone awry, but he cannot grasp what it is. He cannot intervene, either,
because that would imply an understanding of its nature. Kundry's kiss is
his first indication of this, but he does not become the new Grail king at
once. The kiss was just an initiation to be undergone. He must seek and
travel his own road to maturity and experience. He does go to war against
the enemies of the faith, as the missionary Knights of the Grail once did;
he returns as *miles christianus*, a spiritual knight.

Wagner called *Parsifal* his 'world-farewell-work'. Imbued with the sum
of his experience and interpretation of the world, it manifests the inter-
relationship of his works and their condensation: Klingsor is akin to
Alberich in his pursuit of power; Wagner himself related Siegfried to
Parsifal; Gurnemanz is in a line of descent from Hans Sachs and awakens

Kundry in Act III just as Brünnhilde might have been awakened by Wotan; the triple sequence 'day-night-death' in *Tristan* finds its counterpart in *Parsifal*'s 'life-death-redemption', and so forth.

In Act III Gurnemanz and Parsifal champion the storm-tossed Kundry in a humane, sympathetic way and accept her as the feminine principle which Titurel had consistently (and to its detriment) eliminated from his Grail community. As an individual, Kundry is released from the curse of eternal rebirth. As an embodiment of the feminine principle she remains alive and is admitted to the temple. In one simultaneous, mirror-image-like movement, Titurel's coffin is closed and borne away while the Grail shrine is opened. The temple has been demystified. The work's great finale is reserved for the music, and its lingering resonances are conceived of as Wagner's attempt to sketch, in musical terms, the world of the Grail in its ideal state: a world of humane spirituality.

The temple scene in Act I is dominated by the Titurel-Amfortas-Grail axis.

At the end of Act III, Parsifal and Kundry form an axis with the Grail between them.

Just a new constellation?

More:

A new experimental arrangement.

I must conclude by alluding briefly to the recordings made of the productions mentioned and described above. My first *Meistersinger* production exists on CD, and the following were audiovisually recorded: my first *Parsifal* (in 1981), my second *Meistersinger* and first *Lohengrin* (in 1984), and *Tannhäuser* (in 1989).

14

FOUNDATION STONES

To begin by quoting from Richard Wagner's letter to Ludwig II dated 31 March 1880: 'These fruitless efforts to obtain the funds for a permanent foundation, which cannot even grant a condition as wretched as that of the German "nation", are finally driving me mad, and I am resolved, if only so as to hear no more of the whole affair, to end it once and for all.'

It often seemed little short of a miracle that no such 'end' occurred despite changing times and extremely adverse circumstances such as the effects of two world wars, inflation, and the currency reform. If Bayreuth's present and future are relatively secure today, it is no thanks to the imperialistic German Empire, which was uninterested in the festival, nor to the unstable political climate of the Weimar Republic, nor to the official patronage of the Third Reich, which misused the festival for its own megalomaniac purposes. This could be accomplished only by sensible, perceptive and professional management within the free and democratic context of the German Federal Republic.

What ultimately gave rise to the partnership agreement concluded between me and my brother on 30 April 1962 was that the reversionary heirs had no realistic conception, nor could they be persuaded to adopt one, of what would become of the festival management and the festival itself on the death of our mother, Winifred Wagner. It was once more proposed, from 1965 onwards, to set up a family council. My brother-in-law Bodo Lafferentz, who had made previous efforts to that end, resumed his habit of drafting memos to which my brother, in particular, devoted a certain sceptical and ironical attention. Among other things, it was proposed that my brother and I should be debarred from terminating the tenancy agreement through our sisters for three years after our mother's death, this interval to be used to clarify all the procedures and possibilities open to the festival and its future management. Although the aforesaid partnership agreement guaranteed the immediate continuance of the festival in spite of

Wieland's tragic and untimely death, my mother and I were naturally compelled to review the future in the light of that altered situation.

In a letter dated 10 January 1967 Dr Gottfried Breit commented in detail on my mother's proposals to him regarding the possibility of setting up a foundation, their main aim being to preserve the whole of the Wagner estate intact and fulfil the provisions of the will she had made with my father on 8 March 1929. Long and complicated negotiations had to be engaged in before the foundation idea could be put into effect on 2 May 1973 by *all* the competent parties involved. I am bound to state, in retrospect, that the public authorities proved in general to be considerably more reasonable and perceptive as negotiators than the other family heirs. Where my mother and I were concerned, this fully confirmed the expectations we had voiced in advance.

On 18 May 1967, at my mother's instigation, Dr Breit submitted an interesting draft proposal for the establishment of a Richard Wagner Foundation based at Bayreuth. Being not only alive to the crucial importance of this matter but conscious of their Wagnerian heritage, the other reversionary heirs engaged good lawyers to advise them, with the result that sensible and pertinent negotiations were relatively soon under way. My sister Friedelind was advised and represented by Dr Bernhard Servatius, my sister Verena by her husband, Bodo Lafferentz, and my brother's children, who had become reversionary heirs on his death, by Dr Reinhold Kreile. Dr Fritz Meyer was ever ready with advice and assistance in his capacity as executor. Last but not least, our band of helpful expert advisers also comprised Dr Gottfried Breit, a constant source of support to my mother and me and one of those mainly responsible for drafting and finalizing the foundation's charter; Dr Ewald Hilger of the Association of Friends of Bayreuth, who proved an invaluable mediator during our family conclaves; and Dr Konrad Pöhner.

I cannot forbear to mention that grotesque situations sometimes arose at these family meetings, on one occasion because of Udo Proksch, who enjoyed a certain notoriety not only as owner of the Café Dehmel, a well-known Viennese establishment, but as a self-styled professional 'innovator'. (One of his bright ideas was a new, space-saving method of burial by which the dead were to be vertically interred in made-to-measure Plexiglas tubes.) Being then married to a niece of mine, he once felt prompted to attend one of these meetings. His behaviour was governed mainly by a transparent eagerness to see what personal advantages he could extract through third parties. Fortunately, nobody present adopted his 'suggestions' or was willing to sponsor his ideas, so the Festspielhaus continues to occupy its accustomed site to this day. Still an intact cultural concern, it has never had to serve as an aid to a large-scale insurance fraud or some other form of swindle. My nephew Wolf-Siegfried, Wieland's son, shared Friedelind's belief that additional sponsors would be easy to round up if only we set about the task properly, but even he had eventually to acknowledge that this was impracticable. Halfway through the seven years it took to negotiate the foundation into existence, my brother-in-law Bodo took it upon himself to make some additional, seriously-intended proposals to the effect that we should set up a foundation exclusively sustained and financed by the family, and that all members of the family should receive a certain subsistence allowance out of capital receipts and, if need be, have their debts redeemed. His draft proposal for a 'Bayreuth Family Foundation', which he submitted at one of our meetings on 12 June 1970, held out the hope that he would be able to achieve richly remunerative results by personally negotiating with potential backers. He was granted six weeks in which to put this scheme into effect – more than long enough to prove that it was merely wishful thinking.

At last, on 2 May 1973, all the requisite negotiations were complete and the charter of the Richard Wagner Foundation could be signed and sealed. I list the signatories below, together with their relevance to the foundation:

Winifred Wagner, prior heir and person entitled, with certain legal limitations, to dispose of the property;
Dr Bernhard Servatius, authorized representative of Friedelind Wagner, reversionary heir; Verena Lafferentz, née Wagner, reversionary heir; Wolfgang Wagner, reversionary heir – one quarter of the estate each;
Iris Wagner; Wolf-Siegfried Wagner, additionally acting as authorized representative of Nike Wagner; Daphne Proksch, née Wagner – one sixteenth of the estate each;
Dr M. Lugge, Federal Ministry of the Interior;
Dr Kerschensteiner, on behalf of the Bavarian State Ministry of Education and Church Affairs; Hans Walter Wild, mayor of the municipality of Bayreuth;
Dr Ewald Hilger, Association of Friends of Bayreuth;
Winkler, on behalf of the Upper Franconian Foundation and the District of Upper Franconia;
Dr Rudolf Bensegger and Dr Reiner Kessler, on behalf of the Bavarian *Land* Foundation.

The seven public authorities were incorporated in the foundation because they not only enabled the festival to be carried on by directly or indirectly making grants and funds available for the maintenance and renovation of the buildings, but, above all, made a decisive contribution towards the DM 13 million it cost to assemble the whole of the archive. The establishment of the foundation ensured that our subsidies would continue and disposed of the problem presented by increases in the value of the private estate. It has also facilitated further grants and even virtually guaranteed them.

A press release was issued to mark the establishment of the foundation. The following digest embodies its salient points:

The Festspielhaus at Bayreuth was Richard Wagner's private property. It has therefore passed by way of inheritance to his daughter-in-law, Winifred Wagner, and her children and grandchildren. To prevent the estate from being further subdivided and ensure that the Festspielhaus continues to serve the purpose to which it was dedicated by Richard Wagner, the Wagner family has conveyed the building, without charge, to a foundation to be known as the Richard Wagner Foundation. The latter has been established for three main purposes: to enable the Bayreuth Festival to be carried on indefinitely; to conserve Richard Wagner's artistic estate and cultivate an understanding of his works; and to promote the study of the same. The public authorities will have a substantial say in the running of the foundation.

The management of the festival remains in the hands of members of the family. The charter of the foundation provides that, when it becomes necessary to appoint a successor to the present director, Wolfgang Wagner, its management shall pass to some suitable candidate or candidates from within the family.

All the members of the Wagner family who have managed the festival hitherto (Cosima Wagner, Siegfried Wagner, Winifred Wagner, Wieland Wagner, Wolfgang Wagner) have made it their business, sometimes at considerable financial cost to themselves, to build up an extensive archive containing documents and records relating to Richard Wagner's artistic activities. This archive, which has already been available to scholars, will be entrusted to the Richard Wagner Foundation and will remain in Bayreuth. To facilitate this, the Wagner family will sell the archive to the German Federal Republic, the Bavarian *Land* Foundation, and the Upper Franconian Foundation, with the proviso that they entrust it permanently to the Richard Wagner Foundation. The agreed purchase price of DM12.4 million, which will be paid free of interest in three annual instalments, is based on two valuations submitted by the Bavarian State Library and the firm of Stargardt, bearing in mind that the foundation will always preserve the archive intact and may not dispose of it. For that reason, the vendors have accepted a sum considerably less than that which could have been realized had the archive been sold piecemeal.

Richard Wagner's home, Haus Wahnfried, which is to be rebuilt with all possible speed, has been given to the municipality of Bayreuth, also with the proviso that it be entrusted to the foundation on permanent loan and as soon as possible put to use as a Richard Wagner museum.

Finally, the so-called Siegfried Wagner House, at present occupied by Frau Winifred Wagner, has been sold to the municipality of Bayreuth for DM600,000. The foundation will make the fullest possible use of these premises, too, for its own purposes.

In setting up this foundation the family believes that it has acted in accordance with the wishes of Richard Wagner, who expressed similar ideas to King Ludwig II in 1876, and also with those of Siegfried Wagner, who likewise entertained similar plans before the First World War. The Bayreuth Festival, which will continue to be dependent on subsidies from public authorities and private contributors, it being impossible to set ticket prices at a level sufficient to cover costs, will thus retain its special status as an institution run by Richard Wagner's descendants.

Negotiations with the relevant public authorities were not only less than easy at times but extremely time-consuming. However, the good will of all who participated in the said negotiations has finally, after more than three years, conduced to their successful outcome. In this respect, the active assistance of the Association of Friends of Bayreuth is deserving of a special mention.

That the plan for a foundation was far from new, and that Richard Wagner himself had entertained such an idea, is implicit in his letter to King Ludwig dated 21 October 1876, written in Sorrento only a few weeks after the first Bayreuth Festival ended:

[...] Our problem hitherto has been insufficient funds; that was responsible for all the interruptions and delays that made it impossible for me to get everything ready in time, and to carry out indispensable tests and improvements. This can all be different and better in the future, because the most important thing is completed; once the costs of constructing the whole architectonic and scenic apparatus are covered, the costs of maintenance and future use will cover themselves. We should already have covered our costs completely, as I presupposed, had not all my presuppositions been upset by the contemptible calumnies of those frightful newspapers. It was certainly not foolish of me to assume that the success of the first performance, for which all the seats had been sold, would arouse sufficient interest to cause a run on the two succeeding performances, for which many seats were still unsold. But the reviews of that first performance, at which only journalists were present, were so scurrilous that it was only after the second performance and during the third, about which those gentlemen said nothing, that those present formed and disseminated a correct appreciation of everything, with the result that demand became so great that we could, had this been feasible, have given several more performances to packed houses.

My work and activities must in future be safeguarded against such influences and encroachments if I am to take any pleasure in them and preserve the strength to carry them out. I have, therefore, come to the following decisions: the annual festival at Bayreuth must remain a free foundation whose sole purpose is to serve as a pattern for the establishment and cultivation of an original German musical-dramatic art. For this it will be necessary that the fabric of the theatre itself be now disburdened of any charges upon it and guaranteed against all financial losses in the future, with this irrefrangible proviso: that the business itself never be run for private profit, and, more particularly, that the supreme head of the same shall never claim remuneration for his services.

I now propose to see what attitude the 'German Reich' will take in regard to this, for I cannot properly make another approach to my existing patrons except, at most, to ask them for a contribution to costs, which will doubtless be meagre enough. I see, in the first place, two ways of bringing the matter to the attention of the 'Reich': either the application must be made by a Reichstag representative, though I know of none that seems suited to the purpose; or it must be proposed by the Reich Chancellor's office, which would entail my approaching the Emperor, from whom I can hardly expect any profound understanding of the matter. A third course would be that the King of Bavaria, as the protector and custodian of higher German cultural interests, should instruct his authorized representative to submit the proposal in the Bundesrat and to go on from there to the Reichstag. This proposal should read more or less as follows:

'The German Reich government shall take over the Stage Festival Theatre at Bayreuth, together with all its appurtenances, in return for the settlement and payment of all expenses accruing from its construction and not yet covered, and transfer it, as a property owned by the nation, to the management of the municipal authorities of Bayreuth, whose task and obligation it shall be, pursuant to the wishes of the founder of the said theatre and the instructions and statutes to be laid down by the same, to permit annual performances to be held in the style of that which I staged in 1876. The costs of these annual performances shall be covered by the sale of 1000 tickets on each occasion, and also by an annual grant of 100,000 marks from the Reich. On the strength of that grant the Reich shall have the right to allocate the remaining 5–600 seats free of charge to impecunious members of the German nation, this being the best means whereby the whole institution can acquire, outwardly as well, the character of a "national" institution. Associations should be formed in all the countries of Germany to put forward the names of those entitled to admission free of charge, and the governments could give precedence, in awarding the distinction of a free seat, to the winners of first prizes at academies of music and theatre and *Gymnasialschulen* [roughly: grammar schools].'

Such, more or less, should be the wording of the proposal whose acceptance and execution I would regard as the only worthy recognition of my services in this matter. It has only one drawback: that I must entrust its execution to the 'Reich'. It would be better, more fitting, and far more natural if Bavaria and her King could carry it out alone. That would be a boon of inestimably beneficial influence on the future development of Germany's intrinsic nature and ethos, which has been so lamentably undervalued and neglected by her other princes – better than any constitutional body and, more particularly, than all those ubiquitous schools of music and theatre that are establishing themselves under the direction of dogged dilettantes and musicians and journalists eager to find themselves a lucrative niche. They have never exercised a beneficial influence, whereas at my performances everyone, but everyone, learns and is happy to do so!

Such would be my last, heartfelt wish!

My father, Siegfried Wagner, also devoted much thought to a foundation. The extent to which his ideas had matured is illustrated by the following extract from an interview with the *München-Augsburger Abendzeitung* on 26 May 1914:

All that Richard Wagner bequeathed to Bayreuth, that is to say, the Festspielhaus and its grounds, all the objects that belong to the Festspielhaus and the business enterprise, Haus Wahnfried and all its precious manuscripts, all Wagner's mementoes and memoirs, and the very considerable festival assets – all these my mother and I have destined for the German people as a foundation in perpetuity! [...] We shall show ourselves to be custodians of Wahnfried and not allow our idea for a foundation to fall into abeyance. We have resolved that Richard Wagner's Bayreuth does not belong to us; it belongs to the German people, to whom it shall be made over by the inheritors of Wahnfried as 'an eternal Richard Wagner home'.

We began drafting the foundation trust deed with our attorney's assistance on 15 July 1913, and we should have it completed by the beginning of this year's Bayreuth Festival. [...] We shall now let the foundation idea rest, and will not put it into effect until the courts have passed their final judgement on the case of 'Beidler versus Frau Dr Cosima Wagner'.

The stated purpose of the so-called 'German Festival Foundation Bayreuth', established in 1921, was to underwrite the festival financially. Because of the advent of inflation and the thoroughly amateurish way in which it was run, however, it had in the end to liquidate itself without attaining any of its objectives.

Given that all these previous endeavours had failed for a variety of reasons, it was important that my father and mother's joint testament should have laid down a form of 'constitution' for the future running of the Bayreuth Festival by one or more competent heirs, as I have already emphasized sufficiently in the course of this book.

Even after the foundation had been set up in 1973 it took many more years, legally and contractually, to supersede the existing tenancy agreements between my mother, my brother, and myself, and the oft-cited supplementary partnership agreement of 1962, and to replace them with the tenancy agreement now in force between me and the Richard Wagner Foundation.

The following important documents date from this intervening period:

notarial deed forming Wolfgang-Wagner-GmbH [a limited liability company], dated 7 August 1985;

Wolfgang Wagner's pension agreement, limited liability company version, dated 1 August 1986 (new version);

formal consent to the contracts concluded on 1 August 1986 and declaration by Wolfgang Wagner relating to the contracts dated 1 August 1986, both likewise dated 1 August 1986;

final contract relating to documentary material dated 6 April 1987;

agreement on assignment of interest dated 24 March 1987;

conversion of Wolfgang-Wagner-GmbH into Bayreuther Festspiele GmbH – document of 24 March 1987 – with articles of association (shareholders' meeting);

tenancy agreement with the Richard Wagner Foundation dated 6 June 1990.

The eight contracts and documents listed above are selected from among the twenty-six that together form the legal background to my activities in Bayreuth. In the light of the documents listed, it is particularly important that it be made known, at the instance and request of all contributors to the running of the festival, that instead of the fully liable sole proprietor of a company under civil law, I now operate as a shareholder with limited liability, in my case also as sole shareholder.

The remaining documents to which no express consideration has been given here include contractual agreements designed to guarantee the long-term continuance of the festival. They also relate to a supplementary endowment of mine whereby documents important to the festival's history have been entrusted to the historical archive of the Richard Wagner

Foundation. I can state without presumption that I have acted very generously in passing these on. My only guiding principle has been and still is, of course, to secure the continuance of the festival.

Concurrently with the establishment of the foundation I obtained my mother life occupancy of the Siegfried Wagner Haus, and, for my sister Friedelind, the right to occupy the apartment on the first floor of the gardener's house next door to Wahnfried until our mother's death.

From my own point of view, the establishment of the foundation did not alter the situation that had prevailed since 1951: as director of the festival I continue to bear the risks and the artistic responsibilities thereof. It follows that I function as tenant of the premises and not the owner, i.e. the foundation, because it is not the organizer.

Like every cultural institution, the Bayreuth Festival is dependent on public subsidies and private patronage. A so-called festival board was set up as early as 1953. Its sole function is to examine the budgetary estimates and statements of accounts drawn up by the festival management and, if necessary, to adjust them. This is to enable it to vouch for the sums to be raised or requested from the competent authorities. The chairman of the board is the mayor of Bayreuth.

As a non-profit-making corporation, this being the legal status that accorded with the suggestions and wishes of those who contribute to its running costs, the Bayreuth Festival is naturally liable to submit statements of accounts, and is thus subject to the democratically-determined favour or disfavour of the inland revenue department. The granting of public subsidies in the form of deficit financing, too, entails that the commissioner of audits must perform his duties. I have additionally entrusted a private trust company with overall supervision of the festival's administrative and financial management.

At the time of writing, I have been actively engaged in running the Bayreuth Festival for forty-three years. Throughout that time I have always managed to raise the funds required to keep it going, whether from representatives of the public authorities that subsidize it, or from the chairman and board of the private patronage society, the Association of Friends of Bayreuth.

The establishment of the foundation set the seal on Richard Wagner's bequest, and thus on the festival's artistic ideal, which is that it should be 'permanently preserved for all'. The subscribers to the charter not only acknowledged this principle, the very purpose of the foundation, but, in so far as they happened to be members of the Wagner family, were also granted very wide scope for future personal involvement in the festival – though not just because their name was Wagner. The family signatories accepted that they must be professionally competent, in other words, qualified by their personal accomplishments, not by the inherited shape of their chins or noses.

This precluded any form of succession based solely on 'dynastic' considerations and applied to every 'descendant of the four common offspring of Siegfried and Winifred Wagner', in other words, not only to the signatories to the charter but to all the scions of each branch of the family as well. The name Wagner entitles its holder to make suggestions, and even confers privileged status, but not in any prehistoric, quasi-feudal meaning of the term 'succession'.

One could only marvel at the public statements – muddled and obscure but effective in their media-courting superficiality – that emanated from certain members of the family not long after the foundation was established. These tend to recur annually, with almost chronometrical precision, either just before or during the festival season. Their gist has remained more or less the same and continues to betray an alarming gulf between pretension and reality. All that has changed is the nature and tone of the invective employed. Discussion has been replaced by diatribes that have not only made it increasingly difficult to carry on a dialogue over the years, but have rendered it quite impossible.

I am sometimes reminded of Don Quixote's duel with the windmills by the phantasmagoric struggle for 'hereditary rights' and 'power' being waged in respect of the Bayreuth Festival. There is no 'Haus Wahnfried' in the same sense as the House of Habsburg or the House of Windsor, nor is the festival a fief or benefice.

The behaviour patterns exhibited by some members of the family have often given rise to verbal outbursts and aberrations to which the only appropriate response was one of shame, anger, and dissociation. Had they been aimed at me alone, I might perhaps have made less of them, being inured to such things. But when Bayreuth and its leading interpreters and collaborators are morally and ideologically impugned in language that verges on racism, I feel bound to dissociate myself in the strongest terms. I naturally wonder what prompts such onslaughts on the part of one particular person, and can only surmise that they are motivated by a desire to attract the attention that has been denied him in respect of his achievements to date. To accuse him of a pronounced 'image neurosis' would be plainly offensive, so I shall refrain from doing so. Devoid of any genuine sense of responsibility and duty, the great-grandson in question should beware lest the reflected glory of his name and lineage fade to such an extent that it ceases to legitimize his chances of taking over the festival.

I have gained the impression that the embarrassing gulf between what he is and what he claims to be is steadily widening, and that his violent polemics are intended to bridge that gap with the assistance of such sections of the media as will always prefer a sensation to information. I do not complain of this, but I regret it, because he may find it hard to parade himself as a Wagner great-grandson for evermore. What once seemed a natural asset may some day prove to be a stigma.

There is little point in laundering dirty linen in public, and the last thing I want is to recapitulate when, where, or why this person was let down by that. I have no intention of defending myself and no reason to justify myself to anyone, nor would I dream of answering one war of words with another. Anyone who expects me to do so or hopes for details of our family squabbles should consult some other publication. It would go against the grain with me to use an autobiographical book for revelatory purposes. I should certainly prefer it if other members of the Wagner family could finally bring themselves to keep private concerns and festival matters separate, instead of so often mingling the two in a regrettable and unacceptable way. I cannot, however, conceal the fact that some features of these arguments transcend the bounds of an internal family row, so I must devote a little more attention to them.

I have never been able to understand, for instance, why certain of my public statements at press conferences or interviews have been interpreted as meaning that I consider every other scion of the Wagner clan totally and permanently unsuited to working at Bayreuth. All I said at the festival press conference in 1975 was that, objectively speaking and with the best will in the world, I did not *then*, i.e. in *1975*, think it proper to entrust the centenary *Ring* to the next generation of Wagners. And in *1976*, in a very exhaustive interview published in the July number of *Playboy*, I stated among other things that the name Wagner was more of a handicap than a help. 'As things stand,' I went on, 'I can state without exaggeration that if I dropped out tomorrow, none of the younger generation of Wagners, whether female or male, possesses the qualifications to run Bayreuth.' I think it necessary to quote myself verbatim because so many people continue to be afflicted with a strange and regrettably chronic form of word-blindness – one that clouds their understanding of Wagnerian texts and the wording of the foundation charter in equal measure.

I am forever being requested by members of the next generation to enlist them for work at Bayreuth and break them in here. More than that, they insinuate that it is my duty as a conscientious head of the family (which I have sometimes, half-heartedly, been called) to tend and train them to be 'pretenders to the throne'. Apart from the fact that no such duty has ever been incumbent on me, my approach to the management of the Bayreuth Festival is not determined primarily by family or patriarchal factors. There never has been a contractual obligation to pass it on from one generation to the next. Not only is this a pure figment but, even if it had existed, the foundation charter would have invalidated it. Those who seek, indeed, crave employment here have always wanted to take over senior positions or appear in some purely social capacity during the festival. I have had to turn down requests in the first category because their authors were currently incapable of doing justice to the positions they coveted, and in the second because purely social appearances are insufficient in themselves unless backed up by something more substantial than the genetic accident that enables people to wear their name like a badge. I genuinely regret the fact that none of Richard Wagner's great-grandchildren was prepared to work at Bayreuth, perseveringly and all year round, during the relatively drab period when the name Wagner signified no more than an obligation to achieve some solid if rather unspectacular results on a continuous basis. As I see it, there are still only two roads open to a Wagner with aspirations to Bayreuth. Either he legitimizes his claim elsewhere by independently achieving such convincing results that, when I retire, he gains a majority vote in accordance with the democratic provisions of the foundation's charter, or he embarks on his potential career here in Bayreuth, in which case he must work his way up by degrees.

I would gladly revise my existing opinion – indeed, charge myself with gross misjudgement – if it could be conclusively demonstrated that I have failed to discern what is obvious to everyone else. I should be absolutely delighted if non-members of the family, too, were to urge me to acknowledge the outstanding talents and achievements of which everyone speaks, and if I could be convinced that I am mistaken in my present perception of the Wagner name, the festival idea, and the statutes of the foundation. The fact is that most outsiders are still mutely awaiting proof of the aforesaid Wagnerian achievements, and have found no good reason to criticize my management of the festival, whereas the same festival continues to serve my family as a backcloth that will set them off to better effect. But little more emerges from their lips than eloquent self-glorification, and the only form of tenacity they display is an outmoded belief that they are naturally and charismatically predestined to great things – all in all, a process not unlike the one whereby a photographer promises to invest his sitters with 'personality'. It must by now be obvious to all that the mere statement 'I am a Wagner' has long ceased to be an open sesame.

If it has been impossible for me to take one or more of the younger generation into the festival business, either now or years ago, it is because the others would promptly have construed this as favouritism and resented the fact. I was also justified in assuming that self-interest and personal ambition would take precedence over the festival's paramount interests instead of becoming integrated with them. It would not have been long before some 'guardian of the Hoard' reduced his colleagues to 'Nibelungen' and subjected the festival organization to intolerable strains that would quickly have laid it in ruins.

I profoundly regret, in my capacity as a father and uncle as well as director of the festival, that certain members of the next generation can think of nothing better or more intelligent to do than to proclaim, year after year, that fundamental changes should be made to the status for which, as I have tried to show, my brother and I waged such a long and arduous struggle. I cannot help wondering if they really think it appropriate to commend themselves to the foundation board and members of the public, some of whom help to subsidize the festival, as being qualified to assume overall responsibility for Bayreuth. Any reasonably objective person will confirm that I do not cling to tradition and am flexible enough to recognize the signs of the time, from whose exigencies Bayreuth is not exempt. I myself have introduced many changes and am continuing to do so, not half-heartedly, but in accordance with given legal provisions and possibilities. I do not, however, believe that provocative rodomontades or a craving to smash existing structures constitute an adequate policy for the future. Anyone who radically questions the present set-up should be able not only to adduce good rhetorical reasons and arguments for doing so, but also to demonstrate their validity by means of solid achievement. Is it enough simply to be *for* oneself, and to present verbose definitions of what or whom one is *against*? Does pure negation constitute valid criticism and a qualification for future management of the festival? Is 'heartfelt fervour' an adequate substitute for constructive creativity? Do broad theoretical generalizations compensate for a lack of practical experience of the theatre? Is it enough to want to *act* the boss but not to *be* one in the full and thoroughly mundane meaning of the word? Are attacks on non-Christian participants in the festival a special qualification? Is it acceptable, for purely emotional reasons, to want to participate in the work of the Bayreuth Festival when this is largely complete, and to reap where others have sown?

Once again I ask: Is the Wagner name a sufficient qualification for Bayreuth? Have I been remiss or neglectful in some way? Is it possible to 'rear' a festival director? Is the prime concern here the festival management itself, or merely a wish to usurp 'power'? Unfortunately, no means to the latter end is too contemptible to be pressed into service – for instance, the ostracism of my wife, whom my opponents credit with what are doubtless their own motives, spreading malicious rumours and using her as a vicarious target for their aggression.

From 1951 onward my brother and I enjoyed the services of a staff of whom every one deserves to be mentioned with gratitude. The scope of the present book renders this quite impossible, of course, because there are hundreds if not thousands of names associated with particular achievements and anecdotes that would well repay the telling. I could not, in any case, hope even to enumerate all the people I have met during my life. (From the purely statistical aspect, had I encountered only one a day in the course of my life, they would amount to some thirty thousand!)

It is a regrettable fact that one speaks far too often of those who cause annoyance, present problems, or are problems in themselves. Equally, one tends to omit or mention only fleetingly those who do their jobs without fuss, in a 'merely' competent manner. But for them, the innumerable people who are not mentioned here, I could never have fulfilled my allotted task, in so far as it can be regarded as fulfillable. They include administrative assistants, craftsmen, secretarial and box office staff, lighting technicians, make-up artists, dressers, and all those directly involved in the running of the festival. Representing them here are the two with whom I have worked the longest. From 1950 until a few months ago, I was fortunate enough to enjoy the energetic and self-sacrificing assistance of Gerhard Scholz, who had an expert knowledge of the festival's entire financial structure and development. And from 1951 onwards I have been working with Erna Pitz, who has continued, even since her husband died, to give me the benefit of her active assistance and advice, which are based on decades of intimate knowledge of the business.

It would be just as impossible for me to cite the names of all the relevant members of public authorities and thank them individually for their sympathetic and responsive treatment over many decades: representatives of the Federal ministries of the interior and finance, the Bavarian ministries of culture and education, science and art, finance, industry, and transport, the Bavarian audit commissioner's office, the government and district of Upper Franconia, and, last but not least, the municipality of Bayreuth. Our fruitful discussions and negotiations have culminated, ever and again, in the consensus so essential to the existence and vitality of Bayreuth.

Thanks are due in equal measure to the staff of the Bavarian broadcasting service, who have for decades followed the work of the festival and played an invaluable part in making the results of our work accessible to a worldwide audience through their democratic medium. Here, too, I shall mention one name in lieu of all: that of Johann Maria Boykow, who is not only an outstanding expert in his field but a personal friend.

The following section will present a brief survey of the financial management of the Bayreuth Festival and an account of what has been done, where the reorganization of this exceptionally active artistic enterprise is concerned, in the way of capital investment and reconstruction.

It is interesting to compare figures dating from the resumption of the festival in 1951 with present budgetary magnitudes, because the result seems to me symptomatic of the development of the German and world economy. In 1951 expenditure on personnel accounted for only 43.3% of total outgoings, whereas its share in 1988 amounted to 75.5% and has sometimes exceeded 80%.

In 1951 the festival's total expenditure on new productions of the entire *Ring, Parsifal,* and *Die Meistersinger,* as well as a performance of Beethoven's Ninth Symphony – i.e. twenty-one public performances plus one for trades union members – amounted to DM2,535,647.50, that is to say, DM115,256.70 per performance. If one follows the same line of thought and bases one's calculations on the year 1988, for example, the following picture emerges. The programme for 1988 comprised one new production of the four-part *Ring,* of which three cycles were given, five repeat performances of *Parsifal,* six of *Lohengrin,* five of *Die Meistersinger,* and one each of *The Rhine Gold* and *Lohengrin* for members of the German trades union federation, i.e. thirty performances in all. The festival budget for 1988 amounted to DM18,767,804.71. Dividing that sum by thirty, as above, one arrives at a cost per performance of DM625,593.49.

In 1951 we received DM325,317 in public subsidies and DM148,525 from the Association of Friends of Bayreuth. The relevant figures for 1988 were DM7,525,289.34 and DM930,661.50 respectively.

Bayreuth Festival programmes are very largely governed by what is financially feasible. Some of the determining factors are:

The number of soloists in a particular work. Total expenditure on the soloists in a performance of *Die Meistersinger,* for example, is 2.25 times as great as for a performance of *Der Fliegende Holländer.*

New productions. Scenery and costumes for *Die Meistersinger* will naturally cost more than those for *Der Fliegende Holländer.*

The number of rehearsals required by particular works. Where artists are concerned, rehearsals usually start in the middle of June. In the case of a new production of *The Ring* tetralogy, on the other hand, solo rehearsals usually start at the end of April and sometimes even during the previous year's festival.

In the special case of *Tannhäuser,* substantial extra costs accrue from the need to engage dancers. This can entail that we have to forgo refurbishing an expensive work or dispense with a new production altogether.

To facilitate as intensive and efficient a rehearsal schedule as possible, three large multipurpose halls of the same size as the stage have been built on to the Festspielhaus. These serve as large-scale workshops and, when preparations for the festival commence, enable rehearsals to be conducted in conjunction with original scenery up to 4.5 metres in height. These halls or rehearsal stages are on exactly the same level as the main stage, which means that sets can be erected complete, on a far larger scale than is generally possible, and wheeled straight from the hall/rehearsal stage to the main stage with little or no difficulty. Bayreuth is thus spared the problems that beset many other theatres, where scenery has to be built on a smaller scale and laboriously transported from distant store-rooms, often with the aid of elevators.

Rehearsal schedules are systematically mapped out in advance. The result is that we have never had to engage even one more technician than necessary over the years, thereby saving man-hours.

Because we have no evening performances to contend with during the rehearsal period, it is possible to rehearse three times a day on each of the rehearsal stages. Thanks to our three big halls, this means that we can hold twelve full-scale stage rehearsals daily, seven days a week.

The permanent staff of the festival organization, including me, number sixty-four and range from craftsmen and secretarial staff to the janitor and cleaner. Over half of them are craftsmen who, apart from building scenery and doing maintenance work, are employed as stage technicians, especially during the rehearsal period and the festival itself. During the festival season our number of personnel can balloon to as many as 800, including extra choruses and usherettes (the so-called 'Girls in Blue'). Up to thirty-five nationalities are represented in their ranks. I should mention in passing that the bureaucratic regulations in force throughout the modern world impose a special strain on our personnel and accounts departments. Even where EEC nationals are concerned, their administrative problems have not diminished to any appreciable extent.

In order to do full justice to works as demanding as Richard Wagner's, given the concentrated nature of our rehearsal and performance schedules, we had in 1988, for example, to engage an orchestra 189 strong. A further eleven instrumentalists were required for the incidental and intermission music, the fanfares that herald every act instead of a bell and are sounded on the balcony of the 'king's portal'.

From the financial aspect, it is still customary and possible at Bayreuth to remunerate artists according to their roles, and not in keeping with the star system or some form of 'market value'. Singer A (world-famous) and Singer B (a novice) receive the same fee for the same role. This also applies without exception to other leading participants such as conductors, each of whom is paid as much or as little as the other.

Below is a comparative analysis of the contributions to total expenditure accruing from public and private sources:

	1953	1965	1976	1988	1992
Public funds	26.2%	30.5%	38.8%	40.0%	34.3%
Association of Friends of Bayreuth	0.7%	4.9%	4.6%	6.4%	4.07%

I consider it essential that grants from public authorities should never exceed 50%. Bayreuth differs considerably in this respect from the majority of German theatres, some of which are subsidized by as much as 90%.

The historical development of admission charges is briefly outlined below, together with the average price of a ticket:

1951	6 categories	DM15.00–DM50.00	Average: DM29.30
1961	9 categories	DM25.00–DM65.00	Average: DM40.40
1978	25 categories	DM13.00–DM145.00	Average: DM73.20
1992	25 categories	DM17.00–DM225.00	Average: DM159.11

The upward trend clearly indicates that even an artistic enterprise is governed by prevailing economic conditions. To resist such a trend is not, unfortunately, within my power. Richard Wagner's original intention, which was that audiences should attend his festival free of charge, has never been fulfilled, but I have always done my best to structure our tariff in a socially acceptable way, as the broad range of prices illustrates. Bayreuth's tickets are considerably cheaper than those of other major international festivals. In pursuing this pricing policy I have always received the fullest support from our democratic political authorities, so I trust that, despite Germany's present financial straits, the Bayreuth Festival will continue to be assisted in an appropriate manner.

In this connection it may be of interest to give a breakdown of the extent to which, and the way in which, each of our tickets was subsidized in 1992. Expenditure per ticket, which amounted to DM355.18, was financed as follows:

(1)	Festival resources	DM197.84	= 55.7%
(2)	Public subsidies:		
	Federal Government	DM52.74	= 14.85%
	Bavaria	DM52.74	= 14.85%
	Municipality of Bayreuth	DM23.44	= 6.6%
	District of Upper Franconia	DM11.72	= 3.3%
(3)	Private Patrons		
	(Association of Friends)	DM16.70	= 4.7%
Total		DM355.18	= 100%

Thus our own resources, comprising the proceeds from ticket sales and other earnings, accounted for DM197.84 as against a subsidy of DM157.34.

It may be mentioned, for purposes of comparison, that public theatres elsewhere in Germany received a subsidy of up to DM320.00 per ticket at the same period.

The bursary foundation set up at my grandfather's instance on 28 May 1882 is financed by the Richard Wagner Societies. This makes it possible for 200 recipients of the award to attend certain performances free of charge. Members of the German trades union federation have been granted two closed performances at reduced prices every year since 1952 (one in 1951).

It was only to be expected that the Bayreuth Festival would have to walk something of a financial tightrope in the years immediately succeeding 1951. The optimism of the friends who supported us, and of my brother and me, enabled us to survive the financial crises of 1951 and 1952. This was due to the following factors.

The resurrected Bayreuth Festival won full international recognition. This earned my brother and me – those 'inexperienced young people' – a bonus in that no one was willing to allow the road on which we had embarked to become a dead-end. The bank indebtedness of our civil law partnership in 1951 and 1952 was such that it should really have filed a petition in bankruptcy. The situation was not improved when our power supply, which was still largely dependent on steam generators ('locomobiles') dating from the last century and producing direct current, broke down altogether after the final performance in 1952. It had to be completely replaced, wiring systems and dimmer rack included, but our friends did not desert us even then.

On 1 June 1951 Baroness Gerta Louise von Einem, whom I had known for years through her son Gottfried, visited me by appointment for a detailed discussion of ways to obtain the additional funds the festival needed. We agreed that her financial claims against my sister Friedelind (Friedelind took jewellery belonging to Frau von Einem from Europe to the Unites States and sold one piece after the other there) could have absolutely no bearing on the assistance offered us for the festival's benefit. Once that point had been settled, I gave her my permission, in view of our financial straits, to make the requisite moves. When she called on me in my office during the festival we discussed whether Bonn might be enlisted to help finance the festival. Being aware that the Bavarian ministry of culture took a very detached view of the Bayreuth Festival at that time, and knowing the Federal Constitution, I asked if she were in a position to ascertain whether the Federal authorities might do something for Bayreuth despite the statutory cultural paramountcy of the *Länder*. Frau von Einem's response was: 'Wolfgang, we shall see what we shall see.' As a final favour, I asked if she could find out if a few crumbs might charitably be allowed to fall on us from the richly-endowed table of the Amt Blank (Federal ministry for the Marshall Plan).

I was able, in time for the 1952 festival, to obtain a certain sum from Bonn that made it possible for me to acquire some urgently needed lighting equipment without incurring any more debts. Thanks to this special grant, we were able not only to renew the entire lighting system and power supply but to cover all our outstanding bank indebtedness by the time rehearsals began in 1953.

When questioned about the festival's financial position at the 1953 press conference and the annual general meeting of the Association of Friends on 24 July 1953, I was able to state: 'The previous years' debts have been settled, and the festival's future may be regarded as secure, thanks to our acquisition of a subsidy from the Federal Government.'

In October 1953 we set about establishing the festival board mentioned at the outset, which laid down the following ratio for the future subsidization of the Bayreuth Festival:

Federal Government		one-third
Bavarian Free State		one-third
Municipality of Bayreuth	four-ninths	
District of Upper Franconia	two-ninths	one-third
Association of Friends	three-ninths	

By setting the contribution of the private patrons at a fixed percentage, we precluded the arbitrary 'something from everyone' principle.

Many more discussions and negotiating sessions were necessary, especially in regard to the security of investments, before the foundation was established. Declarations of assignment were made in respect of capital appreciation. There was also established a 'Registered Association for the Promotion of the Bayreuth Festspielhaus', which remained in operation for some time, and the registration of land charges was discussed. All incompatible legal agreements were nullified by the establishment of the foundation.

Between 1951 and the end of the decade, when her activities on our behalf ceased, Frau von Einem procured a large number of donations in kind such as diesel generators, pipes, steel sections, sprinklers, and many other things. It was thanks to her multifarious efforts, too, that Professor Arnold Bode of 'Documenta' in Kassel produced a new and interesting décor for the old restaurant building, which also served as an orchestral rehearsal room, with material assistance from the 'Göppinger Plastik' company.

In the following sections I shall briefly summarize the redevelopment of the Festspielhaus and the structural investments that were so essential to the smooth running of the festival.

In recommencing the festival in 1951, we and the municipality agreed that the competent authorities would release the theatre come what might, even though our limited financial resources made it impossible to remedy all its defects. It is well known that the building had, for reasons of economy, been constructed of the cheapest available materials (timber faced with brick). Only the auditorium staircases and structurally important parts of the stage area were of adequate strength and solidity. Very little maintenance work had been carried out between the beginning of the war and 1950, initially because of the impossibility of obtaining the requisite materials, and thereafter because of the consequences of the currency reform. The building was thus in a far from satisfactory condition.

Hans Rollwagen and his mayoral advisers were as aware as my brother and I that, once the festival had been artistically stabilized, immediate efforts must be made to ensure that the structural condition of the Festspielhaus complied with all official requirements and regulations.

The Association of Friends, reassured by the internationally acknowledged success of the festival's resumption, hoped to be able to mobilize private funds for indispensable renovation work and capital investment in addition to the contributions that had already been obtained from commercial firms. At a members' meeting on 25 July 1961, Consul Dr Franz Hilger was able to report that the efforts of Dr Sohl and Professor Burkhardt had yielded very satisfactory results. A campaign to raise money for Bayreuth from German industrial concerns had brought in DM600,000. This sum, added to the DM300,000 already raised, meant that a total of DM900,000 was now available, over and above the other industrial subsidies procured by the Association, for the renovation of the Festspielhaus. In view of this, it was hoped that the Federal and *Land* authorities, too, would contribute large sums. Leading members of the patrons' association offered to reinforce the festival management's own endeavours by initiating the requisite negotiations.

By 8 December I was able to present a preliminary report which outlined the extent of the building work that would be required and, at the same time, mobilized everyone's efforts to carry it out.

My brother would really have preferred to plough all our funds and subsidies into the artistic side of our work, and to execute only those repairs and renovations that were absolutely necessary, instead of investing them in the maintenance and development of the Festspielhaus. It took great patience and persuasion on my part to convince him that any artistic success would be nullified if the building had to be closed on account of its decrepit condition. We could not afford to run that risk under any circumstances. In the event, Wieland freely acknowledged the value of the successive improvements I introduced and was delighted to make use of them.

All the building projects listed here were carried out by the architects Lothar Linder and Helmut Jahn on my instructions and under the joint auspices of my financial department and of the festival office of works that existed from 1961 until the end of 1967. Even after the foundation was established, all structural work including the rebuilding of Haus Wahnfried between 1974 and 1976 was organized and supervised by me and my colleagues in the financial department. The two architects worked for me in a free-lance capacity until March 1976, when Helmut Jahn assumed sole responsibility for structural work after Linder's death.

The municipality of Bayreuth has since 1978 been responsible for the structural maintenance of Haus Wahnfried, now the Richard Wagner Museum and National Archive, and also for the museum complex annexed to the Siegfried Wagner House, which it owns and converted at its own expense. As festival director I continue to supervise structural repairs to the Festspielhaus, both major and minor, because all concerned agree that this is the best way of identifying and executing what needs to be done. I should mention, purely for form's sake, that funds for all the building work carried out to date have been made available on the strength of surveys made by competent authorities, notably the Bavarian Board of Works. Originally conceived of as a makeshift structure, the Festspielhaus has thus been renovated and enlarged, and, to the extent that this is humanly possible, converted into a durable living theatre and cultural monument.

In addition to ensuring that the new buildings and extensions were functional and time-saving in design, we were also able to promote a good working climate by developing the canteen and its garden.

The figures below present a concise overview of the cubic capacity and floor space of the buildings restored and enlarged, together with a breakdown of the way they were funded.

(A) *Converted premises* (gross cubic content):

(1) All buildings of 1876–82	*c.* 88,020 m³
(2) Other buildings and parts of buildings of 1883–1950	*c.* 24,142 m³
Together	*c.* 112,162 m³

(3) Other buildings and parts of buildings   *c.* 55,826 m³
    of 1951–93

Total of present gross cubic content   *c.* 167,988 m³

(B) *Floor space*

    (1) All buildings of 1876–82   *c.* 7,585 m²

    (2) Other buildings and parts of buildings   *c.* 2,858 m²
        of 1883–1950

    Together   *c.* 10,443 m²

    (3) Other buildings and parts of buildings   *c.* 10,579 m²
        of 1951–93

    Total of present floor space   *c.* 21,022 m²

Summary of financing

Construction costs between 1960 and 1992 totalled DM33,297,961.88 and were funded as follows:

Federal Government   DM6,553,300.00 (19.68%)

Bavarian Free State   DM6,553,300.00 (19.68%)

Municipality of Bayreuth   DM1,254,332.00 (3.76%)

District of Upper Franconia   DM282,165.00 (0.85%)

Upper Franconian Foundation   DM100,000.00 (0.30%)

Bavarian *Land* Foundation   DM65,000.00 (0.20%)

Total of public contributions
specifically earmarked for building
purposes   DM14,808,097.00 (44.47%)

Association of Friends of Bayreuth   DM13,963,513.55 (41.93%)

Private donations   DM41,741.00 (0.13%)

Together   DM28,813,351.55 (88.53%)

Funds approved for transfer from
the festival budget   DM1,393,410.33 (4.17%)

Proceeds of television recordings   DM3,091,200.00 (9.30%)

TOTAL   DM33,297,961.88 (100%)

Rebuilding of Haus Wahnfried
(included in the above)   DM3,218,445.63

The Association of Friends of Bayreuth has borne the brunt of the reconstruction costs incurred since the foundation was set up in 1973.

The above expenditure covers measures undertaken to comply with historical monuments legislation, the very stringent and continually updated safety regulations affecting places of public assembly, and the additional and unwelcome expense of sound-proofing. The Festspielhaus stands precisely in the flight path of aircraft approaching Bayreuth Airport, an additional source of disturbance being the international air route between Frankfurt and Prague.

15

MISCELLANY

When my brother presented his new production of *Die Meistersinger* in 1956, audiences were not a little startled by his unexpectedly radical aesthetic refashioning of the work. It had also been Wieland's intention to supplement his statements on the stage with a different orchestral sound. Believing that *Die Meistersinger* had not been composed for a hidden orchestra, he wanted to modify our grandfather's original structure, notably by replacing the forward curve of the abat-voix with the balustrade customary in other opera houses. Acoustic experiments had been carried out on a few mornings during the festival season in 1954, the *Tannhäuser* year, although these applied only to the triple proscenium. When a new lighting system was installed during the 1920s the right-hand space between the main proscenium and the frame in front of it had been rather crudely walled off at right angles, evidently with my father's approval, in order to house some rheostats. After suitable experiments, this right-angled partition and the corresponding area on the left-hand side, hitherto open, were faced with corrugated sheets whose acoustically reflective properties had been gauged with care. Ordinary curtains deaden the sound of any prelude or overture, as everyone knows. This applied as much to the Festspielhaus as to any other theatre, and so, when the original curtain disintegrated from old age, it was replaced with a considerably heavier and denser one. Unfortunately, the sheer weight of the new curtain ripped it during a performance. This meant that it could no longer be used as a 'Wagner curtain', and there was no possibility of opening up the stage after the manner of an iris diaphragm, as my grandfather had intended.

We always consulted Professor Dr Werner Gabler when carrying out acoustic experiments of this kind. In the case of an acoustic alteration as drastic as the one my brother proposed to introduce for *Die Meistersinger*, we were able to show Wieland a solution that enabled the old state of affairs to be reconstructed or preserved with little difficulty. We installed a removable, perforated baffle in the forward abat-voix facing the auditorium. This allowed a more brilliant sound to escape, so the orchestra could remain hidden. A similar perforated sheet, invisible to the audience, was affixed beneath the opposing baffle that extends from the stage over the orchestra. As I ascertained from an original drawing I discovered, my grandfather had installed this, on the strength of experience gained in 1876, for the first performance of *Parsifal* in 1882. Its main purpose was to concentrate the sound of the wind section. Our experiment with perforated baffles met with the full approval of all concerned, especially Wieland. His approval now extended even to the prelude to *Parsifal* conducted by Knappertsbusch, who naturally did his best to prevent any material alterations to the original state of affairs.

It is apparent from some old working drawings that Richard Wagner thought it necessary to enlarge the orchestra pit considerably, and this, given the nature of the premises, could only be done by taking it downwards in steps, in other words, into the under-stage area. In the course of subsequent reconstruction work it proved possible, mainly by installing a regulation fireproof wall at the rear of the pit and removing the ceiling structure, appreciably to enlarge the pit's cubic capacity and, in particular, to create reflective, acoustically non-absorbent surfaces that greatly enhanced the tonal variety achievable by every member of the orchestra.

One of my more memorable artistic experiences occurred in 1991, when I produced *Lohengrin* in the ancient Teatro Greco at Taormina in Sicily. Giuseppe Sinopoli, artistic director of the 'Taormina Arte' Festival, was expecting that great choral opera to be one of the highlights of his programme, and London's Philharmonia Orchestra and the Bayreuth chorus would both be participating at his invitation. For me, the occasion promised to fulfil a long-cherished ambition.

My interest in open-air theatres and their specific qualities had been aroused years earlier. At the end of the 1950s I travelled to Epidaurus to explore the possibility of staging a Bayreuth Festival production in the ancient Greek amphitheatre there. This project, in which my brother was also very interested, could not be realized at the time because of bureaucratic problems. In spring 1958, at the suggestion of Herbert Graf, the builder of the Red Rocks open-air auditorium, invited me to spend a few days in Denver, Colorado, and advise him on the visual and acoustic conformation of the stage, which was over thirty-six metres wide, because the rocks in the background were proving inadequately reflective. The pit, too, presented certain problems. I was accompanied by Dr Werner Gabler, and we later heard that our suggested improvements had been satisfactorily carried out. It had been proposed that the Bayreuth Festival make a guest appearance at Denver, but nothing came of this either, to my regret, nor did I ever fulfil my pet project, an open-air production of Puccini's *La Fanciulla del West* at Red Rocks – 'on the spot', as it were. The main obstacle was an inability to synchronize our programmes, because the temperature at Denver was suitable for open-air performances only during the months of June, July, and August.

One curiosity was that, in order to obtain an entry visa from the American Consulate in Munich, I had to swear the only oath I have ever sworn in my life. Till then I had been ingenious enough to avoid making any such solemn avowal, either in the Labour Service or in the army, so '*Führer, Volk und Vaterland*' had had to dispense with my formal pledge of allegiance. Although my knowledge of German history had inspired an aversion to such things, I was able with a clear conscience to swear on the Bible that I had never belonged to a communist organization and did not sympathize with the adherents of the hammer and sickle. In the aftermath of the notorious McCarthy period, communism was indeed a red rag to the American bull.

Where open-air theatres or amphitheatres are concerned, one more episode springs to mind. During the Bayreuth guest appearance at Barcelona's 'Liceo' in 1955, Dr Gabler and I were invited by the then Falangist governor of the city to look for a suitable site for an open-air theatre among the rocky outcrops of the Montserrat. Although we jointly prepared an interesting preliminary design, this project, like so many others, came to nothing.

My intermittent preoccupation with open-air theatres did, of course, prompt me to consider how one of my grandfather's works, which had been created with a completely different setting in mind, could be staged in a place of that nature.

At Taormina I assumed from the outset that the columns, niches and cornices in the background, which were only partly preserved, could not be incorporated in the action itself. They would function only as an aesthetic framework, and the scenic elements I designed would have to be autonomous in their effect. These elements were cubic structures mounted on ten wagons. Four of them were 5 metres wide, 1.5 metres deep, and 2 metres high, while the other six were half as wide and high. Their difference in height was offset by steps, with the result that the chorus, for example, could be arranged in echelon on a wide variety of horizontal surfaces. The structural elements, all of which were mutually compatible, neither duplicated the existing architecture nor were totally at odds with it. Rather, they formed an attractive contrast to it, and their mobility was an aid to spatial differentiation. The dominant surfaces in Acts I and III were black and shiny enough to reflect the singers, in Act II red and luminous. The excellent acoustics of the Teatro Greco enabled one to hear every last vocal nuance with crystal clarity, as for instance in the Lohengrin–Elsa duet in the bridal chamber scene, for which a simple, stylized, tent-like canopy perfectly summoned up the association between baldachin and bridal chamber seclusion.

The soloists on this occasion were Luana De Vol (Elsa), Siegfried Jerusalem (Lohengrin), Manfred Schenk (King Henry), Uta Priew (Ortrud), Oscar Hillebrandt (Telramund), Eike Wilm Schulte (Herald), and Clemens Bieber, Helmut Pampuch, Robert Riener, and Heinz Klaus Ecker (the four Nobles). I had pre-rehearsed them and a hundred of our choral singers at Bayreuth, just as Giuseppe Sinopoli had rehearsed his orchestra in London, so our work at Taormina was extremely concentrated and economical. We were all so taken with the productive atmosphere and the charm of our surroundings that we still look back on our visit with pleasure.

Rehearsals and performances took place at night, for the most part in complete darkness. Although Sicily's climatic rules were broken by heavy showers that frequently interrupted rehearsals and even threatened to rain off performances altogether, all ended well: we rehearsed as required and gave our performances as scheduled. Rehearsals began at five p.m. and ended at eleven. After that we set to work on the lighting installations, which could only, of course, be tested after dark. Since the performances, too, did not begin until eight-thirty and went on until late at night, dawn was usually breaking by the time we left the theatre.

The costumes for this open-air production, designed by Reinhard Heinrich, were highly effective in colouring and admirably suited to the setting. Despite the dimensions of the stage, our chorus master Norbert Balatsch and his assistants handled their singers with such outstanding success that, as producer, I was able to stage far more action on the steps and horizontal surfaces than I had originally thought possible, for instance when the double chorus appears in Act II ('The dawn fanfare bids us assemble'). I and my assistant, Johannes Taubenschuss, designed a magnificent swan five metres high and eighteen metres square in surface area. Initially concealed behind the fallen columns of the ancient skene, this was hydraulically jacked up into a vertical position in keeping with the music, and was splendidly illuminated. Its appearance and disappearance proved to be extremely impressive and produced the desired dramatic effect.

Another novel device, which many people found particularly successful, was my 'living curtain' composed of two groups of Sicilian *ragazzi*. Maestro Sinopoli felt responsible for their discipline, so rehearsals were often accompanied by lively exchanges in Sicilian. I and my assistants were quite as entertained by these willing and likeable youngsters as they clearly were by the *'tedéschi'* and their own part in the production. The members of each group were attired in stylized grey costumes and carried three-metre poles with flags attached to them. At the beginning of the performance they all stood side by side in a long row extending across the apron of the stage. When the prelude ended the row parted in the middle, like a curtain, and 'rolled back' to left and right in a single, synchronized movement. Depending on the arrangement of the structures on stage and the course of the action, for instance when the crowd assembles outside the minster in Act II, the boys also functioned as a visual cut-off point in the background. The 'curtain' closed as it had opened, but in reverse. My production assistant Stephan Jöris, who had acquitted himself nobly during our guest appearance in Japan in 1989, was a great help to me at Taormina too, and managed to drill the young Sicilians into standing still and performing their evolutions with almost Prussian precision.

All in all, our work at Taormina was a quite exceptional experience. That an opera as romantic as *Lohengrin* could be staged in such an exotic setting, framed by the proud remains of the wonderful old amphitheatre, made for an enduringly memorable production.

Tristan und Isolde was premièred at Milan's La Scala on 5 April 1978. I produced and designed it only because the engagement had been turned down by Patrice Chéreau, whom the conductor, Carlos Kleiber, had originally requested from his colleague Claudio Abbado. It was the opposite of what had happened at Bayreuth: there the stopgaps had been Jean-Pierre Ponnelle and Heiner Müller; at Milan it was my turn. I found it as pleasurable and stimulating to work with the '*Compagnia tedésca*' – a term that became current because of the special circumstances surrounding our rehearsals at the theatre – as I did to converse and rehearse with Carlos Kleiber, Catarina Ligendza (Isolde), Spas Wenkoff (Tristan), Ruza Baldani (Brangäne), Siegmund Nimsgern (Kurwenal), Kurt Moll (King Marke), Gianpaolo Corradi (Melot), Piero di Palma (Shepherd), Giovanni Foiani (Helmsman), and Walter Gullino (Young Sailor).

The word most commonly used and acted upon at La Scala was *sciòpero* [strike] – something both at odds and in harmony with the atmosphere in which we had to operate.

Carlos Kleiber rehearsed the orchestra with truly outstanding success, though his relations with them were appreciably soured by a momentary display of dissatisfaction. Losing his temper with the solo cellist, a celebrated '*professore*' from the Milan Academy of Music, he told him to change places with the tutti cellist at the furthest desk, who had, he said, been playing with admirable intensity. He also found fault on occasion with certain Slavisms in the German pronunciation of our Tristan, who cherished a tenacious belief that he was singing a special Wagnerian brand of German.

Kleiber once asked me during a rehearsal whether Tristan's behaviour in Act I entitles one to conclude that he genuinely loves Isolde. Without disclosing the outcome of our lengthy argument on the subject, I shall leave this extremely interesting and rewarding question to the judgement of the individual reader.

Our presence in Milan coincided with the murder of Aldo Moro, the Italian premier. One result of this was a demonstration that brought everything to a stop and cost us a further day's delay. On one occasion, immediately outside La Scala, my wife Gudrun was pestered by a gypsy woman with a baby in her arms and two children clinging to her skirt. While she was loudly and piteously bemoaning her poverty, one of her offspring appropriated Gudrun's handbag by severing the shoulder strap with a knife. I would never have believed that an allegedly starving mother and her brood could run so fast, but I made no attempt to stop them. I still vividly remembered a similar incident in 1952, when I caught a youngster trying to pick my pocket and was almost lynched by some child-loving Italian onlookers for grabbing hold of him in a rather unceremonious manner. Having reported the theft to the authorities, we were occasionally escorted to our hotel by a police jeep. They were troubled times in general.

Whatever day of the week it was, at least one indispensable group of technicians and stage-hands would be unavailable for work on the rehearsal or main stages. This meant that we ourselves had to transport furniture, props and even pieces of scenery to the places where they were needed. I was impressed and gratified to discover that the best and most helpful amateur stage-hands were Catarina Ligendza and my wife, who was then seven months pregnant.

Another especially salient recollection of those days, from the administrative aspect, was that our fees seemed to take an unconscionable time to come through, and that payment was forever being deferred. Reluctant to keep changing the German currency we had brought with us, we had to run up bills at restaurants. At this time, the most notable characteristic of La Scala's administrative offices was that their leading lights were always either absent or unavailable – unlike their bevy of pretty young secretaries, whose chief qualification seemed to be the charmingly voluble way in which they fended off importunate callers. If our *Tristan* was ready in time, this was due solely to Bianca Zedda, who more than made up for the almost invariable absence of La Scala's artistic director, Claudio Abbado. I saw him only once, and then for barely ten minutes, in the entire course of my sojourn at Milan between 13 March and 5 April 1978.

I found this Italian guest season the least agreeable of any in my experience of the country. Naples, Venice, Bologna, Rome and Palermo had all been far more interesting and congenial, but our '*Compagnia tedésca*' admirably compensated for what was lacking in an otherwise harmonious atmosphere.

Nine months later we were able to pay a glowing tribute to the Italian authorities on the success of their investigation into the theft of my wife's handbag. They had stopped the gypsies on the Italian-Yugoslav border and relieved the woman of Gudrun's passport and driver's licence.

After *Tristan*'s difficult birth in Milan, our daughter Katharina made a gratifyingly easy entrance into the world at Bayreuth on 21 May 1978. Her arrival enriched our life together in a very special way. Although my wife and I were, particularly at that time, being subjected to some very unpleasant and incomprehensible behaviour on the part of my numerous family, my mother showed a growing understanding of the reasons for my divorce. Of Gudrun, whom she had known on and off since 1965, she once told me, very appreciatively, that she admired her most of all for her total commitment to the festival, and for having acquired a comprehensive knowledge of the business lacking in all those who had never been prepared to work for Bayreuth throughout the year. By the time of Katharina's first birthday all our personal differences were buried and forgotten, and my mother enjoyed an exceptionally loving relationship with her twelfth grandchild until the day she died.

It may have been Katharina's antenatal connection with the Milan production of an opera by her great-grandfather that prompted her to ask all kinds of original questions about Wagner and his work at a very early age, displaying some very amusing behaviour patterns in the process. Gudrun and I carefully rationed her early visits to rehearsals at the Festspielhaus and emphasized that she could go only if she made no noise. On one occasion she was sitting on her nursemaid's lap during a *Holländer* rehearsal, quiet as a mouse, with the producer, Harry Kupfer, sitting several rows behind her. When Harry made use of the stage microphone, our four-year-old daughter turned to the perpetrator of all the noise, put a finger to her lips, and signified – with a penetrating 'Ssh!' – that she knew better than he did how to behave in the Festspielhaus.

Katharina played an enthusiastic but totally unaffected part in the television recording of my *Meistersinger* production. She was one of the children who roamed around during the cudgel scene, just as her producer father intended, and she also romped around the festival meadow, first dancing and then watching with interest as events unfolded between Eva, Walter, Sachs, Beckmesser, and all the other mastersingers.

Close attention and personal experience prompted a whole series of questions on her part, sometimes of a novel and surprising nature. She was not only impressed by the sight of people acting but became increasingly interested in what underlay such activities. She once asked a wholly logical, obvious question that would never have occurred to us grown-ups. Eleven at the time, she wanted to attend a performance of *Lohengrin*. Proudly clutching her ticket at lunch that day, she asked us reproachfully why 'Lohengrin' was printed on it in such big, bold letters when the name was a secret and would not be revealed until the end of the opera. She thought it quite absurd that the whole audience should be tipped off in advance. I am reminded here of another remark of hers, uttered during one of her wearisome piano practices and inspired by a certain envy of her brilliant forebears: 'Franz Liszt could play anything he liked, and so could Richard Wagner. I'm the only one that has to play the stupid stuff I'm given!'

For us parents, Katharina's presence in Japan in 1989 and Taormina in 1991 was an illuminating experience. Although we did not influence her in any way, she attended all the rehearsals with the exception of the late-night lighting rehearsals and followed everything with manifest interest and enthusiasm. At Bayreuth she has fewer opportunities to become as closely involved because of her school commitments during the rehearsal period.

Whenever Katharina comes into direct or indirect contact with Wagner in the festival and Festspielhaus environment, what pleases Gudrun and me most of all is that she mingles with us all in an unobtrusive way and makes no attempt to exploit her great-grandchild's status for purposes of self-aggrandizement.

Where keeping quiet at rehearsals is concerned, I had a very odd experience while working on *Die Meistersinger* at Dresden in 1985. We were rehearsing Act I on the stage of Semper's opera house, with the soloists but not yet with orchestra. I often visit the stage and then return to the production desk in the stalls to check on what has so far been achieved. Sometimes I call to the singers or use the microphone to transmit any immediate comments and criticisms. On this particular occasion my assistants were displeased to note that two men, clearly outsiders, had made themselves at home in the centre box of the dress circle and were talking in low voices. At that time, shortly before the opera house reopened, a lot of people were trying to sneak a glimpse of the interior. Very pleasant it was too, secretly lolling in a well-upholstered plush seat and watching other people at work – an innocuous and understandable form of theatre fan's voyeurism. Thanks to the Dresden Opera's senior producer, Joachim Herz, the authority wielded by any producer, even a West German outsider like me, was almost absolute. My two assistants thought I should banish the two uninvited guests from the auditorium. Reluctant to arrogate such domiciliary rights, I left it to them. There followed a largely inaudible exchange of words, after which the men left. My assistants then told me what had happened.

'You can't sit there,' they told the intruders, who were attired in a remarkably similar fashion. 'Oh yes, we can,' the intruders retorted, grinning sardonically. My assistants: 'This is a working rehearsal, no visitors allowed. Kindly leave the box.' The intruders, tersely: 'No.' My assistants: 'Who are you, anyway?' The intruders: 'None of your business.' Before leaving, as they eventually did, they avoided further argument by identifying themselves as professional, official voyeurs, i.e. members of the Stasi. Their final protest: 'We get kicked out even though we were keeping quiet. You should have a word with that short, stout, white-haired gentleman – the one who keeps interrupting. He's making far more noise.'

The opening of the restored Dresden Opera on 13 February 1985 was a source of varied experiences. The organizers of the ceremony had booked us into the newly completed Hotel Bellevue, a luxury establishment just across the Elbe from the opera house, where all the so-called VIPs were staying. We arrived very early, so there were no barriers or security checks in evidence. Once we had signed the register and handed over our passports in the usual way, we went for a stroll. On returning to change for the evening's festivities we were denied access to the hotel by Volkspolizisten and other security men because we had no means of identifying ourselves. The sun had already set and the temperature was dropping rapidly. It looked as if we would be unable to warm up anywhere, either in the hotel or in the opera house, because the tickets were in our room – a tragicomic situation for guests of honour. Then a *deus ex machina* appeared in the shape of a Russian officer with an excellent command of our language. Politely but firmly, he set his implacably conscientious East German colleagues straight: 'You can tell they aren't from here by their clothes. They're guests – let them through.' It was a triumph for the West German clothing industry.

A little while later, as we were walking across the bridge to the opera house, an impressive cortège swept past us – limousines laden with an East–West assortment of dignitaries including Erich Honecker, Berthold Beitz, Helmut Schmidt, sundry Russian guests of honour, Premier Albrecht of Lower Saxony, and their respective ladies.

During the second intermission my wife and I were 'privileged' to attend a reception hosted by Honecker. A guest of honour unknown to me but identifiable by his accent as a native of Saxony, expressed gleeful satisfaction that 'Erich', who was clearly no opera-fan, should have to grin and bear it for so long, and added that 'it served him right'. Art as a form of punishment – a not uninteresting concept, and one that seemed to sum up the feelings of many people present, because there were so many laborious scene changes that the performance dragged on for over four-and-a-half hours. My wife was sitting beside a Russian officer who kept asking her politely in French why the lights had gone up again and what would happen next. The following morning, when I called on Ritter, the technical director, to discuss the staging of my *Meistersinger* at Dresden, he pointed to a framed poster advertising the 1821 première of *Der Freischütz*. 'Well,' he said wrily, 'we certainly achieved one thing: the longest *Freischütz* in history.'

Weber's opera had been chosen for the reopening because it was the last work to be performed at the opera house before it was bombed to destruction on 13 February 1945.

My second encounter with the late Erich Honecker, complete with formal introduction and handshake, occurred at a reception on 11 September 1987, while the East German boss was paying his first official visit to the Federal Republic. Although the invitation coincided with our holidays, which we sorely needed after an arduous festival season and a whole year's uninterrupted work, I accepted it out of curiosity. The Bavarian state chancellery knew that I was the first West German opera producer to have staged a production in East Germany with my wife, so I managed to ensure that we both attended the reception. Apart from Gudrun and Honecker's personal physician, the number of women present could be counted on the fingers of one hand. My wife was the only female *guest* from West Germany, however, because the other women admitted to this predominantly male gathering were there in a party-political or government capacity.

Times had changed with a vengeance. I could not help recalling how hard it had been during the 1950s and 1960s to obtain permission for East German artists to take part in the Bayreuth Festival. Until 1988, or for twenty long years, all those tedious negotiations were in vain. The East German authorities had wanted to secure recognition of their sovereignty by persuading a West German ministry, in this case the Bavarian ministry of culture, to favour them with an official request. I had informed the East German minister of culture that, as director of the Bayreuth Festival, I could not request the Bavarian authorities to do this without forfeiting my artistic independence. It would have been pointless, in any case, because no one on the West German side was at that time prepared to do anything that would have prejudiced the Federal Republic's claim to all-German sovereignty. My failure in this respect prompted me to make up certain deficiencies in Bayreuth's personnel requirements by coming to an arrangement with East Germany's fraternal ally, the People's Republic of Czechoslovakia.

Now, in September 1987, I was tempted by the prospect of observing Franz Joseph Strauss's histrionic talents at first hand, not to mention his metamorphosis from a strict and uncompromising opponent of any concessions to East Germany into a lavish bestower of billion-mark loans. That this spectacle would be set in the lovingly-restored residence of Bavaria's erstwhile kings was an added attraction. The entrance of the guests, as they filed past and shook hands with that strangely-assorted couple, Strauss and Honecker, was so superbly staged that I had, to my chagrin, to concede that all the entrances of the guests in Act II of *Tannhäuser* I had ever seen or produced myself looked grossly amateurish by comparison.

I never dreamed, however, that this festive occasion was a step on the road to the dismantling of the Wall two years later and the reunification of Germany a year thereafter.

On 1 August 1960 the Bayreuth Festival received a visit from King Bhummibol and Queen Sirikit of Thailand, who attended the second performance of *Lohengrin* in the company of Federal President Heinrich Lübke and his wife Wilhelmine. This visit had been arranged during a trip to Bangkok by Hans-Christoph Seebohm, our minister of transport, but at a stage when every festival performance was sold out. Bonn's protocol section naturally expected us to make the centre box available notwithstanding. This was easier said than done. I had to find out whether the purchaser of the seats in the centre, who had legitimately acquired and paid for them, would be willing to exchange them for others. I began by decreeing that the boxes immediately flanking the centre box, which were mainly house seats, should be vacated on the day in question to make room for the theatre-goers whose regular place was in the centre. Polite letters elicited a gratifyingly prompt acceptance of this exchange from all concerned – with the notable exception of two ladies from Oberkotzau in Upper Franconia. Nothing would sway this industrialist's wife and her daughter, neither my personal entreaties nor the intervention of the president of the chamber of industry and commerce, Dr Konrad Pöhner.

Ten minutes before the royal and presidential couples arrived the box was casually inspected by the chief of protocol, Sigismund von Braun. Taken aback by the sight of the two women already ensconced there, he gave them – and me – a tongue-lashing and demanded to know what they were doing there. I, for my part, appealed to his democratic sensibilities, pointing out that they had every right to insist on keeping their seats. Then, as co-host, it was time for me to join my brother at the main entrance and prepare to greet our illustrious guests.

It had been requested that the Thai and German national anthems be played before the performance by *our* orchestra *inside* the Festspielhaus. Wieland and I countered this unwonted suggestion by pointing out that no national anthem had ever been played for any potentate, neither for Kaiser Wilhelm I in 1876 nor even for Adolf Hitler, who had expressly forbidden any form of anthem or ovation inside the theatre. We eventually secured acceptance of our proposal that the provincial police band should give of its best in the Festspielhaus forecourt.

Once we had welcomed the official visitors and the strains of both national anthems had died away, I hurried on ahead, hoping to solve the problem of the unwanted ladies in my own way. In my dinner jacket pocket I had two tickets for a side box. I had not wanted to hand them over in the presence of the head of protocol, feeling that he deserved to be kept on tenterhooks because of his boorish behaviour. He did not discover that the problem was solved until just before the king and the president entered the box. I had explained to the two obdurate ladies that I had seats for them in a neighbouring box, and that they happened, by a fortunate coincidence, to be the ones usually occupied by the Begum and her entourage. They not only exchanged seats in a trice but seemed greatly honoured to do so. In fact, the Begum's usual seat when attending a festival performance was in the front row of the stalls.

Prince Charles's attendance at the third performance of *Tannhäuser* on 6 August 1987 and Queen Margrethe of Denmark's visit in August 1991 were far less formal occasions, and devoid of undue ceremonial.

Whether high commissioners, commanders-in-chief, federal presidents, presidents of the Bundestag, federal ministers, prime ministers, papal dignitaries, ambassadors, parliamentarians, or representatives of a wide variety of religions – all such visitors to Bayreuth were motivated by an interest in art, and their presence never led to any untoward incidents.

Another unique situation arose in 1990, when the festival was attended by the then Czech president, Vaclav Havel, accompanied by Federal President Richard von Weizsäcker and Hans Dietrich Genscher, a long-standing devotee and patron of Bayreuth. The Czech security men, who took their duties very seriously, were unduly protective of their newly-elected head of state, with the result that they took over some of the thirty-six box seats. Other distinguished guests of honour, whom the municipality of Bayreuth had been inviting to the festival since 1951, found their seats already occupied and were prevented from entering the boxes by Havel's security personnel. Their mild resentment evaporated when the misunderstanding was diplomatically dispelled and the Czech bodyguards consented to withdraw, though we naturally had to be careful, Czechs being Czechs, not to revive any memories of 'incorrigible German arrogance'.

The official reception after the first-night performance, held in Bayreuth's Neues Schloss and its neighbouring courtyard, was an unusually free-and-easy function because the guests were so unsure of protocol that none of them knew whom to shake hands with first. Most people assumed that they ought first to pay their respects to the Federal President and President Havel. Their host, Premier Max Streibl of Bavaria, rose to the occasion magnificently. His amiable smile doubtless indicated that, being a native of Oberammergau, he had been inured to such things by the Passion Play.

Only one person has ever busied himself with eggs at the Bayreuth Festival, and that is Mime in Act I of *Siegfried*, where he does so with evil intent. On 25 July 1993, the day the festival opened that *Ring*-less year, a young man from Hildesheim evidently felt an urge to make his presence felt like Mime. It all began when he hoisted a banner inscribed 'Down with the Bosses!' above the heads of the crowd watching the guests of honour arrive. Next, the Green Hill was strewn with neo-Nazi leaflets denouncing 'cultural bolshevism' and 'the decadent political regime' and calling for a 'nationalistic Germany'. The police stepped in and put a stop to these activities, but that was not the end of them. Mikhail Gorbachev had just received an enthusiastic welcome, and a brief photo session was in progress outside the 'king's portal'. With Gorbachev were Premier Edmund Stoiber of Bavaria and his wife, the mayor of Bayreuth, Dr Dieter Mronz, and his wife, and Gudrun and I. All of a sudden three eggs flew through the air. Although a detective tried to fend them off, all of us were splashed with their contents to some extent. The première of *Tristan* was delayed for a few minutes to enable us to remove the worst of the mess from our hair and clothes. The police promptly arrested the egg-thrower, but he had done what he had set out to do, which was to make himself disagreeably conspicuous and abuse an artistic occasion for political purposes. At the same time, is someone who throws eggs truly qualified to become the 'martyr' of some obscure movement?

All three Western high commissioners attended the reopening of the Bayreuth Festival in 1951. This was because, as I have already shown elsewhere, they resembled most other foreigners in harbouring no prejudice against Richard Wagner's Bayreuth. The French high commissioner, André François-Poncet, whom I knew from his visits to Bayreuth before the war, had the very special affinity to Wagner shared by so many of his compatriots. Our then Federal President, Theodor Heuss, had no such affinity. Whenever Bayreuth was mentioned he made a point of declaring that the only Bayreuth he admired was Jean Paul's, and that he could not bring himself to attend the festival. After 1951, however, when he came to recognize the festival's domestic as well as worldwide cultural importance, he always sent messages via an intermediary and wished my brother and me well in our future endeavours. All his successors in office visited Bayreuth, and all, on their own submission, found it an unaccustomed pleasure to share an exceptional artistic experience on equal terms with everyone else, instead of being compelled to preside over an official function.

I am not in any danger of becoming remote or isolated in my capacity as festival director. This is attested by the number of visits I receive annually from colleagues who run other opera houses, festivals, and branches of our transitory art. Whenever time permits, I and my staff engage in interesting discussions and exchanges of ideas with all these visitors from the outside world. Contacts of this type have meant that I am a welcome guest in other continents. Whether in North or South America, South Africa or New Zealand, Japan, Iceland, or Luxemburg, worldwide interest in Wagner's *œuvre* is evinced not only by performances but also by symposia, lectures and discussions in which I take part whenever they coincide with one of my visits. I do so with an open mind, eager to learn whatever I can, because I have always found that Wagner's work possesses supranational status and enjoys the highest esteem abroad – indeed, many would prefer it to be esteemed a trifle more highly in Germany itself. It is half shaming, half gratifying, to reflect that many of the conversations I have had abroad with members of the public and press, and especially with young people and students, were informed by a wider knowledge of the subject and their questions by a deeper understanding of it than I have encountered – and still do, to my regret – in Germany.

Thanks to the hospitality accorded us while travelling abroad, to our impressions of a wide variety of people, and to our familiarity with foreign countries and the mentalities of their inhabitants, my wife and I have seen a whole succession of new and different horizons open up before us.

We have often witnessed productions of Wagnerian works staged with resources and artistic intentions quite different from those to which we are accustomed at Bayreuth. They were a clear insight into what Wagner meant by 'open dramaturgy'. It is the diametrical opposite of what hidebound Wagnerians aspire to when they claim him exclusively for themselves and their existential problems – when they abuse and invalidate his work by stylizing him as a 'redeemer'. That he neither was nor wished to be. On the contrary, he was able to transcend national boundaries through the universally intelligible medium of music. He was not an idol or a guru competent to rule on every sphere of life. It was no accident that we reopened the festival in 1951 under the auspices of the celebrated motto from *Art and Revolution*: 'Just as Greek art embodied the ethos of a fine nation, so must the art of the future transcend all national barriers and embody the spirit of free humanity; its national features must be no more than an ornament, the charm of individual diversity, not an inhibiting restriction.'

We did so in the legitimate hope that Bayreuth would never again give house-room to the narrow-minded and misguided views of those who debased Wagner into a 'religious founder'. We wanted to combat every shade of 'Wagnerism' and sentence it to imminent extinction. I believe that we have succeeded in ridding Bayreuth of the taint of sectarianism. It is reassuring to note that Richard Wagner Societies throughout the world have ceased to indulge in the navel-gazing of an esoteric priestly order, and that they are conscious of the vitality of Wagner's bequest to them. What Wagner not only wanted but accomplished was 'a radical upheaval in our artistic life', coupled with the utopian hope that its effects would extend to politics as well.

The exhibition entitled *'Der Hang zum Gesamtkunstwerk'* [The Gesamtkunstwerk Tendency], an admirable feat of organization on the part of Harald Szeemann, opened in Zurich on 11 February 1983. My grandfather having coined that term, I was invited. It is only when one bears no responsibility for an occasion that one can enjoy and absorb it to the full – sometimes, even, with purely disinterested benevolence. After the inaugural speeches, one of which was delivered by the then Federal President, Walter Scheel, I met Helmut Schmidt, whom Helmut Kohl had succeeded as chancellor four months earlier. Harald Szeemann kindly showed us one or two particularly interesting exhibits, for instance a gas organ constructed by Henri Dunant as a special form of therapy for his mentally ill patients. Helmut Schmidt eyed it dubiously. Always noted for his down-to-earth, realistic cast of mind, the former chancellor suddenly felt called upon to declare that the gas organ was typical of the entire exhibition in that any show devoted to the 'Gesamtkunstwerk' was a load of misguided, utopian nonsense. Harald Szeemann retorted in his dry, Swiss way that the gas organ had, all the same, been built by the founder of the Red Cross, and that no politician could do his job without being guided by a few utopian ideas.

I had another unexpected encounter with Helmut Schmidt and his wife Loki later the same year, this time in Singapore, where my wife and I had been invited to stay by the German ambassador, Dr Wolfram Dufner. Helmut Schmidt had come to Singapore to deliver a political lecture, and it so happened that we shared the same table at dinner one night. It was extremely interesting to eavesdrop on the high-powered political argument that developed between Schmidt and Singapore's foreign minister. They were discussing the international situation, which had been subjected to renewed tension because of the Russians' recent destruction of a South Korean airliner. The foreign minister kept insisting that the Russians only responded to a hard line, and that he considered West Germany's current tendency towards more relaxed relations with the Eastern Bloc a great mistake. Since my table companion, Frau Loki Schmidt, had no wish to take an active part in the politicians' conversation, I talked to her about Singapore's superb botanical gardens, which she had also visited as a matter of course. Having carefully memorized the Latin names of one or two particularly interesting exotic plants, I earned Frau Schmidt's admiration by trotting them out.

My wife and I flew on from Singapore to Japan, where I was to open the Goethe-Institut in Kyoto and deliver a lecture on Bayreuth at the end of October. A few hours before the opening my place was taken by Chancellor Kohl, then in office for just over a year, who had come to Japan at short notice. The director of the Goethe-Institut and his assistants were much embarrassed by this swift and unexpected change of plan because it completely upset their arrangements in regard to protocol. My wife and I arrived in Kyoto on the Shinkansen and were met at the station by a Japanese industrialist who had just contributed a large sum towards the installation of a German–Japanese cultural centre in the former, bomb-damaged Japanese embassy in the Tiergarten in Berlin. So as to spare the Goethe-Institut's nervous master of ceremonies any further headaches about where to put his guests of honour, Gudrun and I seated ourselves in the back row. The Federal Chancellor arrived with a Bundestag deputy from our own constituency, Ortwin Lowack, who drew his attention to our presence and introduced us.

What I found instructive about the whole affair was the contrast between the Germans' remarkably maladroit behaviour and that of the Japanese, which was governed by tradition and ceremonial conventions.

If, on the eve of a birthday ending in a nought, in this case on 29 August 1989, one boards an aircraft that takes the polar route from Europe to Japan and crosses the international date line in the process, it is quite difficult to determine when one's birthday should really be celebrated.

In 1989, at all events, Norbert Balatsch and the festival chorus thought the time had come when we made an intermediate stop at Anchorage. They mustered in the main concourse of the airport, which is dominated by a massive polar bear some four metres tall, and sang me a birthday serenade. The entire Bayreuth Festival ensemble was on its way to Japan to play *Tannhäuser* and give a number of concerts. Needless to say, a huge crowd gathered round and demanded to know what was going on. The members of the chorus and those who were accompanying us as guests had devised a particularly delightful idea in my honour: each of them presented me with a very charming artificial flower which, when put together with the others, formed an enormous bouquet.

We were warmly welcomed by our Japanese hosts on landing at Tokyo's Narita Airport after our twenty-hour flight. The soloists, orchestral players and other participants in the guest appearances were already waiting at the hotel. Having arrived by other flights a considerable time before us, they, too, gathered to pay me a festive musical tribute on my seventieth birthday.

I was given yet another birthday treat during our stay in Tokyo. This took the form of an excellent dinner in a big Japanese hotel, together with an additional musical attraction: Keio University's student choir sang some Wagner choruses in German.

And here I must express my gratitude to the helpful mediator who accompanied us on all our trips to Japan. Natsue von Stegmann, a Japanese married to a German, sang in the festival choir for many years and has continued, even after leaving it, to serve us in the capacity of a translator.

On the occasion of my birthday Federal President Richard von Weizsäcker and his wife invited us to the Villa Hammerschmidt with another thirty-two guests of my own choosing. I tried to do justice to East as well as West, and none of us guessed at that stage, on 5 October 1989, that the 'turning-point' was only five weeks away. It was an all-German gathering of artists notable for its informal and relaxed atmosphere. Also invited were Rudolf Augstein, publisher of *Der Spiegel*, Joachim Fest, author of the definitive biography of Hitler, and the theatre critic Joachim Kaiser, all of whom were amazed at how freely conversation flowed in the presence and official residence of the Federal President. One particularly original feature of this party was that Herr von Weizsäcker showed us a film staged and directed by Werner Herzog, who had made it as a birthday greeting for me during the rehearsal period and festival season at Bayreuth.

Finally, on 10 October 1989, the municipality of Bayreuth gave a party in my honour at the Neues Rathaus. I remember the occasion with particular pleasure because it was yet another demonstration of the close ties that exist between the town and the Bayreuth Festival. The large number of invited guests included prominent local citizens and members of the festival staff. The mayor, Dr Dieter Mronz, and the chairman of the foundation board, Assistant Secretary Franz Kerschensteiner, paid eloquent tribute to the good relations existing between town and festival, which do, after all, go back for more than a century. Responding, I emphasized how much it meant to me, from an immediate, every-day point of view, to be a citizen of Bayreuth as well as the director of a festival with a worldwide reputation.

The only Wagner to have remained true to his birthplace, I feel that I fully belong to it, less as a local patriot than in my overriding perception of the word 'home'. On the one hand, I am closely wedded to the countryside and its people by childhood memories of long standing; on the other, I had and still have the good fortune to be able to work with, and for, the inhabitants of my home town.

Old age is no defence against orders and decorations, as I always say, and my seven-and-a-half decades have garnered me a wide variety of public honours. Although it goes against the grain to vaunt such trophies here, I feel that I should mention them because they were awarded for valid reasons and did not simply drop on me like manna from heaven. Equally, I must enumerate them all because any omissions would unfairly discriminate against the awards I fail to mention. In 1961 I received the Bavarian Order of Merit and Bayreuth's Gold Ring of Honour, in 1974 the Distinguished Service Cross of the Order of Merit of the Federal Republic, and in 1977 the Bareither Mohrnwäscher. In 1984 the French government appointed me 'Commandeur de l'Ordre des Arts et des Lettres' and I received Bavaria's Order of Maximilian for Science and Art and the Wilhelm Pitz Prize. In 1986 the Bavarian Academy of Fine Arts elected me a full member and I received the 'Personnalité de l'année' diploma from Paris. I have since February 1988 been adviser to the Bayreuth University's musical theatre research institute and was in the same year invested with the Bavarian Constitutional Medal in gold. In 1993 the Bavarian Academy of Fine Arts awarded me the Friedrich Baur Prize. Of all the tributes to my work with the Bayreuth Festival, the following have given me especial pleasure: in 1986 I was appointed an honorary member of the Graz Academy of Music and the Performing Arts, in 1987 an honorary senator of the Munich Conservatoire, and in 1988 – in company with the author Peter Härtling and the sculptor Otto Hajek – an honorary senator of Tübingen University.

A young French Wagner fan and student of architecture, who had evolved some very imaginative plans for the area south of Bayreuth's Röhrensee before his final examination, arranged that my wife and I should be invited to Paris for the formal presentation of his diploma. More than that, the faculty appointed me an honorary member of the jury in advance of our arrival. The diploma submission consisted of meticulously detailed drawings and an impressive model for a huge, almost futuristic cultural centre set amid the Berlin lakes. The award ceremony was a gala occasion, and I was agreeably impressed by the friendly relations that prevailed between teachers and students. The atmosphere at the ensuing champagne reception and dinner was splendidly convivial and relaxed, but the real highlight came later that night. Loudly applauded by all the guests, our young friend Olivier Collaudin Verpeaux mounted a fruit box in the middle of a footbridge over the Seine, stark naked but temporarily swathed in a voluminous cloak. When midnight struck, his female fellow students removed the cloak as if unveiling a nude statue. The courageous victim of this student tradition underwent his ordeal on the night of 3/4 March 1990, which was exceptionally cold.

To have a single relationship with the press can be hard enough; to have a threefold one, as I do, is three times as difficult. It is not enough to emulate Mime and be 'doubly sly'.

For one thing, I have a permanent duty to supply information about my sphere of activities as director of the Bayreuth Festival. For another, I have to comment on my work as a producer. Thirdly, I am a member of a 'clan', which means that I am forever being lumped together with its other members and held responsible for all they get up to. My privacy is thus invaded as a matter of course, and journalists have a fondness for treating me like a figure made of glass or wax, to be irradiated or moulded in order to assuage the public's boundless thirst for sensations, or what are considered such.

The following remarks do not, of course, apply to all journalists or other representatives of the media. I have been fortunate enough to encounter many members of their profession whose expert knowledge and genuine perception proved stimulating and enlightening.

In the first place, no one needs to break down any doors at Bayreuth. In my view, there have been no closely guarded taboo zones here since 1951. It puzzles me, therefore, that one particular brand of journalists makes such a habit of reporting on things about which there is nothing to report. I and my colleagues often welcome oral or written inquiries from journalists, only to find that, instead of using our answers, they regale their delighted readers or viewers with fictions of their own for which the preceding interviews and inquiries were merely an aid to the simulation of genuine research. Two recent examples of this phenomenon were an article by Dr Martin Doerry in *Der Spiegel* (No. 30 of 20 July 1992) and the no less arbitrary and malicious farrago presented in the television programme 'Titel-Thesen-Temperamente' [Title, Theses, Temperaments] (10 November 1991) by Tilman Jens, who may possibly have been subjected, and have succumbed, to editorial pressure. A 'free' paraphrase studded with pre-fabricated clichés and characterized by irremediable ignorance, it tendentiously cut or edited my remarks. The 'title' of Jen's contribution, 'War of Succession at Bayreuth', was thoroughly misleading, the 'theses' were presented in an incomplete and biased form, and only the 'temperaments' may have been near the mark. The lamentably threadbare nature of this programme was concealed beneath a wealth of ingenious figments. I would ignore such concoctions if they were not so disastrously far-reaching in their effects.

I am often reminded in this connection of something which Henry Ford said to my parents while they were visiting the United States in 1924, and which I was later told by my mother. At that time the wireless had just firmly installed itself alongside the press as a new, globe-encircling medium. Ford declared that, if he had his way, he would prohibit all news reports if a crisis arose in the world. This would banish war for ever, because no one would know what the crisis was about. The advent of wireless, he said, spelled global disaster, because everyone could now contradict what was said by others to suit his own situation and objectives, thereby presenting himself to an increasingly bewildered public as the sole repository of the truth.

Where Bayreuth and the festival are concerned, there is one age-old trick whose exponents naturally try on again and again. They report some fiction or rumour in the hope of eliciting a denial that will tell them what they really want to know, especially if it is something we would prefer to disclose at a more appropriate time of our own choosing. What is it that motivates this behaviour, an ambition to show oneself better informed than anyone else, or an urge to feather one's nest by disseminating any old rubbish, some of it not entirely implausible? Our society is in the grip of a strange and dismaying tendency: a sometimes violent craving for information, not a hunger for knowledge, a preference for superficial breadth rather than thoroughgoing depth.

I never, in fact, deny anything ostensibly or actually said by me. I am naturally aware that anything published, even the most arrant nonsense, becomes elevated after two weeks to the status of journalistic truth (the difference between truth and journalistic truth being as symptomatic as it is revealing). Konrad Adenauer never allowed himself to be ruffled by anything in this line and calmly declined to issue repudiations. It is very doubtful in any case whether a repudiation will be published. If it is, it generally appears in such an obscure position that the effort of making it bears no relation to its beneficial effect. As for the widespread and brazen practice whereby statements that were never made, or were couched in other words, are invested with specious authenticity by the addition of inverted commas, I shall refrain from commenting on it.

In the second place, I am delighted when critics are provoked by my work. It gives those who consider it beneath their dignity to sound off on the subject, but do so just the same, a chance to earn a living, whereas I, for my part, can honestly say that I never do anything that goes against the grain. Perhaps every critic should take the advice Goethe gives in his autobiography: 'It is not enough to expose defects; indeed, it is wrong to do so unless one can, at the same time, indicate a way of remedying them.'

In the third place, if certain newspapers and magazines survive by retailing bedroom stories, by publishing sensational disclosures, both textual and pictorial, by garnishing them with hypocritical condemnations of perverted proclivities, real or supposed, and by claiming to offer ultimate, 'true' insights into the peaks and troughs of the human condition, it is only natural that they should sometimes plug the gaps in their pages with stories about Richard Wagner and his ramified descendants. They still find it media-effective, even today, to regurgitate accounts of his outrageously (un)bourgeois lifestyle and 'robber knight mentality'. Never has the private life of any other 19th-century artist been the subject of so much nonsensical controversy, which bears witness to the utter philistinism of those who engage in it. It is still asserted that Wagner was the financial bane of King Ludwig II and, ultimately, of Bavaria. This is an even more absurd allegation than most. The furnishings of the royal bedchamber at Schloss Herrenchiemsee cost more than Wagner received from the king in subsidies and gifts over a period of twenty years. It is seldom pointed out that Wagner himself renounced his copyright in many cases and presented the king with several original scores. All this bandying of figures seems downright idiotic after more than a hundred years, especially when it is claimed that some descendant of Wagner's is continuing to benefit from his 'depredations'.

Speaking for myself – and, fortunately, for many others – I do not consider it essential that anyone should gossip or brag about my family in public. Personally, I never do anything to encourage that sort of thing. Anyone exposed to public observation and attention, as I am, naturally has to be prepared for anything, expect little, and fear the worst without flying into a panic. It would be uncharitable to correct everything that is written about me, my family, and my grandfather, if only because those whose livelihood depends on the products I have briefly described might find themselves out of a job.

Under the same general heading come various films about Richard Wagner. In so far as they should not be regarded as altogether fictitious, these are either wholly ludicrous or contain a demagogic mixture of *Dichtung und Wahrheit* [Wagner's monograph on 'Fiction and Fact'].

That is why I have no need to dwell on Hans Jürgen Syberberg or his attitude to Richard Wagner and his family as exemplified by his interview with my mother, then seventy-eight. I should naturally like to comply with Pamina's appeal from Act I of *The Magic Flute*, when Papageno asks 'What shall we speak of now?' and she answers: 'The truth, the truth, were it even a crime!' – but I must, for sound reasons, abide by Clause 3 of my English publisher's contract for this book: 'The Author hereby warrants to the Publishers that the work ... contains nothing obscene, objectionable, indecent, libellous, or otherwise actionable ... and that he will indemnify the Publishers against any loss, injury or damage ... occasioned to the Publishers in consequence of any breach of this warranty.'

Summing up my thoughts on the press and thinking back on my many experiences in that regard, I am reminded of the injunction in Goethe's *Faust*: whenever you cannot fully comprehend something, substitute a fiction of your own.

Until the Berlin Wall went up in August 1961, we at Bayreuth always took it for granted that the Soviet Zone, later the German Democratic Republic, would impose no restrictions on the recruitment of artists and technicians for the festival. It was, however, a not uninteresting fact that for tax purposes, in contravention of official policy, East Germans had had to be treated as foreigners from 1953 onwards. It was apparent from conversations with our East German confrères that GDR citizens were being compelled to relinquish more and more D-Marks to the State Artists' Agency, which countersigned their contracts. At best, they could exchange part of this tithe for Ost-Marks at a rate of 1 : 1.

Fleeced though they already were during the 1950s, GDR festival employees had to fork out a tidy sum to enable their national prize-winner, Dr Max Burghardt, to hold a reception at Bayreuth on behalf of his government. The concessionaire of the festival restaurant, then housed in the chorus hut south-west of the Festspielhaus, was requested to cater for the forthcoming function as lavishly but inexpensively as possible. There was a tremendous fuss when this plan came to the ears of the Verfassungsschutz [Office for the Protection of the Constitution, fulfilling some functions of the Special Branch and MI5], and pressure was put on me to cancel the whole affair. I managed to calm things down by getting the reception transferred to a restaurant near Bayreuth but far enough from the Green Hill. I also pointed out that to cancel it would definitely impair our chances of recruiting singers and instrumentalists from the GDR and run counter to what I had been told by my permanent contacts in Bonn, because our politicians had no wish to disrupt or sever the human relations that still existed between the Federal Republic and the GDR. The same school of thought continued to prevail inside the ministry of all-German affairs after 1966, which was the year before the GDR imposed a total ban on Bayreuth, except for soloists of international repute. There had been no East German musicians in the festival orchestra even between 1962 and 1964.

From January 1963 onwards I negotiated for artists with the new director of the Berlin Staatsoper, Hans Pischner, who acted as his country's representative in that respect. He proved an open-minded and understanding partner in all our dealings, and it was a matter of equal regret to us both when the Iron Curtain descended on Bayreuth, too, after the 1966 festival and remained in place for over twenty years.

Despite this unfavourable development I persevered in my endeavours to resume closer ties throughout the twenty-year ice age. Among other things, I came into contact with Alexander Abusch, the GDR's Franconian-born deputy premier, and with Klaus Gysi, the minister of culture, father of the former chairman of the PDS (Democratic Socialist Party) and present Bundestag deputy. My Dresden productions in 1985 and 1988 were partly motivated by hopes of questioning influential East Germans on the possibility of re-engaging GDR citizens for the Bayreuth Festival, and on the conditions that would obtain. In all my negotiations and discussions I took the line that, if the GDR laid claim to international recognition in the cultural domain, it ought to observe its own, egalitarian, socialist principles, which should preclude it from restricting exit visas to a few prominent artists and foreign exchanger earner.

From the mid-1960s certain problems arose over the engagement of choral singers and technicians. I discussed the matter with Dr Pavel Eckstein, whose knowledge of theatrical conditions in the Eastern Bloc, and, of course, in the Czechoslovak Republic, was second to none. He showed me ways and means of engaging the personnel I needed through the good offices of 'Prago-Concert', the only Czech agency dealing in artists, teachers, technicians, and other professional people. I succeeded in fulfilling this plan, as I also did in Budapest.

The engagement of Milan Malý, chorus master of the Prague National Theatre and the Czech broadcasting network, whom Wilhelm Pitz appointed his deputy, was of exceptional artistic benefit to the festival. In addition, it was very helpful to my relations with 'Prago-Concert' because I had complied with Czech wishes and intentions by engaging someone who would worthily represent his country at international level. This largely dispelled any further difficulties I might have had in engaging other personnel. By virtue of their professional qualifications and great personal commitment, as many as fourteen Czech technicians have made themselves almost indispensable to the running of the festival, and the same applies in equal measure to twenty or so members of our chorus.

After their annual contracts had been renewed without trouble for some ten years, a sudden crisis loomed. Dr Eckstein intimated that it might be advisable under the circumstances for me to visit Prague and pay a personal call on the Czech minister of culture, to whom 'Prago-Concert' was ultimately responsible. This would enable me to restore the situation and tie the knot again.

My wife and I were greeted, on ascending the stairs to the conference room in the imposing Waldstein Palace, by some young and strikingly pretty female interpreters. The room itself had retained its splendour, and the magnificent baroque chairs had been sumptuously re-upholstered in the original style. The minister, who did not keep us waiting long, appeared with some subordinates in tow. Our business discussion lasted about twenty minutes – a very short time, considering that every word had to be interpreted. We drew each other's attention to the difficulties that had arisen and came to a mutually satisfactory arrangement. All that then remained was to set a worthy seal on the favourable outcome of our negotiations, so we were offered some high-proof *eau-de-vie* in addition to the coffee that had already been served. My wife and I only half-emptied our glasses in an attempt to limit the number of times they were refilled and refrain from overstaying our welcome. The young interpreters were soon redundant, because after the second glass the minister and his entourage broke into fluent German.

I had previously visited Hradschin Castle under quite different circumstances. I vividly recall the episode because it was no less memorable than my meeting with the minister.

In mid-March 1939, when I had been in the army for just over three months, I was 'privileged' to take part in the occupation of 'Rump Czechoslovakia', as current jargon termed it. This was a very largely peaceful operation, and one that Adolf Hitler managed to complete without bloodshed or bombardments. Because no skirmishes had occurred, my unit was rerouted outside Prague and stationed at Příbram. On one occasion we were driven into the Czech capital and allowed to go sightseeing. Instead of heading for the beerhouses and other places of entertainment, I, being a loner, preferred to explore the city's streets, bridges, buildings, and – needless to say – Hradschin Castle. While there I was overcome by a very human urge to patronize 'the place that even the Kaiser visits on foot', as they used to say. On leaving I tipped the old woman attendant a couple of German coins. She eyed me closely as I stood there in my army haircut and forage cap. Then, to my astonishment, she said: 'You've got to be a Wagner!'

In 1939, when Germaine Lubin sang Kundry at Bayreuth, she brought her big limousine and her chauffeur, a tall, jet-black Senegalese who always took part in Bayreuth's summer amusements when off duty. One day a deputation of zealous, upright Bayreuth citizens called on my mother and asked her to put a stop to an unpleasant and unpardonable state of affairs. The 'Bürgerreuth', a restaurant overlooking the festival hill, held post-performance dinner dances, and it seemed that the German women and girls who attended them were eagerly competing for an opportunity to dance with the black man, whereas the splendidly Nordic-looking members of the 'Leibstandarte Adolf Hitler' (Hitler's SS bodyguard) were being ignored. My mother disclaimed all competence in the matter. The black man must be an excellent dancer, she said, and besides, he deserved the hospitality due to any visitor to our town. Furthermore, it was clear that National Socialist ideology had still to inculcate any profound awareness of Nordic-Germanic racial superiority.

Anything is possible in our world. This was brought home to me, some two-thirds of a century after my grandfather made it, by the following prophecy in his 'Zur Einführung in das Jahr 1880' (Introduction to 1880): 'If millions were now to be bestowed on us by a new American Croesus, or a Mesopotamian Crassus, they would undoubtedly be taken into the keeping of the Reich, and a ballet would soon be danced on my grave.' He was right: soon after the war ended, Wahnfried was converted into a US officers' club.

To make them go with a Bacchic swing, the dances at the officers' club were usually accompanied by an inordinate consumption of alcohol. And here I cite a tribute to the quality of Wahnfried's wine cellar, which had survived the bombing intact, from Captain Miller, Bayreuth's US commandant. 'Mrs Wagner,' my mother was appreciatively informed by that assiduous sampler of the bottles arrayed there, 'your cellar was better than the Gauleiter's.'

Before the currency reform my brother and I paid a visit to Richard Strauss at his Garmisch home, where we encountered his son Franz and Benvenuto Hauptmann, son of Gerhart, the dramatist, novelist and poet. A press photographer, who happened to be present, took a group picture of us in our capacity as the offspring of artistic and cultural luminaries. All he needed now, he said, when the session ended, was a really apt caption. I promptly suggested a quotation from Act I of Tristan: 'Degenerate race, unworthy of your forebears.' Franz Strauss and Benvenuto Hauptmann did not, unfortunately, appreciate my sense of humour.

16

VIEWING THE FUTURE

Now that I have come to the end of my remarks, I am fully aware how incomplete and imperfect they are. However, I was as little concerned from the outset to achieve perfection in an 'apotheotic' sense as I was to exalt or parade my own importance. This book is not a definitive summary of my life, still less of the Bayreuth Festival, but a caesura, an interim report on what has happened and continues to do so. I am not writing with the detachment of a man nostalgically recalling erstwhile greatness and past achievements. My relations with the present are not merely contemplative. I write as one who is still an active and creative participant. As I see it, therefore, this whole book is a distillation from my active and ongoing experience of life, an open-ended inquiry and statement of accounts. I hope I have succeeded in dispersing, or even dispelling, many of the fog-banks in which Bayreuth continues to be enshrouded from time to time.

My grandmother Cosima wrote, when I was still a baby: 'I am much moved when I look at that little creature whose development I shall not live to see, but who – I feel sure! – will sense my blessing on him in times of trial.' I could not count on that, as the reader will have noticed. Looking back, I am glad that I have never been cast down or consumed by worries and anxieties, even though I have had (and still have) ample reason to be so. I do worry, of course. To deny it would be foolish and inhuman, but I can honestly say that I have never been afraid in my life – afraid, that is, in the sense of natural timidity, submission and surrender, dejection and despair. In that respect I have modelled myself on the grandfather who died thirty-six years before I was born, though not in a presumptuous attempt to imitate him. Had I made material prosperity my foremost aim in life and succumbed to the siren song of Mammon, I could very probably, as an artist and Richard Wagner's grandson, have feathered my nest on a worldwide scale. Instead, I continue to regard the purpose of my activities as the preservation and maintenance of that unique phenomenon, the

Bayreuth Festival. If I direct all my energies to that end, it is not from selfish, 'power-hungry' ambition, but from a sense of responsibility shaped in no small measure by my experience of German history. The disastrous consequences of the Second World War made it seem that the festival was more likely to die than revive. My brother and I succeeded in creating New Bayreuth despite all the obstacles and difficulties I have described, but not from a desire to carry on any old how. We realized that we must not simply jettison the whole Wagnerian legacy like so much unwanted ballast. We had to assimilate it in the broadest and most profound sense. We had to study, examine, and regain it by a process of constructive analysis. We did not fail.

That process, originally initiated and sustained by Wieland and me and perpetuated by me alone since his death, is not complete. Its results, as I have tried to show, are not an assured possession or a comfortable resting-place; it is still in progress. I can justly claim to have succeeded in stabilizing Bayreuth – artistically, legally, financially, and materially – and in creating a basis on which to plan for the future. It was fortunate for us that Hitler's megalomaniac Green Hill project never materialized, because it would have been a travesty of Wagner's original idea. I have not only remained faithful to my grandfather's ideas in respect of the festival and the Festspielhaus. In 1993 I at last managed to unite the hitherto separate archives of the Richard Wagner Memorial and Wahnfried and house them in a research centre designed and built on a human scale. It delights me that my efforts, in which I was assisted by a wide variety of people, should have borne fruit.

As festival director I have always seen myself as a mediator and moderator in the true sense, that is to say, someone who brings, but does not force, people together in 'workshop Bayreuth' so as to create a mutually fruitful field of artistic tension in which Wagner's works can be moulded in advance. Bayreuth is not a hermetically sealed laboratory devoted to some mysterious science that gives birth to *homunculi wagnerienses*. It is not a place where priestly mouthpieces proclaim a doctrine of salvation on behalf of some higher authority, nor is the festival an occult happening. The sole aim of all our joint endeavours is to present living theatre and stimulate independent thought in our audiences. In addition to the other skills and abilities essential to my job, I have a special need for two attributes that happily form part of my physical and mental constitution: strong nerves and a sense of humour. Perhaps this book will have conveyed more than a hint of that.

That I could write it at all I owe as much to foes as friends, as anyone who has read thus far can confirm. I have leafed through mountains of files in the course of my work, reading, remembering, and visualizing –

files that harbour within them what I would describe as mummified life. I had no intention of 'robbing the dead' and was solely concerned with live issues, so I left many things to slumber on in the dusty archives, destined for oblivion, decay, or – at worst – the shredder. Why should I look back in anger, however justified? Most of what has happened, including things that affect the Wagner family's relations with me, is water under the bridge – either that, or I hereby make it so.

I feel that I have failed to devote sufficient space to my sister Verena, to whom I now pay loving tribute, for she and I are the last surviving children of Siegfried and Winifred Wagner.

My brother and I had our disagreements, some of them on matters of principle. It was only natural that friction and differences of opinion should have arisen in the course of such a long association between two equal partners, but any points of detail that divided us were transcended by our fundamental agreement on everything that genuinely affected the festival's existence. Our areas of difference were far fewer than the ties that united us: ours was a collaboration between two individuals, a constructive dialogue between two autonomous personalities. I could cite many examples of our mutual respect and appreciation. What I still find most touching of all is Wieland's birthday present to me after the 1965 festival: three 17th-century copperplate engravings by Lodovico Burnacini. We never exchanged birthday presents as a rule, so this was an exceptional occurrence, a gesture of reconciliation and a heartfelt token of gratitude.

My differences with Friedelind, my elder sister, steadily dwindled as the years went by, especially after the establishment of the Richard Wagner Foundation. Having continued to live in Bayreuth for some time after our mother's death, she spent the last seven years of her life in Lucerne, the place where our grandfather enjoyed his happiest years, where our father was born, and where she, too, pronounced herself 'very happily installed with a view of the lake and mountains'. We did not lose touch. We exchanged letters, telephone calls, and visits. Remote from all controversy and personally reconciled, we had found our way back to each other.

I take an unsentimental view of the future. If I stop here, it is because of my many commitments on the threshold of the 1994 festival. For all the pragmatism inevitably engendered by everyday life, I feel profoundly convinced that my work on behalf of the Bayreuth Festival has helped it, ever and again, to become a symbol of hope in our often cruel and increasingly devastated world. It has, I believe, formed an alliance between reality and the essential utopia without which none of us would really care to live. Bayreuth's relevance to the future does not consist in what has already been accomplished, but, as Wagner himself said, in a striving for the impossible. It was in this utopian hope that, on 22 May 1872, he laid the foundation stone of the Festspielhaus together with some words that convey my meaning better than any long-winded explanations:

> A secret in this stone I lay.
> Here may it rest for many a year,
> for while the stone hides it away
> its message to the world is clear.

APPENDIX I

TOTAL NUMBER OF PERFORMANCES
1876–1993

Total number of performances given at Bayreuth between 1876 and 1993 (discounting Beethoven's Ninth Symphony): **1963**. Of these **717** fell in the years 1876–1944 (*Ring* works: 252; *Parsifal*: 231; *Tristan und Isolde*: 52; *Die Meistersinger von Nürnberg*: 82; *Tannhäuser*: 31; *Lohengrin*: 30; *Der fliegende Holländer*: 39), and **1246** in the years 1951–93 (*Ring* works: 410; *Parsifal*: 199; *Tristan und Isolde*: 106; *Die Meistersinger von Nürnberg*: 150; *Tannhäuser*: 131; *Lohengrin*: 129; *Der fliegende Holländer*: 121).

Of the above **1246** performances, **436** were given under the joint management of Wieland and Wolfgang Wagner (1951–66) and **810** under the sole management of Wolfgang Wagner (1967 onwards).

Wieland Wagner's productions:
Der Ring des Nibelungen, 4 works (2 productions): 113;
Parsifal (1 production): 101;
Tristan und Isolde (2 productions): 33;
Die Meistersinger von Nürnberg (2 productions): 50;
Tannhäuser (2 productions): 58;
Lohengrin (1 production): 25;
Der fliegende Holländer (1 production): 25.
TOTAL: **405**

Wolfgang Wagner's productions (up to 1993):
Der Ring des Nibelungen, 4 works (2 productions): 113;
Parsifal (2 productions): 65;
Tristan und Isolde (1 production): 15;
Die Meistersinger von Nürnberg (2 productions): 86;
Tannhäuser (1 production): 38;
Lohengrin (2 productions): 41;
Der fliegende Holländer (1 production): 13.
TOTAL: **371**

APPENDIX II

CAST LISTS OF WOLFGANG WAGNER'S BAYREUTH FESTIVAL PRODUCTIONS (DIRECTION AND STAGE DESIGN)

*names in parentheses are those of singers who
temporarily stood in for the artists scheduled to appear*

LOHENGRIN

Year	1953	1954
Performances	6	7
Conductor	Joseph Keilberth	Eugen Jochum Joseph Keilberth
King Henry	Josef Greindl	Joseph Greindl Ludwig Weber Theo Adam
Lohengrin	Wolfgang Windgassen	Wolfgang Windgassen
Elsa	Eleanor Steber	Birgit Nilsson
Telramund	Hermann Uhde	Hermann Uhde
Ortrud	Astrid Varnay	Astrid Varnay
Herald	Hans Braun	Dietrich Fischer-Dieskau
1st Nobleman	Gerhard Stolze	Gerhard Stolze
2nd Nobleman	Joseph Janko	Gene Tobin
3rd Nobleman	Alfons Herwig	Toni Blankenheim
4th Nobleman	Theo Adam	Theo Adam Franz Crass
Pages	Lotte Kiefer Gerda Grasser Erika Eskelsen Roswitha Burow	Lotte Kiefer Gerda Grasser Erika Eskelsen Roswitha Burow

Chorus Master   Wilhelm Pitz

Costumes   Fred Thiel

Head of scenery   Otto Wissner
workshops

DER FLIEGENDE HOLLÄNDER

Year	1955	1956
Performances	6	7
Conductor	Hans Knappertsbusch Joseph Keilberth	Joseph Keilberth
Senta	Astrid Varnay	Astrid Varnay
Dutchman	Hermann Uhde Hans Hotter	George London Hermann Uhde Paul Schöffler
Daland	Ludwig Weber	Arnold van Mill Ludwig Weber
Erik	Wolfgang Windgassen Rudolf Lustig	Joseph Traxel
Mary	Elisabeth Schärtel	Elisabeth Schärtel
Steersman	Josef Traxel	Jean Cox

Chorus Master   Wilhelm Pi

Costumes   Kurt Pal

Head of scenery   Otto Wissn
workshops

TRISTAN UND ISOLDE

Year	1957	1958	1959
Performances	6	5	4
Conductor	Wolfgang Sawallisch	Wolfgang Sawallisch	Wolfgang Sawallisch
Tristan	Wolfgang Windgassen	Wolfgang Windgassen	Wolfgang Windgassen (Hans Beirer)
Isolde	Birgit Nilsson	Birgit Nilsson	Birgit Nilsson
King Marke	Arnold van Mill	Joseph Greindl	Jerôme Hines
Kurwenal	Gustav Neidlinger Hans Hotter	Erik Saedén	Frans Andersson
Brangäne	Grace Hoffman	Grace Hoffman	Grace Hoffman
Melot	Fritz Uhl	Fritz Uhl	Fritz Uhl Hans Günter Nöcker
Shepherd	Hermann Winkler	Hermann Winkler	Hermann Winkler
Helmsman	Egmont Koch	Egmont Koch	Donald Bell
Voice of a Young Sailor	Walter Geisler Josef Traxel	Josef Traxel Sándor Kónya	Georg Paskuda

Chorus Master	Wilhelm Pitz
Costumes	Kurt Palm
Head of scenery workshops	Johannes Dreyer Otto Wissner
Scenic consultant	Alfons Klein

Year	1960	1961	1962
Performances	2	2	3
Conductor	Rudolf Kempe	Rudolf Kempe	Rudolf Kempe
Wotan	Hermann Uhde	Jerôme Hines (Hans Hotter)	Otto Wiener
Donner	Thomas Stewart	Thomas Stewart	Marcel Cordes
Froh	Georg Paskuda	David Thaw	Horst Wilhelm
Loge	Gerhard Stolze	Gerhard Stolze	Gerhard Stolze
Fasolt	Arnold van Mill	David Ward	Walter Kreppel
Fafner	Peter Roth-Ehrang	Peter Roth-Ehrang	Peter Roth-Ehrang
Alberich	Otakar Kraus	Otakar Kraus	Otakar Kraus
Mime	Herold Kraus	Herold Kraus	Erich Klaus
Fricka	Hertha Töpper	Regine Resnik	Grace Hoffman
Freia	Ingrid Bjoner	Wilma Schmidt	Jutta Meyfarth
Erda	Marga Höffgen	Marga Höffgen	Marga Höffgen
Woglinde	Dorothea Siebert	Ingeborg Felderer	Gundula Janowitz
Wellgunde	Claudia Hellmann	Elisabeth Steiner	Elisabeth Schwarzenberg
Flosshilde	Sona Cervena	Elisabeth Schärtel	Sieglinde Wagner

|)63 | 1964 |
	2
udolf Kempe	Berislav Klobucar
heo Adam	Theo Adam
arcel Cordes	Marcel Cordes
orst Wilhelm	Hans Hopf
en Neate	Gerhard Stolze
anz Crass	Gottlob Frick
eter Roth-Ehrang	Peter Roth-Ehrang
takar Kraus	Zoltan Kelemen
rich Klaus	Erich Klaus
race Hoffman	Grace Hoffman
tta Meyfarth	Jutta Meyfarth
arga Höffgen	Marga Höffgen
argarete Bence	
arbara Holt	Barbara Holt
isabeth Schwarzenberg	Elisabeth Schwarzenberg
eglinde Wagner	Sieglinde Wagner

Costumes Kurt Palm

Head of scenery Johannes Dreher
workshops and
projection painting

DER RING DES NIBELUNGEN: DIE WALKÜRE

Year	1960	1961	1962
Performances	2	2	2
Conductor	Rudolf Kempe	Rudolf Kempe	Rudolf Kempe
Siegmund	Wolfgang Windgassen	Fritz Uhl	Fritz Uhl
Hunding	Gottlob Frick	Gottlob Frick	Gottlob Frick
Wotan	Jerôme Hines	Jerôme Hines Hans Hotter	Otto Wiener
Sieglinde	Aase Nordmo-Loevberg	Régine Crespin	Jutta Meyfarth
Brünnhilde	Birgit Nilsson (Astrid Varnay)	Astrid Varnay	Astrid Varnay
Fricka	Hertha Töpper	Regine Resnik	Grace Hoffman
Gerhilde	Gertraud Hopf	Gertraud Hopf	Gertraud Hopf
Ortlinde	Frances Martin	Wilma Schmidt	Elisabeth Schwarzenberg
Waltraute	Claudia Hellmann	Elisabeth Schärtel	Anni Argy
Schwertleite	Rut Siewert	Lilo Brockhaus	Erika Schubert
Helmwige	Ingrid Bjoner	Ingeborg Felderer	Ingeborg Moussa-Felderer
Siegrune	Grace Hoffman	Grace Hoffman	Grace Hoffman
Grimgerde	Margit Kobeck-Peters	Elisabeth Steiner	Sieglinde Wagner
Rossweisse	Dorothea von Stein	Ruth Hesse	Margarete Bence

DER RING DES NIBELUNGEN: SIEGFRIED

Year	1960	1961	1962
Performances	3	2	2
Conductor	Rudolf Kempe	Rudolf Kempe	Rudolf Kempe
Siegfried	Hans Hopf	Hans Hopf	Hans Hopf
Mime	Herold Kraus	Herold Kraus	Erich Klaus
The Wanderer	Hermann Uhde	James Milligan	Otto Wiener
Alberich	Otakar Kraus	Otakar Kraus	Otakar Kraus
Fafner	Peter Roth-Ehrang	Peter Roth-Ehrang	Peter Roth-Ehrang
Erda	Marga Höffgen	Marga Höffgen	Marga Höffgen
Brünnhilde	Birgit Nilsson Astrid Varnay	Birgit Nilsson	Birgit Nilsson Astrid Varnay
Forest Bird	Dorothea Sieert Ruth-Margaret Pütz	Ingeborg Felderer	Ingeborg Moussa-Felderer

1963	1964		
4	2		
Rudolf Kempe	Berislav Klobucar		
Fritz Uhl	Fritz Uhl		
Gottlob Frick	Gottlob Frick		
Hans Hotter Jerôme Hines	Theo Adam		
Jutta Meyfarth	Jutta Meyfarth		
Anita Välkki	Anita Välkki		
Grace Hoffman	Grace Hoffman		
Gertraud Hopf	Gertraud Hopf		
Elisabeth Schwarzenberg	Elisabeth Schwarzenberg		
Elisabeth Schärtel	Ursula Freudenberg		
Ruth Hesse	Maria von Ilosvay		
Ingeborg Moussa-Felderer	Eva-Maria Kupczyk		
Grace Hoffman	Grace Hoffman	*Costumes*	Kurt Palm
Sieglinde Wagner	Sieglinde Wagner	*Head of scenery workshops and projection painting*	Johannes Dreher
Margarete Bence	Erika Schubert		

963	1964		
	2		
.udolf Kempe	Berislav Klobucar		
ans Hopf	Hans Hopf		
rich Klaus	Erich Klaus		
tto Wiener	Hubert Hofmann		
takar Kraus	Zoltan Kelemen		
eter Roth-Ehrang	Peter Roth-Ehrang		
arga Höffgen argarete Bence	Marga Höffgen		
strid Varnay	Astrid Varnay	*Costumes*	Kurt Palm
arbara Holt	Barbara Holt	*Head of scenery workshops and projection painting*	Johannes Dreher

DER RING DES NIBELUNGEN: GÖTTERDÄMMERUNG

Year	1960	1961	1962
Performances	2	3	2
Conductor	Rudolf Kempe	Rudolf Kempe	Rudolf Kempe
Siegfried	Hans Hopf	Hans Hopf	Hans Hopf
Gunther	Thomas Stewart	Thomas Stewart	Marcel Cordes
Hagen	Gottlob Frick	Gottlob Frick	Gottlob Frick
Alberich	Otakar Kraus	Otakar Kraus	Otakar Kraus
Brünnhilde	Birgit Nilsson (Astrid Varnay)	Birgit Nilsson Astrid Varnay	Birgit Nilsson Astrid Varnay
Gutrune	Ingrid Bjoner	Wilma Schmidt	Jutta Meyfarth
Waltraute	Grace Hoffman	Grace Hoffman	Margarete Bence
1st Norn	Rut Siewert	Elisabeth Schärtel	Elisabeth Schärtel
2nd Norn	Grace Hoffman	Grace Hoffman	Grace Hoffman
3rd Norn	Aase Nordmo-Loevberg	Régine Crespin	Gertraud Hopf
Woglinde	Dorothea Siebert	Ingeborg Felderer	Gundula Janowitz
Wellgunde	Claudia Hellmann	Elisabeth Steiner	Elisabeth Schwarzenberg
Flosshilde	Sona Cervena	Elisabeth Schärtel	Sieglinde Wagner

1963	1964		
3	2		
Rudolf Kempe	Berislav Klobucar		
Hans Hopf	Hans Hopf		
Marcel Cordes	Marcel Cordes		
Gottlob Frick	Gottlob Frick		
Otakar Kraus	Zoltan Kelemen		
Astrid Varnay	Astrid Varnay		
Jutta Meyfarth	Jutta Meyfarth		
Elisabeth Schärtel	Grace Hoffman		
Margarete Bence			
Elisabeth Schärtel	Marga Höffgen		
Grace Hoffman	Grace Hoffman		
Anita Välkki	Anita Välkki	*Chorus Master*	Wilhelm Pitz
Barbara Holt	Barbara Holt	*Costumes*	Kurt Palm
Elisabeth Schwarzenberg	Elisabeth Schwarzenberg	*Head of scenery workshops and projection painting*	Johannes Dreher
Sieglinde Wagner	Sieglinde Wagner		

Year	1967	1968
Performances	8	7
Conductor	Rudolf Kempe Berislav Klobucar	Alberto Erede
King Henry	Karl Ridderbusch	Karl Ridderbusch
Lohengrin	Sándor Kónya James King Jess Thomas Jean Cox Hermin Esser	James King Jean Cox
Elsa	Heather Harper	Heather Harper
Telramund	Donald McIntyre	Donald McIntyre
Ortrud	Grace Hoffman Astrid Varnay	Ludmila Dvorakova Grace Hoffman
Herald	Thomas Tipton	Thomas Stewart (Dieter Slembeck)
1st Nobleman	Horst Hoffmann	Horst Hoffmann
2nd Nobleman	Hermin Esser Ferdinand Hall	William Johns Hermin Esser
3rd Nobleman	Dieter Slembeck	Dieter Slembeck (Hanno Daum)
4th Nobleman	Heinz Feldhoff	Heinz Feldhoff
Pages	Natsue Hanada	Natsue Hanada
	Lotte Kiefer	Lotte Kiefer
	Elke Georg	Elke Georg
	Margret Giese-Schröder Christel Willenberg	Margret Giese-Schröder

	1972
	6
vio Varviso	Silvio Varviso
anz Crass rl Ridderbusch	Karl Ridderbusch Franz Crass
né Kollo	René Kollo
nnelore Bode	Hannelore Bode
nald McIntyre lf Kühne)	Donald McIntyre
dmila Dvorakova	Ursula Schröder-Feinen
var Wixell	Gerd Nienstedt
ribert Steinbach	Heribert Steinbach
inz Zednik	Heinz Zednik
dolf Gniffke	Rudolf A. Hartmann-Gniffke
inz Feldhoff	Heinz Feldhoff
dmila Erbenova	Ludmila Erbenova
gard Beck	Irmgard Beck
ristel Willenberg	Christel Willenberg
rgret Giese-Schröder	Marianne Dielemann

Chorus Master	Wilhelm Pitz, succeeded in 1972 by Norbert Balatsch
Costumes	Kurt Palm
Head of scenery workshops	Joachim Streubel

DIE MEISTERSINGER VON NÜRNBERG

Year	1968	1969	1970
Performances	8	8	7
Conductor	Karl Böhm Berislav Klobucar	Berislav Klobucar	Hans Wallat
Hans Sach	Theo Adam Gustav Neidlinger	Norman Bailey Theo Adam	Norman Bailey Theo Adam
Veit Pogner	Karl Ridderbusch	Karl Ridderbusch	Karl Ridderbusch
Kunz Vogelsang	Sebastian Feiersinger	René Kollo	Horst Laubenthal
Konrad Nachtigall	Dieter Slembeck	Dieter Slembeck	Dieter Slembeck
Sixtus Beckmesser	Thomas Hemsley	Thomas Hemsley	Thomas Hemsley
Fritz Kothner	Gerd Nienstedt	Gerd Nienstedt	Gerd Nienstedt
Balthasar Zorn	Günther Treptow	Sebastian Feiersinger	Robert Licha
Ulrich Eisslinger	Erich Klaus	Erich Klaus	Heinz Zednik (Franz Klarwein)
Augustin Moser	William Johns	William Johns	Georg Paskuda
Hermann Ortel	Heinz Feldhoff	Heinz Feldhoff	Heinz Feldhoff
Hans Schwarz	Fritz Linke	Fritz Linke	Fritz Linke
Hans Foltz	Hans Franzen	Hans Franzen	Hans Franzen
Walther von Stolzing	Waldemar Kmentt	Waldemar Kmentt Jess Thomas Jean Cox	Jean Cox Ernst Kozub Waldemar Kment
David	Hermin Esser	Hermin Esser	Hermin Esser (Heinz Zednik)
Eva	Gwyneth Jones	Helga Dernesch	Janis Martin
Magdalene	Janis Martin	Janis Martin	Sylvia Anderson (Sieglinde Wagne)
Night Watchman	Kurt Moll	Bengt Rundgren	Bengt Rundgren

1973	1974	1975
7	6	7
Silvio Varviso	Silvio Varviso	Heinrich Hollreiser
Karl Ridderbusch Theo Adam	Theo Adam Karl Ridderbusch	Karl Ridderbusch Theo Adam
Hans Sotin	Hans Sotin	Hans Sotin Kurt Moll (Karl Ridderbusch)
Heribert Steinbach	Heribert Steinbach	Heribert Steinbach
Rudolf A. Hartmann	Jozsef Dene	Martin Egel
Klaus Hirte	Klaus Hirte (Benno Kusche)	Klaus Hirte
Gerd Nienstedt	Gerd Nienstedt	Gerd Nienstedt
Robert Licha	Robert Licha	Robert Licha
Wolf Appel	Wolf Appel	Wolf Appel
Norbert Orth	Norbert Orth	Martin Finke
Heinz Feldhoff	Heinz Feldhoff	Kurt Rydl (Heinz Feldhoff)
Hartmut Bauer	Hartmut Bauer	Hartmut Bauer
Jozsef Dene	Nikolaus Hillebrand	Nikolaus Hillebrand (Kurt Rydl)
René Kollo Gerd Brenneis	Jean Cox René Kollo Gerd Brenneis	Jean Cox Hermin Esser
Frieder Stricker	Frieder Stricker Heinz Zednik	Frieder Stricker (Heinz Zednik)
Hannelore Bode	Hannelore Bode	Marita Napier
Anna Reynolds	Anna Reynolds	Anna Reynolds
Bernd Weikl	Bernd Weikl	Bernd Weikl

Chorus Master	Wilhelm Pitz, succeeded in 1972 by Norbert Balatsch
Costumes	Kurt Palm
Set realization	Rüdiger Tamschick

DER RING DES NIBELUNGEN: DAS RHEINGOLD

Year	1970	1971	1972
Performances	3	3	3
Conductor	Horst Stein	Horst Stein	Horst Stein
Wotan	Thomas Stewart Theo Adam	Theo Adam Thomas Stewart	Thomas Stewart Theo Adam
Donner	Gerd Nienstedt	Gerd Nienstedt	Gerd Nienstedt
Froh	René Kollo	Harald Ek	Heribert Steinbach
Loge	Hermin Esser	Hermin Esser	Hermin Esser
Fasolt	Karl Ridderbusch	Karl Ridderbusch	Karl Ridderbusch
Fafner	Bengt Rundgren	Peter Meven	Hans Sotin Kurt Moll
Alberich	Gustav Neidlinger	Gustav Neidlinger	Gustav Neidlinger Franz Mazura
Mime	Georg Paskuda	Georg Paskuda	Heinz Zednik
Fricka	Janis Martin	Anna Reynolds	Anna Reynolds
Freia	Margarita Kyriaki	Janis Martin	Hannelore Bode
Erda	Marga Höffgen	Marga Höffgen	Marga Höffgen
Woglinde	Hannelore Bode	Elizabeth Volkman	Yoko Kawahara
Wellgunde	Inger Paustian	Inger Paustian	Ursula Rhein
Flosshilde	Sylvia Anderson (Faith Puleston)	Sylvia Anderson	Ilse Gramatzki

1973	1974	1975
2	3	2
Horst Stein	Horst Stein	Horst Stein
Theo Adam Donald McIntyre	Donald McIntyre Theo Adam	Donald McIntyre Theo Adam
Gerd Nienstedt	Gerd Nienstedt	Gerd Nienstedt
Heribert Steinbach	Heribert Steinbach	Heribert Steinbach
Hermin Esser	Hermin Esser	Hermin Esser
Karl Ridderbusch	Karl Ridderbusch	Karl Ridderbusch
Hans Sotin (Hartmut Bauer)	Kurt Moll	Kurt Moll
Gustav Neidlinger Franz Mazura	Franz Mazura (Karl Heinz Herr)	Gustav Neidlinger Franz Mazura
Heinz Zednik	Heinz Zednik	Heinz Zednik
Anna Reynolds	Anna Reynolds	Anna Reynolds
Hannelore Bode	Hannelore Bode	Rachel Yakar
Marga Höffgen	Marga Höffgen	Marga Höffgen
Yoko Kawahara	Yoko Kawahara	Yoko Kawahara
Ursula Rhein	Ursula Rhein	Trudeliese Schmidt
Ilse Gramatzki	Ilse Köhler	Hanna Schwarz

Costumes	Kurt Palm
Head of scenery workshops and projection painting	Rüdiger Tamschik

Year	1970	1971	1972
Performances	2	4	3
Conductor	Horst Stein	Horst Stein	Horst Stein
Siegmund	Helge Brilioth	Helge Brilioth Hermin Esser	James King Hermin Esser
Hunding	Karl Ridderbusch	Karl Ridderbusch	Karl Ridderbusch
Wotan	Thomas Stewart Theo Adam	Theo Adam Thomas Stewart Donald McIntyre	Thomas Stewart Theo Adam
Sieglinde	Gwyneth Jones	Gwyneth Jones Janis Martin	Gwyneth Jones Janis Martin
Brünnhilde	Berit Lindholm	Catarina Ligendza Berit Lindholm	Catarina Ligendza
Fricka	Anna Reynolds	Anna Reynolds	Anna Reynolds
Gerhilde	Elisabeth Schwarzenberg	Elisabeth Schwarzenberg	Elisabeth Schwarzenberg
Ortlinde	Gildis Flossmann	Ursula Rhein	Ursula Rhein
Waltraute	Wendy Fine	Sylvia Anderson	Michèle Vilma
Schwertleite	Sylvia Anderson	Glenys Loulis	Katherine Pring
Helmwige	Liane Synek	Wendy Fine	Leslie Johnson
Siegrune	Inger Paustian	Inger Paustian	Anna Reynolds
Grimgerde	Faith Puleston	Faith Puleston	Ilse Gramatzki
Rossweisse	Aili Purtonen	Sieglinde Wagner	Sieglinde Wagner

1973	1974	1975
2	3	3
Horst Stein	Horst Stein	Horst Stein
Gerd Brenneis James King	Gerd Brenneis	James King Hermin Esser
Karl Ridderbusch	Karl Ridderbusch	Karl Ridderbusch
Theo Adam Donald McIntyre	Donald McIntyre Theo Adam	Donald McIntyre Theo Adam
Gwyneth Jones	Marita Napier	Marita Napier
Berit Lindholm Catarina Ligendza	Roberta Knie	Gwyneth Jones
Anna Reynolds	Anna Reynolds	Anna Reynolds
Elisabeth Schwarzenberg	Hannelore Bode	Rachel Yakar
Ursula Rhein	Ursula Rhein	Irja Auroora
Eva Randová	Eva Randová	Eva Randová
Katherine Pring	Heljä Angervo	Ortrun Wenkel
Marita Napier	Brenda Roberts	Jeanne Hieronymi
Anna Reynolds	Anna Reynolds	Anna Reynolds
Ilse Gramatzki	Ilse Köhler	Trudeliese Schmidt
Sieglinde Wagner	Ingrid Mayr	Hanna Schwarz

Costumes	Kurt Palm
Head of scenery workshops and projection painting	Rüdiger Tamschick

Year	1970	1971	1972
Performances	2	3	4
Conductor	Horst Stein	Horst Stein	Horst Stein
Siegfried	Jean Cox	Jean Cox	Jean Cox
Mime	Georg Paskuda	Georg Paskuda	Heinz Zednik
The Wanderer	Thomas Stewart Theo Adam	Theo Adam Thomas Stewart	Thomas Stewart Theo Adam Donald McIntyre
Alberich	Gustav Neidlinger	Gustav Neidlinger	Gustav Neidlinger Franz Mazura
Fafner	Bengt Rundgren	Peter Meven	Heinz Feldhoff
Erda	Marga Höffgen	Marga Höffgen	Marga Höffgen
Brünnhilde	Berit Lindholm	Catarina Ligendza Berit Lindholm	Catarina Ligendza
Forest Bird	Hannelore Bode	Elizabeth Volkman	Yoko Kawahara

'73	1974	1975
	3	2
orst Stein	Horst Stein	Horst Stein
an Cox	Jean Cox	Jean Cox
einz Zednik	Heinz Zednik	Heinz Zednik
eo Adam onald McIntyre	Donald McIntyre Theo Adam	Donald McIntyre Theo Adam
ustav Neidlinger anz Mazura	Franz Mazura (Rolf Kühne)	Gustav Neidlinger Franz Mazura
einz Feldhoff	Heinz Feldhoff	Nikolaus Hillebrand
arga Höffgen	Marga Höffgen	Marga Höffgen
rit Lindholm tarina Ligendza	Brenda Roberts	Gwyneth Jones
oko Kawahara	Yoko Kawahara	Yoko Kawahara

Costumes   Kurt Palm

Head of scenery   Rüdiger Tamschick
workshops and
projection painting

DER RING DES NIBELUNGEN: GÖTTERDÄMMERUNG

Year	1970	1971	1972
Performances	2	3	3
Conductor	Horst Stein	Horst Stein	Horst Stein
Siegfried	Jean Cox	Jean Cox	Jean Cox
Gunther	Norman Bailey	Franz Mazura	Franz Mazura Thomas Stewart
Hagen	Karl Ridderbusch	Karl Ridderbusch	Karl Ridderbusch
Alberich	Gustav Neidlinger	Gustav Neidlinger	Franz Mazura Gustav Neidlinger
Brünnhilde	Berit Lindholm	Catarina Ligendza Berit Lindholm	Catarina Ligendza
Gutrune	Janis Martin	Janis Martin	Janis Martin
Waltraute	Anna Reynolds	Anna Reynolds	Anna Reynolds
1st Norn	Marga Höffgen	Marga Höffgen	Marga Höffgen
2nd Norn	Anna Reynolds	Anna Reynolds	Anna Reynolds
3rd Norn	Liane Synek	Wendy Fine	Ursula Schröder-Feinen
Woglinde	Hannelore Bode	Elizabeth Volkman	Yoko Kawahara
Wellgunde	Inger Paustian	Inger Paustian	Ursula Rhein
Flosshilde	Sylvia Anderson	Sylvia Anderson	Ilse Gramatzki

1973	1974	1975
3	3	2
Horst Stein	Horst Stein	Horst Stein
Jean Cox	Jean Cox	Jean Cox
Franz Mazura Gerd Nienstedt	Franz Mazura Gerd Nienstedt	Franz Mazura
Karl Ridderbusch	Karl Ridderbusch	Karl Ridderbusch
Gustav Neidlinger Franz Mazura	Franz Mazura (Klaus Hirte) (Rolf Kühne)	Gustav Neidlinger (Klaus Hirte)
Catarina Ligendza Berit Lindholm	Gwyneth Jones	Gwyneth Jones
Eva Randová	Eva Randová	Eva Randová
Anna Reynolds	Anna Reynolds	Anna Reynolds
Marga Höffgen	Marga Höffgen	Marga Höffgen
Anna Reynolds	Anna Reynolds	Anna Reynolds
Marita Napier	Marita Napier	Marita Napier
Yoko Kawahara	Yoko Kawahara	Yoko Kawahara
Ursula Rhein	Ursula Rhein	Trudeliese Schmidt
Ilse Gramatzki	Ilse Köhler	Hanna Schwarz

Chorus Master	Wilhelm Pitz, succeeded in 1972 by Norbert Balatsch
Costumes	Kurt Palm
Head of scenery workshops and projection painting	Rüdiger Tamschick

PARSIFAL

Year	1975	1976	1977
Performances	8	7	5
Conductor	Horst Stein Hans Zender	Horst Stein	Horst Stein
Amfortas	Bernd Weikl	Bernd Weikl	Bernd Weikl
Titurel	Karl Ridderbusch	Karl Ridderbusch Matti Salminen	Karl Ridderbusch Matti Salminen
Gurnemanz	Hans Sotin	Hans Sotin Theo Adam	Hans Sotin Theo Adam
Parsifal	René Kollo	Peter Hofmann René Kollo	René Kollo Hermann Winkler (Manfred Jung)
Klingsor	Franz Mazura	Franz Mazura	Franz Mazura
Kundry	Eva Randová Ursula Schröder-Feinen	Eva Randová (Regine Fonseca)	Eva Randová
1st Knight	Heribert Steinbach	Heribert Steinbach	Robert Schunk
2nd Knight	Nikolaus Hillebrand Kurt Rydl	Heinz Feldhoff	Heinz Feldhoff
1st Squire	Trudeliese Schmidt	Carol Richardson	Ilse Gramatzki
2nd Squire	Hanna Schwarz	Adelheid Krauss	Hanna Schwarz
3rd Squire	Martin Finke	Heinz Zednik	Heinz Kruse
4th Squire	Martin Egel	Martin Egel	Martin Egel
1st Flower/I	Rachel Yakar (Hannelore Bode)	Rachel Yakar	Norma Sharp
2nd Flower/I	Trudeliese Schmidt	Carol Richardson	Carol Richardson
3rd Flower/I	Hanna Schwarz	Adelheid Krauss	Hanna Schwarz
1st Flower/II	Yoko Kawahara	Yoko Kawahara	Carmen Reppel
2nd Flower/II	Irja Auroora	Irja Auroora	Inga Nielsen
3rd Flower/II	Alicia Nafé	Alicia Nafé	Ilse Gramatzki
Contralto Solo	Ortrun Wenkel	Ortrun Wenkel	Hanna Schwarz

1978	1979	1980	1981
5	5	4	5
Horst Stein	Horst Stein	Horst Stein	Horst Stein
Bernd Weikl	Bernd Weikl	Bernd Weikl	Donald McIntyre
Matti Salminen Heikki Toivanen	Matti Salminen	Matti Salminen	Matti Salminen
Theo Adam Hans Sotin	Hans Sotin Theo Adam	Theo Adam Hans Sotin	Hans Sotin
Peter Hofmann Manfred Jung	Siegfried Jerusalem Manfred Jung	Siegfried Jerusalem Manfred Jung	Manfred Jung
Franz Mazura	Franz Mazura	Franz Mazura	Leif Roar
Dunja Vejzovic	Dunja Vejzovic	Dunja Vejzovic (Regine Fonseca)	Eva Randová
John Pickering	Toni Krämer	Volker Horn	Toni Krämer
Heinz Feldhoff	Karl Schreiber	Dieter Brencke	Heinz Klaus Ecker
Ilse Gramatzki	Ilse Gramatzki	Ilse Gramatzki	Marga Schiml
Hanna Schwarz	Hanna Schwarz	Hanna Schwarz	Hanna Schwarz
Helmut Pampuch	Helmut Pampuch	Helmut Pampuch	Helmut Pampuch
Martin Egel	Martin Egel	Martin Egel	Martin Egel
Norma Sharp	Norma Sharp	Norma Sharp	Norma Sharp
Carol Richardson	Carol Richardson	Carol Richardson	Carol Richardson
Hanna Schwarz	Hanna Schwarz	Hanna Schwarz	Hanna Schwarz
Carmen Reppel	Carmen Reppel	Carmen Reppel	Mari Anne Häggander
Kumiko Oshita	Marga Schiml	Marga Schiml	Marga Schiml
Ilse Gramatzki	Ilse Gramatzki	Ilse Gramatzki	Margit Neubauer
Hanna Schwarz	Hanna Schwarz	Hanna Schwarz	Hanna Schwarz

Chorus Master	Norbert Balatsch
Choreographic assistant	Riccardo Duse
Costumes	Reinhard Heinrich
Assistant set and projection designers	Rüdiger Tamschick Michael Tietjens Florian Eickelberg

Year	1981	1982	1983
Performances	7	7	7
Conductor	Mark Elder	Horst Stein	Horst Stein
Hans Sachs	Bernd Weikl	Bernd Weikl	Bernd Weikl
Veit Pogner	Manfred Schenk	Manfred Schenk	Manfred Schenk
Kunz Vogelsang	David Kuebler	David Kuebler	András Molnár
Konrad Nachtigall	Martin Egel	Martin Egel	Martin Egel
Sixtus Beckmesser	Hermann Prey	Hermann Prey	Hermann Prey
Fritz Kothner	Jef Vermeersch	Jef Vermeersch	Jef Vermeersch
Balthasar Zorn	Udo Holdorf	Udo Holdorf	Udo Holdorf
Ulrich Eisslinger	Toni Krämer	Toni Krämer	Toni Krämer
Augustin Moser	Helmut Pampuch	Helmut Pampuch	Helmut Pampuch
Hermann Ortel	Sándor Sólyom-Nagy	Sándor Sólyom-Nagy	Sándor Sólyom-Nagy
Hans Schwarz	Heinz Klaus Ecker	Heinz Klaus Ecker	Heinz Klaus Ecker
Hans Foltz	Dieter Schweikart	Dieter Schweikart	Dieter Schweikart
Walther von Stolzing	Siegfried Jerusalem	Siegfried Jerusalem	Siegfried Jerusalem
David	Graham Clark	Graham Clark	Graham Clark
Eva	Mari Anne Häggander	Mari Anne Häggander	Mari Anne Häggande
Magdalene	Marga Schiml	Marga Schiml	Marga Schiml
Night Watchman	Matthias Hölle	Matthias Hölle	Matthias Hölle

1984	1986	1987	1988
6	5	6	5
Horst Stein	Horst Stein	Michael Schønwandt	Michael Schønwandt
Bernd Weikl	Bernd Weikl	Bernd Weikl	Bernd Weikl
Manfred Schenk	Manfred Schenk	Manfred Schenk	Manfred Schenk
András Molnár	Kurt Schreibmayer	Kurt Schreibmayer	Kurt Schreibmayer
Martin Egel	Martin Egel	Martin Egel	Robert Riener
Hermann Prey (Hans Günter Nöcker)	Hermann Prey	Alan Opie	Alan Opie
Jef Vermeersch	Jef Vermeersch	Jef Vermeersch	Jef Vermeersch
Udo Holdorf	Udo Holdorf	Udo Holdorf	Udo Holdorf
Peter Maus	Peter Maus	Peter Maus	Peter Maus
Helmut Pampuch	Helmut Pampuch	Helmut Pampuch	Helmut Pampuch
Sándor Sólyom-Nagy	Sándor Sólyom-Nagy	Sándor Sólyom-Nagy	Sándor Sólyom-Nagy
Heinz Klaus Ecker	Heinz Klaus Ecker	Heinz Klaus Ecker	Heinz Klaus Ecker
Dieter Schweikart	Dieter Schweikart	Dieter Schweikart	Dieter Schweikart
Siegfried Jerusalem (Jean Cox)	Siegfried Jerusalem	Reiner Goldberg (William Johns)	Peter Hofmann Reiner Goldberg
Graham Clark	Graham Clark	Graham Clark	Ulrich Ress
Mari Anne Häggander	Mari Anne Häggander (Lucia Popp)	Lucy Peacock	Lucy Peacock
Marga Schiml	Marga Schiml	Marga Schiml	Marga Schiml
Matthias Hölle	Matthias Hölle	Matthias Hölle	Matthias Hölle

Chorus Master	Norbert Balatsch
Costumes	Reinhard Heinrich
Assistant set designer	Rüdiger Tamschick

TANNHÄUSER

Year	1985	1986	1987
Performances	7	7	6
Conductor	Giuseppe Sinopoli	Giuseppe Sinopoli	Giuseppe Sinopoli
Tannhäuser	Richard Versalle	Richard Versalle	Richard Versalle
Elisabeth	Cheryl Studer	Cheryl Studer	Cheryl Studer
Venus	Gabriele Schnaut	Gabriele Schnaut	Gabriele Schnaut (Sophia Larson)
Hermann, Landgrave	Hans Sotin Matti Salminen	Hans Sotin	Hans Sotin
Wolfram von Eschenbach	Wolfgang Brendel	Wolfgang Brendel	Wolfgang Brendel
Walther von der Vogelweide	Robert Schunk	Robert Schunk	Kurt Schreibmayer
Biterolf	Siegfried Vogel	Siegfried Vogel	Siegfried Vogel
Heinrich der Schreiber	András Molnár	Kurt Schreibmayer	Clemens Bieber
Reinmar von Zweter	Sándor Sólyom-Nagy	Sándor Sólyom-Nagy	Sándor Sólyom-Nagy
Young Shepherd	Brigitte Lindner	Brigitte Lindner	Brigitte Lindner
Pages	Brigitte Lindner	Brigitte Lindner	Brigitte Lindner
	Irene Hammann	Irene Hammann	Hannelore Weber
	Gitta-Maria Sjöberg	Sara Jane Clethero	Ulrike Heyse
	Lene Farver	Lene Farver	Christine Beckmann

1989	1992	1993
5	7	6
Giuseppe Sinopoli	Donald C. Runnicles	Donald C. Runnicles
Richard Versalle Reiner Goldberg	Wolfgang Schmidt	Wolfgang Schmidt
Cheryl Studer	Tina Kiberg	Tina Kiberg
Ruthild Engert-Ely	Uta Priew	Uta Priew
Hans Sotin Manfred Schenk	Manfred Schenk	Hans Sotin Manfred Schenk
Wolfgang Brendel	Eike Wilm Schulte	Eike Wilm Schulte
William Pell	Richard Brunner	Richard Brunner
Siegfried Vogel	Ekkehard Wlaschiha	Ekkehard Wlaschiha
Clemens Bieber	Clemens Bieber	Clemens Bieber
Sándor Sólyom-Nagy	Sándor Sólyom-Nagy	Sándor Sólyom-Nagy
Joy Robinson	Christiane Hossfeld	Christiane Hossfeld
Joy Robinson	Susan Roper	Franziska Wallat
Hannelore Weber	Christiane Rost	Juliane Heyn
Ulrike Heyse	Simone Schröder	Simone Schröder
Lene Farver-Sonne	Elisabeth Zenkl	Gertrud Spitzer

Chorus Master	Norbert Balatsch
Venusberg choreography	Iván Markó
Costumes	Reinhard Heinrich
Assistant set and projection designer	Johannes Taubenschuss

PARSIFAL

Year	1989	1990	1991
Performances	6	5	5
Conductor	James Levine	James Levine	James Levine
Amfortas	Bernd Weikl	Bernd Weikl	Bernd Weikl
Titurel	Matthias Hölle Siegfried Vogel	Matthias Hölle	Matthias Hölle
Gurnemanz	Hans Sotin	Hans Sotin Manfred Schenk	Hans Sotin Manfred Schenk
Parsifal	William Pell	William Pell	William Pell
Klingsor	Franz Mazura	Günter von Kannen Bodo Brinkmann	Franz Mazura
Kundry	Waltraud Meier	Waltraud Meier	Waltraud Meier
1st Knight	Richard Brunner	Richard Brunner	Richard Brunner
2nd Knight	Sándor Sólyom-Nagy	Sándor Sólyom-Nagy	Sándor Sólyom-Nagy
1st Squire	Carmen Anhorn	Carmen Anhorn	Alina Wodnicka
2nd Squire	Annette Küttenbaum	Annette Küttenbaum	Annette Küttenbaum
3rd Squire	Helmut Pampuch	Helmut Pampuch (Peter Maus)	Helmut Pampuch (Peter Maus)
4th Squire	Peter Maus	Peter Maus (Robert Riener)	Peter Maus (Robert Riener)
1st Flower/I	Christiane Hossfeld Rebecca Littig	Christiane Hossfeld	Christiane Hossfeld
2nd Flower/I	Carmen Anhorn	Carmen Anhorn	Alina Wodnicka
3rd Flower/I	Alexandra Bergmeister	Alexandra Bergmeister	Alexandra Bergmeister
1st Flower/II	Hilde Leidland	Rebecca Littig	Rebecca Littig
2nd Flower/II	Deborah Sasson	Marie-Claire O'Reirdan	Marie-Claire O'Reirdan
3rd Flower/II	Jane Turner	Jane Turner	Jane Turner
Contralto Solo	Hitomi Katagiri	Hitomi Katagiri	Hitomi Katagiri

1992	1993		
5	5		
James Levine	James Levine		
Bernd Weikl	Bernd Weikl		
Matthias Hölle	John Tomlinson Matthias Hölle		
Hans Sotin Manfred Schenk	Hans Sotin		
Poul Elming Placido Domingo	Placido Domingo		
Franz Mazura	Franz Mazura		
Waltraud Meier	Deborah Polaski		
Richard Brunner	Richard Brunner		
Sándor Sólyom-Nagy	Sándor Sólyom-Nagy		
Alina Wodnicka	Christiane Hossfeld		
Annette Küttenbaum	Hilde Leidland		
Helmut Pampuch	Helmut Pampuch		
Peter Maus	Peter Maus		
Christiane Hossfeld	Christiane Hossfeld		
Alina Wodnicka	Hilde Leidland	*Chorus Master*	Norbert Balatsch
Alexandra Bergmeister	Alexandra Bergmeister	*Flower Maidens choreography*	Iván Markó
Rebecca Littig	Rebecca Littig		
Marie-Claire O'Reirdan	Marie-Claire O'Reirdan	*Costumes*	Reinhard Heinrich
Jane Turner	Jane Turner	*Assistant set and projection designer*	Johannes Taubenschuss
Hitomi Katagiri	Sarah Fryer		

THE JOINT WILL OF SIEGFRIED AND WINIFRED WAGNER, 8 MARCH 1929

WILL

This day, the eighth day of March One thousand nine hundred and twenty-nine, 8th March 1929, the following persons appeared before me, Counsel of Justice Joseph Leuchs, Notary of Bayreuth, at the notarial chambers, Bayreuth II:

Siegfried Wagner, poet and composer of Bayreuth 59 years old, and his wife Winifred Wagner 31 years old, both known to me personally and both of sound mind.

In that these persons, appearing before me have expressed their desire to make a will the following persons were present as irreproachable witnesses:

1. Mr Ernst Beutter, bank manager of Bayreuth,
2. Dr Fritz Meyer, lawyer of Bayreuth.

both are also personally known to me.

In the presence of both witnesses the married couple Wagner produced to me the public document annexed to this deposition and made the verbal declaration that this represented their joint last Will.

All participating persons were present throughout the whole transaction.

Read out by the Notary, affirmed by the married couple Wagner and signed personally by them and also by both witnesses.

sig. Siegfried Wagner   sig. Winifred Wagner
sig. Ernst Beutter   sig. Dr Fritz Meyer

sig. J.R. Leuchs,
Notary.

L.S.

Joint Will of the married couple Siegfried and Winifred Wagner.

Mr Siegfried and Mrs Winifred Wagner declare their last Will to be as follows:

The married couple hold the matrimonial estate in accordance with the law relating to administration and usufruct thereof.

I

If Mr Siegfried Wagner predeceases Mrs Winifred Wagner, then the estate will devolve in accordance with the following provisions:

1. Mrs Winifred Wagner is the heir-in-tail of the entire residue of Mr Siegfried Wagner.

   The reversionary interest will devolve, per stirpes upon the joint descendants of the married couple Wagner. The reversionary interest will vest upon the death or remarriage of Mrs Winifred Wagner.

   If Mrs Winifred Wagner remarries or waives her inheritance then she will solely be entitled to the statutory share. In that case the heirs in tail will be the sons and daughters of the married couple Wagner. The reversioners will be their joint descendants who are alive at the time the reversioner vests. The reversioner will vest when all sons and daughters of the married couple Wagner are dead.

   If the sons and daughters of the married couple Wagner waive their intended inheritance then they will receive the statutory share only, Mrs Winifred Wagner will be the sole beneficiary.

2. The beneficiaries will be made subject to the following duties as regards the Festival Theatre. The Festival Theatre is not to be sold. Instead, it is to be maintained for the purpose determined by its founder, that is for the celebratory performance of the works of Richard Wagner.

   If the heirs do not comply with this duty then the consequences will be the same as those under number 1 above where waiver of the heirs-in-tail or reversioners interests has occurred.

   If the fulfilment of this duty, despite best endeavours, proves impossible for the persons so charged then a committee made up of the following persons will determine the further regulation and fate of the Festival Theatre to the exclusion of the courts and with binding effect on the participating persons.

   Mrs Winifred Wagner, insofar as she has not remarried, and after her departure the eldest descendant of Mr Siegfried Wagner at that time, as chairman, the eldest member of the faculty of law at Erlangen, Mr Ernst Beutter, bank manager of Bayreuth, and after his departure or becoming incapable, Dr Fritz Meyer, lawyer of Bayreuth, after his departure or incapability, the President of the Academy of Art and Science in Munich. If a member appointed to this committee is unable for any reason whatsoever to act then their replacement will be chosen by the Chief Executive Mayor of Bayreuth. The determining factor in the decision making of the committee is to be the consideration that the Festival Theatre should remain a stronghold of genuine German art for posterity.

If all persons mentioned in this Will waive their inheritances and as a result the statutory inheritance provisions come into effect then the duties as to the Festival Theatre will be retained. The performance of this duty can be required by the municipality of Bayreuth (§2194 BGB).

If through default of all beneficiaries, or one of them, the heirs-in-tail, reversioners or statutory heirs do not carry out this duty the municipality of Bayreuth shall, as legatee, be granted ownership of the Festival Theatre. The municipality of Bayreuth will, in that case, be made expressly subject to the duties mentioned above.

II

Mrs Winifred Wagner, as heir-in-tail is not subject to the provisions of §2116, 2117, 2118, 2119 BGB. This will also apply, where the heir-in-tail Mrs Winifred Wagner waives her inheritance, to the descendants of Mr Siegfried Wagner, who will, under those circumstances, become the heirs-in-tail.

III

If Mrs Winifred Wagner predeceases her husband then Mr Siegfried Wagner will be the sole beneficiary. If one of his descendants should require their statutory share from their mother's estate, then that descendant will also receive the statutory share from Mr Siegfried Wagner's estate. In addition, after the death of his wife, Mr Siegfried Wagner will have the right to revoke this will without having to waive his right to the property acquired (§2271 BGB).

IV

This Will shall have no validity or effect where the marriage of the spouses is terminated for any reason (§2268 BGB) or if Mr Siegfried Wagner, has, at the time of his death, the right to sue for divorce based on his wife's fault and the petition for divorce or judicial separation has been issued.

V

All dispositions under this Will are concurrent in the sense of §2270 BGB. It is to be assumed that one disposition will not be met without the other also being met.

Mr Siegfried Wagner's right of revocation (number III) will subsist.

VI

Mr Ernst Beutter, bank manager of Bayreuth is appointed as executor, if he should no longer serve, his replacement will be Dr Fritz Meyer, lawyer of Bayreuth.

Bayreuth, the 8th March 1929

sig. Siegfried Wagner   sig. Winifred Wagner

Certified:

Bayreuth, the 18th October 1932
The Public Records Official at the Lower District Court Registry.
Justiz-Obersekretär.

INDEX

Abbado, Claudio, 257–8
Abendroth, Hermann, 64, 69
Abusch, Alexander, 275
Adam, Theo, 109, 137, 156
Adenauer, Konrad, 272
Adler, Witiko, 181
Adorno, Theodor W.: 146; *Versuch über Wagner*, 215
Albrecht, Premier, 261
Albrecht-Potonié, Lotte, 102
Aldenhoff, Bernd, 109
Altmeyer, Jeannine, 183
Ammer, Heike, 201
Anders, Peter, 62
Appia, Adolphe, 19
Araiza, Francisco, 178
Arendt, Benno von, 23
Armann, Gudrun, *see* Mack, Gudrun
Armstrong, Karen, 180
Augstein, Rudolf, 269
August, Carl, Grand Duke of Weimar, 29

Bach, Johann Sebastian: 212; *St Matthew Passion*, 9
Bahlsen, Dr Hans, 102
Balatsch, Norbert, 157, 159, 170, 192, 198, 256, 268
Baldani, Ruza, 257
Balslev, Lisbeth, 178
Barenboim, Daniel, 179, 181–2, 195–7, 201–3, 216
Barnett (engineer), 188
Barth, Hanna, 145
Barth, Herbert, 66, 145–8
Bauer, Oswald Georg, 2, 135, 146, 149–50, 192, 208, 225
Bauvais, Peter, 190
Bayreuth Blätter, 18

Bayreuth Festival: 'New Bayreuth', 4, 19; 'Incorporated Association of Friends of Bayreuth', 9, 13–14, 102, 34; finances, 12, 21, 102, 146, 244, 247–52; and Gertrud Wagner, 14–5; first festival (1876), 17; during 2nd World War, 57; centenary publications, 66; trusteeship, 83, 99; management, 87–8, 97–8; administration, 100–1; re-opening, 105–7; and the press, 144–5, 148; Exhibitions, 152; production teams, 156; master classes, 183–4; German Festival Foundation Bayreuth, 236; staff, 245; admission charges, 246; celebrity visits to, 263–5; and East Germany, 274–5
Beaufils, Marcel, 147
Becht, Hermann, 182
Becker, Heinz, 147
Beethoven, Ludwig van: 26; *Ninth Symphony*, 105, 121, 125, 144
Beidler, Franz Wilhelm, 81, 82–5, 88, 98
Beirer, Hans, 108
Beitz, Berthold, 102, 104, 261
Béjart, Maurice, 112
Benackova-Cap, Gabriela, 220
Bensegger, Dr Rudolf, 232
Beresford, Hugh, 157
Bergman, Ingmar, 165
Bernstein, Leonard, 161, 163
Bhummibol, King of Thailand, 263
Bieber, Clemens, 195, 201, 256
Bjoner, Ingrid, 183
Björling, Sigurd, 107
Blech, Leo, 107–8
Bloch, Ernst, 9, 26, 146
Bode, Professor Arnold, 248
Böhm, Karl, 108, 136, 162, 205
Böhm, Karlheinz, 162

Böhm, Thea, 162
Bonhoeffer, Dietrich, 71
Borchmeyer, Dieter, 147
Borkh, Inge, 110
Bormann, Martin, 45, 48
Bornemann, Barbara, 201
Bornemann, Walter, 114
Boulez, Pierre: conducts *Parsifal*, 5, 7, 9, 164,
    208; and *The Ring*, 134, 141, 147, 165,
    167–9, 171, 173–4; and Wieland Wagner,
    137; and Carlos Kleiber, 163; Bayreuth
    Festival Master Classes, 184
Boykow, Johann Maria, 243
Brand, Dr, 44, 47–8
Braun, Sigismund von, 263
Breit, Dr Gottfried, 10–11, 184, 231
Brenner, Peter, 181
Brillioth, Helen, 163
Brouwenstijn, Gré, 108, 110
Buchenberger, Bertha, 104
Bülow, Cosima von, *see* Wagner, Cosima
Bülow, Hans von, 28
Bumbry, Grace, 179
Bundschuh, Eva-Maria, 196
Burghardt, Dr Max, 274
Burkhardt, Professor, 249
Burnacini, Lodovico, 280
Busoni, Ferruccio: *Faust*, 179, 192

Callas, Maria, 109
Castelberg, Herr von, 13
Cebotari, Maria, 59
Chamberlain, Eva, *née* Wagner, 18, 23–5, 30,
    33, 35, 37, 81
Chamberlain, Houston Stuart, 18–19, 25,
    29–30, 35, 37
Charles, Prince of Wales, 264
Chéreau, Patrice: and *The Ring*, 141, 147,
    163, 166, 169, 171–4, 181, 188, 192, 223;
    and *Die Welt am Sonntag*, 164; and Pierre
    Boulez, 165; and Gottfried Wagner, 176;
    Tristan und Isolde, 257
Churchill, Sir Winston, 47
Clark, Graham, 182, 196
Clay, Lucius D., 88
Cluytens, André, 121, 124, 208
Coenen, Ernst, 147
Connell, Elizabeth, 201
Constantin, Prince, 29
Corradi, Gianpaolo, 257
Cosi fan tutte, 64
Cox, Jean, 156, 164, 172, 222
Cox, John, 181
Cullberg, Birgit, 8, 112

d'Agoult, Comte de, 28
Dahlhaus, Carl, 146–7
Danzher, Dr Helmut, 8
Das Rheingold, 115, 133–4, 140, 166, 170–1,
    173, 181, 195, 197
Dehmel, Wolfram, 5
Der Bärenhäuter, 65
Der Fliegende Holländer: Vienna production
    (1967), 13; and King Ludwig II, 17;
    Cosima Wagner produces (1901), 18;
    1940, 58; Wieland Wagner designs for
    (1942), 65; Birgit Nilsson in, 108; Leonie
    Rysanek in (1959), 110; 1963, 113; 1960,
    114; and Wolfgang Sawallisch, 114;
    Wolfgang Wagner produces, 122, 150–1,
    204; 1959, 129; 1960, 131; in Munich
    (1864), 135; 1990, 152; Wieland Wagner
    produces, 156; recordings, 162; 1978,
    177–8; Peter Schneider, 191; Dieter Dorn
    produces, 198–200; costs, 244
Der Hang Gesamtkunstwerk (exhibition), 267
Der Ring des Nibelungen: 1876, 2, 17; Wieland
    Wagner produces, 5–6, 112–13; Cosima
    Wagner produces (1896), 18, 20; and
    Cosima Wagner, 19; 1940, 58; Wieland
    Wagner designs for, 66, 116; Alfred
    Rosenberg on, 68; première, 83; re-
    opening of the Bayreuth Festival, 105–6,
    109, 115, 117, 146; Birgit Nilsson in, 108;
    recordings of, 111, 181; Joseph Keilberth
    conducts (1952), 118; Herbert von Karajan
    conducts, 120; Knappertsbusch conducts,
    124; 1959, 129; Wolfgang Wagner
    produces, 130–3, 138–9, 150, 164–5, 168–
    74, 176; Richard Wagner, 134–5, 144;
    Vienna State Opera, 136; history, 140;
    casting, 141, 166–7; centenary, 149, 240;
    and Carlos Kleiber, 163; Georg Solti, 186–
    7; Peter Hall, 188; cast lists, 189–90; Peter
    Schneider, 191; 1983, 192; 1988, 195–6;
    cast lists (1988), 197–8; after Wieland's
    death, 204–5; 1985, 220; interpretations,
    223; costs (1951), 244
Die Feen, 213
Die Hamletmaschine, 203
Die Meistersinger von Nürnberg, Cosima
    Wagner produces (1888), 18; 1944, 63;
    1943, 64; Wolfgang and Wieland Wagner
    (1943), 69; re-opening of the Bayreuth
    Festival, 105–6, 115; Hans
    Knappertsbusch conducts, 107, 117;
    Joseph Greindl in, 108; Hans Sachs in,
    109; recordings, 111, 229; and Wolfgang
    Sawallisch, 114; 1956, 122; conductors,
    1959–61, 125; 1959, 129; first